Poverty: America's Enduring Paradox

BOOKS BY SIDNEY LENS

Sidney Lens

Poverty: America's Enduring Paradox

A History of the Richest Nation's Unwon War

Thomas Y. Crowell Company

New York · Established 1834

*To
Sophie,
my mother,
the little immigrant lady who
arrived in 1907 and died in 1954
without ever catching the gold ring*

ACKNOWLEDGMENTS

My sincere thanks to five professors for taking time out from busy schedules to read this book and give me their reactions: Robert J. Lampman and Jack Barbash of the University of Wisconsin; Arthur Mann of the University of Chicago; Staughton Lynd of Chicago State College; and Donald M. Bluestone of Roosevelt University. Any errors in fact or interpretation that still remain are, of course, my own responsibility. I am also grateful to the Newberry Library in Chicago for providing excellent facilities for research, and to the Institute for Research on Poverty of the University of Wisconsin, and its director, Harold W. Watts, for getting me off to a flying start by letting me browse through its shelves. Most of all I want to express my affectionate gratitude to Shirley, my wife and beloved back-seat driver.

CONTENTS

CAT WITH NINE LIVES

In the image it has of itself, America has been the land of promise. Here have been relief and opportunity for countless injured and oppressed who were vegetating or starving elsewhere. An eighteenth-century immigrant to the New World, St. John de Crèvecoeur, could note of his fellow immigrants that "everything tended to regenerate them, new laws, a new mode of living, a new social system; here they are become men; in Europe they were so many useless plants, wanting vegetable mold and refreshing showers. They withered and were mowed down by want, hunger, and war; but now by the power of transplantation, like all other plants, they have taken root and flourished." This indeed is what Americans have believed their country has done for immigrants throughout the three and a half centuries they have plowed the fields and raised the spires to fashion, at least statistically, the wealthiest society of all time.

Yet concomitant with promise and wealth there has always been poverty in America, not only episodic and incidental but extensive and deep-rooted, not only the poverty of the "lazy" and "unfit," but of the most determined and hard-working. The indices that record economic growth may have moved generally upward, but innumerable millions have remained mired in misfortune despite their most zealous efforts to climb out of their circumstance. True, except for the

Negro (and the Indian) there have been no segments of this society that have remained poor throughout the American saga; in this respect the United States is different from most cultures.

But the most remarkable feature of American history has been the endless capacity of poverty for reincarnation. It dies off in one form, comes to life in another. It dies off for one sector of the population, re-emerges for others. What makes it all the more remarkable is that it has endured against innumerable and almost continuous antipoverty programs. Government agencies or elements of "the establishment" have been formulating and directing wars on poverty from the earliest colonial days. Admittedly, the phrase "war on poverty" was not invented until the Madison Avenue prophets put their imagination to the task in recent years, and the word itself—"poverty"—had a different connotation for hundreds of years from the one it has now. But society was not inactive. As a matter of fact, viewed in the glow of retrospect, many of the earlier antipoverty programs were far more dramatic than present ones, yet the cat—poverty—has had nine lives, and more.

The first war on poverty, though no one thought to give it that name, was the settlement of America itself. Unlike the present one, it was not a single, preconceived blueprint drawn by a central agency, but took many forms ranging from the profit-conscious plan of the Virginia Company to William Penn's "holy experiment" in "Pennsilvania." Yet it was probably of greater historical significance, given the state of technology, than the Kennedy-Johnson war more than three centuries later. It certainly carried a greater sense of excitement. A ballad by Michael Drayton, sung at the time the 120 adventurers were leaving for Jamestown in 1606, referred to "Virginia— Earth's only Paradise." James River, a London actor, pictured America as a lush land where Indians go "forth on holy days to gather rubies and diamonds by the seashore." Their dripping pans were said to be pure gold, even their prisoners were "fettered in golde." This was heart-warming intelligence to the unemployed of London who slept forlorn on the city's streets.

"Crimps"—called "newlanders" on the Continent—exceeded one another in depicting the New World to potential immigrants. "They would convince one," writes Frank R. Diffenderfer, "that there are in America none but Elysian fields abounding in products which require no labor; that the mountains are full of gold and silver, and that the wells and springs gush forth milk and honey; that he who goes there as a servant becomes a lord; as a maid, a gracious lady; as a peasant, a nobleman." Though there was a pound of deception to such claims there was also an ounce of truth, enough to raise the temperature of hope appreciably.

Closer to our own times the Homestead Act, vetoed by President Buchanan in 1860 and passed under President Lincoln two years later, was expected to be a "war" of greater dimensions than the unfocused assault of the 1960's. Beginning with George Henry Evans' cry, "Vote yourself a farm," two decades earlier, the demand for free land stirred desire and enthusiasm on a scale that would make today's Head Start seem irrelevant. The emancipation of the slaves, which liberated one of every nine Americans from bondage, taken together with the proposal of some left-wing Republicans to give each Negro "forty acres and a mule" was a program of visionary, almost utopian, dimensions. Even the discordant regulatory and welfare measures taken by the Progressives under Teddy Roosevelt and Woodrow Wilson raised blood pressure more than the New Frontier or the Great Society. To socialist William English Walling, it appeared that progressivism was moving the nation toward the nirvana of socialism itself. He waxed lyrical in 1914 that "President Wilson agrees with ex-President Roosevelt that governments must place human rights above property rights." There has been no end of wars against poverty, both by official agencies and highly placed men of power.

It is denigrating, in fact, to the American past to suggest that concern for the poor is a recent phenomenon. As dour as he was, Cotton Mather (in the words of Robert H. Bremner) "dreamed of a city in which each house would have an almsbox bearing the message 'Think on the Poor.'" William Penn proposed that "money, instead of being hoarded or spent on impious luxuries, should be used for comforting the poor." Benjamin Franklin, looking beyond both, conceived of a society in which "preventing poverty" was "a more sensible course than relieving it." Jefferson sketched a plan for distributing the public domain so widely that the nation would rest on a base of near-equal farm owners.

Reporting on more recent concerns, John Simpson Penman noted in a 1915 book that "since Henry George wrote his *Progress and Poverty* some forty years ago, the problems of poverty have awakened a public interest and have become the burning question of the 20th century. . . . Men are conscious of the sufferings and misery of the poor as never before in history." Even Herbert Hoover alluded to the abolition of poverty as the great national objective. Accepting the Republican nomination on August 11, 1928, he said, "We in America today are nearer to the final triumph over poverty than ever before in the history of any land. The poorhouse is vanishing from among us. We have not yet reached that goal, but given a chance to go forward with the policies of the last eight years, we shall soon with the help of God be within sight of that day when poverty will be banished from this nation."

Not all plans carried equal conviction. Some were the platitudes of political expediency, others were the sentiments of true idealism. The point is that with cyclical regularity, as if the clock were preset, there has been a national reawakening of conscience to "do something" for the poor. Yet, as the Bible reminded us a long time ago, poverty is still with us.

II

A history of this tenacious phenomenon—a limited one, needless to say, since almost all history is in some way related to it—must begin with a definition, or at least with some way to identify our quarry. What exactly is poverty? By what measuring stick do we call one man poor and another not poor?

If we assume, as most scholars do today, that poverty is synonymous with want, the question arises, What is want? A man wants material things such as food, clothing, and shelter merely to keep body and soul together, to survive. But he has certain psychological wants that are often more meaningful to him than his physiological ones. He wants to be creative and important, or if he cannot rise to such heights in the world of reality he at least wants an opportunity for vicarious creativity and importance. Until a few years ago authorities in Chicago denied relief to indigent families who owned television sets on the theory they were not yet in need so long as they possessed "property." But for a man who was unemployed and had nothing to do with his time except enjoy forms of escapism on the picture tube, this was as cruel as denying him bread. Whether he withered away physically or psychologically might be important for statisticians who classify such matters but it made little difference to the man in need.

On the other side of the ledger physical want is often tolerable, even ennobling, if accompanied by psychological satisfaction. A young revolutionary—say, of the Students for a Democratic Society or the Student Nonviolent Coordinating Committee—who lives on a bowl of chili and sleeps on the floor of his organization's office may receive more than enough spiritual joy from his labors and sacrifices to compensate for physical hardships. The fact that he has no TV set and not much bread has little relevance to poverty, for if he is in want it is by his own design. The same may be said of the pacifist in jail who goes on a hunger strike. He is certainly a problem for society, for its conscience as well as for its stability, but again he is not "poor" simply because he is starving.

Thus, the term "want" may be slightly more specific than the term "poverty," but it is just as elusive of scientific definition. Not only does it depend on the physical-psychological syndrome, but it is relative as to place and time. A man in want can easily be identified: his clothes are shabby, his table and cupboard are bare, his exchequer is depleted. But want is absolute and want is relative. Not long before he died, Jawaharlal Nehru, prime minister of India, was embroiled in a debate with an old nemesis, Ramonohar Lohia, a Socialist member of parliament. Lohia charged that 260,000,000 people in that despairing country were existing on six cents a day. Nehru vehemently denied this claim as a "damn lie"—the figure, he said, was fifteen cents. The minister of planning took issue with both men, asserting that the true amount was ten cents a day. Clearly, in such a milieu, a man who earned a dollar a day could be classed above the sociological poverty line. But what is "non-poor" in India obviously is very poor in the United States, France, or Italy, where a man with an income so small is considered as poor as the proverbial church mouse.

The standards by which want is measured differ also as to time; in a fluid, or relatively fluid, society expectations rise with each generation. The radio or television set that is a luxury at one point becomes a necessity a decade or two later. Thus the eighteenth-century frontiersman who lived in a mud hut without any conveniences but owned his own patch of land was a notch or two above want in the thinking of indentured servants, Negro slaves, or paupers who were his contemporaries. On the other hand, a slum tenant who lives in modern Harlem in a flat that boasts electricity and flush toilets, and who receives a $150 relief check each month is definitely poor. A man who owned an automobile fifty years ago was affluent, whereas automobiles today are considered a virtual necessity and millions who own secondhand jalopies may in fact be below the poverty line.

For hundreds of years in the American experience poverty was considered coterminous with pauperism. A person was poor only if he or she was lame, blind, insane, widowed, or aged and unable to provide for rudimentary needs. He was poor, in other words, if he needed a handout to survive. Then, at the end of the nineteenth century and early in this one, the national conscience extended the boundaries of poverty to include those who were, as Jacob Hollander, a professor at Johns Hopkins put it, "inadequately fed, clad, and sheltered." In this new view, which prevails to the present, a man did not have to be dependent to be poor; he might have a job or a small farm yet be desperately in need. The connotation of poverty made the big leap to include *inadequacy*. The arithmetical criterion for "inadequacy" in 1962, according to architects of the antipoverty program such as Robert J. Lampman, was a family income of less than $3,000 a year.

Even this definition, however, does not satisfy many critics who would extend the border much further. For Roy Wilkins of the National Association for the Advancement of Colored People, poverty is "a kind of anguished culture that is almost impossible for people outside to comprehend." This "anguished culture" is something apart from a "wrinkled belly," for though one contributes to the other they are not the same thing. The anguished culture has something to do with mood, with inequality, hopelessness, anxiety. As Michael Harrington defines it, in the same vein, poverty is a condition of men who "are dispossessed in terms of what the rest of the nation enjoys, in terms of what society could provide if it had the will." There is a "sense of outrage" to this phenomenon that goes beyond materialist borders.

Men of this school argue that poverty is not an arbitrary term translated into so many dollars and cents, but a concomitant of the human spirit. How else, they ask, can one explain the Black Rebellion of 1967, in which cities like Detroit were plagued by riots, vandalism, and burning? The worst disturbance that summer came not in Mississippi, where some Negroes were starving, but in the liberal auto center where much had been done to alleviate destitution. Yet many an auto worker with earnings of $100 to $125 a week and more participated in the riots. By mathematical yardsticks such men could not be considered poor. Evidently, however, they felt themselves part of an anguished culture that could not be appeased with wages alone.

To choose one of these three definitions—that poverty is dependency, that it is want, that it is a subculture—is very important for those prescribing an antidote. But for the chronicler they either limit the subject unnecessarily or widen it too far.

One kind of "dependence," for instance, is that of the maladjusted —the lazy, the drunk, the neurotic. If we widen the concept of poverty to include these we are forced to grapple with the chicken-and-egg conundrum: Is a person poor because he has become a drunkard or drunk because he is unable to escape poverty? Sincere prohibitionists believed for a long time that if distilled spirits could be withheld from those tempted by them the nation would take a long step toward curing indigence. But the greatest surge of poverty in American history, from 1929 to 1933, occurred at a time when the first (and only) nationwide prohibition law was on the books. The thesis of Social Darwinism, that poverty is incurable because it is the result of a natural selection, would send us far afield into either biology or psychoanalysis. According to this school the lazy, the ne'er-do-wells, the inebriate, the inefficient, the cowardly are consigned by a judicious nature to the place they belong, at the bottom of the ladder. This is a theory that has endured in the recesses of popular thinking since long before there were theoreticians to promulgate it and long after it was scientifically discarded. Yet apart from the fact that Social Darwinism does not tell us why "unfit" sons of "fit" fathers escape their just fate when they inherit their sires' money, it fails to account for the circumstance that there are fewer "unfit" at one time (during prosperity) than at others (during depression), or in the United States than in China. In any case, what the "unfit" contribute to their own misery is a subject for exploration into areas other than politics or history.

A different form of immiseration—that due to nature's hostility—is also ungermane to this tale, since politics can deal with it only peripherally at best. To focus on it at length limits the subject too much. Within six months after the first 104 settlers arrived in Jamestown in 1607, fifty-one were dead. Of the 100-odd in the original Plymouth contingent, half succumbed, according to William Bradford, within three months. Nature vented its fury on succeeding generations through epidemic, plague, fire. An epidemic in Virginia during the 1670's killed off 50,000 head of cattle, imposing commensurate hunger on the people who owned them, and another one in Maryland in 1695 took twice that toll. Three large fires in Boston in 1685 caused destruction estimated at £150,000 ($750,000). From 1607 to 1680, by the estimate of Albert Bushnell Hart, "perhaps 80,000 persons were actually landed in the New World." Of these from a third to a half died within a few years from hardship and disease, particularly malaria, with the attendant impoverishment of their families. But by and large, after early difficulties, nature has been beneficent to America, submitting quietly to steady conquest. Pauperization due to epidemics, tornadoes, fires, floods, and similar disasters has been episodic, seldom widespread.

Rather than define poverty abstractly, then, it is preferable for our purposes simply to identify its many forms either by their salient characteristic or by their immediate cause. Here we can find a common link and an explanation for its tendency to reincarnate. For whether the cause is social malfunction, such as depressions, or personal misfortunes, such as blindness, man—generic man—plays some role either in originating or continuing the resultant poverty. In every case he could have avoided or greatly mitigated it through a common social effort. There never has been a time in American history, for instance—except during the early Indian wars or for a few decades of colonial time—when society was incapable, from a material standpoint, of raising the income of its helpless blind or maimed much closer to the general average. And, as the last three decades have shown, depressions can be bypassed if the nation is willing to manage its economy. There is a man-made element to poverty, at least the poverty that has occupied national attention.

From this focal point we can prepare a list of the various types of poverty encountered in American history. Without in any way trying to be exhaustive, and conceding that the types blend and intertwine, here is a list of the dramatis personae of our play:

The poverty of the landless or dispossessed farmer.

The poverty of those dislocated by war.

The poverty of the helpless or semihelpless.

The poverty of the enslaved—red, white, and black.

The poverty of the economically manipulated—e.g., the backwoods-man saddled with heavy mortgages, the nineteenth-century agrarian weighted down by high freight rates.

The poverty of the politically manipulated—such as the returning Revolutionary soldier whose Continentals were worthless because the government wouldn't redeem them.

The poverty of the propertyless—e.g., the underpaid worker divorced from the means of production.

The poverty of joblessness due to depression, technological change, or business failure.

The poverty of the racially exploited—Negroes.

The poverty of the ethnically exploited—immigrants.

The poverty of the socially forgotten—e.g., the Southern poor white, the American Indian, the "invisible poor."

What we propose to do is to trace briefly the emergence of these poverties, as well as the alternating efforts to ameliorate or abolish them. It will appear, alas, an endless tale, moving back and forth from promise to blighted hope up to this very day. The promise of a better day was inherent in America—the subject in fact of Thomas More's dream of Utopia—but in the process of laying stakes for future affluence the forefathers devised means for blighting the hopes, temporarily or for long periods, of black men, tenants, indentured servants, and some frontiersmen. The boon of land made available by the Revolution offered opportunity to some but ended in a freezing out of many others. And so it has been throughout American history, even into the late 1960's, when *Fortune* magazine could list 153 persons worth $100 million or more, and the Citizens Board of Inquiry into Hunger and Malnutrition in the United States could report that the number of hungry in America "reaches well into the millions. And we believe that the situation is worsening."

A single thread seems to run through the story of poverty: that each of the forms listed above is somehow related to generic man's own failings, his unwillingness or inability to implement the precepts of *brotherhood* which he speaks of endlessly on holidays and religious occasions. The ethic of the family, in which all members, young and old, share adversities as well as joys, is not duplicated in the ethic of society, where indifference is more pronounced than concern. Thus, while the percentages may have changed, there is poverty today amidst plenty just as there was poverty amidst scarcity. Viewed from a different angle, the poor and their spokesmen periodically have gained sufficient power to modify their plight, only to find subsequently that their power has been whittled away and their efforts either Pyrrhic or only partly successful.

At any rate the story will tell itself.

Chapter 2

ROOTS AND RESEMBLANCES

Like so much else in early America, the story of poverty is umbilically linked to old England. In a sense—a limited one—America was England's antipoverty program, and for some Englishmen, such as Sir Thomas More, a dream of the beautiful, povertyless tomorrow. It was in England that vast changes in production and trade spawned a class of insecure people willing to emigrate from their misery. It was in imitation of the English way of life that new aristocracies emerged in the colonies and, concomitantly, new classes of poor. And it was from the England of Queen Elizabeth that Americans borrowed the techniques and principles for dealing with poverty that were to be their guideline for two centuries.

Long before America was colonized it was the substance for English visions of paradise. Sir Thomas More's witty book *Utopia*, published in 1516 in Latin, relates conversations between the author and a mythical sailor, Ralph Hythlodaye, who voyaged to the New World with Amerigo Vespucci, where he visited an island of peace and plenty called Utopia. Here, in a milk-and-honey surrounding, according to the mariner, everyone had a job, land was owned in common, children received public education, and the work day was only six hours, allowing leisure "for the free liberty of the mind." Hythlodaye contrasts this enchanting place with the appalling

11

poverty of England, where men were being thrown off the land by the tens of thousands and the cities were filling with beggars and vagrants.

More envisioned in this great, mysterious, and boundless territory, sighted only a generation before by Columbus, a final surcease from the plague wracking England, landlessness. In Sir Thomas' thinking, the single cause for man's ills was the lust for land. The rich, tempted by greed, used devious means to accumulate more acreage for themselves while denying it to the poor; and from this original sin flowed all others, including crime and poverty. This may or may not be sound social theory, but it certainly reflected conditions in England at the time.

Insofar as its economy was concerned, though not its people, Dame Fortune was smiling on the island nation. As Flemish wool manufacture expanded on the Continent, the demand for the raw commodity, as well as its price, was rising apace. Here was a source of easy money if the English lords of the land could only find the acreage to raise sheep. As it turned out, sheep and men were incompatible, for to make room for the four-legged animals the men of power had to uproot the two-legged ones. By devices called enclosure and rack-renting, they evicted unfortunate husbandmen from the villages by the thousands. In appeasing their lust for land and profit, the gentry of England blanketed their nation with a pall of poverty.

Sheep, said Thomas More, became more important than people. "Your sheep," he wrote, "which are naturally mild and easily kept in order, may be said now to devour men and unpeople, not only villages, but towns, for, wherever it is found that the sheep of any soil yield a softer and richer wool than ordinary there the nobility and gentry, and even those holy men and abbots . . . stop the course of agriculture, destroying houses and towns . . . that they may lodge their sheep in them. . . . When an insatiable wretch, who is a plague to his country, resolves to inclose many thousands of acres of land, the owners, as well as tenants, are turned out of their possessions by tricks, or by main force, or, being wearied out with ill-usage, they are forced to sell them. By which means those miserable people, both men and women, married and unmarried, old and young, with their poor but numerous families . . . are all forced to change their seats, not knowing whither to go. . . ."

Ironically, England in the sixteenth and seventeenth centuries was headed toward a rosy future. The old order, stagnant and immobile, was in the process of being replaced by mercantilism, the merchant society, and both tradesmen and adventurers often pocketed staggering fortunes. Typically during the reign of Queen Elizabeth, pirates like Drake and Hawkins despoiled Spanish settlements and ships of £12,000,000. In a three-year voyage from 1577 to 1580 to the coast of South America, Drake showed a profit of £600,000 ($3,000,000) on an investment of £5,000 ($25,000). Even a few people of low estate were climbing the economic ladder. A widowed Quaker, Joan Dant by name, began life as a peddler and accumulated £9,000 as a moderately affluent merchant. From the time of Elizabeth's accession in 1558 to 1695 merchant enterprise grew from a paltry £50,000 to £4,000,000. The demand for investment capital was so great that joint stock companies such as the East India Company had to be formed to pool resources. From 1660 to 1688 national wealth quintupled, according to Louis Hacker, from £17,000,000 to £88,000,000.

It was all wonderful and breath-taking, except that as England grew more affluent it spawned a wider and more insidious pauperism. The population, of course, had always been poor, in the sense that the average man lived from hand to mouth. But in earlier times he had had a certain security; he had had a few patches of land to work and a reasonable expectation that he would continue to work them. But wool, England's chief export for a long time, made a shambles of the former way of life. By age-old custom each village had a commons, used by the lowly as well as the mighty to graze cattle. Presumably the commons was commonly owned, but in their zeal to find pasture land for their sheep, the gentry built enclosures—fences—around this common property to make it their own. Tenants and small farmers were left to graze their cattle on already inadequate holdings, or slaughter them, and in many cases give up their land. It was an act of unbridled robbery, often denounced by men of conscience like Sir Thomas More and even the monarchy, yet in the end economics proved stronger than morality.

A petition to the House of Commons by farmers from Wootton Bassett, quoted by Leo Huberman, sheds light on the farmers' problem. It reads as follows: "That whereas the Mayor and Free Tenants of the said Borough . . . had and did hold unto them free common of pasture for the feeding of all sorts of other beasts . . . one Sir Francis Englefield . . . did enclose the said park . . . and this did continue so long, he being too powerful for them, that the said free tenants were not able to wage law any longer; for one John Rous, one of the free tenants, was thereby enforced to sell all his land (to the value of £500) with following the suits in law, and many others were thereby impoverished. . . ."

A 1581 pamphlet complained that "where 40 persons had their livings, now one man and shepherd have all . . . by these enclosures men do lack livings and be idle." As the peasants fled (in many places a quarter to a half of them), a not unhappy landlord cried "Good riddance!" and razed their cottages to the ground. Both Henry VII and Henry VIII, alarmed by the steady exodus, enacted laws to stem the tide. They prohibited destruction of "houses of husbandry" and limited the ownership of sheep to two thousand head, but it was all unavailing against the tide of economic progress. Henry VIII's confiscation of the immodest holdings of the Catholic Church, far from alleviating the plight of the landless, exacerbated it. The properties were either granted outright to court favorites or sold at minimum price to speculators, and the latter took advantage of the changeover to consolidate land strips and drive still more tenants from house and hearth.

Enclosure continued in England, and to a lesser extent in France and the Continent, from the sixteenth to the early nineteenth century. An eighteenth-century ditty, expressing the bitterness of the displaced, went like this:

> The law locks up the man or woman
> Who steals a goose from off the common;
> But leaves the greater villain loose
> Who steals the common from the goose.

Another device for dispossessing the land tillers, probably more pernicious, was rack-renting. Here too custom, usually believed to have the effect of law, had been designed for stability. Annual rents were considered fixed and relatively unchangeable, so that a tenant could expect to farm his acreage indefinitely and even pass it on to his son on the payment of a small fine. But the landlords raised rents and fines sky high, and tenants without the wherewithal either gave up their holdings willingly or were dispossessed. A 1533 petition by residents of Whitby listed five lords who had increased rents two to eight times. In the face of this economic pressure, villages were depopulated, except for sheep and shepherds, and hordes of people either starved, stole, or begged to keep body and soul together. Sheffield, whose population in 1615 was listed as 2,207, reported 725 subsisting on charity. In Scotland, where forcible eviction took place much later, a Member of Parliament stated in 1698 that "the number of beggars . . . is reckoned at not less than 200,000," a rather ominous number considering how small populations were at that time.

Thus, while the first taste of individualism was a boon measured in terms of trade and accumulation of bullion, it was a bitter brew for countless small people, whose immiseration was a necessary condition for a cheap labor force in the cities. Want and need had, of course, been constant handmaidens of the old society; they were joined now by massive destitution. The mercantile society eventually would merge into the industrial society; the city and town would eventually find jobs for the displaced villager. For the time being, however, no such prospect loomed on the horizon.

"The Land growes weary of her Inhabitants," observed John Winthrop, the future leader of New England.

II

In due course, a century and a quarter after the enclosures began to spread pauperism far and wide, England formulated what was probably the modern world's first antipoverty program—Queen Elizabeth's poor laws. Like its future offspring this Elizabethan war on poverty was distinguished by the fact that it shied from fundamental measures such as refashioning social institutions or altering the status of the rich, as revolutionaries might propose. Instead it limited itself solely to ameliorating the plight of the poor. If the good Queen had read More's *Utopia*, she had no intention of revising the English way of life so that land would be owned in common. She had neither intention nor desire to retrieve stolen lands or in any way to clip the wings of the wealthy. On the contrary, implicit in this as in other antipoverty plans was the conviction that the upper classes had an inalienable right to pursue their riches. Society's obligations to the poor ended at the water's edge of public assistance. Thus the 1601 poor laws substituted a collective alms box, sustained by the state's taxing power, for individual giving.

Queen Elizabeth, the last of the Tudor monarchs, ruled from 1558 to 1603. In this period England rose to greatness, defeating the Spanish Armada, sending her adventurers throughout the New World, laying the seeds of empire, growing in stature both materially and spiritually. This was the age of Shakespeare and Bacon, of intellectual and scholarly probing, a time, in other words, when conscience was stirred by the winds of national pride. The Queen's program for the poor was promulgated in that spirit.

In previous days, until the middle of the sixteenth century, distressed villagers could look to their landlord for some relief. The Church too was a refuge for the hungry, raising and disbursing monies on their behalf. In fact its levies eventually acquired the force of law, since anyone who refused to pay could be ordered to do so either by the bishop or by a civil magistrate.

The Church, however, was being divested of much of its own riches by Henry VIII, and the landlord, as already noted, was in the process of evicting tenants rather than worrying about their welfare. It fell to the state, therefore, to deal with what no one else was equipped to do. It could have shirked this obligation, of course, but the convergence of mercantile political doctrine with religious belief dictated otherwise. To help the helpless was considered synonymous with the word of God in the sixteenth and seventeenth centuries, and no one questioned it. And since the state, under mercantilist precepts, viewed itself as a totalitarian directing agency for all national endeavor, it was only natural it should assume this duty as well. The state set prices, fixed wages, determined apprenticeship rules and quality standards, chartered stock companies, granted patents for land. Poor relief became another facet of its activity.

But if the principle of assistance was fully accepted, the question of who would benefit from it was troubled—then and for hundreds of years to come, both in England and America—by a certain ambivalence in popular thinking. No one denied that the helpless, the sick, the aged, and so forth were worthy of society's generosity. But under the Protestant ethic work was considered among the highest virtues, akin to motherhood, and idleness among the most flagrant sins. Time and again this double standard emerges, in the writings not only of stark conservatives but of liberals as well. As forward-looking as he was, for instance, John Locke proposed in 1697 that "all men, sound of limb and mind, begging in maritime counties out of their own parish shall be seized by an officer of the parish or by an inhabitant and brought before the next J.P. and be sent . . . to the next seaport town, there to be kept at hard labor till some of H.M. Ships coming in, give an opportunity of putting them on board, where they will serve three years under strict discipline at soldiers pay." The Puritan Thomas Shepard, in a letter to his son at Harvard, 1672, urged him to "abhor therefore one hour of idleness as you would be ashamed of one hour of drunkenness." And when Cotton Mather saw beggars on the streets of Boston he fumed that "our Lord Jesus Christ himself had expressly forbidden us to countenance" them. Those who do not work, he said, should not eat. Such stigmas against idleness prevailed for centuries and are evident in virtually all the legislation dealing with poverty.

As early as 1531, under Henry VIII, beggars too old to work were granted licenses to ply their calling within fixed boundaries, but under the same act able-bodied idlers were ordered lashed or imprisoned. For their sinfulness they might be tied to a cart tail, whipped, and made to pledge under oath they would return to their birthplaces to find honest labor. The second offense was punished by having an ear cut off; the third, frequently, by execution. An act of 1547 subjected vagrants to branding and two-year terms as servants. This was repealed as too severe, but in 1572 the rulers of England decreed that idlers must be put out for one year's service with a responsible property owner, and if none could be found the criminal was to be whipped and have his right ear "burned through the gristle." For the third offense, again, death was the ultimate reward. If this seems sadistically harsh, it should be noted by way of extenuation that as good Christians the English combined punishment with opportunities for redemption. In a sort of pre-New Deal W.P.A., they opened workshops for the unemployed to which the government supplied wool, hemp, and iron so that surplus laborers might be employed at useful endeavor.

Finally in 1601, under Elizabeth, all these principles of poor relief were woven together into a single fabric. These laws, modified from time to time in both England and America, were to remain the guidelines of public assistance to the destitute for more than three centuries. They provided that each parish select two to four householders who, together with the church warden, were to act as overseers of the poor. Among other duties they were to impose a weekly tax on constituents to purchase flax, hemp, wool, and other materials to make work for the idle. Children whose parents could not provide for them were to be hired out as apprentices, to prepare them for a later useful life. And the helpless—the dependent—were to be supplied with relief in the form of money, food, shelter.

The poor laws were in many respects a model of moderation. Such punitive practices as the whipping of paupers and fining of beggars were abolished. Almshouses were set up for the sick and infirm, and the children who were forced to live in them were given a rudimentary education. If the attitude toward the able-bodied seems harsh, it must be noted, on the other side, that the sense of liability to the helpless was taken with at least as much seriousness as it is today. In the years 1665 and 1666, during the reign of Charles II, when war, plague, and the burning of a large part of London had reduced one-fifth of England's population to pauper status, poor rates were raised so high that almost half the King's income—£700,000 annually—was assigned to relief.

But liberal as these laws were, they could not cope with the scourge of unemployment; almshouses and forced labor were no substitute for a patch of land. For the economically disadvantaged, therefore, the colonies in America soon beckoned like a beacon—even for those who could not muster the courage to make the fearsome voyage overseas. And for the monarchy, settlement of the New World held promise not only as a source of minerals, furs, timber for the royal navy and for trade, but also as a means of coping with potential social explosions of the jobless. Sir Humphrey Gilbert, the explorer who first set foot on Newfoundland, suggested in 1574 that "we might inhabit some part of these Countryes [in America] and settle there such needy people of our country which now trouble the commonwealth and through want here at home are enforced to commit outrageous offences, whereby they are dayly consumed by the gallows." Among the stated objectives of the joint stock companies that were given charters by James I to colonize Virginia was one to rid England of its "superfluous twigs." The Spanish minister to England, Velasco, reported to his monarch in 1611 that the "principal reason for colonizing these parts is to give an outlet to so many idle, wretched people as they have in England, and thus prevent the dangers that might be feared of them."

That too, of course, could be considered a war on poverty, though no one in 1611 really thought of it quite that way.

Chapter 3

ANTIPOVERTY—OLD STYLE

England was a century behind Spain and Portugal when the first Stuart, James I, took the throne, but she claimed an area in America a hundred times larger than her own. Sir Francis Drake, after a marauder's trip to South America, is said to have landed in a bay north of the present San Francisco in 1572 and named the country he was annexing for Queen Elizabeth Nova Albion—New England. More than a decade later, Sir Walter Raleigh arrived with a fleet on the other side of the continent, now North Carolina, and designated it Virginia, after the "Virgin Queen." Most of what is now the United States and Canada was viewed as the English bounty, the only obstacle in the way to effective seizure being a million Indians, and in the more limited area that was actually colonized—bounded by Maine, Florida, and the Appalachian Mountains—200,000. The red men, however, were not considered a decisive obstacle. In granting a patent to explorer Sir Humphrey Gilbert in June 1578, Elizabeth authorized him to seize "any remote barbarous and heathen lands not possessed by any Christian prince or people." James I, when he issued charters for colonizing Virginia, narrowed this order somewhat to the "superfluous lands" of the natives. In either case there would be land aplenty, if it could be secured, for limitless numbers of English poor who hungered for it at home. And clearing that wilderness offered the prospect of full-time work indefinitely for any who sought it.

A couplet distributed by the London Company in 1630 to lure immigrants read:

> In England land scarce and labour plenty
> In Virginia land free and labour scarce.

Yet, as it turned out, the mere availability of land was no sure-fire guarantee against poverty. In the seventeen colonial decades some men would become rich (or richer) because of the land; many, poor before, would become independent; but large numbers would be catapulted into new forms of poverty. This was to be, in the circumstances of the seventeenth and eighteenth centuries, a land of promise, but not Sir Thomas More's Utopia.

England's men of power understood that by opening up America they were offering a mecca to the poor—draining off, as the London Company put it, "the fuel of dangerous insurrections." Their first concern, however, was for themselves. The monarchs doled out America's largesse in large chunks to the high and mighty. The whole area from Maine to the middle of South Carolina, two hundred miles inland, for instance, went to two stock companies made up of the biggest entrepreneurs of the time on condition they would pay James I one-fifth of the gold and silver they found there. One of these charters—for the Massachusetts Bay Company—was given to twenty-six men, mostly affluent Puritan merchants, with the intervention of no less a personage than the Earl of Warwick. The Carolinas went to eight proprietors, including the future Earl of Shaftesbury. Maryland was given to Lord Baltimore and the Calverts; Pennsylvania, to William Penn; New York (and New Jersey), to the Duke of York.

Inevitably, however, some of the land trickled down to the lowly. When a doughty band of religious mavericks, under Roger Williams, sought another place to live they simply occupied Rhode Island. Thomas Hooker and his friends took over Connecticut. The Crown later sanctified these acts of seizure, but originally the two groups were nothing more than high-class squatters. Individually and in groups squatters also found haven in large parts of Maine, New Hampshire, New Jersey, Pennsylvania, the Carolinas, and elsewhere; there was just too much land available to deny them access to it and most of them eventually won title to their holdings. In addition, the 100,000 servants who came here in the seventeenth century had to be assured some means of securing farms once their bondage was over; otherwise they might as well stay at home. In Maryland, by tradition and law, each servant was given, on the completion of his term, fifty acres, an ax, two hoes, and three barrels of corn. In New England the General Court sent groups of settlers to establish villages of thirty-six square miles, each family in the group being entitled to a patch of land and use of the common.

Those who could pay their own fare (half to two-thirds of the 750,000 who crossed the ocean from 1607 to 1770) were guaranteed 100 or more acres at low cost or free. Shareholders in the London Company that settled Virginia were granted 100 acres in "fee simple" beforehand, another 100 when they were "seated," plus 50 acres for each person brought over. During the eighteenth century the Crown granted 50 acres to anyone who could pay five shillings and agree to build a house and cultivate three acres. Pennsylvania offered 500 acres to anyone transporting his family to America; Maryland bestowed 100 acres each for husband, wife, and servant, on condition the family pay ten pounds of wheat rent for every 50 acres. Freeholds were assigned in Carolina based on 100 acres for the man, his wife, each child, and male servant, and 50 acres for a female servant. In New Jersey a man with his own gun and six months of supplies was given 150 acres, with a similar amount for each servant and Negro, and half as much for each woman in the family. Captain John Smith's statement in 1616 that land in America "costs nothing but labor" was an exaggeration no doubt, but not a flagrant one. Put in a nutshell, the moguls of England bartered away unimproved land, useless unless worked in any case, for settlers to work it.

It was a marriage of two needs: John Bull needed muscle to become a great colonial power; most of the 750,000 Englishmen and Europeans who emigrated needed a haven from their tumultuous despair. Early in their history the Puritans of Massachusetts pleaded with philanthropists in England to send poor children overseas, "they being superabundant [in England]" and "we wanting hands to carry on our trades, manufacturing and husbandry." The shortage of labor was endemic to the American scene throughout most of the colonial period. William Fitzhugh, a rich Virginia planter who owned 24,000 acres in 1684, for instance, could put only 300 to the plow because his whole estate, including two stores and a mill, had to be worked by twenty-nine slaves. This was a universal problem. Land without labor was useless, and to recruit labor the large landowners, in the early days at least, had to offer land as the carrot.

II

Here begins a peculiar tale both of escape from poverty and immersion in it. History seemed to be moving in opposite directions simultaneously: relieving destitution for many formerly oppressed in Europe, creating new forms for those settled here.

One of the possible sources of labor obviously was the Indian. But the settlers found to their chagrin that he was not easily domesticated. "When they [the Indians] hired themselves out as servants," records V. F. Calverton, "they did so with the utmost reluctance and upon many occasions robbed and sometimes even killed their masters. It did not take the whites very long to realize that the Indians were impossible as servants or in any other menial capacity." An advertisement in the *Boston News-Letter* of October 1707 read: "Run away from her master Baker. A tall, lusty Carolina Indian woman named Kezia Wampum, having long, straight Black Hair tyed up with red Hair Lace, very much marked in the hands and face. . . ." Indian slavery survived for a long time; as late as 1708 South Carolina held 1,400 natives in bondage as against 4,100 Negroes. But it was not a dependable supply of labor, and in any case was meager against the need. Colony after colony, dispirited by the "conspiratorial tempers" of the natives, abolished the practice as unfeasible.

If there was no hope of subduing the red man, then labor must be recruited from the disaffected of Britain. Until 1665 there was manpower aplenty to be secured this way, particularly after the crimps had finished picturing America as the golden highway. The tobacco culture of Virginia alone absorbed 1,500 to 2,000 emigrants annually from 1635 to 1705. Most of this class came willingly. The servant made a contract with a ship captain to be put out for a given number of years of bondage—usually four to seven, sometimes longer—in return for passage. The captain would tear the contract into jagged halves, giving the emigrant one part—an indent—and keeping the other. A second type of servant was the "redemptioner" or "free willer" who pledged to sell himself on arrival, not beforehand, the ship captain to be reimbursed by the purchaser. A third, smaller group, though still numbering tens of thousands, were those who came not by their own decision. They were either kidnaped on the streets of London or the Continent (the word evidently derives from "kid nabbers"), or criminals sent overseas by the Crown. The utilization of prisoners for labor in the colonies began almost at the outset of the American experiment. Scotsmen captured in the battle of Worcester were dispatched to Virginia in 1610. The following year the governor, Sir Thomas Dale, urged the king "to banish hither all offenders condemned to die, it would be a readie way to furnish us with men, and not allwayes with the worst kinde of men either for birth, spiritts or Bodie." Richard B. Morris estimates that as many as 50,000 involuntary servants were shipped to the colonies, 20,000 of them to Maryland alone. Odd as it may seem, there were convicts in England who, when given the choice, preferred to remain in prison rather than become one of "His Majesty's seven-year passengers." A certain Philip Gibson, sentenced to death for street robbery, accepted hanging in preference to bondage.

How many white indentures—temporary slaves—came over is a subject of dispute, but it is generally agreed that no fewer than one-third and perhaps half of the immigrants during the colonial period were of this class. During the seventeenth century they were more numerous than Negro slaves. Virginia in 1671, for instance, estimated the number of white slaves at 6,000 (13 per cent of the population) as against 2,000 Negroes.

Whatever its long-term opportunities, temporary servitude was a harrowing experience. To begin with, there was the voyage. Ordinarily the trip lasted six to twelve weeks, but it might take longer. "These slave ships," writes Calverton, "were literal prisons in which men, women, and children grew sick, suffered, and died." The average cargo was 300 people, but it was not unusual to have double that number aboard. The servants wore the same clothes four weeks to four months running, lay flat for days when the small vessel was in heavy seas—sometimes next to a corpse—and went hungry or starved with painful frequency. "There are many instances," writes James Truslow Adams, "where passengers almost fought for the bodies of rats and mice, a number where cannibalism was threatened, and one, at least, where it was practiced." On one ship carrying Scotch-Irish refugees the "maddened passengers" ate six dead humans and were in the process of carving up a seventh when another ship came by and offered supplies. The number of dead was appalling. On one voyage of 400 Palatines in 1709, 20 per cent expired. Of a cargo of 150 servants in 1730 only thirteen survived to see the new land. Another in 1745, with 400 Germans aboard, recorded fifty alive at the end. But terrible as these losses were in human terms, the ship captains and merchants were not unrewarded. The cost of transportation was £4 to £5 per person, while the average white slave brought twice to four times that amount on the open market.

On arrival in America the indentured servant would be marched to the magistrate's office to take an oath to the king, then put on the auction block. If there was no buyer, the shipmaster would turn him over to a "soul driver" to be dragged through the countryside and offered for sale. On one occasion a quick-witted servant sold his soul driver while the latter was asleep and made his escape. Not infrequently, as with black slaves, families were broken up, children going to one master, the wife to another, and the husband to a third. A Philadelphia gentleman who purchased a man, wife, and daughter found that they were his own father, mother, and sister.

Though, unlike Indians and Negroes, the white slave was a Christian, he did not on that account receive any preferred treatment. A letter written late in the eighteenth century made an interesting comparison between white and Negro bondsmen: "Negroes being a property for life, the death of slaves in the prime of youth or strength is a material loss to the proprietor; they are, therefore, almost in every instance, under more comfortable circumstances than the miserable European, over whom the rigid planter exercises an inflexible severity. They are strained to the utmost to perform their allotted labour."

Since this was an age before sociology, no survey exists on the ill-treatment of indentures, but the subject comes up constantly in colonial accounts. The Virginia Assembly noted in 1662 that "the barbarous usage of some servants by cruell masters bring soe much scandell and infamy to the country in generall that people who would willingly adventure themselves hither, are through feare thereof diverted, and by that means the supplies of particular men and the well seating of his majesties country very much obstructed." Occasionally servants were beaten to death. There is the tale of Elizabeth Abbott of Virginia, who was found dead with "her flesh in some places . . . raw and very black and blew . . ." after continuous whippings. She had fled to the woods and expired after fourteen days. Cases of inadequate food came to court dockets over and over again, and laws were enacted in Maryland and Virginia to remedy the situation. Servants ran away so often that Virginia passed a bill adding twice the time lost by flight to the term of service. A repeat of the offense was punishable by branding on cheek and shoulder.

Apart from the ordeal of heavy work, inadequate food, and punishment, the white slave was restricted in his personal life as if in a prison. He could not buy or sell anything, especially liquor, or leave his master's home without permission. Marriage was prohibited, so that, as might be expected, bastardy became a frequent crime, all the more so since female servants were at the mercy of masters, who as one writer notes, "if inclined to licentiousness, would not be slow to use it." In 1663 fourteen cases of bastardy were tried in just one Virginia court. The legal code provided that if the master was responsible for the illegitimate child the servant was taken from him and resold by the parish, the money going for the youngster's support. If the illegitimacy was not the master's doing, additional time was added to the servant's bondage as punishment. The father, if known, was made to pay for the child's rearing; the mother was always flogged and fined as a reminder of her sins.

It can be argued, of course, that white servitude was temporary, but four to seven years can be interminable under certain conditions, and in not a few instances the indentures took measures against their plight. Some committed suicide. Some fled, every now and then taking a Negro slave along. Thus an advertisement in the *Pennsylvania Gazette* of October 8, 1747, reads: "There went away with Ann Wainwright, White Servant, a Negro slave Woman belonging to June Bailard." Still others plotted revolt. So fearful were the colonial aristocrats of placing weapons in the hands of their indentures that when Governor Nicholson of Virginia proposed military service for servants, the House of Burgesses turned him down because "they might be tempted to seek to obtain their freedom by slaying their masters."

III

The garish story of Negro slavery forms a special chapter in the history of American poverty. With the growing labor requirements of the colonies, white slavery and native labor became inadequate, particularly in the South. Furthermore, the indentured servant was relatively expensive. During the seventeenth century the cost of transport plus commissions ran from £10 to £12 per indenture and the cost of "freedom dues"—the food, clothing, tools, and sometimes a cow—the master was required to provide at the end of bondage, came to an equal sum, for a total of around £22. A young Negro slave, by contrast, could be bought for £18 to £25 (by 1770, £50 to £80) and not only work for life but produce salable progeny. It was an excellent arrangement both for the wealthier planters and the merchant capitalists involved in the trade. The Royal African Company, given a monopoly in 1672, was big business, with £111,000 capital. By 1750 slave traders, with investments of £800,000, were earning yearly profits of £1,200,000 and providing spin-off affluence for many middle-class families in Newport, Rhode Island, and in Bristol and Liverpool in England. In the century from 1686 to 1786 something like two million Africans were spirited away from the Black Continent, approximately 250,000 of them winding up on the American mainland. It was a boom business. Connecticut, which had only thirty Negro bondsmen in 1720, listed 6,500 in 1775. At midcentury one out of every seven New Yorkers was a Negro. The largest concentration, of course, was in the South, especially after the cultivation of rice and indigo was begun. South Carolina held within its borders 32,000 blacks in 1724 and 90,000 forty years later, approximately two-thirds the total population.

The black man comprised a sector outside society—poor, hopeless, mistreated, living in hovels, with virtually no legal rights. Some Americans entertained ideas of liberating the Negro after a specific period, just as the white slave was freed. Thus George Fox, leader of the Quakers, admonished his followers: "It will doubtless be very acceptable to the Lord if it be that masters of Families here would deal so with their servants, the Negroes and blacks whom they have bought with their Money to let them go free after a considerable Term of Years if they have served them faithfully." Noah Webster proposed "to raise the slaves by gradual means to the condition of free tenants." But generally such notions were considered dangerously idealistic. The Negro not only remained a slave for life, but his status was inheritable; his children too became bondsmen at birth. To make sure that there would be no question on this score, Maryland and Virginia early passed laws sanctioning this situation, to be followed in 1698 by Massachusetts, in 1704 by Connecticut and New Jersey, in 1706 by Pennsylvania and New York, in 1712 by South Carolina. As time passed, until the Revolution, even manumission was made more difficult, so that the Negro was offered no escape either for himself or endlessly into future generations. He sang a doleful song, as he worked the fields, attesting to his plight:

> De night is dark, de day is long,
> And we are far from home.
> Weep, my brudders, weep!

The horror began with being kidnaped in Africa by other tribesmen. In these wars, spurred by slave merchants, in the insurrections that followed, the transportation to the coast for shipment, and the voyage itself, at least three black men died for every one who made it. Aboard ship alone the loss was titanic: of the 60,000 slaves sent to the colonies by the Royal African Company from 1680 to 1688, 14,000 perished. Once in the colonies "so severe was the change from native to European ways," writes Curtis P. Nettels, "that about half of the Negroes died within three or four years after their removal from Africa." After being sold on the auction block they were treated to the usual infamies accorded men without rights. Even the Quakers, progressive in other matters, decreed in 1693 that Negroes "gadding about" be taken to jail, left without food or drink, and whipped with 39 lashes the following morning. Runaway slaves in Virginia not infrequently had their ears nailed to the pillory and then cut off.

The Negro's life naturally was not confined to having his ears cut off or being whipped. Some observers honestly believed they lived better than if they had been free. Thus the Reverend Hugh Jones, describing conditions in 1724 in Virginia, writes: "The Negroes are very numerous, some Gentlemen having Hundreds of them of all sorts, to whom they bring great Profitt; for the Sake of which they are obliged to keep them well, and not over-work, starve or famish them, besides other Inducements to favour them; which is done in great Degree, to such especially that are laborious, careful and honest. . . ." On the other hand, "when they are free they know not how to provide so well for themselves generally; neither did they live so plentifully nor (many of them) so easily in their own Country where they are made Slaves to one another, or taken Captive by their Ennemies."

Many Negroes—and hundreds of clergymen who sympathized with their plight—evidently did not agree with this estimate, for suicide, flight, and revolt were recurrent. Whole families of Negroes made compacts to deliver themselves beyond this world to the grace of God. One mother, it is recorded, strangled every one of her thirteen children, before taking her own life. A document advising planters how to handle would-be suicides noted that Negroes sometimes "stifle themselves by drawing in the tongue so as to close the breathing passage, others take poison, or flee and perish of misery and hunger."

Occasionally the Negro rose in armed rebellion. Early on the morning of April 8, 1712, a group of slaves in New York City, armed with knives, guns, and clubs, set fire to a house and waited for whites to cluster around it. Thereupon they killed nine and wounded seven. When they were captured six of the slaves committed suicide, twenty-one were hanged, burned, or broken on the wheel. More serious was a revolt in September 1739. When the governor of Spanish Florida promised Negroes freedom in his territory, a sizable band near neighboring Charleston, South Carolina, attacked an arms magazine, killed its two guards, and with the weapons seized moved westward toward the Edisto River. On the way, with colors flying and drums beating, they enrolled more recruits, shouted for liberty, and burned everything in their path, as if in scorched-earth war. Thirty white men were killed, though one slaveowner was spared because he was said to be "kind to his slaves." Seventy of the rebels were hanged or gibbeted alive; ten were never accounted for. Perhaps they escaped to Florida. All told there were forty revolts or conspiracies by Negroes in colonial days.

IV

If slavery was a unique type of poverty, in the sense that it rested on the totalitarian exercise of power by the owner, there were enough other subtle and traditional types from 1607 to 1776 to remove the gloss from the "American promise." Not that every day was dire, or the horizons hopelessly gloomy; on the contrary, no place on earth, at the time, offered such possibilities or excited such optimism. A Pennsylvania immigrant, writing to friends in England at the beginning of the eighteenth century, said that American "farmers or husbandmen live better than lords. If a workman only work for four or five days a week he can live grandly." While this was buoyant exaggeration, wages here were in fact 30 to 100 per cent higher than in the old country, and land ownership sufficiently widespread to offer comfort to sizable numbers. Yet there was a machine at work in the colonies manufacturing misery even while lifting the plight of the majority notch by notch. The domain of poverty extended beyond the one-fifth in slavery (black and white) to significant sections of the four-fifths that were free.

To begin with, the freeholder or squatter had to contend with the elements. He had to clear his land and pray that his first crops would not be destroyed by plague, famine, or fire. Ordinarily, in the earlier days particularly, he lived with his family in a tent or cave, or in a hut with clapboard roofing and windows made of paper weatherproofed with lard. His furniture was rudimentary, his clothes homespun. Though he was armed with hope for tomorrow, his condition in the present was highly tenuous.

Another threat to security was the red man, who stubbornly refused to be Christianized, domesticated, enslaved, or cheated of his heritage. He fought the white man's incursion with massacres, skirmishes, and at least four major wars. And though the white man always won, the cost was sometimes staggering. Of the 80,000 inhabitants of New England in 1675–76, more than 600 were killed fighting the Wampanoag chief, Metacom (called "King Philip"), and his allies. (An equivalent loss for the whole United States today would be 1,500,000 killed in action.) Hundreds of houses were razed and at least twenty villages destroyed. It was two decades before they were fully rebuilt, and forty years before New Englanders advanced again into the contested central and southern parts of their domain. Those who had lived in the area were reduced, despite Puritan efforts at relief, to stark dependency for a considerable period.

The more significant forms of poverty, however, were the result of economic and political manipulation. In the ceaseless contest for power, some men acquired vast tracts of land or became great merchants; others were victimized by devalued prices, high interest rates, limitation of land settlement, increased rents, and resistance to squatters' rights.

Generation to generation, aggregates of wealth grew larger and more concentrated. By 1676 there were thirty merchants and landholders in Massachusetts with fortunes of £10,000 to £20,000 ($50,000 to $100,000). A half century later, through political control of the legislatures, the wealthy scions were able to reverse the old custom of assigning new villages to actual settlers. Instead, land speculators were permitted to buy them for resale. Thus there grew up in New England a class of men, known as the "river gods" or "lords of the valley," who pre-empted vast areas. Colonel Jacob Wendell of Boston bought 24,000 acres of what was to be a new township in western Massachusetts. Colonel Israel Williams of Hatfield held property in no fewer than a dozen towns. In 1721 John Reed, a prominent councilman of Boston, was permitted, with a few partners, to purchase 106,000 acres for the incredibly low sum of £683. It created a scandal in the colony but twenty-eight years later, when Reed died, he left enormous estates in Connecticut, Massachusetts, and New Hampshire.

Polarization of land wealth in New York, taken from the Dutch in 1664, was even more pronounced. By "investment, chicanery and corruption," writes Mary Beard, the men of power in this colony——about thirty—were able "to engross from one-half to two-thirds of the land." The tract of the Van Rensselaers near Albany ran 700,000 acres; that of the Van Cortlandts, 140,000; the Beekmans, 240,000. Robert Livingston garnered an estate sixteen miles long by twenty-four wide. Under Lord Cornbury's governorship, one group of speculators, known as the "little nine partners," secured a grant of a million acres.

In Maryland and the South, the trend was fairly similar. Those with capital and political influence acquired massive estates. Thomas

Berewood in 1731 was ceded 10,000 acres by the proprietor in Maryland, and Charles Carroll and Daniel Dulany were even more fortunate. At midcentury a man named Richard Bennet was the proud owner of a dozen plantations in Virginia and Maryland. When Robert Carter died in 1722, he left an estate of 300,000 acres, a thousand slaves, and £10,000 in cash. A group of favored Virginia gentlemen, including George Washington, who formed the Ohio Company somewhat later, were allocated 200,000 acres out west, with a pledge of another 300,000 if they would settle 100 families there within seven years. Holdings of 20,000 to 100,000 acres in South Carolina, while not commonplace, still were not rare. In North Carolina influential cronies of the Crown or governor were favored with colossal and often undefined tracts. A group around Henry McCulloch received a million and a half acres; another band of speculators, a half million.

The inevitable consequence of such land accumulation was the crystallization of an eighteenth-century *rentier* class. The land was there and seemingly limitless, but not so easy to come by as in the past. For one thing, price rose astronomically; in Maryland, it tripled from 1730 to 1769. For another, men like Carroll preferred leasing acreage to tenants at fixed rent to putting it up for sale. It was evidently more profitable, since lands that brought him no income at the beginning of the century in 1784 produced no less than 50,000 pounds of tobacco in rent. The German emigrants in particular, ignorant of the language and customs, were amenable to this leasing system, and the large owners were quick to take advantage of it. The result then was a spiraling of tenancy, with all the pitfalls and injustices that this system normally spawns.

Colonial history is studded with disputes between landlord and tenant, often flaring into armed revolt. In 1751 tenants on the estate of Robert Livingston in New York refused to pay their fees on the ground that Massachusetts had promised them title to the land they worked. An antirent revolt, under the leadership of William Prendergast in Dutchess County, New York, involved 1,700 tenants. When it was suppressed eighty were arrested, pilloried, fined. Prendergast was sentenced to be hanged, but no one could be found to act as executioner. To avoid further riots the governor had him pardoned. Tenants of the Van Cortlandts complained that their tenure was insecure, and when they failed to get satisfaction, took to arms. Excessive rents, high taxes, heavy interest on loans, overcharges at the landlord's store were so onerous that hardly a year passed without some disturbance on tenanted farms, particularly in New York and New Jersey.

As a corollary to such problems there were perennial arguments over who owned a specific piece of land. A band of Germans in 1710 made an arrangement with the English Board of Trade whereby they would work a tract at Schoharie, New York, until they paid off the equivalent of their passage. On arrival, however, the governor assigned them a plot nearer New York City and put them under the tutelage of Robert Livingston, the great landowner, who promptly cheated them in the sale of food and the advancement of credit. When the distraught Germans demanded the territory promised them, they were met by troops and dispersed. Most of them sought refuge in New Jersey and Pennsylvania, but the few who proceeded to Schoharie to claim their rights were met by an impostor who alleged prior ownership. In South Carolina, after the Yamassee Indians had been driven out, it was decided to settle the territory with 500 English Protestant families. But when the immigrants showed up the proprietors refused either to confirm the titles or give them their money back. The fleeced victims soon spent their money and were forced into such "want and poverty that they are daily . . . perishing and those that have anything left [are] removing off the province to the great weakening of the same." Land titles were a constant source of litigation, not only with squatters but with those who felt they had legitimate claims. Throughout the 1740's, up to 1754, the titles of small farmers in New Jersey were adjudged faulty. "Persons who had long holden under the proprietors," reported E. J. Fisher, "were forcibly ejected . . . while those who had courage to stand out, were threatened with, and in many instances, received personal violence."

An everlasting war continued between the mighty and the powerless, often resulting in the destitution and even imprisonment of the latter. In 1745 a squatter in New Jersey named Samuel Baldwin was clapped in jail for cutting trees allegedly belonging to the proprietor. Friends and neighbors soon rescued him, only to be imprisoned themselves, and in turn set free by larger mobs. London was considering sending troops to quell the revolt when the French and Indian War made it expedient to forget the matter. The poor argued too over quitrents due proprietors and the Crown—some £37,500 annually. The rent collector, when money was scarce, insisted on payment in currency or coin; the farmer offered payment in wheat, tobacco, or rice. If the rent collector agreed, haggling ensued as to how to grade the commodities and how much they were worth. When rents went unpaid, especially in depression periods such as 1703–13, 1720–34, and 1756–65, the farmers resisted collection and the proprietors' agents sought to have the property foreclosed.

The poor of colonial days felt themselves squeezed by fraudulently assessed taxes, manipulated prices, and the shortage of currency. In five Piedmont counties of North Carolina during the 1760's and 1770's, taxpayers were bilked ceaselessly by unscrupulous collectors who charged more than legally due. Defaulted farms were sold by insiders to friends at deflated prices and then resold at extortionate profits. If a farmer sought the aid of a court this is what he might encounter, according to one contemporary report: "For entering the judgement on the court docket and issuing the execution—the work of one long minute—the justice of the peace demands forty-one shillings and five pence. Unable to pay the fee, the unfortunate debtor is confronted with the alternative of a distraint or twenty-seven days work on the justice's plantation. But even after he has worked out his debt to the justice the poor man's account is not settled. There is still the damned lawyer's mouth to stop. . . . You empowered him to confess that you owed five pounds, and you must pay him thirty shillings for that or else go to work nineteen days for that pickpocket . . . ; and when that is done you must work as many days for the sheriff for his trouble and then you can go home to see your living wrecked and tore to pieces to satisfy your merchant."

A typical example of poverty by economic and political manipulation, duplicated elsewhere and at other times repeatedly, was that imposed on the backwoods tobacco growers of Virginia. It began with the Navigation Acts of 1660, which gave English merchants a monopoly over the crop. In the next years the price of this "noxious weed," driven down by the monopolists, fell from threepence a pound to a half-penny. But when farmers tried to sell their tobacco to other colonies, instead of the mother country, a tax of one penny per pound was levied on such trade, making it prohibitive. Simultaneously London traders completed the squeeze by raising the price of finished goods; and as the farmers fell into debt, they were harried further by exorbitant interest rates. Those who sought to emigrate westward were stopped by a law that set the border of the colony close enough to the seaboard to protect fur trade with the Indians. "The poverty of the country is such," proclaimed Nathaniel Bacon, who led the small planters in revolt, "that all the power and sway is got into the hands of the rich, who by extortious advantages, having the common people in their debt, have always curbed and oppressed them in all manner of ways."

Another sore point, translating itself into impoverishment for the small farmer, was that of "cheap" versus "sound" money, which was to bedevil the American yeoman up to the Populist era and beyond. The man who acquired land needed credit for tools, cattle, and supplies. It was usually available only from the planter or merchant on the seaboard, at 6 to 8 per cent. The debts were listed in fixed sums of money—so many pounds and shillings—but since currency was short they were redeemed instead in farm produce. When prices fell, however, a frequent affliction, that meant that more corn, wheat, or tobacco was due than originally borrowed. The situation was made worse by the fact that the farmer ordinarily had only a single outlet for his crop; the merchant he dealt with paid him lower prices for his crops than if there had been competition, and charged him higher prices for the finished goods he needed. In this double bind of credit and prices, many an agrarian went under, defaulting on his holding.

To remedy the situation there were many cries on the part of the lowly for land banks, particularly when currency was in short supply or about to be withdrawn, as at the end of Queen Anne's War in 1713. Under this scheme, the colonial governments were urged to issue bills on their own, lending it to farmers at much reduced interest rates. Such injections of money into the colonial bloodstream, it was felt, would lead to controlled inflation, raise prices, and give the debtor a decided advantage in repaying his obligations. Deacon Sam Adams, father of the leader of the Revolution, organized such a bank in Massachusetts in 1740 and issued £49,250 in loans to a thousand farmers at 3 per cent. Parliament in London, however, put the land bank out of business and the good deacon, with others who had stood surety, was financially ruined.

In a dozen different ways, then, the colonial masses were whipsawed by manipulation, and many succumbed to it. The mere fact that land was available did not mean that the landless were always able to get their hands on it; or if they did, that they could rise above the burden of depreciated prices, high taxes, currency shortages, and legal litigation. The misery of America was not equal to that of the Old World. But there were not a few who might have seconded this anguished cry of an eighteenth-century Philadelphian: "O these Liars. If I but had wings to fly, I would soon hie myself from hence to Europe, but I dread the tempestuous ocean and the pirates. . . . Whosoever is well off in Europe better remain there. Here is misery and distress, same as everywhere, and for certain persons and conditions incomparably more than in Europe."

V

For all those in want as a result of servitude or debt, the colonial world, like the old one, had naught but indifference. The only segment for which it showed concern was the poor who were unable to work. The lame, the blind, the sick, the aged had their needs appeased much as today and in the same fitful manner. The colonists carried over from England the Elizabethan principle of providing for the helpless.

On the other hand, in tune with the Calvinist ethic, there was an almost sadistic attitude toward the able-bodied idle, who were deemed lower than worms. In part this was a reaction against the idle nobility back home, who lived by the sweat of other men's brows. In part it arose from the needs of the frontier. There was so much work to be done and so few hands to do it, and so much fear of the Indian at the gate, that those who did not labor or were unwilling to share in defense were considered the most antisocial of people. No distinction was made between those who were jobless because they were shiftless and those who, at a particular time or a particular place, were actually unable to find employment. The harsh attitude encompassed both types and was considered justified even by good men like William Penn.

As the New England Puritans put it, idleness was the "parent of all vices." How deep this notion penetrated the culture is evidenced by this self-castigating rhyme, from late in the colonial period, of a burglar awaiting execution:

> With honest labor earn your bread,
> While in your youthful prime;

Nor come you near the harlot's bed,
  Nor idly waste your time.

The dreadful deed for which I die,
  Arose from small beginning;
My idleness brought poverty,
  And so I took to stealing.

The fate of an idler, like that of ordinary criminals, was whipping, imprisonment, or being bound out as a servant. It was not unusual in staid Boston and other New England towns for able-bodied paupers to be sold at public auction for temporary servitude. In 1697, the courts of Chester County, Pennsylvania, bound out thirty-three orphan children for service lest they become addicts to the vice of idleness. Where the punishment was neither servitude nor flogging the culprits were clapped in jail, as in the old country. Their number was never very great since work was available and wages quite good compared to England. But war, poor crops, and other misfortunes made the economic tempo uneven, periodically producing a certain amount of joblessness. Doubtless there were the chronically lazy, but they were probably only a minor burden.

As the number of able-bodied idlers grew toward the end of the century and into the eighteenth, it became too expensive to lodge them in prisons. Instead workhouses were constructed and the ne'er-do-wells forced to labor for their keep. Connecticut put one such workhouse into operation in 1727; Boston opened another in 1729.

Punishment was supplemented by a peculiar form of prevention. Towns took special precautions to restrict the right of settlement. Strangers were permitted residence only if the town was assured they would not become public wards. Severe as this sounds there was pragmatic logic to it: if a town was duty bound to care for all the destitute, it could be wiped out financially by pauper immigrants from other places. Estimates of poor relief costs in New England placed the figure at 9 to 33 per cent of all local expenditures, a tidy enough sum to evoke the specter of bankruptcy if it were permitted to grow. It should be emphasized that the largest "cities" would hardly qualify now as more than good-sized villages. Newport boasted 96 souls in 1640 and 2,600 by 1690. Boston, the great metropolis of early colonial times, listed 1,200 people in 1640 and 7,000 a half century later. Philadelphia had a mere 4,000 inhabitants and Charlestown

1,100 as late as 1690. A few dozen additional paupers in any of these cities could spell the difference between an empty treasury and an adequate one. In the smaller ones the hazard was even greater.

Thus in America as in England measures were taken to control movement. In May 1636 Boston selectmen forbade anyone to put up a stranger for more than two weeks without official permission. Three or four years later it became standard practice, if a stranger sought the right to settle, to have a townsman put up security for him. By 1647 the provisions were tightened further, forbidding anyone to rent or sell a dwelling or a shop to a newcomer without approval from the selectmen. In the space of two decades, from the mid-1660's to the mid-1680's, more than two hundred persons were excluded from Boston by the selectmen.

Such practices obviously were not limited to Massachusetts. Peter Stuyvesant decreed in 1642 that no stranger could be harbored in New Amsterdam for more than a single night without having his name recorded. Though few people abided by this decree New York City by 1676 rigorously enforced a law that vessel captains list their passengers with the Recorder. As a main port of entry, New York had good reason to fear being swamped. So did small Rhode Island, which urged its towns to require bond from prospective inhabitants. In 1675 the overseers of Portsmouth were instructed "to take care that strangers be not entertained in this town but according to order."

On the other hand, though we cannot be sure, concern for the destitute in colonial times probably matched or outstripped that of any other period. The Social Darwinism that has always undergirded attitudes toward the needy—namely, that they are poor because they are unfit—was less pronounced when the population was smaller and relief more personal. Early records of Portsmouth, Rhode Island, tell us of measures taken from 1644 on to provide for "ould John Mott" that are perhaps typical. "Ould" Mott evidently was incapable of further labor, and his son, though willing to contribute a cow and corn for his father's support, presumably had limited resources. The town therefore boarded Mott with a local citizen to whom it paid £9 annually for "diett and washing." The next year it voted to indemnify Mott's caretaker five shillings a week "out of the tresurie . . . so farr as the tresurie will goe." There were only seventy-one freemen in Portsmouth as late as 1655, so that it is conceivable that the "tresurie" was not sufficiently overflowing to take care of too many cases such as "ould John Mott." But it is significant that the citizens considered support for a senior citizen a social rather than an individual commitment.

In the ensuing years Portsmouth doled out forty bushels of corn to a Mr. Balston to pay for Mott's "home rome dyate lodging and washings." Mott, it seems, was the town's charge for thirteen years, a constable regularly collecting fees for his welfare. At one time it was decided to build a stone house for the old man's "more Comfortable beinge." On another occasion, in 1654, Portsmouth offered to pay Mott's passage to Barbados Island so that he could live out his days in a warmer climate. It assured him return fare if he decided not to stay in the West Indies. Whether Mott went and came back or decided to stay at home is not clear. He continued, however, to receive help for some additional years.

The Elizabethan philosophy was taken as a matter of course in the New World. The Plymouth Assembly passed a poor law in 1642; Virginia, in 1646; Connecticut, 1673; Pennsylvania, 1688; Massachusetts, 1692. According to Carl Bridenbaugh, historian of early city life, Charlestown "alone failed to take any official cognizance of its pauper problems in this period." In New England, where administration was lodged in the town meeting, taxes for poor relief were levied by selectmen or overseers; in the southern colonies, where the vestry ruled each parish, the methods of collection were slightly different but with the same purpose. In New York the Common Council instructed aldermen in each ward to prepare a list of needy for the mayor, who provided for them out of the public till. Somewhat later the aldermen were permitted to draw funds themselves for this purpose, the total in 1688 being £20. Bostonians were evidently more generous—or more in need—for the cost of charity in that city in 1700 was £500, and after 1715 usually £2,000 annually.

The simplest form of aid was the "putting out" system. A widowed lady in Hadley, Massachusetts, for instance, was boarded with one freeholder after another for two-week periods. Ordinarily the "putting out" was for a whole year, with the selectmen paying from the levies they collected for food and lodging, and the town providing medical care and clothing. Those who were not entirely helpless were given small stipends and continued to live in their own homes. Records in Boston show such entries as a payment of £6 to Edward

Weeddine in 1663 to assure "dyete and lodging" for a lady named Elizabeth Ward, and to the Widow Blore, who was given five shillings a week "in mony & one Load of Wood for the winter" to take care of Mary Chelsam.

In larger communities this system proved inadequate, so that almshouses began to appear as early as 1660. Boston completed a frame almshouse in 1662, financed by a few hundred pounds in legacies from two prominent citizens as well as other gifts. It was occupied in 1665, when the selectmen "admitted Mrs. Jane Woodcock, widow." The building burned down in 1682 and was replaced three years later by a brick structure costing £1,000. At first the "honest poor" and criminals were housed together, but a separation was made in 1712. In New Amsterdam, before it became English property, the deaconry built a house for the poor in 1653 and two years later bought a "bouwerie" near Hellgate which they called the poor farm. Upkeep was provided through voluntary contributions deposited in church poor boxes.

At times, after a war with Indians, for instance, when refugees became a serious problem, the structure of poor relief was strained to the utmost. Newport, with almost no paupers before 1675, levied £800 that year, as fugitives arrived from Providence, Warwick, and Westerly. Boston appealed to Ireland for help in January and July 1677, and its selectmen distributed provisions donated from overseas to the homeless fleeing the frontier.

In embryo, then, most of the means for caring for the destitute were already in evidence early in colonial history. A system comprising relief, almshouses for the "honest poor," workhouses for "idlers," prisons for vagabonds, and public hospitals for the ill, as well as private and religious charity, differs only slightly from the more complex structure of the twentieth century.

And like the present system, it did not abolish poverty. It simply ameliorated it. The first important *new* approach to the problem was a strange experiment by the proprietor of Pennsylvania, William Penn, and his Quakers.

Chapter 4

THE HOLY EXPERIMENT

Once the sluice gates of religious dissent had been opened in seventeenth-century England, some men began to question not only the dogma but the social principles of the Church. Sects such as the Diggers and Levellers reverted to a Christian communism, characteristic of the Middle Ages. They interpreted the Biblical concept of brotherhood and "the poor shall inherit the earth" literally, not figuratively. "At this very day," preached one of their leaders, Gerard Winstanley, "the poor people are forced to work for 4 d. and corn is dear. And the tithing-priest stops their mouth and tells them that 'inward satisfaction of mind' was meant by the declaration, 'the poor shall inherit the earth.' I tell you the scripture is to be really and materially fulfilled . . . the poor people you oppress shall be the saviours of the land . . . and break to pieces the bands of property." In this scheme of things poverty would not be ameliorated but totally eliminated by assuring that "no man shall have any more land than he can labour himself . . . neither giving hire nor taking hire." The Christian communists were a left wing in Cromwell's revolution; afterward some came to America where they organized small communities in which land was owned in common.

Less extreme was a sect originally called Children of the Light, then Friends of Truth, and finally Society of Friends, but usually re-

ferred to as Quakers, presumably—according to one version—
because George Fox, their founder, once warned a judge who was
trying him to "tremble at the word of the Lord." The Quakers too
practiced a primitive Christianity, insisting on equality between all
Christians in religious and social matters. But in the mundane area of
economics, the Quakers did not go so far as the Diggers and Levellers. They were reconciled to class differences in wealth and property, so long as the upper classes accepted as a fundamental duty the
extirpation of poverty. Where the Christian communists, in other
words, urged equality, the Quakers proposed mitigating inequality.
The rich were exhorted to eschew all frivolity, extravagance, and
conspicuous consumption, so that the first call on their surplus funds
could go for the less fortunate.

Other sects, of course, also spoke of "concern" for the poor, but no
other group either in England or America took this task so seriously.
The abolition of poverty was for the Quakers a religious mission,
God's word translated into practice, flowing inexorably from their
thesis that all men were equal before the Lord. According to the
Friends, every person had his own relationship with God, requiring
no intermediaries, such as priests, to interpret it for him. That empathy was expressed in an Inner Light guiding the individual toward
self-development, love of his fellow men, avoidance of self-
indulgence. Virtue could not be forced on any man from the outside
by the strictures of priests or magistrates, but only from within by his
own conviction. Thus there was no need for ornate churches, paid
clergymen, or mellifluous sermons. Each man had his own access to
God and in that sense was his own Christ. "Are all Christians
priests?" asked George Fox, the Quaker leader. "Yes. All Christians."
Even women.

The Quakers held "meetings"—not "services"—in a meeting
room, sitting in silence, communing with the Inner Light until constrained to share their concerns with others. They would not pay
taxes to the Church of England, for to do so would concede the
state's right to determine a man's religion from without. They would
not bear arms or make war, for that was an abomination of the Com-
mandment "thou shalt not kill." They would not swear an oath in court
or on affidavit, since swearing was a blasphemy. They would not remove their hats for lord or king, since all men were equal before
their Maker. For the same reasons, they addressed everyone by the

singular "thee" and "thou," ordinarily reserved for children and those of lesser rank, rather than the deferential plural "you." They made decisions not by majority vote but by consensus, heeding all views, listening to long discussion, until a "sense of the meeting" was arrived at.

The doctrine of the Inner Light had significant practical implications ranging far beyond dogma. If men communed with God in their own special way, society must be tolerant of all religious beliefs; and if they were all equal in the eyes of the Lord, they must also be equal before the law. This thesis, novel in the seventeenth century, imposed certain duties on the state toward its citizens, the foremost of which, as the Friends saw it, was to help them overcome the major impediment in their lives, poverty. "Let all the poor, the blind, the lame, and the crippled be cared for," read a Quaker pamphlet, "so that . . . you can claim to be the equals of the Jews; for they had the Law, which provided for widows, orphans, and strangers. Whoever closes his ear to the poor, closes it to the Law."

Time and again Fox and his Friends petitioned Parliament to take forthright measures on behalf of the paupers, estimated at one-fifth of the English population, and in the absence of state measures undertook programs of their own. "And many times," recorded Fox in his Journal, "there woulde bee two hundred beggars of ye world (there for all ye country knewe wee mett about ye poore) which after ye meetings was donne, freinds woulde sende to ye bakers & give ym each a loafe a peice bee ym as many as woulde."

Leading Quakers formulated elaborate plans for relief. One of them, by John Bellers, was hailed a century and a half later by Robert Owen, Karl Marx, and Eduard Bernstein as the genealogical forerunner of modern socialism. It carried the unwieldy but informative title: "Proposals for raising a Colledge of Industry of all useful Trades and Husbandry, with Profit for the Rich, a Plentiful Living for the Poor, and a Good Education for the Youth." Bellers, it should be stressed, was not averse to "profits for the rich," but it would have to be concomitant with a "plentiful living" for the less fortunate; this was the essence of the Quaker credo. In justifying his "Colledges of Industry" Bellers presented an analysis of the economic problems of England much as Leon Keyserling would those of the United States today. With 7,000,000 inhabitants, he pointed out, England could increase its national income by £3,900,000 a year if it created jobs for its 500,000 unemployed. Adding this to the £1,300,000 annual cost for supporting paupers, he showed that the total loss was £5,200,000. "Colledges of Industry," therefore, would not only make work for the workless but make England itself more affluent.

II

Among those who accepted Quaker doctrine and transplanted it to America in the form of a "Holy Experiment" was William Penn, the eldest son of a distinguished English admiral. Joseph Dorfman describes him as "the greatest intellectual figure that trod colonial soil in the 17th century." Tall, lithe, an excellent oarsman, a good swordsman, he was, in the words of John Fiske, "a picture of manly beauty, with great lustrous eyes under wide arching brows, a profusion of dark hair falling in curls upon his shoulders, a powerful chin, a refined and sensitive mouth." He was in addition as competent a scholar as an athlete. He spoke six languages fluently and was one of the most prolific writers of his time. His best known work, *No Cross, No Crown,* penned while imprisoned in the Tower of London, was a masterful polemic against the established Church written in the passionate prose of the true believer.

As sometimes happens with sons of the upper class, young Penn rebelled against the established order in which his father had found such distinction. The elder Penn, Sir William, was a man of pragmatic flexibility, less concerned with conviction than finding his own place in the sun. As one of the youngest admirals in royal navy history, he had fought with Cromwell against the king not because of ardor for the Puritan cause but because his fellow officers had joined it. When the time seemed propitious he offered his fleet to the exiled monarch, Charles II, in 1654, and for this generous act was eventually lavished with large estates in Ireland as well as the eternal friendship of both Charles II and his brother the Duke of York (James II).

But young William, though he had the facility for remaining on good terms with those with whom he disagreed, showed an early trend to kick over the traces. In 1655, at the age of eleven, he had a religious experience while in his chamber which led him to believe "that the seal of Divinity had been put upon him at this moment, and that he had been awakened or called upon to a holy life." Six years later, while at Christ Church, Oxford, he fell under the influence of dissenters, and either was expelled for an ecclesiastical prank or withdrawn by an irate father lest he become even more wayward. To reorient him, the admiral tried persuasion, beatings, turning the boy out of the house—the doors of which were usually reopened by a more tolerant mother—and finally dispatched him to France. For the next few years William studied law and theology, traveled some more in Europe, and might have evolved along more traditional lines if he hadn't met an old Quaker friend, Thomas Loe, while on a business mission for his father in Cork, Ireland. Henceforth the young man, who was on intimate terms with kings, dukes, and riches, was never distracted from his course.

Being a Quaker in the seventeenth century was akin to being a Communist nowadays but much more dangerous. The Conventicle Act of 1664 made it a crime to worship God except through the Church of England and many thousands were arrested for violating it. One day in September 1667 Penn was attending a meeting of dissenters when soldiers invaded the premises and arrested those present for "riotous assembly." He was soon released after penning a note to a high official of his acquaintance. Not many months later, however, he was again imprisoned, this time for writing a pamphlet that incurred the displeasure of the Bishop of London. Even the son of a highly placed admiral was forced to remain in jail nine months for such an offense, though his imprisonment had the happy side effect of reconciling him with his father. In 1670, arrested once more for attending a meeting, Penn refused to take an oath of allegiance and was thrown into Newgate for six months, the worst of English prisons, usually reserved for felons and pickpockets.

If this sort of thing could happen to a man of cavalier upbringing and the highest connections, lesser men were in greater hazard. In the forty years after the English civil war thousands of Quakers were jailed, their property sequestered, and by Penn's estimate 5,000 died of disease and malnutrition while in prison. Auguste Jorns, historian of the Quaker social doctrines, makes the more modest claim that "at least 12,000 Quakers suffered severe prison sentences, as a result of which more than 300 died."

Under such persecution the Friends—now established in Holland, Germany, and to a small extent Russia—sought surcease in America.

They settled in Massachusetts, Rhode Island, New Amsterdam, Maryland, and Virginia, but except in Rhode Island they were treated with less than robust enthusiasm. Two Quaker ladies, Mary Fisher and Ann Austin, who arrived in Boston in 1656, were hustled off to jail for five weeks and then deported to Barbados. When a few days later eight more Friends set foot in the city they too were imprisoned. By order of the general court fines of £100 were levied on any shipmaster who dared land a member of this sect, and the Quaker himself was publicly whipped. A later law increased the punishment: the miscreant's tongue was to be burned through with a hot iron, and his ears cut off. If he was foolhardy enough to return he was executed. A diehard Quaker, Mary Dyer, was twice sentenced to hanging under this law, reprieved the first time with the rope already around her neck, hanged the second when she ventured back to the colony. Though Massachusetts was the most vigorous in persecuting Quakers, every colony with the exception of Rhode Island enacted legislation to harass them.

Penn, noting these developments from afar, remained determined to establish in the New World a Holy Experiment where virtuous men could build a virtuous society. All his adult life, he recorded years later, he had had an "opening of joy as to these parts," that would not be dissuaded by temporary adversity. He remained convinced that "governments, like clocks, go from the motions men give them. . . . Let men be good, and the government can not be bad; if it be ill, they will cure it." All that was needed was a place where the Quakers could put these maverick notions to the test of reality. An opportunity offered itself in 1673, when Lord Berkeley sold half ownership in New Jersey to two Quakers. But the project was bedeviled at the outset by quarrels between the partners as well as quarrels with neighboring New York. Penn was called on to adjudicate the intramural disputes among his fellow Friends, and later became the leading trustee administering West and East New Jersey. But the caviling made self-government impossible and the land itself proved less attractive than anticipated.

In 1680, then, Penn petitioned his father's friend, Charles II, for a vague territory still sparsely settled "bounded on the east by the Delaware River, on the west limited as Maryland, and northward to extend as far as plantable." Since the Stuarts owed Sir William Penn's estate some £16,000, they turned over this great territory, 55,000 square miles of fertile soil and rich minerals, to the admiral's heir in lieu of the debt. Here, in 1681, the "second founder" of Quakerism began his experiment to forge a virtuous society on the bedrock of virtuous men.

III

Like most antipoverty programs, before and after, the Holy Experiment did not begin as a specific program of laws or a minimum-income target. It was the *élan* of Quakerism translated into daily political life, the application of virtue to the mundane enigma called society, and it spelled itself out as it went along.

This special characteristic of the experiment was evident in the first brochure published by Penn to attract settlers. Never in the history of the lusty profession of advertising has there been such a deliberate undersell of the product as in *Some Account of the Province of Pennsylvania.* "I shall say little in its praise," wrote Penn, "to excite desires in any. . . ." Unlike the flamboyant outpourings of the old crimps and newlanders, this was a sober document offering land on easy terms in return for settlement. The well-to-do could purchase 5,000 acres for £100 and an annual quitrent of a shilling per 100 acres. Anyone with the wherewithal for his own passage was offered up to 200 acres at a rental of a penny an acre. And indentured servants were guaranteed 50 acres on completion of their service.

If these terms were on the same order as those in other colonies, leading to the usual class stratification (almost half the land purchased in 1681–82 went to forty persons), there were two major points of difference. In the first place, Pennsylvania (and Delaware, acquired by Penn from the Duke of York in 1682) opened its doors to *all* Christians, including non-Englishmen, on a basis of full equality. It was the only colony to do so, and though the open doors were not pried ajar for Jews and other non-Christians, the colony gave refuge to more "foreigners"—Germans, Swedes, Finns, Dutchmen—than any other. It stands as a monument to Penn's theories of religious tolerance that when the American Revolution broke out in 1776 Pennsylvania and Delaware, the original proprietary domain of Penn, were the only two states in which there was total equality between all Christian groups, whether English or European.

Secondly, the right to vote, usually limited by property and religious qualifications, was even more liberal than in Connecticut, most democratic of American colonies at the time, and, on a per capita basis, offered ten times as many people the franchise as back home in England. Democratic prerogatives were so far in advance in Pennsylvania, writes V. F. Calverton, "that at the time of the Revolutionary War most Pennsylvanians could find little reason to grow enthusiastic about fighting for liberty, and the colony entered the fray with marked reluctance." For the small freeholder the ballot was an important shield against official abuse and the various forms of manipulation that might plunge him to the lower depths.

The Quaker *élan* was evident too in the framework of government Penn drafted and the first code of laws that accompanied it. Though they would seem pedestrian today, they were models of democracy, far ahead of their times in the seventeenth century. The legislative prerogative was vested in a bicameral body, elected by the people, subject to the veto of Penn and his governor. Though this structure was in the tradition of other colonies, it contained additional democratic safeguards which eventually were incorporated into all American constitutions under the general heading of checks and balances. Among other things, provision was made whereby the form of government itself could be amended, and procedures were spelled out for impeaching elected officials guilty of misdeed.

More directly affecting the common man was the code of laws. Here one sees, approaching from the horizon, a new insight into penological problems: the Quakers, by and large, sought to reform rather than punish, to persuade rather than imprison. During the seventeenth century, it must be recalled, the onus for crime lay with the individual. But the Friends assessed at least part of the blame on environment. Thus Penn abolished imprisonment for small debts (though not for larger ones), a scourge that plagued Americans into the 1830's. The number of crimes for which capital punishment could be inflicted was reduced from the 150 in England to just two, murder and treason. The property of executed men, ordinarily seized by the state, was deemed inheritable by the next of kin. The customary practice of charging prisoners for food and lodging was revoked, and stern steps were taken to separate criminals from the insane. Above all, the jails were transformed from filthy, abysmal dungeons such as London's Newgate, where men simply vegetated, into workshops, where the emphasis was on spiritual rehabilitation. "Visitors from Europe," writes John Fiske, "remarked upon Philadelphia prisons as the best in the world. Philadelphia also had the only lunatic asylum in America that was managed upon something like modern methods. It had, moreover, an excellent hospital, a reform school, and no city in the world devoted a larger share of time and thought to philanthropic purposes."

The Holy Experiment, like Puritan New England, sought a sense of community; but where class cleavage was accepted as ordained by the Puritans, Penn's Quakers stressed collective responsibility for reducing inequality. God had never ordained, said Puritan John Cotton in 1638, "that democracy be a fit government either for church or commonwealth," for if the "people be governor, who shall be governed?" Help for the poor in Massachusetts, therefore, was something of an afterthought, as in old England. But for the Quakers, though theory and practice were never totally attuned, it was the center of concern, the essence of Christianity.

In the Quaker schema it was sinful to charge what the traffic would bear for any commodity; economic relations had to be based on the ethic of Christianity, not the ethic of the market place. It was also an abomination of God's will to frolic in luxury, for the monies spent in such wantonness were due the poor not as a privilege but as a right. "Clothe the naked and feed the hungry from what is left over," said Penn and Fox. "The poor," wrote Penn on another occasion, "are the hands and feet of the rich. It is their labor that improves countries; and to encourage them is to promote the real benefit of the public." At every monthly meeting of the Quakers, help for the poor was a major point on the agenda. Men in difficult straits presented their problems to the group or, if embarrassed, arranged for another member to report on their behalf. The meeting then voted sums for food, shelter, and coal, to be dispensed by a caretaker. Help was not confined to Quakers exclusively but often included people who did not belong to the Society of Friends, and not infrequently ranged beyond welfare. Minutes of the Friends show sums allocated for loans at a liberal interest rate (2 per cent), for gifts, and in some cases for dowries of £40 each. "They have become," wrote an eighteenth-century doctor about the Quakers, "the only people on earth free from poverty."

When a Friend was out of work, efforts were made to place him at a job or, if that was not possible, to supply his family with raw materials to spin yarn at home. Such matters too came up at the monthly, quarterly, and annual meetings. Article 23 of Penn's constitution required that lists be kept of jobs available for domestic servants, stating the wages, paydays, and similar data. When a fire swept someone's home, money was made available through a special fund to rebuild. Both in this and in relief measures what was unique was not that aid was given, but first that it was given by *voluntary* subscription, and second, that the aim was to help a man help himself. Here in fact was the essence of the Holy Experiment—to create conditions so that men could become self-reliant, as well as live in a measure of dignity.

It began with childhood. Among the first laws passed in the Quaker colony was one requiring parents to see to it that their children could read and write by their twelfth year, on penalty of a £5 fine. A year after Philadelphia was laid out in checkerboard symmetry, the building of schools commenced, both public and private, almost all of them coeducational. Both the sons of the poor and the sons of the rich were required to learn a trade so that "the poor may work to live, and the rich, if they become poor may not want." Concern for the individual included his funeral. If poor, he was buried with simplicity but dignity in the Quaker graveyard, members of his Meeting, without distinction as to status, being required to attend.

Concern is the key word for describing the Holy Experiment; it is a word that Quakers use to this day to express that empathy with other human beings that is ordained by the Inner Light. It manifested itself in dealing not only with each other but with the Indians and, to a lesser extent, the Negroes. Pennsylvania was not the only colony that paid the red man for his land; other colonies, notably New York, followed a comparable course. Historians are agreed, however, that Penn and his governors were meticulous in avoiding deception or debauchery. They neither plied the natives with drink nor drove a bargain to which they did not adhere. The French philosopher Voltaire, alluding to one of the treaties between the Quakers and an Indian tribe, called it "the only treaty between savages and Christians that was never sworn to and that was never broken." During all the years that the Quakers held sway over public affairs in Pennsylvania and for decades afterward, they lived in peace with the Indians. The Friends, to this day, point to the seven decades of harmony as convincing proof for their pacifist theories of nonviolence.

The Quaker approach to Negro slavery was less exemplary, but even so showed a measure of concern that prodded them toward a progressive position. They could assuage their conscience about white indenture on the handy theory that it was temporary. But the black man in bondage was a stark affront to their stated thesis that all men were equal before the Lord. Yet slavery was an institution thousands of years old and so universally accepted that it seemed indestructible; the Friends edged away from it with marked ambivalence.

The statutes of the Free Society of Traders in 1682 called for liberating black slaves after fourteen years of bondage, but the regulation was generally disregarded. A community of German Quakers, headed by Penn's friend Francis Daniel Pastorius, petitioned the Yearly Meeting in 1688 to abolish slavery on the grounds that it was an offense against the Biblical maxim "Do unto others as ye would that they should do unto you." Pastorius denounced the kidnaping of blacks in Africa as un-Christian, a blot on the Quaker reputation. Judgment was suspended by the Meeting, but five years later Friends were urged to buy slaves only for the purpose of freeing them, and to discourage with all their power further imports. Beginning with 1705, sterner measures were taken, and in 1711 a law, subsequently vetoed by the Crown, was passed forbidding importation. Three years later a law imposing a prohibitive £20 duty for each black brought to the colony from abroad was also rejected by the queen. By the time of the Revolution, the Quakers had long since given up the reins of power, but it is worth noting that from then to the Civil War they were without question the most active religious sect working for emancipation.

IV

For all that, the Holy Experiment did not succeed. The virtuous men, instead of building the virtuous society, lost their virtue as they became more affluent. In some measure the failure was due to Penn's absence from his colony. After a two-year stay, he returned to England in 1684, expecting to be gone for only a few months, but for a variety of reasons, including financial woes at home, he did not come back to Pennsylvania for fifteen years. Meanwhile he tried to rule by long distance, but it was a losing battle. Jealousies and rivalries consumed those Penn left in charge. The caliber of governors and judges, with some exceptions, was decidedly below par. At one point the Council, the upper legislative body, refused to follow Penn's instructions to submit its legislation to the Crown, as provided by the colony's charter, and the Assembly, the lower body, feuded with its rival constantly. The situation became so ominous Penn appointed a non-Quaker, a Puritan, to act as his deputy.

The Quakers themselves began to dispute whether it was right for them to act as a governing force, or whether their religion made it impossible. A schism that exposed the dilemma of a pacifist group holding state power developed within the Society in 1692. A man named Babbitt and a few friends, it seems, stole a ship in the Philadelphia harbor. It was a scandalous situation, but as absolute pacifists the Quakers were troubled about forming an armed posse to catch the criminals. One faction opted for practical police measures, another for friendly persuasion. Before a decision was reached a fearless Quaker climbed aboard ship and, with neither gun nor sword, prevailed on the culprits to disperse. The armed posse, formed meanwhile, pursued the bandits into the woods and wounded some. This incident became a *cause célèbre* and plunged the Society into severe factionalism for a long time.

After a while men's passions, including Penn's, outweighed their virtues. Penn and the colonists were at each other's throats, the one demanding his quitrent, the others refusing to pay. As they became wealthier, Quakers veered from their original ideals. Some trafficked in slavery, despite the injunction of the Yearly Meetings. The more prosperous began wearing ostentatious clothes and setting an ostentatious table. Penn himself was of this ambivalent character: he urged moderation but built himself a home worth £7,000, wore costly wigs, set his table with silver dishes, rode in a luxurious coach, and operated an estate of eight thousand acres. He became, as Benjamin Franklin observed a long time later, "less of a man of God . . . and more of the man of the world." His sons, who ruled after his death in 1718, were even less men of God. When the American revolutionaries confiscated their estate during hostilities, it was found to be worth £1,000,000.

Before long the fabric of the Holy Experiment began to disintegrate. Laws against illegal trade were violated wholesale, lawlessness became a problem. After 1701, as the humanitarian colony was flooded with runaway servants and other pariahs, criminal laws became increasingly harsh, including whipping, branding, mutilation. By 1767 capital punishment was levied for sixteen crimes, as against two originally. Quaker ardor was never entirely dissipated, either during the fifty years that they ruled the colony or afterward, but the sense of purpose and the idealism were gone. Making money, rather than the virtuous society, became the daily guideline, and poverty remained for many the daily curse. Looking back at this period, members of the Society of Friends say of their ancestors that "they came to America to do good—and did very well." Or, "They believed in 6 per cent and God—in that order."

V

Apart from the Holy Experiment, the only event approximating an antipoverty program in colonial times was the founding of Georgia fifty-one years later. In certain respects it was more liberal than the Quaker colony: it did not permit slavery within its borders, it accepted non-Christians (Jews) as equals, it operated on a nonprofit principle. But the charitable impulse in Georgia was too closely linked to mundane considerations to give it that nobility of purpose that prevailed in early Pennsylvania. Had Georgia not been a buffer zone between rival empires, the utopia of outcasts would not have been established. This marred the project from the beginning and finally led to its eclipse as a philanthropic venture.

Between South Carolina, which belonged to England, Florida, which belonged to Spain, and Louisiana, which was the property of France, was an uninhabited oasis which any of the three powers could use as a military springboard against the other. In 1715 the English had been given quite a scare when the Yamassee Indians, spurred on by the Spaniards, had overrun a section of South Carolina and killed hundreds of whites. The Yamassees in due course had been set on their heels, with the aid of troops from Virginia and North Carolina, but fear of Spanish designs ran high in London. To occupy the area between South Carolina and the possessions of the two other powers became therefore a fervid goal for empire-minded Englishmen.

One of these, James Edward Oglethorpe, a Member of Parliament for ten years and an ex-army officer who had fought with distinction against the Turks, conceived the weird idea of mating geopolitics with the rehabilitation of criminals. The use of English convicts for labor in America was a practice as old as colonial settlement; some 50,000 of this class were in fact dispatched across the ocean to provide additional muscle power. Under a law passed in 1717 judges were empowered to assign convicts to the New World for seven years of servitude—"His Majesty's Seven-Year Passengers," they were called—or, if under a death sentence, for fourteen years. What Oglethorpe proposed was to bring them here as freemen, not as servants, and in addition to include the many insolvent small debtors who had been recently released by Parliament in an act of benevolence, but who were nonetheless still mired in penury. In return the emigrants need only pledge to do military duty in defense of the Crown's imperial interests.

It was an alluring idea which seemed to give everyone what he wanted—the king a buffer zone, the philanthropists an opportunity to reprieve and rejuvenate criminals and debtors, and the emigrants not only their freedom but land. In 1732 George II deeded the group around Oglethorpe a territory between the Altamaha and Savannah rivers, to be run as a nonprofit colony. They were to administer the new Crown jewel for twenty-one years, with absolute powers to enact all laws (subject to the king's veto), dispense justice, distribute land, raise funds, impose taxes. No pretense was made at democracy, but then the derelicts who were recruited had known little of this joyous commodity back home either. On the other hand, this was the only colony established neither as a religious haven nor as a means of making money. The trustees were charged with the business of security—and philanthropy—with no one to earn so much as a penny for his labors. The money was provided by Parliament, which allocated between £8,000 and £26,000 annually, and by private donations of £20,000, which Oglethorpe raised from reform-minded associates.

The experiment began with a fanfare of exaggeration. Georgia, read the advertisements soliciting settlers, had "such an air and soil [it] can only be described by a poetical pen." It was a "future Eden," a "paradise with all her virgin beauties," the "most delightful country in the universe." Despite the flamboyancy, however, the offer had solid aspects to it. Passage to the "land of liberty and plenty" was paid for by the philanthropists, so that the newcomer did not have to bind himself for years of servitude. Once in Georgia—appropriately named after the king—the ex-convict would work on a community farm for a year, then receive gratis a plot of fifty acres, plus a sixty by ninety foot lot in town on which to build a home. Not only land, but food, clothing, and tools were his for the asking. To make sure that enough people came, the trustees of Georgia also appealed to non-convicts in Germany, Switzerland, Scotland, and elsewhere on somewhat different terms. Anyone bringing ten servants with him was allotted five hundred acres; the servants themselves, after four years of bondage, were to be given twenty-acre holdings with only quitrent to pay. No one was to be excluded on grounds of religion except Catholics, who were deemed unreliable for any war against Catholic Spain. For the same reason Oglethorpe prohibited not only Negro slaves but free Negroes. The founder of Georgia was no antislaver in principle: he owned a farm in South Carolina that utilized slaves and was associated with the Royal African Company which trafficked in black bondsmen, but exigency dictated barring black men lest they prove untrustworthy in manning the military outposts.

Hopes ran high as Governor Oglethorpe sailed with 130 carefully screened persons in the autumn of 1732. It was believed the warm climate was perfect for silk to rival Italian silks, and give labor, part time and full time, to 40,000 people. The prospect for growing grapes on "the finest land on all the continent" and creating a wine industry also seemed propitious. But the trustees and Oglethorpe had seriously miscalculated the land's potential. Georgia, it soon became apparent, was not the place for either silk or grapes, and the planting of rice—soon to become its main product—was difficult because of the hot climate and malaria. Instead of tens of thousands then, fewer than 2,500 ex-convicts could be lured to the "future Eden," and many of them either died or fled northward to South Carolina. The fifty-acre plots for the former prisoners and the twenty-acre holdings for freed servants proved inadequate to eke out even a minimum living.

As of 1741 Georgia accommodated a mere 1,500 to 2,000 people. A report to the trustees complained that "the colony is reduced to one-sixth of its former number. . . . The few who remain are in a starving and despicable condition." An attempt was made to liberalize conditions for the settlers by raising the grant to servants to fifty acres and lifting restriction on the sale of land and inheritance. But it was a losing battle. Georgia could not survive on the institutional frame elaborated for it by Oglethorpe, and it soon began to take on all the vices Oglethorpe had sought to avoid.

Before long the sale of rum to Indians, so carefully proscribed originally, was legalized. Slavery was introduced in 1749 under pressure from the colonists, and six years later a slave code was promulgated as extreme as any in the southern colonies, providing among other things for invading Negro homes without warrants, and punishment of the black man with impunity. Instead of basing itself on convicts and philanthropy, the colony now invited large landowners from South Carolina and England to work the wonders of large-scale enterprise.

By 1751 the original venture was a shambles. Georgia reverted to the Crown to become a royal colony on an economic and political model unintended by Oglethorpe. Rice production, Negro slavery, and large plantations became its dominant characteristics, the liberation of the poor a fond memory.

The next phase in the "war against poverty" was to wait until the Revolution.

Chapter 5

FREE BUT NOT EQUAL

Two days before Congress proclaimed the end of the "War of the Revolution" in April 1783, Elijah Fisher, an American soldier, was released by the British from the "old Jersey prison ship." No one greeted him as a war hero, no one provided him with funds to go home. On his way back to Boston, begging food along the way in taverns, he sat down to ruminate his plight: "The 16th I come down by the market and sit down all alone, almost discouraged, and began to think over how that I had been in the army, what ill success I had met with there and also how I was wronged by them I worked for at home, and lost all last winter, and now that I could not get into any business and no home, which you may well think how I felt; but then came into my mind that there were thousands in worse circumstances than I was, . . . and after that I felt as contented as need to be."

Elijah symbolized a widespread condition. The Revolution, which in the long run was as significant an assault on poverty as any event in American history, in the short run had strewn it far and wide. The economic terrain of the thirteen colonies, loosely assembled in federation, was torn up, bulldozer fashion, by the staggering dislocations customary for war periods. Some men had filled their hats to the brim with great wealth; many, like Elijah Fisher, had lost what

57

little they had—and worse, were in debt. "The spirit of enthusiasm which overcame everything at first," commented General George Washington, "is now done away with."

The soldier, waiting to be mustered out, painfully aware of the inflation that laid siege to his farm and the hunger that gripped his family, must have looked with dismay at the unconscionable profiteering around him. For far too many patriotism had taken a back seat to profits. Otis & Andrews of Boston, without flinching, had sold a million dollars' worth of clothing to the government at tidy markups of 100 to 200 per cent. Other gentry were buying flour for $5 a barrel, reselling it at $28 to $34 to a hard-pressed government always on the brink of bankruptcy. Even some of those whose contribution to the Revolution was sizable stuffed their own exchequers handsomely. Robert Morris, who advanced his own money to the cause when its finances were low and guaranteed loans with his own credit, also enriched himself. "At the beginning of our revolution," John Adams wrote of him, "his commerce was stagnated, and as he was overtraded, he was much embarrassed." But as custodian of the new nation's treasury he sold matériel and arms to Congress at a lusty enough profit to make himself rich. By the standards of the time such conflicts of interest were not considered particularly venal; yet it is a fact that in the midst of widespread hardship some people on the inside were able to feather their own nests. Men like Silas Deane and even John Hancock fattened their resources appreciably.

At the other end of the spectrum, the harvest of sacrifice all too often was pauperism. Men flocked to the colors in a cascade of enthusiasm to begin with—50,000 in New England, 20,000 in Pennsylvania. But as conditions deteriorated in the homesteads where wives tried to work farms without male labor, desertions from the army reached alarming proportions. Bounties had to be offered potential recruits or old veterans to lure or keep them in the fold. In 1779 Virginia promised 300 acres of land plus $400 to each volunteer. That same year the Continental Congress authorized General Washington to offer $200 to each new recruit. Yet the bounties and the meager pay (often defaulted) were unavailing against enervating inflation. Congress and the states had printed $438,000,000 in paper currency which in due course became so worthless that a bowl of toddy in Virginia sold for $1 in silver but $500 in paper. A pair of stockings in Philadelphia cost $300 in 1781, tea sold for $90 a pound. Laws were desperately enacted requiring everyone to accept Continental money, but the slide in value could not be checked: in July 1779 the Continental was worth seven cents in specie; six months later, three cents; and a year later, a penny and a half. The most descriptive way to call something worthless was to say it was "not worth a Continental."

The runaway inflation, of course, simply signified that Congress had no resources except good will. Even that melted away as federal debts mounted and Congress defaulted on $6,000,000 in back wages to its soldiers. Washington pleaded that at least a token be given to those being disbanded, but the men were sent home, as one officer put it, "without pay, and without even thanks, for eight years of toil and dangers." A captain who had been forced to sell his property said that if it were not for his army rations his family would face literal starvation. "Not a day passes my head," reported another officer, "but some soldier with tears in his eyes hands me a letter to read from his wife painting for the distresses of his family in such strains as these, 'I am without bread, and cannot get any . . . we have no wood, neither can we get any. Pray come home.' " It reached such a state of affairs that in June 1783 mutinous soldiers in Philadelphia took over the arsenals and drove Congress out of town.

Debt fastened on the common man with such savage grip that, according to J. B. McMaster, one half of Vermont "was totally bankrupt, the other half plunged in the depths of poverty." Had the laws that required imprisonment for debt been rigorously enforced in New Hampshire in the autumn of 1785 "it is probable that not far from two thirds of the community would have been in prisons." As merchants and bankers demanded "hard money" in payment for old obligations, the common man found himself in a hopeless state. He held mountains of depreciated paper, taken in good faith, that now were worthless and unredeemable. An artisan named Trevett created a *cause célèbre* in Newport, Rhode Island, when he offered a butcher paper money for a cut of meat and was refused. The butcher was taken to court, but when the judges held him not guilty, public indignation became so heated the legislature was forced to call a special session and remove four judges from office. The poor came to anger often during the "critical years" from 1783 to 1788, sometimes taking arms to redress their grievances. The worst such outbreak occurred in Massachusetts in 1786 when Captain Daniel Shays led 2,000 insurgents against the commonwealth. The rebels invaded the courts, broke up its sessions, burned barns, seized what they could of the property of the wealthy, and held parts of the state for months.

The malaise of the critical period was so deep that on the one hand officers of the army such as Major John Armstrong, Jr., urged Washington to establish a military dictatorship—which he vehemently rejected—and on the other, armed mobs in a few areas threatened the new order from the left. The Constitutional Convention was in large measure a hurried reaction to a discontent of the poor that overflowed into the streets.

II

Had it not been for the safety valves opened by the Revolution, America probably would have confronted a "second revolution," much as are some of the new nations being born today; or disintegrated like wet paper, each state becoming a separate country, as Latin America was to do a half century later. Fortunately the Revolution, though it is generally thought of as a struggle for independence, was in a true sense an antipoverty program as well. It carried no specific name, like Holy Experiment, nor did any single oracle, lay or religious, proclaim it as such. But the leveling tendency was unmistakable, especially in the earlier stages when the firebrands were in charge. Thus, the original version of the Pennsylvania constitution of 1776 carried this egalitarian statement of social philosophy: "An enormous proportion of property vested in a few individuals is dangerous to the rights and destructive of the common happiness of mankind; and therefore every free state hath a right to discourage possession of such property." Benjamin Franklin espoused the doctrine that no man ought to own more property than he needed for a livelihood; the rest, he said, rightly belonged to the state. John Adams fumed at "the dons, the bashaws, the grandees, the patricians, the sachems, the nabobs, call them what name you please," who denied economic rights to the underprivileged. The Revolution was being fought not only against the Tories of England but against the wealthy at home, and disrespect for the rich became flagrant. The Pennsylvania constitution, which came close to guaranteeing universal male suffrage, was called by its enthusiasts a "good one for the poor man," but bad for the "few overgrown rich." The "spirit of independence," noted Colonel John Randolph of Virginia, "converted into equality, and every one who bore arms, esteems himself upon a footing with his neighbors."

By the time the war had spun itself to a desultory end in 1783, the radicals were on the wane and some, like John Adams, were transmigrating to the right. Yet the momentum was not entirely spent, and Benjamin Rush, a Jeffersonian, could cry with fervor that the "American war is over but this is far from being the case with the American Revolution." As men like Rush saw it, there was unfinished business on the agenda requiring answers to slavery, education, debt, landlessness, the franchise, all of which related directly to the issue of poverty.

No one man was responsible for the reforms that followed the war and salved lower-class wounds, but the mood was embodied in a thin, long-legged intellectual with red hair and blue-gray eyes—Thomas Jefferson. The third President was one of that rare species, a scholar turned political leader. Like Benjamin Franklin, his interests ranged far and wide, embracing among other things science, literature, the fine arts, architecture. He published books and articles not only on politics but on Greek, neo-Platonism, steam engines, biology, archaeology, theology. The buildings he designed for the University of Virginia and for a friend in Fluvanna County, as well as his own Monticello atop the Blue Ridge, ranked architecturally with the best in the country. Even more he was an aristocrat, born and reared in wealth, who matured into the most fervid enemy of all things aristocratic except the "aristocracy of talent." Unlike Sam Adams, who reveled in sharing a beer with thorny-handed members of the Sons of Liberty, Jefferson was shy in personal relations with the common man. His identification with the under classes was a mental rather than emotional process; he had probed the subject philosophically, not empirically. Yet, as author of the Declaration of Independence, governor of Virginia, member of Congress, envoy to foreign capitals, and Secretary of State under Washington, he was as consistent a spokesman for the disadvantaged as the Revolution produced.

This evolution was not entirely accidental. From his father, a giant of a man spiritually as well as physically, Tom acquired a democratic bent and a taste for books early in life. Peter Jefferson, civil engineer, justice of the peace, farmer, colonel of the militia, was an unusual

man who read to his family at night in front of the log fire from the
works of Shakespeare, Swift, and Addison. The Blue Ridge was then
on the western frontier, and though the elder Jefferson by wealth
and status should have been a Tory, he was imbued with that democratic spirit so common in such areas. Young Tom seems to have
been infected by the same virus. In between reading the classics on
the 1,900-acre family plantation, he rubbed shoulders with rough and
tumble backwoodsmen in buckskin breeches and hunting shirts
who evidently "had little use for government of any sort." From his
father and from his surroundings then, Tom imbibed an individualism
later expressed in that famous maxim, That government is best
which governs least.

Peter Jefferson died when Tom was only fourteen, leaving the boy
in charge of the family plantation. Three years later he enrolled at the
College of William and Mary in the colonial capital, Williamsburg,
and by the time he was twenty was adept in Latin, Greek, and French
(later three other languages), natural science, and mathematics. A
remarkable young man, he was also a fine violinist, dancer, singer,
horseman, and athlete, a combination of physical and intellectual
attributes that made him both personable and persuasive.

How highly he was held in esteem by colleagues is evidenced by an
anecdote related by John Adams. Adams tells how when he and
Jefferson sat down to write the Declaration of Independence each
suggested that the other prepare the draft.

"What can be your reasons?" asked Jefferson.

"Reason first," replied Adams, "you are a Virginian, and a Virginian ought to appear at the head of this business. Reason second—
I am obnoxious, suspected, and unpopular. You are very much
otherwise. Reason third—you can write ten times better than I can."

On finishing college Jefferson entered a law office and became at
the age of twenty-four a practicing barrister, the usual gateway for a
political career. Thus it was from the thinker's perch, rather than the
journeyman's bench, that he elaborated the leveling principles that
were his hallmark. Jefferson was a subpar administrator. At one stage
of the Revolutionary War as governor of Virginia he was maladroit
in raising troops and organizing defense against Lord Cornwallis. In
1781, after offering large bounties of clothing, money, and land to
raise 500 soldiers, he was able to recruit only seven, and two immediately deserted. In his personal life he was similarly a poor manager.

One of the reasons he was not able to free his slaves, as he wished, was because they were by law security on his debts, and he was seldom out of debt. But as a political philosopher Jefferson was among the greatest of his time; his imprint on the American tradition was so great that to this day his name is synonymous in the national lexicon with true democracy.

The cornerstone of that philosophy was that the United States could flourish only if it became and remained a nation of small agrarian producers. Unlike the English thinker John Locke, who argued that the government "cannot take from any man any part of his property without his own consent," Jefferson interpreted the eighteenth-century dictum "preservation of property" to mean that society also had a duty to reduce inequality in the distribution of wealth. "I am conscious," he wrote in 1785, "that an equal division of property is impracticable." But it was the government's responsibility to take measures so that "the consequences of this enormous inequality producing so much misery to the bulk of mankind" be mitigated.

In contrast to the individualism of Locke and Adam Smith, Jefferson conceived of society as an organic whole, and government as a collective repository for the people's welfare. Where Locke spoke of "life, liberty and *property*," Jefferson wrote "life, liberty and *the pursuit of happiness*." (Italics added.) There is a subtle difference here that is the essence of modern liberalism and all antipoverty programs. Every man is due basic liberties, including that of owning property, but where it impinges on the "happiness" of others the community, through its government, must take action to create a balance between the two. Under Adam Smith and Locke, there were to be no restraints on aggrandizement, except the restraints of the market and natural selection. Under Jefferson's schema, the sanctity of property was relative, not absolute; the government must protect it, but not to the point where one man has too much and another too little. So that while Jefferson believed it was "impractical" to have an "equal" division, he proposed many measures to narrow the gap between the haves and the have-nots. One of the means, he said, "of lessening the inequality of property is to exempt all from taxation below a certain point, and to tax the higher portions of property in geometrical progression as they rise." This is a more extreme nostrum than the progressive *income* tax; it is a progressive tax on wealth, something that the nation has not adopted to this day, except insofar as inheritance is concerned. Another measure in this leveler's faith was "to provide by every possible means that as few as possible shall be without a little portion of land. The small landholders are the most precious part of a state." When he drafted the Virginia constitution of 1776 Jefferson inserted a provision that "every person of full age . . . shall be entitled to an appropriation of fifty acres. . . ."

Building on Locke's edifice, the Virginian added the dimension of collective concern for the dispossessed, leading him to what was in the eighteenth century the upper stratosphere of reform. He espoused free education, prison reform, full male suffrage, emancipation of the slaves. In drafting the Declaration, for instance, he slipped in a passage denouncing the English monarch for waging "cruel war against human nature itself, violating its most sacred rights of life and liberty in the persons of a distant people who never offended him, captivating them into slavery in another hemisphere, or to incur miserable death in their transportation thither." Only the sensitiveness of Georgia and South Carolina forced him to withdraw the offensive paragraph. To undergird the democratic process he favored education for everyone. "No other sure foundation can be devised," he wrote in 1786, "for the preservation of freedom and happiness." His later proposal for "Establishing Elementary Schools" in Virginia was a detailed exposition of universal, state-financed education— decades ahead of the times.

Had the radical wing, typified by Jefferson, Patrick Henry, and Samuel Adams, held sway after the war and during the Constitutional Convention, the Jeffersonian doctrine might have been translated into many more benefits for the dispossessed. But the high ground, after the war and up to the nineteenth century, was held by Washington's right-hand man, Alexander Hamilton, who believed that government must serve the few as against the many. The reforms that emerged therefore were compromises, of considerable portent for the future, yet incomplete for the present.

III

The one attack on poverty that had results both enduring and substantial was the opening of land to the landless. Mixed with Jefferson's dream of constructing a nation on the bedrock of small landholders were political and geopolitical motives, such as punishing the Tories or thwarting the territorial ambitions of England, Spain, and France. There was also the irrepressible pressure of land speculators like the Ohio Company, as well as the need for revenue. But if motives of security and profit blended with Jeffersonian idealism, the fact is that the Revolution made land available on a grand scale. It effectively opened the frontier beyond the Appalachians, a single act by which it more than doubled its original empire. It seized the holdings of American Tories, the proprietors, and the Crown, and sold much of it in small parcels at low cost. And it removed a number of old and onerous practices that tended to reinforce aristocracy. Taken together, these measures offered opportunity to the poor on a scale hitherto unknown anywhere in the world.

It is generally forgotten that during colonial days lower-class Americans directed their wrath more against native aristocrats than the gentry in London. A ceaseless conflict between the tidewater and the backwoods, the borrower and lender, the landlord and tenant, the rich and the poor had torn the turf of the American scene and often spilled over to violence—sometimes, as in Bacon's rebellion of 1676, revolutionary violence aimed at seizing the government. Britain's intemperate passage of the Stamp Act and the restrictive legislation that followed deflected hostility from the native aristocracy to the mother country. But the militants of the Revolution, the men who engaged in boycotts, dumped tea in Boston Harbor, and formed themselves later into "committees of safety," did not forget— or forgive—their home-grown rich even while fighting a war against England.

During that war Massachusetts seized every acre of those who fought for Britain, including the Pepperell holdings which ran 30 miles along the coast. Pennsylvania, in ironic turnabout, sequestered farms of the William Penn family valued at $5,000,000, for which it paid $650,000. New York, the bastion of landed aristocracy, grabbed such precious morsels as the 300-square-mile manor of the Philipse family, the De Lancey riches, and all told nearly half the acreage of the state, though some of this was given to rich patriots like the Livingstons. New Jersey laid hand on 500 large holdings, Virginia confiscated the 6,000,000-acre Fairfax estate. The suggestion by the Continental Congress in November 1777 that states appropriate the property of those who adhered to the king was accepted with lyrical enthusiasm by all except South Carolina. Twenty-nine landowners lost their patrimony in New Hampshire, 490 in Pennsylvania, 55 in New York. By the end of the war 5,000 loyalists complained that they had been deprived of assets valued at $40,000,000 to $50,000,000. It was as extensive a land seizure as any in the annals of the Western Hemisphere, comparable to those of Lázaro Cárdenas in Mexico and Fidel Castro in Cuba a long time later.

The confiscated Tory estates, as well as the unallocated lands that belonged to the Crown and proprietors, also unceremoniously seized, were sold by the thirteen states for much needed revenue— New York realized more than $3,000,000 thereby, Maryland more than $2,000,000. In the process large holdings were carved into tracts suitable for small and middle-sized farms. Thus the fiefdom of James De Lancey was broken up into 275 separate farms by New York, that of Roger Morris into 250, with limits of 500 acres on each parcel. In a single year New York put five and a half million acres on the auction block at bids of a couple of shillings an acre. The effect, of course, was that many land-hungry tenants or artisans with a taste for rural living were given a chance to satisfy their urge on a grand scale. The Revolution, too, acted kindly to another segment of the poor, the squatters, offering them pre-emption rights on generous terms. In Virginia, squatter families were permitted to retain 400 acres each, provided they agreed to farm for a year and plant corn. A law of 1781 authorized squatters to buy land at $5 for a 100-acre parcel, payable in two and a half years. Taken together with the many land assignments in the hands of returning soldiers, the result was a substantial fattening of agrarian democracy.

Four other changes wrought by the Revolution had similar consequences. One was the automatic death of quitrent. Under the old system freeholders in most colonies were required to pay the Crown or the proprietor an annual quitrent of a penny an acre, a shilling per hundred acres, or similar sums. These exactions had been sweepingly evaded, as William Penn learned to his dismay during the Holy Experiment, but collections nonetheless usually ran to about $100,000 a year. With the outbreak of hostilities it was simply assumed that liabilities to the king and his cronies were canceled, and they naturally lapsed.

So too with the vexatious law on naval stocks. To ensure the supply of masts for the royal navy, colonists had been prohibited from cutting white pine trees until the king's representative had designated which ones he wanted for the English fleet—free of charge, of course. Again, it was a statute more observed by the breach than by enforcement, but it was an irritating claim against the farm population, and no one shed any tears when it passed into limbo during the Revolution because the British could not compel compliance.

With independence, too, the states began to divest themselves of two carry-overs from the ancient feudal order which were meant to concentrate land ownership in as few hands as possible. Under the law of entail, initially enacted in thirteenth-century England, a man could put a "tail" on land given someone else, say his son, so that it was inalienable. It could be neither sold nor given away, only inherited by "heirs of his body." Under the law of primogeniture the property left by a man without a will went to the eldest son exclusively. (New England, more liberal on this score than its sister states, permitted other children to share in the inheritance, but allotted the eldest son a double legacy.) The fruit of entail and primogeniture was sometimes bitter: a family that could no longer farm its holdings, because of health or financial reasons, was nonetheless proscribed from selling it or borrowing against it. When a father died intestate the oldest son fared well, but the other children, unless they had received property during their father's lifetime, were plunged into an abyss of poverty. The two laws promoted the kind of inequality that the English and American gentry were pledged to sustain, and levelers like Jefferson to abolish. Legislators, wrote Jefferson, "cannot invent too many devices for subdividing property. . . . The descent of property of every kind to all the children, or to all the brothers and sisters, or other relations in equal degree, is a politic measure, and a practical one." In 1776 he introduced a law in Virginia whereby property could be sold in fee simple, forever inheritable by the heirs of the purchaser. South Carolina already had such legislation on the books; five others—Pennsylvania, New York, Georgia, Maryland, North Carolina—followed suit within the next decade. Within fifteen years of the Revolution all states had also abolished primogeniture.

The most significant result of the Revolution, both for the poor and for the nation per se, was the breaching of the barrier by which England had hemmed in its colonists east of the Appalachians. Beyond the watershed, from West Florida to the Great Lakes and from the Alleghenies to the Mississippi, were 488,248 square miles of land (as against 341,752 square miles of the original states). The British, with pragmatic flexibility, had encouraged the opening of this territory when it was claimed by France and Spain. But with the resounding victory of England in the French and Indian War the great domain was closed off. By a royal proclamation of 1763 settlement was limited to the mountains, and eleven years later, smitten by vengeance against the truculent colonists, the English not only further restricted white settlement but placed the section north of the Ohio River under the suzerainty of the province of Quebec. The effect was to stifle the aspirations of the yeoman class, eying the great prairies explored by La Salle, Thomas Walker, Christopher Gist, and Daniel Boone, as well as those of the large speculators. The Mississippi Company, the Company of Military Adventurers, the Loyal Company, the Illinois Company held grants of 200,000 to 12,000,000 acres beyond the Alleghenies, but they were worthless unless England permitted people to settle there. So was the enormous tract, now West Virginia, that enterprising Pennsylvanians had bought from the Indians in the hopes of establishing a new colony, Vandalia.

It is painful to speculate what might have happened to the fledgling nation if somehow this lush real estate had not fallen into its hands. Not only would expansion westward have been debarred but it is almost certain that the tenuous confederation of thirteen states would have splintered beyond repair, and the "American promise" shriveled to the dull despair of eighteenth-century Europe. Fortunately, all the cards seemed to fall into place for the Americans. To checkmate the British, Patrick Henry of Virginia dispatched George Rogers Clark, barely twenty-six, and a band of 250 men into the northwest to seize outposts and wrest control from England. The rival claims of those states that asserted title to areas beyond the Appalachians from old, vague royal grants were bypassed when little Maryland in 1779 refused to ratify the Articles of Confederation until the other twelve states agreed to make the northwest *common* property. Virginia and Connecticut, after holding out for a few million acres each to reimburse citizens for property losses and veterans who held land warrants, ceded the rest to the federal government. Then in a stroke of diplomatic genius the Americans, playing on the rivalry of England, France, and Spain, were able to convince the British to cede the whole territory to them in the Treaty of Paris.

Even so there were more hurdles to overcome. The Indians were encouraged by all three European powers, with weapons and matériel, to resist militarily the tide of American settlement. So fierce was this resistance that from 1795 to 1809 the United States, victorious in battle, imposed ten humiliating treaties on the Indians in the northwest alone. Efforts by the English to induce Kentucky and Vermont to secede from the Union likewise were frustrated as were similar blandishments by the Spaniards. Above all, the "west" began to fill out with American settlers; by 1783 there were already 25,000 there, the largest segment in Kentucky, where Revolutionary soldiers were given land warrants by Virginia in lieu of pay and bounty. And once the war was over the tide became inexorable. Hardy families by the thousands moved through Wilderness Road or down the Ohio River into Kentucky—some 967 boats, carrying 18,370 persons and 7,896 horses, passed by Fort Hamar in just a single year ending November 1788. By 1790 Kentucky boasted a population of 74,000 and was about to enter the Union as an independent state. Tennessee had 35,000. The year Marietta, Ohio, was laid out—1788—some 10,000 people passed through it.

With the region marked for effective U.S. ownership, there were still a few pitfalls in the way of enlightened policy. Had the thirteen states followed European precedent, they might have designated it a colony, to be ruled in dependent status indefinitely. Jefferson, in drafting the Ordinance of 1784, however, proposed to divide the northwest into ten states with such esoteric names as Sylvania, Chersonesus, Assenisipia, Illinoia, Metropotamia, and Pelisipia. Here, as well as in Kentucky and Tennessee, slavery would be forbidden after 1800. The proposed ordinance fell two votes short of acceptance (seven states favored it as against the needed nine), but three years later the famous Ordinance of 1787 laid the framework for national policy. Slavery was outlawed north of the Ohio. Three to five states were to be carved out of the northwest, instead of Jefferson's ten, and when any of these subdivisions held 60,000 eligible voters it would become a state "on an equal footing with all others." The franchise was granted anyone with fifty acres.

Only in the distribution of the vacant land was the post-Revolutionary policy wanting. Here a bitter dispute erupted between those who looked on the territory as a source of revenue for the states and those who looked on it as a means of spreading agrarian democracy.

Alexander Hamilton suggested that land be sold in large holdings at an "advantageous" price. Jefferson favored giving it away, later swung around to selling it but in relatively small plots at low cost. The final policy, contained in the Land Ordinance of 1785, was a compromise, though heavily weighted toward Hamilton's position. It provided for the government to lay out in neat survey rectangular communities of thirty-six square miles—like the old New England townships—putting aside one thirty-sixth of each to support public schooling. Half of each township would be sold at auction at a minimum of $1 an acre (later $2), the other half in sections one mile square. It was a system made to order for the land jobbers, especially those who bought for a song land warrants owned by ex-soldiers. Even a single section, 640 acres, cost $1,280, far beyond the resources of the average individual.

Yet the best laid plans of mice and men went awry. Under relentless pressure Congress was forced to reduce the size of holdings for sale to 320 acres in 1800, 160 acres in 1804, and finally 80 acres by 1820. Furthermore the surveys and elaborate plans for the sale never worked out as originally contemplated. Men simply settled on lands beyond those surveyed. Before Congress' program got under way, there were already 7,000 persons on unsurveyed territories. Many more were to follow, and though the government sometimes used force to evict them, it was also made to recognize their claims by periodic pre-emption acts that made it possible to gain title at so much per acre.

Thus the frontier, despite the peculations of the big companies, not only deepened the democratic spirit but offset poverty measurably. By 1790 some 221,000 pioneers were ensconced in the sprawling paradise beyond the Appalachians. "The practical liberty of America," wrote an Englishman in 1817, "is found in its great space and small population. Good land, dog-cheap everywhere, and for nothing if you will go for it, gives as much elbow room to every man as he chooses to take. . . . They come, they toil, they prosper. This is the real liberty of America."

IV

Apart from the reforms affecting land ownership, the revolutionary new nation liberalized voters' rights, modified imprisonment for debt, and struck a few modest blows against slavery, but in every case it stopped at the point of amelioration, short of basic reversal.

Restrictions on the ballot had never been so severe in the colonies as in England, yet in all thirteen the franchise was tied to ownership of a certain amount of property, and office holding to considerably more. Benjamin Franklin once told the delightful story of a man who by virtue of owning a mule earned the precious right to cast a ballot. But when the mule died, his right perished with it. "I wonder," mused Franklin, "who had the vote, the man or the mule?"

To have jumped in one giant step from a franchise tied to property to a franchise based on citizenship was evidently too drastic for eighteenth-century American leaders to contemplate. Four states in fact made no change at all in voting prerogatives. New York and Massachusetts continued a hierarchical system favorable to the affluent. In the latter state, for instance, wealth of $300 was needed to cast a ballot, $500 to $1,000 to run for Congress, $1,500 to $3,000 to become a senator, and $5,000 to stand for governor. As late as 1790, reports Curtis P. Nettels, "only one adult male in ten in New York City could vote for a governor." This was a battle still to be won, an armor only partly pierced. Yet, in irregular fashion, there were many changes for the better. Pennsylvania's constitution of 1776 granted the ballot to any male who paid taxes, and equalized representation between the backwoods areas and the eastern ones—what we would today call the principle of "one man, one vote." Delaware, North Carolina, and New Hampshire followed suit in their constitutions, and New Jersey reduced the property qualification to £50. Georgia lowered it from the ownership of fifty acres of land to £10 of any kind of property. In addition the number of officeholders to be elected rather than appointed was gradually increased to include the governor—in Massachusetts and New York—judges, and other officials. Pennsylvania took a decisive step forward when it declared all free men eligible to hold public office regardless of wealth or religion, and Delaware when it banned all religious tests. Thus, in the push and pull between the Jeffersonian and the Hamiltonian approaches, reform was inevitable, yet incomplete.

Another social sector in which improvement was ambiguous was in relief of the debtor. The abolition of imprisonment for debt, one of the more onerous burdens on the poor, had to wait until the Jacksonian era more than a half century after Lexington and Concord. A man could be clapped in jail for owing someone a few dollars, and while incarcerated, to add insult to injury, be forced to pay his own upkeep. How extensive was this type of punishment is indicated by the fact that as late as 1785, even in Philadelphia, half the inmates of the prisons were there because they violated the debtors' code. New York jails in 1787–88 housed 1,200 men unable to pay obligations, sometimes as small as $5. The numbers doubtless would have been greater if the Pennsylvania and North Carolina constitutions hadn't been modified after 1776, limiting imprisonment to those who failed to turn over their assets in settlement of debts or who had engaged in fraud. New York in 1789 passed a law limiting imprisonment to thirty days if the debt was less than $50. A Pennsylvania bill in 1792 required that creditors pay part of the upkeep for imprisoned defaulters. Following Shays' Rebellion in Massachusetts a law was enacted granting freedom to debtors who swore they could pay neither their bills nor their upkeep while in jail.

A more direct assault on the problem, presumably aimed at amelioration of the debtor's plight, and one that was to titillate the imagination of poor men for a century and a quarter, was the printing of paper money. It is not difficult to prove, as many scholars have done, that this panacea offers only temporary help at best, but behind the demand for cheap money has always been the desire to redistribute income in favor of the lower classes. At any rate, as has happened every generation or two, the cry went up during the critical period from 1783 to 1788, just as it had in Deacon Adams' day and just as it would through much of the nineteenth century.

Currency manipulation during the war had been so farcical it almost cast from view the grim torment that accompanied it. The states, just as Congress, had issued vast sums of paper—$250,000,000 —all of which had reached an absolute nadir in value. Paper had depreciated by 1780 so that Virginia and Georgia dollars were worth but one-tenth of a penny in silver; those of New York, three-quarters of a penny; and of Maryland, two and a half cents. As usual, commodity prices rose more rapidly than the earning power of the lower classes, placing them on an endless merry-go-round of debts. Attempts to correlate the price of paper with that of silver—such as $1,000 in paper for $1 in silver—invariably failed.

Yet, in the depression of 1785–86, as the impact of postwar dislocation hit the economy full blast, paper money again became the rallying cry of the underprivileged. If only the pernicious merchants could be made to take paper as legal tender, inflation could be kept within decent bounds, and the debtor could repay in depreciated money the more expensive money he had borrowed. This radical demand bedeviled eleven of the thirteen states—only Connecticut and Delaware escaped the swirling tornado—and forced seven to accede. North Carolina printed large amounts of currency which it used to purchase tobacco at double its price in specie. South Carolina took coercive measures forcing planters to take paper at its stated value. "Hint clubs" reminded merchants that they had better accept the money or face the prospect—as in colonial times—of having their homes burned down. Georgia put a unique twist in its campaign: any merchant who was unwilling to sign an affidavit that he had always accepted paper script was denied the right to export. Pennsylvania trod more carefully, issuing a million dollars in bills of credit but not designating it as legal tender. New Jersey passed paper money legislation twice, since its first bill was vetoed by Governor William Livingston.

It was in Rhode Island and Massachusetts that the tumult reached a shrill blast. Both had been occupied for a long time by the British. Their economies were in tatters and their people perhaps the most debt-ridden in the nation. But where the Massachusetts legislature, founded on the conservative constitution of 1780 and in the hands of the right wing, refused to back off from "sound money" policies—provoking rebellion in the western sections—the Rhode Island legislature was controlled by the radicals and forced to give way. Sound-money proponents who at first dominated the small state's law-making body were turned out of office in the 1786 elections and a half million dollars in script was printed and offered as loans to farmers with real estate as security. A forcing act provided that if a creditor refused to take paper money the debt was automatically canceled.

The plan foundered, of course, on the shoals of commercial apprehension. Merchants refused to take the rag paper, farmers in reprisal withheld their milk, pigs, and grain from the market, seeking in vain to sell them in other states. In desperation they dumped milk, let their produce rot, and burned their corn. But economic reality was working against the cheap-money enthusiasts. Script issued in May at a dollar was worth only sixteen cents six months later. The same fate befell other currencies issued with nothing but a prayer behind them. The cacophony of thirteen states with thirteen different paper-money values trying to trade with each other was just too much for economic efficiency. It remained for Alexander Hamilton and the federal government that emerged after the Constitutional Convention to fashion a sound money, but it is worth noting that while the Washington Administration paid full value on redeemed long-term bonds in the hands of the wealthy, the Continentals, held by many poor, were left unredeemed.

Another muted cry of the Revolution, similarly related to the extirpation of poverty, was for emancipation of the slaves. Many good men saw the inconsistency between all men being created equal and some being treated as property. Jefferson naturally was one. Patrick Henry, two years before hostilities, put the question forthrightly: "Is it not amazing," he asked, "that at a time, when the rights of humanity are defined and understood with precision, in a country above all others fond of liberty, that in such an age and in such a country we find men . . . adopting a principle [slavery] as repugnant to humanity as it is inconsistent with the Bible and destructive to liberty?" Thomas Paine, the redoubtable pamphleteer, urged not merely freedom for the slave but a generous gift of land to sustain him, an idea which the left-wing Republicans plagiarized ninety years later, after the Civil War. Even Washington, no rabble rouser, called for abolition "on the score of human dignity" and on the more practical ground that "nothing but the rooting out of slavery can perpetuate . . . our union." A strain of idealism motivated the Continental Congress of 1774, even before independence, to proclaim that "we will neither import nor purchase any slave imported after the first day of December next." Five days before Lexington, devout Quakers met at the Sun Tavern on Second Street in Philadelphia to form "The Society for the Relief of Free Negroes unlawfully held in Bondage." New Yorkers led by the conservative John Jay ten years later founded a society for manumission of slaves, and within a few years similar groups were proclaiming the message in six other states. If Americans, said Jay, did not free their Negroes, their "prayers to Heaven for liberty will be impious."

But as with so many other progressive developments the practical concerns of some people coalesced with the idealistic concerns of others to force a modification of attitudes. For one thing the English were offering slaves freedom if they deserted to the British cause. When Lord Dunmore, royal governor of Virginia, in November 1775 proclaimed liberation for all blacks who could reach his lines, thousands responded. "Slaves flock to him in abundance," observed Edmund Pendleton, a prominent Virginia citizen. And though British officers blatantly reneged on their promises by selling slaves into the more terrifying bondage of the West Indies, the number of blacks who sought escape must have been high. Jefferson estimated it in 1778 at 30,000; by 1783 the figure was believed to be as high as 100,000—one out of every five or six black slaves. British ships leaving New York harbor after the Treaty of Paris carried 3,000 Negroes in their bunks. Five thousand left with the British fleet when it evacuated Savannah in July 1782.

British inducement, thus, was one factor in relaxing the yoke of slavery. Another was the urgency of manpower for Washington's army. In this war as in all others many a patriot preferred that others fight for him, while he confined support to verbal pyrotechnics in the rear. Enlistment tapered off after the first burst of nationalism, and despite bounties of land and cash, the number of recruits for the armed forces was less than overwhelming. To offset the terrible problem of desertion, the states devised a scheme for sending substitutes. A New York law of 1776, followed by others elsewhere, permitted drafted men to send alternates in their place, black or white. Lucky was the owner therefore who had a slave to offer for his country. In addition a number of states, unable to meet their soldier quotas, passed specific laws for the enrollment of Negro slaves, offering emancipation in return for military service. Rhode Island and Massachusetts took such action in 1778, Maryland in 1780, New York in 1781. Congress pleaded with the southern states to do likewise, even offering $1,000 to Georgia and South Carolina for each Negro set free to serve in the armed forces, hoping thereby to recruit 3,000 men. The offer was turned down, but Negroes, free and slave both, formed sizable segments of certain contingents, and often fought with great distinction.

Historian John C. Miller estimates that northern battalions included an average of fifty Negroes each and that at the battle of Monmouth Courthouse, 700 black men fought with the patriots. "It began to appear that Ethiopia as well as America was in arms." They joined, these Negroes, not out of overpowering love for their masters or the cause of a nation that held them in bondage, but because at the end of the rainbow was the cherished promise of freedom. Freedom and a musket went together. Generally the northern states promised liberation at the end of three years of military service; Virginia required only that the slave serve "honorably." At least 5,000 black brethren, mostly in integrated units, tasted gunpowder with white comrades on the glory road to freedom.

If there was a mixture of idealism and practical motive in enrolling the Negro for war, the impulse carried over for emancipation. It was strongest, as might be expected, in those states where there was little to lose. Vermont, for instance, never recognized the institution of bondage; its 1777 constitution prohibited the enslavement of anyone "born in this country or brought from over sea." Vermont, however, had virtually no slaves within its borders. At the time of the Revolution there were 4,000 black bondsmen in Rhode Island, 5,000 in Massachusetts, 6,000 each in Pennsylvania and Connecticut, as against 200,000 in Virginia and 100,000 in South Carolina. Obviously there was a threshhold for idealism; it was less painful to the exchequer to free 4,000 or 6,000 pieces of property than 100,000. The pace of emancipation seemed to move with the account ledger. Pennsylvania in 1780, Connecticut and Rhode Island in 1784 legislated for gradual abolition. In Massachusetts the task was accomplished by judicial fiat, when judges ruled that the reference to "free and equal" in the Constitution applied to all men, regardless of skin pigment. In a historic decision, Chief Justice William Cushing, in ruling against an owner who beat his slave, held that the "idea of slavery is inconsistent with our own conduct and Constitution." By 1804, when New Jersey instituted gradual emancipation, all states above the Mason-Dixon line were committed to abolition.

Southward, however, the institution clung with stubborn tenacity. Despite the abolitionist views of men like Jefferson, Washington, Randolph, Mason, and Madison, Virginia would go no further than to legalize manumission by enlightened owners, providing they gave security that the freed slave would not become a ward of the public. And by 1808, with the invention of the ingenious cotton gin, sentiment somersaulted in the opposite direction, a grim testament to the influence of the pocketbook on humanism. Elsewhere, especially in Georgia and South Carolina, slavery was too serious a business to be jibed at. Theorists even contrived a kind of moral sanctity for it by quoting the Bible. As one congressman was heard to say many years later: "God Himself, after he had rescued the children of Israel from the house of bondage, sanctioned and recognized slavery both in principle and practice."

Fortune was more benign in dealing with another type of poverty, that of the white slave—the indentured servant. Here there can be no question that the good will of men was very much less important than the strictures of economics. The institution had simply run out its time, like a horse-drawn carriage challenged by the automobile. It was already much withered when the Revolution broke out, having tapered off at the end of the seventeenth century. With Negroes available in grand numbers southern planters lost interest in white servants whose term of service was limited and who were less tractable to heavy field labor, especially the female indentures. The servants themselves were disenchanted with the South because policies of land engrossment left little opportunity to obtain freeholds. Except in Pennsylvania, white slavery was in eclipse. Britain's decision at the end of the war to prohibit further transport of indentures— because it needed workers at home for its own new factories —contributed as much to the demise of this form of bondage as any action taken by the Americans.

In the flush of revolution, Maryland passed a law limiting servitude for whites to a maximum of four years. Societies sprang up in a number of states, similar to the ones dealing with Negro slavery, to lighten the burden for indentures. Many such men gained their freedom—though it was illegal for them to enlist—simply by running off to the army. Citizens in New York, witnessing the arrival of a shipload of servants in 1784, proclaimed that "traffick in White People" clashed with the principles of liberty, and forthwith paid their passage and set them free. The institution of white bondage lingered for another generation but the laws of economics as well as the nobility of reformers had already sounded its death knell.

By haphazard and abbreviated steps, then, the founding fathers fabricated an antipoverty program inherent in the principles of revolution. The aristocratic wing—for there was one, as witness the debates of the Constitutional Convention or the monarchistic notions of Alexander Hamilton—deplored many of the leveling measures. Devereux Jarratt of Virginia spoke for a considerable faction when he expressed concern that "high republican times" were bringing about "more levelling than ought to be, consistent with government." But the Revolution's momentum could not be checked entirely, and it produced a war on poverty as dramatic as any in American annals.

Chapter 6

BITTER FRUIT

A smuggler by the name of Samuel Slater arrived in the United States in 1789, the same year Washington was inaugurated President, with an illicit item that was to help change the American way of life. Born in Derbyshire, England, and barely twenty-one, Slater was smuggling not diamonds or dope, or any other physical substance for that matter, but a plan—in his head—for a labor-saving machine. The reason he dared not put the plan to paper was that the insular British, jealous of their lead in the Industrial Revolution, had taken stern measures to prevent its secrets from being exported, either physically or as drawings. Even artisans who worked on such machines were prohibited from emigrating to other countries for fear they would divulge industrial intelligence. Young Slater, an employee of an English factory, had read an advertisement of the Pennsylvania Society for the Encouragement of Manufactures and the Useful Arts offering $500 for improvements in textile machinery. Disguising himself as a farm boy, he thereupon made his way to London, then New York, and, with the help of an American Quaker, the "father of American manufactures" set up a mill in Pawtucket, Rhode Island, dredging his memory to reproduce water frames and spinning and carding machines.* Nine small children tended the factory.

* Some historians contend that such mills already existed in the South, before Slater, but most assign him priority for the innovation.

79

It was an inauspicious beginning for the incredible national face lifting that impended. In the ensuing decades the technological and social logic of labor-saving machinery would reshape the United States into a fantasy of hope and tragedy, upsetting all inherited guidelines. Machines, first driven by hand when James Hargreaves invented the jenny in 1764, then by water power, steam, and finally coal and electricity, were destined to father innumerable cities, shift the locus of economic decision from rural to urban areas, draw to the nation tens of millions of immigrants, divorce a section of the producing class—the laborers—from ownership of the tools of production, and sire new types of poverty considerably worse than anything men would endure on the farm.

The machines stirred imagination and prodded mechanically minded geniuses to invent ever more complex and efficient varieties. But for decades after Samuel Slater, well into the nineteenth century, there was severe controversy as to whether the game was worth the candle. What Jefferson had seen of the factory system in England and France had convinced him that it drained the spirit out of women and small children, and reduced breadwinners "below the means of supporting life, even by labor." In discussing the matter with Washington and Hamilton he continued to opt for a nation based on small landholders. He had faith neither in the monied classes, which lived off other people's labor, nor in the proletariat, which he feared would be corrupted by nonownership of property. "I consider the class of artificers," he argued, "as the panders of vice, and the instruments by which the liberties of a country are generally overturned." Though the future President and leader of republicanism eventually made his peace with the labor-saving machine, many men long afterward opposed the factory system, as John B. McMaster tells us, on the ground "that the country was new, that the West was yet to be settled, that the Government had vast tracts of land for sale, and that no steps ought to be taken toward the establishment of any industry which, by gathering men and women in towns and villages, stopped the purchase of public lands and hindered the movement of population toward the Mississippi. Others of the same mind looked on the employment of girls and young children in mills as ruinous to good morals and education."

The other side of the argument, the one that prevailed, was brilliantly defended by that young financial genius who was the keystone of Washington's cabinet, Hamilton. Only thirty-four when he was appointed Secretary of the Treasury, the handsome redhead born in the West Indies, had strong leanings toward the "rich and well-born." Communities, he told the Constitutional Convention, "divide themselves into the few and the many. The first are the rich and well-born, the other the mass of the people . . . turbulent and changing, they seldom judge or determine right. Give therefore to the first class a distinct, permanent share in the Government." The factory system he envisioned would make this class paramount. In the process it would encourage immigration, utilize the skills of women and children not currently employed, and increase demand for raw materials to feed the factory.

Far from being shocked by the human results of the British industrial system, Hamilton was elated by them. In his voluminous "Report on Manufactures," December 5, 1791, he noted that four-sevenths of the workers in British mills were women and children "rendered more useful, and the latter [children] more early useful, by manufacturing establishments, than they would otherwise be." Carefully but fastidiously the man from the West Indies began fashioning a nation along the businessman's—rather than the small farmer's—pattern. To assure a supply of labor for that businessman he placed obstacles in the path of would-be small farmers. Land of the public domain was to be sold in large plots unavailable to the poor man's pocketbook. By funding the $56,000,000 debt of the national government and the $18,000,000 debt of the various states, Hamilton made it possible for entrepreneurs to accumulate venture capital. By doubling the duties on finished goods, he offered protection to new industries; and by establishing a United States Bank in a country that had only four functioning banks, he made credit available to the business community. The radicals opposed such measures not only because they were not consonant with their image of a nation of small landowners, but because they raised prices on consumer goods that could be bought cheaper from Europe, increased taxes on the poor, and created a class of pauperized laborers in the city slums.

The onrush of manufacture, however, could not be slowed by abstract doctrine. The machine saved time and produced mountains of goods, a circumstance against which philosophic argument, no matter how cogent, could not persevere. In the following decades, stimulated by the War of 1812, during which British goods were unavailable, the factory system spread wings like a great eagle sure of its course. The Commonwealth of Massachusetts, which had issued but three charters for manufacturing companies from 1789 to 1796, issued 133 in the decade from 1810 to 1819. By 1830 there were 795 cotton mills in the United States, valued at $45,000,000; by 1860 there were 1,091, worth more than double that amount, employing 122,000 laborers. Other industries showed the same glowing development, pig iron production, for instance, rising from 54,000 gross tons to 564,000. On the eve of the Civil War, 140,000 industrial establishments were operating with a capital of more than a billion dollars, and employing 1,300,000 workers.

II

The Industrial Revolution was not simply an addition to American life, it was a rearrangement of everything from living habits to ethical values. When Washington became President only 130,000 people lived in the six cities with 8,000 or more population. When Lincoln became President there were 5,000,000 people in the nation's 141 cities. No city had as many as 75,000 inhabitants in 1790; Manhattan alone had 813,669 in 1860; Philadelphia, 566,000; Baltimore, 212,000. Moreover, in such places as New York, St. Louis, and Chicago half or more of the population were foreign-born, a cluster of unassimilated immigrants more concentrated than anything known previously. Of the 622,924 people in Manhattan in 1855, 52.3 per cent had been born overseas—28.2 per cent in Ireland and 15.7 per cent in Germany.

Throughout this period, as throughout colonial days, labor was always in short supply and had to be imported from Europe. But the number and utilization changed dramatically. From about 5,000 a year in the decade from 1790 to 1800, immigration rose to peaks of 100,000 in 1842 and 427,833 in 1854. Virtually all the immigrants in the colonial period had found their way to the farm, as servants, tenants, or owners. Now almost twice as many came to the cities as the farm, working in factories, on construction projects such as the Erie Canal and the new turnpikes, and in transport, the vast majority of them common laborers.

Statistics alone did not begin to explain the change. Farm life was individualistic: a man owned or rented a certain acreage, planned, planted, harvested, and marketed in his own way, by his own decision. The laborer on a construction project or in a factory lived under a collectivist star, his work necessarily coordinated with that of others. Except for a certain freedom in choosing his job, one that was frequently imposed on him by necessity, the decisions affecting his work were made by others. The laborer on a plantation in colonial times or the typical journeyman employed by a master made a contract for a full year. During that time he could not quit, nor be fired except for specified causes. Sometimes he received his pay every three months, often at the end of the year. In the new era the laborer was more free, more mobile. He could work or not work—idleness was no longer punished by imprisonment, whipping, or the workhouse; he could shift from one employer to another, one city to another, and arrange for whatever wage he could negotiate. His freedom, however, included a dubious prerogative—the right to starve.

The feudal serf of Europe had lived in a stagnant society, tied to his land, prohibited from moving to another village except with the permission of his lord; but he enjoyed a measure of security under the shelter of lord and clergyman. When and if conditions became dire, these men were under obligation, by lay and religious tradition, to alleviate his condition. In the American colonies, the indentured servant and Negro slave, distressing as was their circumstance, were assured a minimum wherewithal by their masters. Whatever the state of the national economy there was a roof over their heads and a little food on the table. The poor backwoodsman, both in colonial and postcolonial days, might be victimized by natural disasters such as drought or tornado, but societal plagues such as depressions did not reduce him to actual starvation. The land almost always provided a few blessings of corn and potatoes to keep body and soul together.

The proletarian of the industrial era was not so fortunate. In the depression periods, which enervated the nation every decade, he was forced to scrounge for food on a soup line provided haphazardly by a benevolent charity or his city. That those soup lines were not overly lavish is attested to by the costs of the public soup house opened in the basement of Albany's city hall in 1838. The $1,098 it spent for a period of nearly four months provided each member of the 291 families with "a large piece of bread" and one pint of soup, at less than a penny per day per person. "This year," wrote a Philadelphian during the 1819 depression, "the question is how to exist." He meant it literally, not figuratively. Typical of the fate that tens of thousands of urban poor were to meet in depressed times was seen in the study by a Philadelphia committee which showed that employment in thirty industries had fallen from 9,672 in 1816 to 2,137 in 1819, and total wages from $58,000 to $12,000. A report from Cincinnati described "distress as beyond conception. Marshall and Sheriff sales are almost daily." Not a few people left for the backwoods to grow food. Newspapers pleaded for clothing, as many others, unable to buy wood, faced the prospect of freezing. The Society for the Prevention of Pauperism noted that in gay New York one out of fifteen persons (8,000 out of 120,000) had been reduced to the state of pauperism, and 12,000 to 13,000 were receiving poor relief.

The strain on the human psyche was equally vexing. One day God was in his heaven and all was right with the world; the next, disaster struck. "We are settling down better than was hoped for . . . ," editorialized the *Niles Register* in 1817, "the trial of war and the trial of peace have passed. It remains that we . . . march steadily on the high destinies that await our country." Three years later John Quincy Adams, future President of the United States, noted that "there has been within these two years an immense revolution of fortunes in every part of the Union; enormous numbers of persons utterly ruined; multitudes in deep distress; and a general mass of disaffection to the government, not concentrated in any particular direction, but ready to seize upon any event and looking out anywhere for a leader." A "deeper gloom hangs over us," read a newspaper dispatch from Lexington, Kentucky, "than was ever witnessed by the oldest man. The last war was sunshine, compared with these times."

The panic of 1837, even more than the depression of 1819, was a shattering event for the foreign-born working masses, for with only a short interruption in 1842–43 it was to last for eight years and resume soon thereafter. In May 1837 the banks called a halt to specie payment, refusing to honor their paper notes. Six hundred closed their doors in a single year. By January 1838 there were tens of thousands unemployed in New York alone and 200,000 city people living "in utter and hopeless distress with no means of surviving the winter but those provided by charity." One third of the laboring class was idle, most of the rest working part time. By 1839 wages had fallen 30 to 50 per cent, and in the next two years there were actual cases of families starving and freezing to death. At one time nine-tenths of the New England factories were out of operation. This was the period when Horace Greeley urged the jobless to "fly, scatter through the country, go to the Great West, anything but stay here."

Thus the Industrial Revolution, glorious as it was for national development and for the fabrication of an economy of gadgetry, piled an additional and more wretched poverty on top of the others. For a century, that poverty was concentrated in the immigrant.

III

The glamorized myth fashioned by comfortable historians is that millions came to the promised land to make their fortunes. But this is only partly true. Though land was available out west and wages were higher than in Europe, the five million immigrants who arrived from 1818 to 1863, a huge majority Irish and German, came not because life here was good but because life on the old continent was intolerable. The Irish faced recurring famine such as the one of 1816–17; the Germans were victims of unsettlement that followed abortive revolutions in 1830 and 1848. Not a few, of these and other nationalities, were running away from military service in their home country.

On arriving in New York or one of the lesser ports of entry, the immigrants' vision of the beautiful tomorrow began to dim somewhat. No Grover Whalen greeted them with keys to the city. Instead, runners boarded their ships to lure them to boardinghouses around Greenwich Street where the price was usually three to four times normal rates. Other runners, Irishmen for the Irish, Germans for the German, dinned their ears with offers of work hundreds of miles away that ranked, presumably, with the wonders of paradise, but never turned out that way. Frequently, as an inducement, immigrants were given "free" chits for transport to a job beyond Albany, say, only to find on arrival that they had to pay these fares and the chits were worthless.

Moreover the land of opportunity looked on these polyglot immigrants with abiding suspicion. The new arrivals were required to make surety that they would not become public charges within the ensuing two years. Speculative bond brokers soon appeared who took over this load for "a trifling payment." In some instances the shippers paid $1 to $10 for each immigrant as a tax against potential indigence. Far from rolling out a welcome mat second- and third-generation natives often complained that Europe was "casting upon us the refuse of her Alms Houses and Prisons."

This was to be a persistent castigation long into the twentieth century. Thomas Richard Whitney, charging the American Mechanics' Union in 1856 to defend native mechanics against the competition of foreign-born, asserted that immigration "imparts nothing to the genius of this country, saps the fountains of honest industry, and brings the deserving to want." The new laborers, he said, not only were willing to work for a pittance to undersell the native craftsmen, but used a dozen artifices to milk the country as well. By way of evidence he referred to a German cabinetmaker "on Ann Street" who, "under a plea of destitution, obtained all his winter fuel, with other necessaries, from the Alms-House department of the city," even though he worked with three apprentices making furniture in his "spacious loft." Another mean creature, also a German, "kept his two children constantly . . . begging for broken victuals from door to door" despite the fact that he had eight to ten hands working for him manufacturing clothing.

One of the less amusing features of the antiforeign cabal throughout the nineteenth century was the tendency to blame the immigrant for everything from hives to job stealing. Mayor Aaron Clark of New York, elected on the Native American ticket in 1837, told his council that the immigrants "necessarily drive our native workmen into exile, where they must war again with the savage of the wilderness. . . . It is apprehended they will bring disease among us; and if they have it not with them on arrival, they may generate a plague by collecting in crowds within small tenements and foul hovels." It was the immigrant's fault, said the Mayor, that the almshouses were so full, that "petitions signed by hundreds, asking for work, are presented in vain," that "private associations for relief are almost wholly without funds." Samuel F. B. Morse, Native American Party candidate for mayor the term before Clark's, wrote two brochures with the tantalizing titles "Imminent Dangers to the Free Institutions of the United States through Foreign Immigration" and "Foreign Conspiracy Against the Liberties of the United States."

In point of fact, of course, the immigrant worked for low wages not because he wanted to replace a native but because he could not do better, and far from being a "conspirator" against others he was victim of a thousand greeds. One of the most debilitating features of his life, to begin with, was the slum in which he lived. As the cities were saturated with people, it became a sellers' market for those who had apartments to rent. Many an enterprising building owner converted a single unit house into two, three, and four tiny apartments—"the smallest proportions capable of containing human life within four walls," as Robert Ernst puts it in his study of immigrant conditions from 1825 to 1863. When such converted buildings proved insufficient to accommodate the need, multistory tenements rose which were in every respect just as bad or worse,—overcrowded, lacking ventilation or sunlight except in the front and back rooms, shoddily constructed, festering holes for disease, frustration, and crime.

A Lowell, Massachusetts, citizen reported in 1847 that in one such tenement apartment "I found one of the families to consist of a man, his wife and eight children—four of whom were over fifteen years of age—and four adult boarders. . . . This by no means furnishes the worst case." In the Irish-German Tenth Ward of New York density per acre grew from 54.5 persons in 1820 to 171 just twenty years later. When the buildings filled overground, people rushed to occupy the cellars. New York reported 7,196 people living in dank apartments underground in 1843, but 29,000 a couple of years later. The chief of police in that city noted in 1850 that one out of twenty people was confined to a cellar, the average per room was six people, the maximum twenty. The former peasant of Ireland or Germany, accustomed to light and fresh air, had difficulty adjusting to the funereal darkness, so much so that, according to labor historian Norman Ware, the life expectancy of an Irishman after he moved into the Boston slums was fourteen years.

"In these places," summarized Horace Greeley, "garbage steams its poison in the sun . . . thieves and prostitutes congregate and are made . . . disease lurks. . . ." Tuberculosis, cholera, typhoid, pneumonia, and scrofula were particularly in evidence, taking their heaviest toll on children under five.

Not only the cellars of the tenements but other units as well were prey to water and refuse filtering in through the wall cracks, roaches and rodents multiplying in haughty abundance. The water had to be drawn from outside hydrants, privies were usually behind the building. The "contents, instead of being drained or carried away, frequently overflowed to the surface and created breeding places of disease." As late as 1857 a mere 138 miles of sewer had been laid in New York City's 500 miles of streets, and conditions in other cities were even less inviting.

Perhaps it was worse in Europe; nonetheless for the immigrant poor the American paradise was a daily tussle with tragedy. Figures for the decade after 1849 in New York (they are unreliable before that) indicate that three-fourths of those admitted to the almshouses and seven-eighths of the clients relieved by the Association for Improving the Conditions of the Poor were foreign-born, mostly the unfortunate Irish. More than a third of the insane enrolled in the city's lunatic asylum had lived in the metropolis less than a year, a large proportion young women. The cause was ascribed by a physician to "the combined moral and physical influence of their leaving the homes of their childhood, their coming almost destitute to a strange land, and often after great suffering." The conditions in most asylums and almshouses—inadequate staffing, overcrowding—were, as they are today, a source of constant complaint by reformers. One writer tells of a man of "excellent character" who after losing his business and voluntarily placing himself in an almshouse "was so horrified at the abominations and corruptions of the motley herd, by whom he was surrounded, that he refused sustenance, and actually starved himself to death."

If the slum was the locus of city poverty, its actual source was the wage system. Because of the usual shortage of labor—except in time of depression—American wages were better than those of England or Europe. Yet in the absence of trade unions for the unskilled, their living standards hovered around the destitution level. In March 1851, Horace Greeley published in his *New York Tribune* an estimate of what a family of five would need as a minimum budget. The figure, $10.57 a week, included, apart from food, clothing, fuel, and rent, only twenty-five cents for wear and tear on furniture and twelve cents for the daily newspaper, nothing else. Yet, to Greeley's dismay, of nine crafts listed in the iron and steel industry not one averaged $10.57 a week. The common laborer was paid 89 cents a day, just half the minimum budget, and "catchers, bar mills" 69 cents, a third of what was necessary. "I ask," wrote Greeley, "have I made the workingman's comfort too high? Where is the money to pay for amusements, for ice cream, puddings, trips on Sunday up or down the river, in order to get some fresh air; to pay for the doctor or apothecary, to pay for pew rent in the church, to purchase books, musical instruments?"

In Massachusetts, where mill rates were highest, men earned about $5 a week at mid-century, women about $2, and children, who constituted 40 per cent of the work force, 50 cents plus board. Top wages for a female operative in Philadelphia was $1.50, out of which she paid 50 cents a week for lodging plus additional money for wood. The workday averaged twelve and a half hours in 1830; eleven hours a day, after much industrial agitation and strikes, thirty years later. It was not unusual then to hear friends of labor as well as apologists for the slave system call the free laborer's plight worse than that of the Negro. "A common slave in the states of Virginia, Tennessee and Kentucky," charged the Reverend M. Ely, "is much better compensated for his labor by his necessary food, clothing, lodging and medicines, than many respectable workers and daughters in this city [Philadelphia], who apply themselves diligently to their work, two hours for every one occupied by the Negro in his master's service."

Nor do wage rates alone convey the corollary effects of the industrial system on the immigrant's life, his frequent sense of insecurity and hopelessness, his lack of control over his destiny. A large number of the new proletarians in the first half of the nineteenth century were Irish, fleeing famine and the loss of land in their home country. Once here, they formed the backbone of the labor force that built the canals, turnpikes, and railroads, much as Negroes today are the backbone of the service industries. Their condition was far from enviable. Here is the way Matthew Carey, a businessman, described it in 1830: "Thousands of our labouring people travel hundreds of miles in quest of employment on canals at 62½, 75 and 87½ cents per day, paying $1.50 to $2 a week for their board, families behind, dependent on them for support. They labour frequently in marshy grounds, where they inhale pestiferous miasmata, which destroy their health, often irrevocably. They return to their poor families, broken hearted, and with ruined constitutions, with a sorry pittance, most laboriously earned, and take to their beds, sick and unable to work. Hundreds are swept off annually, many of them leaving numerous and helpless families. Notwithstanding their wretched fate, their places are quickly supplied by others, although death stares them in the face." Those working on turnpikes earned even less, 50 to 75 cents a day, "exposed to the broiling sun in summer, and all the inclemency of our severe winters."

The argument was often advanced, then as later, that the deprived were wretched because of their own improvidence, worthlessness, and dissipation. Figures were adduced on the increase of gambling, prostitution, and drunkenness as proof positive of the poor man's dissoluteness. "They love to clan together in some out-of-the-way place," said a leading philanthropist, Robert M. Hartley, "are content to live in filth and disorder with a bare subsistence, provided they can drink, and smoke, and gossip, and enjoy their balls, and wakes, and frolics, without molestation." A statistic of mid-century showed that seven-eighths of the occupants of city prisons were there for overimbibing firewater.

But it was a matter of interpretation, of course, as to which came first, frustration or dissipation. On the other side of the philosophical fence Matthew Carey pointed out that the "industry, morals and virtues of the poor are underrated." He gave an instance where 1,100 women in hard times applied for employment "at the apartment of the Provident Society" to make shirts at 12½ cents each, even though none would receive more than four (50 cents' worth of work) and most only two. "This bears the most overwhelming testimony to their intense distress, and their untiring industry," he concluded.

A single girl, said Carey, who depended for a livelihood on her wages, had one of four choices if she wanted to survive: beg, depend on overseers of the poor ("a species of begging"), steal, or sell herself into what was then a lively profession, prostitution. The *Boston Daily Times* of July 17, 1839, quoted a doctor that "there used to be in Lowell [Massachusetts] an association of young men called 'The Old Line' who had an understanding with a great many of the factory girls and who used to introduce young men of their acquaintance, visitors to the place, to the girls for immoral purposes. Balls were held at various places . . . and after the dancing was over the girls were taken to infamous places of resort in Lowell and the vicinity and were not returned to their homes until daylight." In one week seventy people, mostly girls, applied to a single physician for remedies for venereal disease. It may or may not be relevant, but wages for these factory girls were cut three times between 1832 and 1840.

The lot of working children was particularly appalling. A labor paper in Philadelphia, the *Mechanics' Free Press*, charged in 1830 that the hours of work for youngsters were so long "no more than one-sixth of the boys and girl [sic] employed in such factories [cotton mills] are capable of reading or writing their own name. We have known many instances where parents who are capable of giving their children a trifling education one at a time, deprived of that opportunity by their employer's threats, that if they did take one child from their employ (a short time for school) such family must leave the employment—and we have even known these threats put into execution. . . ." A New York police report of 1852 indicated that 10,000 abandoned, orphaned, or runaway youngsters were living on the streets, sleeping haphazardly in privies, hallways, or barges, any place where their little bodies could fit. Parents tried valiantly to assert the social controls they were accustomed to in Europe, but in the turbulent, overcrowded situation of the burgeoning cities here, many children, says Robert Ernst, gained their views of life from "flash-men, engine-runners, cock-fighters, pugilists and pickpockets. . . ."

The advance of industry penetrated everything, including the home life, and converted thousands of homes into miniature factories. Much of the manufacture in the nineteenth as well as the early twentieth century was performed in households on a contract system, especially in the needle trades. Matthew Carey describes a room on the east side of Eleventh Street in Philadelphia, fifteen feet by eleven, where two couples and four children lived and did homework. One woman spooled, the other spun; between them they earned twenty to twenty-five cents a day, but since both husbands had been unemployed for weeks—this was 1829—it was the only income for eight people. In another such home a charitable organization found the McGiffie family with the father emaciated, the mother "lying in a state of insensibility—one child . . . dead, the other dying." Not all homeworkers, naturally, were in this extreme condition, yet the household system with all its vices and tragedies was a familiar feature of American life until two generations ago. It was, as Jefferson had foreseen in his early opposition to industrialism, a barren harvest of a system in which the producing class, divorced from ownership of the means of production, lived in continuing insecurity.

To be sure, not all workers lived at the lowest threshold. Natives fared better than immigrants, skilled workers better than the unskilled. A craftsman earned $7 to $10 a week in the 1830's, enough to maintain a decent standard, particularly if one of the children was working. Even so, as Philip S. Foner reports in his extensive history of the labor movement, large numbers of people were unable to keep from debt. In New York City in 1828, 71,576 poor people shuttled back and forth to the pawnshop seeking loans on 148,890 articles. The fruits of city life and industrialism, at least in the beginning, were not the abundant life but increased pauperism. "Thirty years ago," wrote a labor reformer, George Henry Evans, in 1844, "the number of paupers in the whole United States was estimated at 29,166, or one in three hundred. The pauperism of New York City now amounts to 51,600, or one in every seven of the population."

Chapter 7

OF TIME AND PATIENCE

From 1801 when Jefferson took office to 1841 when Van Buren left it, the nation was ruled by six Presidents whose hearts were as close to the lower classes as any in its history. Jefferson, Madison, Monroe, John Quincy Adams, Jackson, and Van Buren were men of populist belief who generally won the heartiest plaudits of the poor. When Jackson vetoed the bill to recharter the Bank of the United States in July 1832 he sounded like a disciple of Fanny Wright, the most flamboyant revolutionary of the period. "It is to be regretted," he said, "that the rich and powerful too often bend the acts of government to their selfish purposes. . . . When laws undertake . . . to make the rich richer and the potent more powerful, the humble members of society, the farmers, mechanics, and laborers, who have neither the time nor the means of securing like favors to themselves, have a right to complain of the injustice of their government."

Van Buren's opposition to the bankers, his espousal of a "comfortable" wage for the workingman, and his executive order for a ten-hour day without any reduction in pay for federal employees on public works, won lyrical praise from the most radical elements of the period. "I wish to thank you in the name of liberty and humanity," wrote Orestes Brownson, an ex-leader of the New York Workingmen's Party, "for the firm stand you have taken during the struggle which has been going on for some time between the Democracy and the moneyed power of this country . . . you are now indeed with the people and Sir, the people will sustain you."

Yet sympathetic as they were to the underprivileged, none of these Presidents formulated a program that can even remotely be called an antipoverty program. The times were not yet ripe for such eccentric concepts as minimum wages, guaranteed annual incomes, or social security. Only a few decades before, the Americans had waged a great struggle around the banner of individualism. It had been taken for granted since 1776 that this was the cure for whatever ailed society. A citizen must be free from the restraints of kings, lords, or centralized governments so that he might get ahead on his own. That government was best that governed least. For the confirmed democrat central authority was a malignant disease, and while Jefferson, Madison, and Monroe found it necessary at times—as in the purchase of Louisiana or in governing the public domain—to bend this doctrine appreciably, it was one of those ordained principles that could be tampered with only after excruciating rationalization. The way of life was individualistic, since 80 or 90 per cent of the people lived on the farm, and the doctrine of a revolutionary government inevitably was tailored to that measure. In old England and under the king in colonial days the grubby finger of government had injected itself into everything—it regulated commerce, manufacture, and settlement, it set maximum wages, apprenticeship rules, quality standards, selling prices. Freedom meant precisely the right to be free of such domination.

This individualist credo carried over into the conventional wisdom on poverty. "I think the best way of doing good to the poor," Benjamin Franklin wrote in the eighteenth century, "is, not making them easy *in* poverty, but leading or driving them out of it." The emphasis was on self-help and voluntarism. The task of the affluent and of government was to make it easier for people to help themselves, not to help them per se—unless, of course, they were senile, lame, blind, crippled, orphaned. Franklin's philanthropy included formation of clubs for self-help; raising money for libraries, the Pennsylvania Hospital, and the university; organizing volunteer fire departments; arranging to have the streets paved and lighted.

Such was the tradition under which the nineteenth century operated, a tradition that constantly came into conflict with the collective way of life in city and factory, but that nonetheless survived to set limits on government action. During the industrial depression of 1819 one of President Monroe's associates, John Quincy Adams, argued that the "government can do nothing, at least nothing by any measure yet proposed. . . ." In point of fact government—federal, state, and, above all, local—did many things to mitigate the situation, but the actions were within a certain frame, circumscribed by the philosophical mandate of individualism. Government yielded to necessity and pressure, but only up to a certain point.

The depression of 1819 illustrates this thesis convincingly. Banks were failing by the dozen, cotton prices had fallen 50 per cent, sheriffs were foreclosing farms in increasing number, imprisonment for debt was mounting alarmingly. There were 14,537 actions for debt in Philadelphia alone that year and 1,808 men in prison for being in arrears. The federal government, however, stood above the maelstrom, as if nothing were happening. In his Message to Congress, December 1819, Monroe hardly mentioned the event. A year later, though the depression was still on, he spoke eloquently about "the prosperous and happy condition of our country." When 30,000 people in nine states sent petitions to Congress for relief, their pleas were not even read on the House floor, and resulted in no legislation. Yet, on the other hand, each of the three levels of government took certain steps to lighten the load.

A federal act of 1820 reduced the price of public land from $2 an acre to $1.25 and authorized sale in patches as small as eighty acres. Men in default to the federal treasury for farm purchases were permitted by the President to keep that portion commensurate with payments already made—at the new price of $1.25—forfeiting only the unpaid portion. Since this type of debt had risen from $3,000,000 in 1815 to $18,000,000 in 1819, it was a concession that affected many people. Another one sanctioned payments in any bank notes that were "in good credit in the district" rather than acceptable universally. Again, since many banks had closed their doors, leaving the notes they had issued in clouded state, this too gave succor to many.

The cry of the debtor was particularly heeded at the state level. When the Bank of Kentucky suspended payments, the state itself formed a Bank of the Commonwealth, authorized to issue up to $3,000,000 in notes, with nothing behind it but $7,000 for printing expenses. Any creditor who refused this money would have to wait two years "for an execution." Illinois and Tennessee also opened state banks, circulating notes on real estate security and requiring creditors to take them on pain of waiting two years for a court judgment. Indiana and Kentucky imposed stay laws on debts; Missouri established a loan office to help those in dire straits. Seven states exempted debtors from imprisonment, three others abolished it for anyone who turned over his property. Pennsylvania freed all female debtors.

On the local scene, Baltimore set up twelve soup stations for the poor in 1820, Philadelphia distributed a pint of soup per person, New York enlisted its butchers and churches to raise money for soup houses. Everywhere some provision, public and private, was made for people in want, however inadequate it might be. But this was the dividing line: relief was conceived of as a temporary emergency measure. It was "antipoverty" only in the immediate, not in the long-term sense.

The gains made by the common man that had long-term significance were along the brittle edges of his problem—in reinforcing democracy—rather than at their core, in placing a floor under want. Suffrage was extended widely in this period, imprisonment for debt abolished, the criminal code modified, prison reform instituted, compulsory education introduced. The leveling winds of democracy blew steadily, gaining impetus from the frontier states on the one hand and the radical parties—especially the Workingmen's parties of the 1820's—on the other. Indirectly they undoubtedly affected the poor appreciably, but it was like giving a man the tools without the raw materials to work on.

Inexorably, the right to vote or run for office was removed from the embarrassing proscriptions of the pocketbook. The fourteen states that joined the union from 1789 to 1840 began with an advanced view of democracy, granting suffrage to all male whites, regardless of land or wealth. In the original thirteen states property and religious qualifications eroded slowly, but by 1850 only North Carolina was a holdout, and it too fell in line six years later. Property restrictions for office holding, such as the £1,000 needed to run for governor in Massachusetts and the £10,000 in South Carolina, were similarly removed, and the selection of electors for President was taken from the hands of state legislatures and put into those of the voters. It was incomplete suffrage—women and Negroes were still barred from voting—but much more complete than in the past.

In another field, the barbarism of early penal codes gave way to more humane treatment. Within a decade or two of the new century flogging, the pillory, branding, cropping of ears were abolished in favor of fines and imprisonment. Simultaneously the cry went up to remodel the prison system. Such groups as the Philadelphia Society for Alleviating the Miseries of Public Prisons agitated ceaselessly against conditions where inmates were forced to pay for their own food and lodging, were kept unsegregated as to sex, age, or the nature of their offense, and were crowded into small cells with no work to do. The result was a wave of reform along two lines. At the Auburn and Sing Sing penitentiaries in New York, prisoners were confined to small cells but put to work in a variety of shops during the day, more than paying for their "free" upkeep. Under the Philadelphia system the men and women were kept in orderly, clean cells, but under solitary confinement with a "small walled courtyard" for each inmate for exercise. Neither system was satisfactory; the latter produced extreme mental anguish by denying prisoners all human contact, and the former was amenable to corruption and considerable brutality. Yet, such was the nature of the old jails that the new ones were improvements.

Imprisonment for debt, a self-defeating penalty since men in jail could hardly earn the money to pay obligations, fell to the pressures of groups such as the Humane Society and the Boston Society for the Relief of the Distressed. The tales of woe they could point to convinced even the most wary that the system was more vengeful than useful. During 1816, for instance, some two thousand New Yorkers languished in jail for this crime, one of them for three years, another for six. A man in Vermont was held for owing 54 cents to two creditors; another in Philadelphia, for 2 cents. Thirty-five hundred were imprisoned in Boston in a period of two and a half years, a thousand in Philadelphia and nearly that many in Baltimore in a single year, many hundreds of them with piddling obligations of less than $25. From time to time, particularly when there was economic crisis, the laws had been liberalized, but that was not enough. Beginning with Kentucky in 1821, Ohio in 1828, New Jersey in 1830, New York in 1832, bills were enacted abolishing imprisonment for debt entirely.

Another achievement of the era was the inch-by-inch advance toward a free, compulsory education system. Jefferson had urged in one of his letters that Americans "establish and improve the law for educating the common people. . . . The tax which will be paid for this purpose, is not more than the thousandth part of what will be paid to kings, priests and nobles, who will rise up among us if we leave the people in ignorance." But it took a bit of doing to implement this advice, for while people favored education in the abstract they were not overly anxious to tax themselves for what they considered tangential luxuries. The New England common schools, provided since the seventeenth century, thus deteriorated from neglect, their buildings grim and unpainted, their teachers poorly paid and poorly trained. In the Middle Atlantic states free schooling was available only to the children of paupers. In the South, despite the pleadings of Jefferson, free education was little more than a cherished principle, and in the West it was handicapped by the shortage of teachers and the difficulties of assembling children in thinly inhabited communities.

Step by step, nonetheless, the modern educational edifice came into view. De Witt Clinton's Free School Society in New York, a private philanthropy which received state and local aid, established the first free school in 1809 and gradually took charge of public education for the city. Under the proddings of men such as Horace Mann of Massachusetts and Henry Barnard of Connecticut, organizations such as the Pennsylvania Society for the Promotion of Public Schools, the American Lyceum, and the Western Academic Institute, and the pioneering work of the State of Michigan, many businessmen and the public generally were finally drawn to invest in a crusade against ignorance. In her *Freedom's Ferment*, Alice Felt Tyler quotes as the eventual public consensus this stanza sung by advocates of the free schooling system in New York during the 1840's:

> Then free as air should knowledge be—
>   And open Wisdom's portal,
> To every thirsty, earnest soul,
>   Who longs to be immortal.
> Here rich and poor stand side by side,
>   To quaff life's purest chalice,
> And never dream that deathless names
>   Belong to cot or palace.

The first timid steps toward compulsory education included state and municipal grants to existing religious, charity, and private schools. Next, a more formidable obstacle was hurdled when laws were enacted permitting, then *requiring*, communities to levy taxes for education. Finally, in rapid-fire order came cancellation of tuition fees, formation of boards of education, establishment of teacher-training schools, and legislation making it mandatory for all children to have some schooling. Before long, too, there were institutions for the deaf and dumb, for the blind, and for juvenile delinquents, such as the New York House of Refuge. By the Civil War the foundation for the modern school system had been firmly laid in all the northern states and in some of the southern ones.

Necessity as well as common sense propelled communities to take on collectivist functions which hitherto had been off limits. Thus, in the wake of a yellow fever epidemic in 1794, which killed 732 of New York City's 50,000 people, the state organized Governor's Island as a quarantine area for new arrivals, and the city leased five acres of land, called Belle Vue (forerunner of the famous hospital), for fever patients. From 1795 to 1822 the city faced five such epidemics and in 1832 an attack of Asiatic cholera, factors that greatly influenced the passage of laws requiring a health officer and commissioners of health for the city.

But advanced as were the improvements in democratic structure, poverty relief remained strangely anachronistic. Upper-class opinion on the subject was typified by what Samuel Rezneck calls the "time and patience" school. With time and patience, said such men, depressions would disappear, the plight of the lowly ameliorate, and government had no right to bestir itself on this issue. Reflecting such sentiments was an editorial in the *New York Gazette* in 1819 denouncing the "rant in most of our prints about our distresses. . . . Trade will regulate itself. Banks will soon become more useful, and merchants more wise. . . . There is no real distress in the country, and we hope to hear no more of it." A statement by the New York Association for Improving the Conditions of the Poor in 1857 undoubtedly commanded wide support. "The doctrine so pertinaciously urged," it said, "that a man has a right to work and wages from the government, or from any one, whether his services are needed or not, originated in those countries where the subject held land of a superior, to whom he owed subjection as a bondsman and became a vassal or slave under the absolute control of his master. . . . The theories in question are mainly urged by our foreign-born citizens, who would introduce here the wrongs and oppressions of their native land, from which they have come hither to escape." *Laissez faire* was a sanctified byword of early industrialism and that meant leaving the poor, like the rich, to make their own way. What changes there were in the old Elizabethan system of poor relief, therefore, were dictated only by the enlargement of the problem rather than by any new ideas on the subject.

The equation of poverty with pauperism, the concept that people were entitled to aid only if destitute, remained the guidelines for nineteenth-century America. What changed simply were the forms by which the poor became public charges. The main method of relief in the past, when life was almost entirely rural, had been "home relief." Overseers of the poor provided money and necessities to the indigent either in their own homes or, if physically unable to care for themselves, in the homes of others. To guard against being burdened by wandering paupers from elsewhere, communities placed restrictions on settlement and required a certain period of residency before anyone was eligible for relief. A modification was made in this pattern when it became obvious there were too many nonresident paupers floating about. State governments were forced to lend a hand. New York's Governor John Jay, as early as the 1790's, for instance, secured an appropriation to aid "such poor . . . as shall not have gained any settlement in this state."

Home relief, however, modified or not, was inadequate to deal with a growing problem. The emphasis shifted therefore to placing the poor in almshouses or putting them out on "contract" and "auction." The advantage of the almshouse (or poor farm) was that the pauper could perform a little work there, such as spinning, cooking, picking fruit, farming, and similar tasks, keeping costs down. The well-operated poor farm at Poughkeepsie, New York, boasted that it spent only $25 a year—50 cents a week—for the upkeep of each of its inmates: "our house of industry affords an opportunity to economize and to support our paupers at least 50 per cent less than formerly." The almshouse was a place where society could pack its poor out of sight and usually out of mind. Whatever the original motives for building them, the trend was usually toward overcrowding and neglect. Reformers throughout the nineteenth century complained of the bad food, intermingling of sexes and ages, the filth, and other vices to which a system of this kind lent itself. Mixed, as in a cook's brew, were the orphaned children, drunks, vagrants, prostitutes, the infirm, and lunatics. The Boston House of Industry in 1834 reported a hundred children, some only infants, and sixty insane among its variegated population. There were exceptions to the rule, of course, as for instance the Baltimore almshouse built in 1821, where the sexes were segregated in separate wings, youngsters were given an opportunity for schooling, the insane were isolated, and workshops and gardens made life a little more pleasant. By and large, however, there was scant difference between an almshouse or poor farm and a prison, especially, as sometimes happened, when the almshouse or poor farm was leased to a private entrepreneur to operate at a profit. A report of a state senate committee in New York during the 1850's doubtless summarized the general situation when it complained of "filth, nakedness, licentiousness . . . and . . . gross neglect of the most ordinary comforts and decencies of life."

Under the contract system the community placed its needy in the care of householders at a specified weekly, monthly, or annual fee. The town of Beekman in Dutchess County, New York, reported paying $32 annually for each person over twelve farmed out and $16 for each child below that age. One farmer in Amsterdam agreed to accept all the town's idle under his tutelage for a flat fee of $350 a year. Written agreements with the contractors spelled out areas of responsibility, such as the one in 1820 between Fitchburg, Massachusetts, and the local undertaker, who was "to Board, Clothe and Comfortably provide for, in sickness and health the persons hereafter named . . . and if any of the above named persons should decease within the course of the year, the town to be at the expense of burying, and the doctor's bill if any of them are sick. . . . The undertaker to have the benefit of the labor of said Paupers, and receive his pay quarterly." This was hardly more than a partnership between the community and one of its citizens in an indentured servant system.

Under the auction system men, women, and children were placed on the block, much as Negro slaves, and auctioned off to the person willing to accept the lowest amount for his care. The bidder himself was sometimes only a notch or two above that of the man he "bought," so that in an indirect way he was relieving his own misery. Again, corruption and neglect were almost invariable by-products of such an arrangement. "Notwithstanding the large amount raised in this county, for the support of the poor," charged Abijah Hammond, a respectable citizen of Westchester County, New York, "they are neither fed, clothed, nor treated like human beings. . . . Most of the parish poor are now sold, as the term is, that is, bid off, to those who agree to support them on the lowest terms, to purchasers nearly as poor as themselves, who treat them in many instances more like brutes than like human beings; and who, instead of applying the amount received from the poor-master, for the comfort of the pauper, spend it to support their families, or, which is too often the case, in purchasing ardent spirits. . . ."

In due course humanitarian pressures forced modification of many of these practices. The extension of orphanages, insane asylums, and houses of correction drained away people from the almshouses and jails to institutions better suited to their problems. The "sale" of paupers was curtailed and more almshouses and poor farms built. But essentially, despite all the democratic advances of the pre-Civil War period, poor relief—and above all its philosophic underpinning—stood little altered from what it had been a century before.

II

What did change was the scale and character of private philanthropy. "Throughout the 19th century," writes Robert H. Bremner, leading historian on the subject, "the charitable response of the American people was almost as generous as their pursuit of gain was selfish." Philadelphia, with a population of 130,000 in 1829, listed thirty-one institutions ranging the spectrum of human misfortune. There was the Provident Society for employing the poor, an orphan society, an association for the care of "Coloured Orphans," an "Indigent Widows and Single Women's Society," a City Infant School Society, an Institution for the Deaf and Dumb, a Society for Alleviating the Miseries of Public Prisons, and so on.

A host of professional altruists fashioned hundreds of organizations to alleviate distress. They included such men as Joseph Tuckerman and William Ellery Channing of Boston, and Thomas Eddy, John H. Griscom, Robert M. Hartley, Charles Loring Brace of New York, among many others. To radicals such as Henry David Thoreau, these "do-gooders" or "bleeding-hearts" were simply salving their consciences for having robbed the poor in their capacity as employers or landlords. Thoreau mocked "a charity which dispenses the crumbs that fall from its overloaded tables, which are left after its feasts!" and Ralph Waldo Emerson warned the "foolish philanthropist" to stay away from him. There was nothing particularly generous, in their view, about men who gave away a twentieth or a tenth of their earnings to charity while retaining the rest of their ill-gotten gains for themselves. But among the philanthropists were some who combined charity with reform, and who in their own way considered themselves the true benefactors of the lower classes.

Typical of this element was an American success story named Thomas Eddy.

One of a brood of sixteen children of fecund Philadelphia Quakers, Eddy's first years were spent on the wrong side of the American Revolution. His mother, a stouthearted lady who carried on the family hardware business after the father died, was "induced to quit the city on account of the bitter spirit of persecution of the Whigs [the advocates of independence] against the Tories," of whom she was a member in good standing. Two of Eddy's friends were executed by the patriots after Philadelphia was retaken, and one of his brothers, "without being admitted to a hearing," was banished to Winchester, Virginia, because of his antirevolutionary views.

Young Tom, barely twenty-one in 1779, deeply religious, hied himself to New York, then occupied by the British. In his memoirs he tells of having to sell his horse in Rahway and arriving in the great port city with barely $96 in his pocket. But opportunity was not far away, for before long Tom and a brother were buying and selling imports from Ireland, amassing enough money for a comfortable stake. It was during this period that Eddy had a brief encounter with the prison system. One day while crossing into New Jersey to see the girl he later married, Tom was seized by the Jersey militia and confined to a "foul and noxious" cell, six feet by seven. Though he was freed after eight or ten days when his British friends arranged to exchange him for two patriots they held in their custody, it was a memory that lingered with Eddy and spurred his future labors for reform.

British evacuation of New York, after the American victory, was a sad day for the young Tory and a catastrophe for his growing business. Many of his friends fled to Halifax, but Eddy sweated out the "trying period," and in a few years was again prospering in an insurance business. Alexander Hamilton's funding of the national and state debt finally gave Eddy the opportunity to make a financial killing. The funding, he writes, "afforded an opportunity for people to speculate in the public lands. In this business I made a good deal of money." He was now a man of substance, director of an insurance company, treasurer of a navigation firm, and "being in easy circumstances," his biographer, Samuel L. Knapp, records, "had leisure to turn his attention to those charities that are of permanent benefit to mankind. . . . He found, as every wise man will, that if there are inevitable evils in the world, yet much may be done by way of softening them, or preparing the mind to bear them."

This is a perceptive insight into the mentality of philanthropy, perhaps an unintentional one. The "evils" of society, it contends, are "inevitable," ergo the best that can be done is to "soften" them. In the gospel of benevolence inequality is an enduring assumption. John Winthrop, one of the first colonial philanthropists, equated the word "charity" with "love," but he distinguished with sanguine emphasis between the "high and eminent" who were ordained thus by God's will and "the poor and inferior sort." There was to all this a streak of self-ennoblement, as if to say: "God has chosen me to a higher order than the unfortunates below me, I must therefore ameliorate their plight through charity."

At any rate, whatever Eddy's motivations, one of his first ventures early in the century was to establish a state penitentiary for New York. This was a time, it should be recalled, when towns still had stocks, whipping posts, and pillories, and when burning the forehead or hand of a condemned man, flagellation with the cat-o'-nine-tails, and cropping ears were common practices. With the help of General Philip Schuyler, a New York senator, Eddy was able to secure an appropriation from the state to build a prison along humane principles. As a religious Quaker he focused on "amendment [reform] of the offender" more than on punishment. Each prisoner was assigned his own cell, put to work in workshops, and fed considerably better than in the city jails. "Such cleanliness, order and moral discipline," writes Knapp, "marked the penitentiary system under the administration of this untired philanthropist that those formerly dissipated and sickly were made sober and healthy."

Eddy, like his fellow philanthropists, was an admixture of compassion and self-righteousness. He believed, with prevailing respectable opinion, that "misery is ordained to be the companion and punishment of vice." When he bemoaned horse racing as a "source of vice and criminality," or damned the demon rum and dram shops, he was hoping to save the poor from temptation. When he joined the New York Bible Society, which translated the Bible into a hundred languages, he expected that Bible reading would help the poor overcome their moral defects. He also founded a savings bank in 1819—then an innovation—was governor of a hospital, worked to modify the penal code, wheedled money from the legislature to buy eighty acres of land at Bloomingdale for an insane asylum, gave considerable aid to the Indians, and helped erect a free school for poor children. With John Griscom he established the New York House of Refuge, first reformatory for juveniles in the country, and with Griscom too he initiated in 1817 the Society for the Prevention of Pauperism in New York City.

This society was Eddy's major accomplishment, and gives us a glimpse into the thought processes of nineteenth-century philanthropy. Its purpose, as set out in the prospectus, was to investigate "the circumstances and habits of the poor" so as to devise "means for improving their situation, both in a physical and moral point of view. . . ." The leaders of the society were not insensible to the need for relief, especially during depression periods, but they regarded it as a temporary expedient. And true to their individualistic precepts, they ascribed the poverty by and large to the pauper's own moral defects, rather than to flaws in the societal system.

The ten causes of poverty listed by the society in its first compendium on the subject read, except for the last one, like a catalogue of individual sins and weaknesses:

1st. Ignorance, arising either from inherent dullness, or from want of opportunities for improvement.

2nd. Idleness. A tendency to this evil may be more or less inherent. . . .

3rd. Intemperance in drinking. This most prolific source of mischief and misery drags in its train almost every species of suffering which afflicts the poor. . . .

4th. Want of economy. . . .

5th. Imprudent and hasty marriages.

6th. Lotteries.

7th. Pawnbrokers. The establishment of these offices is considered as very unfavorable to the independence and welfare of the middling and inferior classes.

8th. Houses of ill fame. The direful effects of those sinks of iniquity upon the habits and morals of a numerous class of young men, especially sailors and apprentices, are visible throughout the city. . . .

9th. Is not the partial and temporary good which [the numerous charitable institutions of the city] accomplish . . . more than counterbalanced, by the evils that flow from the expectations they necessarily excite; by the relaxation of industry, which such a display of benevolence tends to produce . . . ?

Lastly. Your Committee would mention WAR, during its prevalence, as one of the most abundant sources of poverty and vice, which the list of human corruption comprehends. . . .

The cure for these ten plagues, according to the society, lay in changing the poor man's habits, beginning with visits and "friendly" advice on how to live a life free from drink, the pawnshop, and similar temptations. The role the society saw for itself, as David M. Schneider records it in his graphic *History of Public Welfare in New York State*, was "to encourage and assist the laboring classes to save their earnings by the establishment of a savings bank; to prevent the access of paupers who were not entitled to settlement in the city; to suppress street begging; to aid in furnishing employment to those unable to procure it by establishing houses of industry and by supplying materials for domestic labor; to promote the increase of churches and Sunday schools; and to further the suppression of liquor shops in the city."

Such objectives were sternly espoused by virtually all philanthropists. In a land of opportunity where some became rich in the twinkle of an eye, the man who could not make it was obviously a misfit; and while the charity reformers felt sympathy for him and were ready to aid him materially, they placed even greater emphasis on his moral uplift. Probably the outstanding spokesman for this thesis was Robert M. Hartley, founder of the New York Association for Improving the Conditions of the Poor, and the major figure in the world of philanthropy before the Civil War. Like Eddy, he was a successful businessman—a merchant—and like Eddy, do-gooding became his full-time vocation. During the 1830's he was an official of the City Temperance Society, in which capacity he visited distillery owners in the vain attempt to dissuade them from selling their "poison." Subsequently, being convinced that aid to the poor was being dispensed solely for relief rather than moral regeneration, he called together kindred spirits in 1843 to establish A.I.C.P. Its central principles

dominated welfare horizons for a long time. The first of these principles was that relief was due the impoverished not as a right but as
"a favor"; second, that indiscriminate aid pampered the needy and
contributed to rather than cured indigence; and third, that private
charity was preferable to public relief because it was personal and
grappled with root causes.

During the depression that began in 1854 the A.I.C.P. carried on
relentless criticism against the relief committees established in
twelve of the twenty-two city wards because they committed such
"indefensible indiscretions" as urging the poor not to pay their rent.
The opening of soup kitchens was denounced on the "sound social"
principle that "the poor should not be aided in promiscuous masses
. . . but by personal visits at their homes." In the year ending November 1, 1855, the New York A.I.C.P. visited 15,549 families and
doled out $95,018 in aid—a massive operation at the time—solely on
an individual basis.

Given the dominance of laissez-faire theories, it was probably inevitable that private charity, with its emphasis on moral uplift,
should loom so large. The number of organizations formed to soften
the impact of poverty seemed to grow in direct proportion to the fortunes of the *nouveaux riches*. As the century wore on there were innumerable movements specializing in one field or another. There
were thirty or forty almsgiving societies in New York City alone during the 1840's. Every community seemed to have a Society for the
Relief of Distressed Debtors (later called the Humane Society); a
Provident Society to find jobs for the jobless; a Bible Society to bring
the comforts of religion to the materially deprived; a Children's Aid
Society, modeled after the one set up by the pioneer in this field,
Charles Loring Brace; a Young Men's Christian Association; a prison
reform group; societies for the handicapped; immigrant aid groups
established on an ethnic basis; temperance unions; and hundreds of
others.

III

One of the most sustained, if indirect, crusades to relieve poverty in
the nineteenth century was waged against what a Methodist bishop
called the "demon rum." The crusaders at their peak numbered an

army of a million zealots, and were able to enact prohibition laws or local option bills in Maine, New York, Vermont, Rhode Island, Michigan, Connecticut, New Hampshire, Tennessee, Delaware, Illinois, Indiana, Iowa, Wisconsin, and the Territory of Minnesota. The roster of temperance men included philanthropists like Eddy and Hartley; abolitionists like William Lloyd Garrison and Arthur Tappan; advocates of free land like Gerrit Smith; innumerable clergymen like Lyman Beecher; reformers like Benjamin Rush and Anthony Benezet; scores of aristocrats and businessmen like Stephen Van Rensselaer; and heaven only knows how many ex-drinkers eager to prove to others the error of their ways. It was altogether a remarkable chapter on behalf of the downtrodden.

The correlation between drink and dependency, of course, needed no documentation, since city prisons, as Thomas Eddy found, overflowed with drunks who often formed a majority of their population. Americans were hard drinkers by tradition. "No keel of a vessel could be laid," read a temperance booklet, "no frame of a house or barn reared, in any of the Atlantic States; no log house be put together west of the mountains, without the presence of several gallons of New England Rum, Jamaica Spirits, or Western Whiskey." A colonial jingle indicated to what lengths doughty inhabitants would go for intoxicants:

> If barley be wanting to make into malt,
> We must be content and think it no fault,
> For we can make liquor to sweeten our lips,
> Of pumpkins, and parsnips, and walnut-tree chips.

Everyone, it seemed, drank—young people at dances, judges, ministers, legislators, laborers. The habit was evidently on the upswing in the nineteenth century. Estimates of drinking quotients, according to Alice Felt Tyler, showed that the average citizen consumed 2½ gallons of alcohol in 1792; 4½ gallons in 1810; and 7½ gallons by 1823. The census of 1810 listed no fewer than 14,000 distilleries in the United States, producing 25,000,000 gallons of firewater. A small city like Albany, with 20,000 inhabitants, reported 500 habitual drunks and 4,000 "tipplers." In 1818 New York City boasted 1,600 grocery stores that sold liquor, in addition to the many taverns and saloons. The statistics were enough, if we may use a pun, to make the head swim.

Concern with the demon rum, of course, was age-old. In colonial days courts often required drunkards to wear the letter D, just as paupers sometimes were made to embroider P on their clothing. The Continental Congress, in the midst of revolution, passed a resolution urging the states to put "an immediate stop to the pernicious practice of distilling grain, by which the most extensive evils are likely to be derived, if not quickly prevented." The Quakers, under the exhortations of Anthony Benezet, and the Methodists voiced disapproval of both the manufacture and use of liquor before the turn of the century. The crusade received its greatest spur, however, from the writings of a true Jeffersonian democrat, Dr. Benjamin Rush.

A member of the College of Physicians and Surgeons in Philadelphia, Rush wrote a well-rounded *Inquiry into the Effect of Ardent Spirits Upon the Human Mind and Body,* which was a runaway bestseller; it was reprinted in eight editions and had sold 172,000 copies by 1850. He did not argue that drink was harmful on all occasions, but he said it had deleterious effects on those who took it habitually or were novices. Reciting in medical terms the deplorable record of mortality among drinkers, he urged those who needed stimulants to rely on cider, wine, beer, tobacco, and coffee.

The early temperance advocates, following Rush's advice, campaigned for self-control rather than abstinence. They were not teetotalers. But early in the century temperance coalesced with religious revivalism, and became subject to revivalism's flamboyant oratory. Thus, by way of example, declaimed Reverend John Pierpont: "If I be willingly accessory to my brother's death, by a pistol or cord, the law holds me guilty; but guiltless if I mix his death drink in a cup. The halter is my reward if I bring him to his death in a bowl of hemlock; if in a glass of spirits, I am rewarded with his purse. Yet who would not rather see his child die by hemlock than by rum?"

With the Reverend Lyman Beecher in the vanguard, the Congregationalists and Methodists formed the Massachusetts Society for the Suppression of Intemperance in 1813. Similar societies soon swarmed through the country, though their sensational climb did not begin until 1825. Beecher that year preached six sermons on abstinence which rallied men everywhere. "Let the temperate cease to buy," he cried, "and the demand for ardent spirits will fall in the market three-fourths, and ultimately will fail wholly, as the generation of drunkards shall hasten out of time. . . . Let the consumer do his duty, and the capitalist, finding his employment unproductive, will quickly discover other channels of useful enterprise." He compared spirits with slavery as "sinful, impolitic, and dishonorable. That no measures will avail short of rendering ardent spirits a contraband of trade is nearly self-evident."

It was a call for the most massive boycott of the century, comparable in some respects to the boycotts of Sam Adams against British manufacture three-quarters of a century before, and it drew to its colors college presidents and clergymen by the hundreds. A year later Dr. Justin Edwards founded the American Society for the Promotion of Temperance, complete with offices, secretaries, revivalist lecturers, and newspaper publicity campaigns. In its ten years of existence it exhorted citizens everywhere to sign a pledge for total abstinence, and with considerable success. By 1829 there were 1,000 local societies, 100,000 members; five years later, 5,000 groups with a million adherents were scattered throughout the nation but were strongest in the North and Northwest. Housewives were induced to boycott groceries that sold the evil drink; students were organized at Amherst, Oberlin, and elsewhere. To attract those sympathetic to temperance, various hotels boasted that no intoxicants could be bought on their premises.

The movement foundered for a while in the 1830's but was revived in 1840 along new lines. A group of six friends who frequented a local tavern in Baltimore to gamble and drink were converted by a reformer to take the pledge. Subsequently they formed their own society. The Washington Temperance Society, as it was called, unlike its predecessors, had no religious base or clerical roots; it was solely a movement of reformed drinkers to reform others who imbibed, and as such it succeeded beyond all expectations. A year after being founded it had enrolled 23,000 in New York, New Jersey, and Pennsylvania alone. Two years later it reported, perhaps with some exaggeration, that a half million drinkers had taken the pledge. Everywhere the temperance people, like true evangelists, held parades and demonstrations, but with no religious overtones. Children in the vanguard, wearing satin badges, sang the stanzas of the Cold Water Army and signed a cold-water pledge as follows:

> We do not think,
> We'll ever drink,

Whiskey or Gin,
Brandy or Rum,
        or anything,
    That'll make drunk come.

The sustained agitation by these and other groups was eventually converted to political coin. Almost all states introduced bills to license liquor dealers, though this proved an inadequate deterrent because the fees were too small. Massachusetts in 1838 outlawed the sale of retail liquor in any amount less than fifteen gallons, obviously an insuperable hurdle for the common man—undoubtedly its main aim. It was repealed two years later under a barrage of petitions and public discussion. Some states gave local communities the option to determine whether to be wet or dry. But the pioneer of prohibition was Maine, where feeling was so intense local groups pledged on their honor not "to vote for a man for any civil office who is in the habit of using ardent spirits or wine to excess." In 1846 Maine became the first state in the Union to boast a prohibition act, followed thereafter by thirteen others.

Prohibition seemed to be America's destiny. Fortunately or unfortunately, however, except in Maine, New Hampshire, and Vermont, enforcement was lax, and the Civil War drew the nation's attention to other matters, thereby writing a temporary finis to temperance. By this time a counterreaction had set in, many influential people arguing that government supervision of private habits was an encroachment on liberty. Critics insisted the Maine law was unconstitutional, and one writer, Edward Payson, questioned whether "a great moral evil, whose cancerous spots have for thousands of years penetrated the body politic through and through, and for hundreds of centuries have clasped it round and round, [can be] susceptible of a radical and nearly instantaneous cure."

At any rate there is no convincing proof that the temperance crusade alleviated or eliminated poverty to any measurable extent. The causes seemed to lie deeper than the demon rum.

Chapter 8

VOTE YOURSELF A FARM

The first unions of workingmen in the United States were formed during the 1790's, small, simple affairs without paid officeholders, headquarters, national affiliations, or, except for a general sympathy for Jeffersonianism, ideology. The members were skilled craftsmen—carpenters, masons, printers, shoemakers, sailors. Their single weapon was the turnout—strike—and their objectives were limited to shorter hours and higher wages. Dues were six to ten cents a month, initiation fees forty to fifty cents. These first societies, as they were called, were obviously not formidable factors in the war against poverty. In fact they had difficulty surviving when in 1806 the Philadelphia courts ruled that a union of shoemakers was a conspiracy and had to be disbanded.

As the years passed, however, the trade union movement took on meat and marrow, reaching a peak of 300,000 members in 1834 and embracing not merely the skilled but many unskilled, such as the 2,000 girls in Lowell, Massachusetts, mills or the women and children in a Paterson textile mill. In New York City two of every three laborers belonged to unions, many who had never been enrolled before—weavers, milliners, cigarmakers, plasterers. Simultaneously the labor movement's horizons widened to include political goals, and among its leaders there emerged a radical cadre that spoke a lan-

112

guage not very different from that of Karl Marx a generation later. "What distinguishes the present from every other struggle in which the human race has been engaged," wrote Frances (Fanny) Wright, "is that the present is evidently openly and acknowledgedly a war of class, and that this war is universal."

The radicals talked of finishing "the glorious work of the Revolution," and invariably proposed nostrums for full economic equality to supplement political equality. In time they promulgated plans for utopian socialist communities, "phalanxes," agrarian groups, socialized boarding schools, producers' cooperatives, and more. Where the philanthropists stressed self-help and moral regeneration in which the individual was the key, the radicals stressed programs in which government, as the collective spokesman, or groups of people aligned together, were the primary agents for change. The former presupposed continuation of laissez-faire capitalism, the latter its demise.

The radicals were not without influence. Their friends often included men in the White House, as well as writers like Emerson, Thoreau, Walt Whitman, Horace Greeley, and innumerable clergymen, but they never gained a consensus for their social blueprints. One radical concept, however, trimmed down from revolutionary and egalitarian to reformist dimensions, became a milestone in the struggle against poverty.

II

Residents of New York City woke one morning in March 1845 to find walls plastered with a circular that bore the intriguing headline: "Vote Yourself a Farm."

"Are you an American citizen?" ran the text. "Then you are a joint owner of the public lands. Why not take enough of your property to provide yourself a Home? Why not Vote yourself a farm? . . .

"Are you a party follower? Then you have long enough employed your vote to benefit scheming office-seekers; use it for once to benefit yourself. Vote yourself a farm.

"Are you tired of slavery—of drudging for others—of poverty and its attendant miseries? Then, Vote yourself a farm. . . .

"Are you endowed with reason? Then you must know that your right to life hereby includes the right to a place to live in—the right to a home. Assert this right, so long denied by feudal robbers and their attorneys. Vote yourself a farm."

The circular was a reprint from a radical sheet, *Working Man's Advocate*, available at ten to the penny and eventually to be sold by the hundreds of thousands. Editor and publisher of the *Advocate* was a man of pleasant face, symmetric features, a beard that looked like a woman's braid stretching from ear to ear around the chin, and thin but wide lips, named George Henry Evans. In his time Evans had been beguiled by other panaceas for rescuing the workingman from the tyranny of the Industrial Revolution, but this one was to leave its mark.

Born in Herefordshire, England, in 1805, Evans was brought to the New World by his parents and at the age of fourteen was apprenticed to a printer in Ithaca, New York. Printshops in those days seem to have been matriculation schools for radicals, perhaps because they developed the habit of reading. George Henry nursed himself on the writings of Tom Paine, worked as a delivery boy, pressman, compositor, and editor, and—in the words of his equally famous brother, Frederick, who became Elder of the religious movement known as the Shakers—emerged "a firm and consistent infidel." After roaming about for a while young George Henry landed in New York City late in 1829, just in time for the excitement of the first labor parties the world had ever seen.

The Working Men's Party of New York had begun innocently in a mass meeting of 5,000 laborers called that April to protest employer efforts to lengthen the workday from ten hours to eleven. Following a quick victory in their campaign, thoughts turned from the ten-hour day to political action, just as was happening in Philadelphia and dozens of other cities. The leader of the "Workies" in this early period was a self-educated machinist, Thomas Skidmore, who held the revolutionary view that there was no cure for man's misfortunes unless property was equally divided. Specifically he urged government to give, free, to every man over twenty-one and to every unmarried woman 160 acres of land to be held as long as they tilled the soil. The practice of selling or renting land would be illegalized forever, and those who currently owned more would be permitted to deed to their children, on death, only the standard 160 acres. Thus within a single generation a universal equality would settle over the United States, assuring the abundant life for all.

Within three months Skidmore was replaced as party leader by Robert Dale Owen, son of the British socialist who had established a utopian community at New Harmony, Indiana, and Fanny Wright, a red-headed dynamo who was considered the most dangerous radical of her time. To Owen and Fanny the solution to man's ills lay not in property division but in establishing free boarding schools in which the children of the rich and those of the poor would be taken from home at age two to be reared and educated together. Through community living in the formative years, they felt, the class struggle between workers and employers would be superseded by an egalitarian harmony. It was to this faction that George Henry Evans attached himself when he began publishing, in a musty little office on Thompson Street, the *Working Man's Advocate,* the most influential labor paper of the period. Its original slogan, expressing prevalent leftist sentiment, read: "All children are entitled to equal education; all adults to equal property; and all mankind to equal privileges"; and its first editorial proclaimed in apocalyptic prose that "the working classes have taken the field and will never give up the contest until the power that oppresses them is annihilated."

The Workies in general, however, and the "free enquirers"—as the Owen-Wright faction was called—in particular, enjoyed only a brief day in the sun. They seeded the ground for reforms such as abolition of imprisonment for debt, but disappeared in a rampage of schism. Before long there were four workingmen's parties in New York, none receiving enough votes to make any difference. Evans, though he continued to endorse the usual labor planks, such as the ten-hour day and opposition to the Second Bank of the United States, deduced from these experiences, first, that labor should work within the two major parties, putting forth its own candidates only as a last resort, and second, that poverty would always be endemic to the system unless workingmen could escape to the public domain. "The poor," he wrote in March 1833, "must work or starve in the manufactories as in England, unless they can cultivate the land."

During the 1830's Evans' star was in eclipse. He continued to espouse the cause of trade unions, endorsed the Equal Rights Party ("loco-focos"), and Jacksonian democracy, but his paper went out of print at mid-decade, and from 1835 to 1841 he concentrated his energies on tilling a forty-acre farm in a backwoods section of New Jersey. Then in 1841 he returned to the fray, and with the aid of "very good friends to the cause" began publishing a monthly, the *Radical Continuation of the Working Man's Advocate.*

The forties were a distinctive period in American history. As John R. Commons notes, they "far outran the other periods in . . . unbounded loquacity." It was the time of the "talk fest" and "hot air." William Lloyd Garrison was pursuing his crusade against slavery; Horace Greeley and Albert Brisbane were initiating their Fourierist phalanxes; the reformers of New England were occupied with Brook Farm; the temperance movement and spiritualism were clearly on the upswing. On any given day a city had its fill of lectures on women's rights, protests against capital punishment, talks on phrenology, and what have you. In the backwash of the 1837 panic men were turning to every conceivable nostrum for relief. Horace Greeley, the tribune of this era, became the exponent of every ism then known, except spiritualism and free love.

The 1840's were also a time of deteriorating conditions for the poor. Immigration rose by 300 per cent, from 600,000 in the previous decade to 1,700,000 (and 2,600,000 the following decade). The urban areas, where poverty was concentrated, nearly doubled in population from 1840 to 1860. And with the expansion in number came an expansion of misery. Dr. Henry Clark reported visiting a house on Half-Moon Place in Boston with three cellar apartments, one of which was occupied each night by no fewer than 39 persons. In another the "tide had risen so high that it was necessary to approach the bedside of a patient by means of a plank which was laid from one stool to another; while the dead body of an infant was actually sailing about the room in its coffin." Poverty and pauperism had existed before but they now took on an impersonal character, as if mass-produced on a machine. In the lodging cellars that dotted the city a class structure prevailed even in misery: the "affluent" paid 37½ cents a week for board and lodging, sleeping on straw and eating at what was called the "first table," where food was slightly less noxious. The second class paid half that amount but were accommodated on the bare floor without the luxury of straw. The third class paid only nine cents a week but were not guaranteed any floor space unless second-class spaces were unfilled.

"There is not a State's Prison or House of Correction in New England," wrote a Lowell, Massachusetts, doctor, "where the hours of labor are so long, the hours for meals so short, or the ventilation so much neglected as in all the cotton mills with which I am acquainted." Slaves in Richmond's tobacco factories worked 10 hours a day but Lowell's free workers toiled 12 hours ordinarily and 13½ hours in April. Girls in these plants were forced to live on company premises, crowded an average of six to a room "of moderate dimensions" which in the view of one authority was less healthful than that of the average jail. William Henry Channing's biting indictment of city civilization, flamboyant though it was, was not entirely exaggerated. "Its factories," he wrote, "change into brothels; its rents to distress warrants; its railroads to mighty fetters binding industry in an inextricable net of feudalism; from under the showy robes of its success flutter the unseemly rags of ever-growing beggary; from garret and cellar of its luxurious habitations stare out the gaunt forms of haggard want. . . ."

III

Revulsion against the factory system in England had once taken the form of machine-breaking; armed bands of Luddites, around 1811, descended on Nottingham mills in the dark of night to destroy their equipment. In land-rich America, during the first half century of the Industrial Revolution, the same revulsion converted to "back to the farm" movements. It was an idea that had occurred to Jefferson and Skidmore, to Robert Owen in the 1820's when he organized his utopian communities, and to that star-studded group of Associationists—Albert Brisbane, Greeley, Henry James, Nathaniel Hawthorne, Emerson, Margaret Fuller, Bronson Alcott, George Ripley, to name a few—who sponsored thirty-four phalanxes in the 1840's.

George Henry Evans' new agrarianism was in the same tradition, a retread in fact of the works of Skidmore, Tom Paine, and others, its saving virtue being that it was far more effective. "If any man has a right on the earth," Evans wrote in his magazine, *Radical*, "he has a right to land enough to raise a habitation on. If he has a right to live, he has a right to land enough for his subsistence. Deprive anyone of these rights, and you place him at the mercy of those who possess them." And for Evans land reform was not merely a means of uplift for the proletarian who fled to the farm but for the one who remained in the city as well.

The reason wages were low, said Evans, was that there was a "surplus of mechanics" in the cities. That oversupply was due to the circumstance that "speculators and wild beasts" had seized the public lands while "thousands of God's children have not where to lay their heads." The unconscionable frauds of the land jobbers hemmed people to the cities, so that supply of labor far outstripped demand, and wages were kept at subsistence level. The way around this problem, of course, was to break the backs of the speculators by making land available to the people free. As some disenchanted proletarians left for rural areas, the relative shortage of laborers in the city would force wages up to a decent level.

One Sunday in February 1844, Evans called together five friends in a room behind John Windt's small printshop in New York to form a movement, the National Reform Association, around these principles. The men were all skilled mechanics, former members of the Workies and the loco-focos; Windt was the first president of the printers' union. The specific scheme they elaborated, as spelled out in the revived *Working Man's Advocate* and in another reform publication, *People's Rights*, was not particularly novel but it had the merit of simplicity and symmetry. The federal government would lay out in the public domain Rural Republican Townships six miles square, each subdivided into 144 quarter sections of 160 acres each. The center of each township would contain five-acre lots for homes and stores, as well as a 30-acre park to house the public office building. So far there was little difference from the New England townships of the old Puritans. The point of departure, however, was in the distribution of land. Evans opposed government sale of the public domain, either at low or high prices; if it were cheap, he said, the speculators would grab it, and if dear the workingman could not afford it. The only sensible solution therefore, in Evans' opinion, was to give the land away and make it inalienable—neither to be rented, sold, nor seized in lieu of mortgage or debt. Every landless person willing to settle and work a quarter section would receive one, no more, no less, free of charge. According to a circular distributed in April 1844, "The Safety Valve," there was enough land in "the possession of the general government (leaving Oregon and Texas out of the question) to allow every family in the United States two hundred acres each, besides all the land now held in private property in the twenty-six States and Territories."

Evans' plan was not hard to sell. It used typically American rhetoric—equality, inalienability, individuality—and it could be compressed into that single, attractive slogan, "Vote Yourself a Farm." By September 1845 national reform groups were functioning in twelve New York counties and six or eight states. The *New York Courier and Enquirer* called the plan "wild," "utterly senseless," "fatal to society," "thoroughly destructive to all social and civil interests," but it won converts in high places. Gerrit Smith, a philanthropist and landowner, defrayed the losses of Evans' paper and offered 200 acres to city workers willing to accept them on his northern New York estate. The plan failed, partly because those who came were not accustomed to farming and the land itself was not particularly fertile, but Smith continued his agitation and became a spokesman for the National Reformers in Congress when he was elected in 1852.

The most important convert, of course, was Horace Greeley, publisher of the most widely read periodical of the time, the *Tribune*, and one of the most colorful figures in American history. Greeley's father had been cut adrift by the depression of 1819 and forced to change status from small farmer to day laborer. Just how much this affected young Horace is not certain, but he seems to have developed a boundless love for minority causes. As a boy of thirteen he resolved never to drink whiskey; as an adult he became a prohibitionist. On settling in New York in 1831 he made his way to the vegetarian boardinghouse of "Doctor" Graham. At one time or another Greeley and his *Tribune* spoke out for Associationism, socialism, protectionism, abolition of capital punishment, and, on meeting George Henry Evans, for National Reform. "Make the Public Lands free in quarter-sections to Actual Settlers and deny them to all others," wrote Greeley, "and earth's landless millions will no longer be orphans and mendicants; they can work for the wealthy, relieved from the degrading terror of being turned adrift to starve. When employment fails or wages are inadequate, they may pack up and strike westward to enter upon the possession and culture of their own lands on the banks of the Wisconsin, the Des Moines or the Platte, which have been patiently awaiting their advent since creation. Strikes to stand still will be glaringly absurd when every citizen is offered the alternative to work for others or for himself, as to him shall seem most advantageous."

In a nation as richly endowed as the United States such words had the pungent quality of realism and George Henry Evans was able to transmute them, with dexterity and tenacity, into political capital. Recalling what he considered the mistake of the old workingmen's parties in operating outside the two-party system, Evans decided to proselytize within them. Each Democratic or Whig candidate was solicited to endorse land reform in writing, and on doing so received the support of the Vote Yourself a Farm contingent. To assure bargaining power, Evans had each applicant for membership in the National Reform Association commit himself not to "vote for any man, for any legislative office, who will not pledge himself, in writing, to use all the influence of his station, if elected, to prevent all further traffic in the Public Lands . . . and to cause them to be laid out in Farms and Lots for the free and exclusive use of actual settlers." Later Evans added the ten-hour day and the ideas of inalienability and limited holdings to the membership pledge. With a little—and growing—army behind him he was sometimes a balance of power between the parties, enough so to get favorable replies from many prospective legislators. Where no friendly candidate was available the National Reformers occasionally ran their own, usually with pathetic results. Their independent selection for mayor of New York in 1845, Ransom Smith, for instance, garnered 117 votes out of 20,000 cast. Two years later they were happy to endorse the Whig nominee who gave "favorable" replies to their questions.

Evans was also shrewd enough to hitch his chariot to other popular causes. The New England Working Men's Association had been formed around the single issue of winning the ten-hour day. The National Reformers joined with it to initiate industrial congresses which met annually from 1845 to 1856 and attracted quite a few trade unions, especially in the early period, around both issues. Through this amalgamation Evans also gained a bridge to the prominent Brook Farm writers. Simultaneously he joined hands with the anti-rent groups in Albany County, New York; Thomas H. Dorr's People's Party in Rhode Island, formed to secure manhood suffrage; and the antislavery movements of Michigan, Wisconsin, Indiana, and Massachusetts. Though Evans had reservations about most of these causes as inadequate, he was flexible enough to blend them with his own. National Reform, he wrote in 1846, initiated an era in which there "will be but two parties, the great Republican Party of Progress and the little Tory Party of Holdbacks."

No one was as yet thinking of a "Republican Party" as those words were written, but true to Evans' prophecy many National Reformers were prominent figures in siring the new party during the next decade. By a dozen different routes the program for free, inalienable, and limited homesteads insinuated itself into the bloodstream of the Republican Party, side by side with the issues of slavery and preserving the Union. Andrew Johnson, future President, introduced a homestead bill in Congress that same year, 1846, and Horace Greeley introduced one two years later. Wisconsin came close to enacting legislation in 1851 limiting land holdings to 320 acres. Galusha Grow, called by some the "father of the Republican Party," made his first important speech in Congress in 1852 on the subject "Man's Right to the Soil." Alvin E. Bovay, leader of one of the coalitions that merged into the Republican Party, had long been associated with Evans and his movement. The Vermont convention of the new party in 1854 came out for free grants of land to actual settlers, and the Pennsylvania Whigs, as they shifted to the Republicans, hoisted banners reading "Free Men, Free Labor, and Free Land." Evans was four years dead when the Republicans held their Chicago nominating convention in 1860—he died in 1856 at the age of fifty-one—but William H. Seward, one of the leading contenders, had been a pioneer supporter of land reform and Lincoln was considered favorably disposed. Four of the forty-four songs produced by the Republicans during their 1860 campaign dealt with homestead, and two years later, when they came to power, they made it the law of the land, one of the major pieces of legislation in the nation's history.

IV

"Here," writes Helene Sara Zahler, historian on the subject, "ends the story of the political efforts of National Reform. Its issue had been adopted by a major party. Although never able to win more than a local rural election land reformers had brought considerable pressure on legislators." They had transformed the word "donation" into "homestead," and had "made free homes on the public domain a right of the actual settler instead of an act of charity to the poor."

But the Homestead Act embodied only one of Evans' three principles—free land to the man who settled it. The other two principles, fundamental to abolition of poverty in his view, nonalienation and equality, fell by the boards. In typical political compromise, the Republicans spat simultaneously in both directions—giving homesteads to many poor but not withholding large holdings from the rich. The idea that no one be permitted to sell, rent, or mortgage his quarter section was dropped as too radical. The government continued to make large grants to railroads as an inducement to build more trackage, and speculators were able to gobble up millions of acres from the public domain by a variety of techniques.

By 1890, twenty-eight years after the Homestead Act was passed, some 372,659 titles had been granted to settlers, embracing 48,000,000 of the one billion acres in the public domain. Two million people were the beneficiaries, but in the same period the nation's population grew by 20,000,000. Moreover the railroads, with the aid of bribed congressmen, were able to garner four times as much land as the 372,659 families combined. Three western carriers, chartered between 1862 and 1864, were given not only federal loans for each mile of track laid but outright gifts of 70,000,000 acres.

The National Labor Union at its 1867 convention in Chicago, just five years after the Homestead Act was passed, noted with dismay the trend toward speculation. "The course of our legislation recently," it stated in one of its resolutions, "has tended to the building up of greater monopolies, and the creation of more powerful moneyed and landed aristocracies in the United States than any that now overshadows the destinies of Europe. Eight hundred millions of acres of the people's lands have been legislated into the hands of a few hundred individuals, who already assume a haughty and insolent tone and bearing towards the people and government, as did the patricians of ancient Rome. These lands are held unimproved, and mainly for speculative purposes . . ."

What had begun as a revolutionary doctrine to achieve equality ended as a reform with enough loopholes for any land jobber to crawl through. Evans had elaborated a timetable by which in 1900 the United States would be a "Nation of Freeholders," free from poverty, but while the Homestead Act did bring benefits to millions, it fell far short of the objectives foreseen by the man who elaborated the idea.

Chapter 9

"NO MORE DAT!"

A white man—his name is unknown—came to Clarke County, Alabama, in the year 1873 carrying a bundle of small colored stakes. Calling on freed Negro slaves, this sorcerer explained that he had been charged by the President of the United States to pass out these little items to black men so that they could at long last become owners of a patch of land. All they had to do, he said, was drive a stake into whatever farmland suited their purpose and by that simple act, with the blessings and protection of the President, the land would become theirs. The price for this wooden manna was a mere $3 and those who did not have such large sums were permitted to buy their ticket to paradise for the bargain figure of a single dollar.

"Many of the credulous and trusting colored people . . . ," records T. H. Ball, "bought these little stakes, stuck them on the lands of their white neighbors, and some began to work their newly acquired plantations, with what results need not be told."

This fraud, one of thousands perpetrated on the black man, was crude but on balance less painful than the deception by the nation itself. Eleven years before, as the culmination of eight decades of various forms of agitation, President Lincoln had issued the Emancipation Proclamation decreeing that as of January 1, 1863, all slaves in the rebel states "shall be, then, thenceforward, and forever free." A

123

joyous Negro told a meeting in Washington, December 31, 1862: "Onst the time was, dat I cried all night. . . . De nex mornin my child was to be sold, and she was sold, and I neber spec to see her no more till de day ob judgment. Now, no more dat! no more dat! no more dat! Wid my hands agin my breast I was gwine to my work, when de overseer used to whip me along. Now, no more dat! no more dat! no more dat! . . . We'se free now, bress de Lord. Dey can't sell my wife and child no more, bress de Lord! No more dat! no more dat! no more dat, now! Preserdun Lincum have shot de gate!"

A couple of years later that persistent agitator, William Lloyd Garrison, whose voice and pen did more than those of any other man to rouse the nation's conscience against slavery, liquidated his American Anti-Slavery Society. His life's work, Garrison felt, had been finished.

But by 1877 it was clear that that work had only begun. The presidential election campaign that year between Republican Rutherford B. Hayes and Democrat Samuel Tilden had been thrown into the House of Representatives over contested results in Oregon, South Carolina, Florida, and Louisiana. Tilden needed a single electoral vote to win; Hayes needed all twenty. To get them the Republican candidate promised the three southern states to withdraw all federal troops from the South, leaving the destiny of the area again in the hands of those who had fostered slavery. From thenceforward and for many decades to come, the Negro lost his vote and whatever dream he cherished for material security.

II

There exists no more disheartening chapter in the war on poverty than this aborted effort to lift the American Negro to economic citizenship. Most white people of the South had no stake in slavery; on the contrary they were its victims almost as much as the black man was. Nor did they gain any advantage from the failure of Reconstruction and the enduring torture of the former bondsmen.

As of 1860 there was one slave for every two white men in the fifteen slave states—four million as against eight million. But, and this is the crucial point, only 384,000 southerners owned any slaves at all and the vast majority of these were marginal owners of one to ten bondsmen. A mere 10,781 plantations boasted fifty or more slaves; only 1,733 a hundred or more.

Moreover, the slave economy, by retarding development in everything but cotton kept millions of whites in a state of wretchedness, almost as unenviable as that of the Negro. A Missouri writer who made a study of Deep South manufacture in 1847 concluded that whites who did not own slaves "possess, generally, but very small means, and the land which they possess is almost universally poor and so sterile that a scanty subsistence is all that can be derived from its cultivation." Since the more fertile soil belonged to those with slaves this "must ever remain out of the power of those who have none."

William Gregg of the South Carolina Institute claimed in 1851 that nearly half of that state's 274,563 white population were "substantially idle and unproductive, and would seem to have sunk into a condition but little removed from barbarism." Whatever benefits the rich South Carolinian reaped from slavery, vast numbers of poor whites were "whiling away an existence but one step in advance of the Indian of the forest." They survived on occasional jobs, hunting, fishing, small trade with slaves, or minor thievery. Sometimes, he said, they entered into league with black men to steal together.

Industry, of course, did penetrate to an extent below the Mason-Dixon line. But the southern worker, competing with slave labor and having few unions to defend him, reaped a harvest of subpar wages. At a time when men in the cotton and wool factories of Lowell were earning 80 cents a day, similar operatives in Tennessee were receiving 50 cents. Women in Lowell were paid $2 a week; in the South, $1.25. In North Carolina, according to one writer who lived there, factory labor—either slaves rented to industrialists by their masters, or free whites—cost $110 to $120 a year. "It will cost at least twice that sum in New England."

The overwhelming mass of southerners clearly had nothing to gain from slavery; only the subliminal drive of the "pecking system" can explain why they fought and died to uphold it. Deep in the human psyche there must exist a need for miserable men to be aggrandized by the greater misery of others, for without this psychological mechanism the poor white, far from opposing his black brother, would have developed a compassionate community with him.

For the rich white too there was some question whether slavery was plague or windfall. The price of Negroes kept going up, particularly after 1808 when slave trade was abolished and the supply depended largely on home breeding in old tobacco states such as Virginia. A prime field hand in Georgia could be purchased for $300 in 1792, but the price—though it fluctuated downward in bad times—had risen to $1,000 by 1819, $1,200 by 1853 and $1,800 on the eve of the Civil War. To this must be added interest on capital, taxes (since the slave was property, just like a textile spindle), insurance against death, illness, injury, or flight, as well as a modest upkeep. The plantation owner tied up great sums in his chattels which could have been used more effectively in improving the land. Where the northern capitalist paid nothing for labor but weekly wages and could invest his capital in labor-saving machines, the southern slave-owner carried the albatross of an inelastic labor system which kept him so heavily in debt to his banker there was little left over for technological improvement.

Many students of the subject believe that the southerners would have been better off freeing the slaves and rehiring them on a daily wage. Hinton Rowan Helper, in his widely acclaimed book of 1856, *The Impending Crisis*, admonished the southerners that "but for chattel slavery you might be enjoying the things upon which your fellow little bourgeoisie in the North are fattening." But the slave-holders had become wedded to a way of life, heedless of its long-term consequences. Sensitive and intelligent individuals not only rationalized slavery as morally superior to "wage slavery" but as, of all things, a cure for poverty. Some southern enthusiasts shared a "purple dream," as Stephen Vincent Benét called it, that the slave society would spread to Mexico and form a great empire that would dominate world-wide trade. This empire would abolish poverty not merely in its own sphere but throughout the planet. A rabid slaver, George Fitzhugh, compared the southern system with Horace Greeley's "socialist" phalanxes. "A Southern farm is a sort of joint stock concern or social phalanstery," he wrote, "in which the master furnishes the capital and skill, and the slaves the labor, and divide the profits, not according to each one's in-put, but according to each one's wants and necessities."

The defenders of southern virtue wove a web of intricate argument for their cause. "The difference between us," boomed Senator James H. Hammond of South Carolina, "is that our slaves are hired for life and well compensated; there is no starvation, no begging, no want of employment among our people. . . . Yours are hired by the day, not cared for, and scantily compensated, which may be proved in the most deplorable manner, at any hour in any street of your large towns." General Benjamin F. Stringfellow, using the language of Marxism, claimed the system of servitude superior in that it substituted class harmony for class struggle. "In the South," he said, "no struggle between labor and capital can arise. Where slavery exists, capital and labor are one, for labor is capital. There the capitalist, instead of exhausting his laborer, must strengthen, protect and preserve him, for he is his money. The interest of the laborer and the capitalist, the slave and his master, are identical; they cannot conflict. The prosperity of the master is the happiness of the slave, for his condition is improved as his master prospers; the master prospers as his slave is healthy, vigorous and happy."

Such fervid defense on the philosophical plane could be buttressed with innumerable instances of paternalism in personal relations. Francis Scott Key of Maryland, who had misgivings about the institution and had freed seven of his Negroes, nonetheless explained to a friend in 1838 that he was proslavery because he "could not, without the greatest inhumanity be otherwise. I own, for instance, an old slave, who has done no work for me for years. I pay his board and other expenses, and cannot believe that I sin in doing so."

In self-interest the slaveowner often showed more humanity than the employer of free labor. When a canal was dug through the swamps of Louisiana to Lake Pontchartrain in 1835, for instance, it was necessary to import hundreds of Irishmen for the work because slavers would not hire out their Negroes for labor that endangered their lives. Dr. Richard Arnold, during the cholera epidemic of 1849, wrote a friend: "I wish an Abolitionist could see the care and attention bestowed upon our Negroes. . . . A manufacturing cotton lord can easily fill the place of his dead operative and he loses nothing by his death. A planter loses so much capital by the death of every one of his operatives, and hence to save his capital is to save his Negroes."

The record of the times are filled with anecdotes that dispute the image of harsh masters, applying the lash, starving and working their Negroes to the edge of death. On the plantation where Booker T. Washington was born in Franklin County, Virginia, the master and his sons worked side by side with the six slaves. "In this way we all

grew up together, very much like members of one big family . . . ,"
says Washington. "On some of the large estates in Alabama and Mississippi which were far removed from the influence of the city, and
sometimes in the midst of the wilderness, master and slaves frequently lived together under conditions that were genuinely patriarchal." Though it was illegal to teach a Negro how to read and
write, not a few masters did, and some gave special instruction in
higher education to young blacks of talent. A slaveowner named
John McDonough introduced in 1825 a system of self-government for
slaves on a plantation near New Orleans, including trial by a jury of
peers. Jefferson Davis is said to have copied this design for his two
farms in Mississippi. A master in North Carolina was noted for feeding his slaves exactly what his own family ate, housing them in well-
built bungalows, providing them with "plenty of firewood . . .
good shoes and ample clothing." When sick, the Negroes were attended to by the best physicians in the area. Ailing children were
taken to the master's home and treated with the same care as his own
youngsters. Every adult black man was given a "patch of ground" to
cultivate for himself and time to work it.

The record of slavery is not one solid mass of brutality. Some servants, it is true, were worked to death within six or seven years, but
these were exceptions, not the rule. Others were sold away from
their families never to see wives or children again. On the other hand
many lived in puritan monogamy with kith and kin by their side till
the end of their days. Though work was usually barren and unre-
warding, some black men were given assignments of responsibility,
such as foremen, "head of the culinary department," or similar posts.
Slavery was a lifelong servitude without pay, but some owners, such
as the one in Savannah described by Ulrich B. Phillips, permitted
their chattels to earn cash working holidays, Sundays, and nights "at
rates of 37½ cents to 50 cents per day or at job prices for ditching,
woodcutting, blacksmithing, cooperage and the like, or by selling
produce, including corn and hops." There were not a few instances
where owners (e.g., James G. Birney of Alabama) took their bondsmen north in order to free them. As of 1860 there were 262,000 free
Negroes in the South, one for every sixteen slaves, and that year another 3,018 were emancipated.

III

Clearly there was no uniformity to the slave system; it was diverse enough so that one could find testimony for any point of view.

When the balance sheet is drawn, however, the chattel slave lived in the most demeaning poverty the nation has ever known. Whatever apologia is contrived for the institution, the fact is that the slave, no matter how hard or zealously he worked, could seldom raise his living standard beyond bare necessity. If there were a few who subsisted on the same diet as their masters, the vast majority tasted little but corn meal and bacon or salt pork. "All that is allowed," reports an ex-slave of his previous circumstance, "is corn and bacon, which is given out at the corncrib and smoke-house every Sunday morning. Each one receives, as his weekly allowance, three and a half pounds of bacon, and corn enough to make a peck of meal." On thousands of plantations the slave never ate meat, milk, fruits or eggs, and fresh vegetables only rarely.

The typical shelter—"quarters"—was a cabin of "crudely cut, loose-fitting clapboard" without lining "so that only the thickness of a single board kept out the winter's air and cold." "Small, low, tight and filthy, their houses can be but laboratories of disease," wrote an Alabama physician. (Contrary to legend, the slave suffered appreciably from such enervating ailments as malaria, yellow fever, cholera, as well as mental illness; and his mortality rate was about a third higher than that of whites.) Often there were no windows, roofs leaked, chimneys, made of mud and wood, disintegrated. There were exceptions, of course, but on the other hand there were conditions so mean as to be barbaric—such as a certain Georgia plantation where the slaves were allotted neither chairs, tables, plates, knives, nor forks. "They sat . . . ," writes Kenneth M. Stampp, "on the earth or doorsteps, and ate out of their little cedar tubs or an iron pot, some few with broken iron spoons, more with pieces of wood, and all the children with their fingers."

As for clothing, apart from hand-me-downs given to house servants, the typical ration was a few yards of "Negro cloth" such as calico or linsey-woolsey, one or two pairs of pants a year, a woolen jacket, a pair of shoes. Frederick Douglass in his autobiography says that he "was kept almost in a state of nudity" as a child, "no shoes, no stockings, no jacket, no trousers; nothing but coarse sack-cloth or tow-linen, made into a sort of shirt reaching down to my knees. This I wore night and day, changing it once a week."

The tyranny of the system is attested to by the cost of upkeep. Stampp lists maintenance records of a number of plantation owners indicating, in his view, "that the yearly charge for the support of an adult slave seldom exceeded $35.00 and was often considerably less than this." Costs at the Virginia plantation Marlbourne, of Edwin Ruffin, averaged less than $25 for the five years from 1844 through 1848; James Hamilton, only $18.33 per slave per year over a forty-year period. James A. Tait of Alabama estimated his expenses, including food, clothing, medical care, and taxes, as $34.70; and Thomas Pugh of Louisiana, as $23.60.

Worst of all, a fact about which statistics are mute, was the insecurity of chattels who belonged even to the most benign of masters. No heart-rending story can be imagined as poignant as that described by a reporter for the *New York Daily Tribune* (March 9, 1859) of the auction of 436 men, women, children, and infants of the Major Butler estates at the race course near Savannah, Georgia. None of the Negroes had ever been sold before, but now that the Major was dead, his sons decided to get rid of the estate, including, of course, its most valuable property, the slaves.

As the auction approached, every hotel in Savannah was jammed by the speculators who had come from as far away as Virginia and Louisiana, lured "by the prospect of making good bargains," while the black families huddled at the race course for a week or more in pitiful anxiety over their fate. Would they be separated from their wives, their children, their parents, the girls they loved? The Butlers had promised that they would be sold "in families" but a family was considered to be a man and wife.

As the speculators lit cigars and consulted their catalogues, "the Negroes were examined with as little consideration as if they had been brutes indeed; the buyers pulling their mouths open to see their teeth, pinching their limbs to find how muscular they were, walking them up and down to detect any signs of lameness, making them stoop and bend in different ways that they might be certain there was no concealed rupture or wound; and in addition to all this treatment, asking them scores of questions relative to their qualifications."

The reporter overheard Elisha, chattel No. 5 in the catalogue, trying to convince a "benevolent looking middle-aged gentleman" to "purchase him, with his wife, boy and girl, Molly, Israel and Sevanda, chattels Nos. 6, 7, 8. The earnestness with which the poor fellow pressed his suit, knowing, as he did, that perhaps the happiness of his whole life depended on his success, was interesting, and the arguments he used were most pathetic." With all his passion Elisha tried to show that this was a hard-working family that should be purchased as a whole: "Sho' you won't find a better man den me; no better on de whole plantation; not a bit old yet; do mo' work den ever; do carpenter work, too, little; better buy me, Mas'r; I'se be good servant, Mas'r. Molly, too, my wife, Sa fus rate rice hand; mos as good as me. Stan' out yer, Molly, and let the gen'lm'n see."

When the sale was over—it brought $303,850—Mr. Pierce M. Butler, now of Philadelphia, gave each Negro as he was led away a gift of four twenty-five-cent pieces.

Chapter 10

FORTY ACRES AND A MULE

Unscrambling the organism of slavery after two and a half centuries was obviously a complex matter, and unscrambling it in such a way that the Negro would win not only his physical freedom but protection against new forms of poverty was even more so. To begin with, many Americans did not believe it possible—or desirable—to assimilate the Afro-American into the white man's culture. Thus in 1817 when a group of notables, including Henry Clay, Daniel Webster, James Monroe, and John Marshall, formed the American Colonization Society, they urged as a solution sending manumitted Negroes back to Africa. Under the plan 52,000 blacks a year, at a cost of one million dollars, would be returned to the ancient habitat of their forefathers. The panacea did not catch fire, since the society was never able to raise more than $43,000 in any one year—usually much less—and all told dispatched a mere dribble of 8,000 blacks overseas, mostly to Liberia.

Nonetheless the idea of colonizing the Negro out of sight and out of mind persisted in high places up to and beyond the Civil War. Even that slender, devoted Quaker, Benjamin Lundy, who did yeoman's work for the antislave cause in the 1820's with his speaking tours and his paper *Genius of Universal Emancipation,* suggested that the slaves be freed only "gradually" and then be removed to

Haiti, Texas, or Canada. Lincoln too favored colonization; his friend and adviser Francis Preston Blair proposed in November 1864 that "a portion of Texas on the Rio Grande" be put aside as "a refuge for the freedmen of the South to go to. . . ." ° When Congress freed the slaves of the District of Columbia (April 1862) it allocated $100,000 to find a separate haven for them.

The prevailing sentiment held that the Negro was a secondary concern, distinctly subordinate to political expediency. For the most part the northern elite opposed slavery *as an institution* and declaimed against its extension to territories not yet formed into states, but it had no compelling feelings about the black man as a human being. It is worth noting that though the North and West had long abolished slavery, only six states, all of these with small colored populations, had granted the franchise to black men. New York required that a Negro own $250 in property to exercise his right, and Ohio bestowed suffrage solely on mulattoes with more white blood than black.

The war itself was fought not, as commonly believed, to unfetter the slave but to "preserve the Union." "I have no purpose either directly or indirectly," Lincoln told the nation as he was inaugurated March 4, 1861, "to interfere with the institution of slavery in the states where it exists. I believe I have no right to do so, and I have no inclination to do so." When General John C. Frémont, harried by guerrillas in Missouri, declared free all slaves belonging to rebel owners in the area, Lincoln revoked the order, as he did a little later when General David Hunter issued a similar proclamation for bondsmen in Georgia, Florida, and South Carolina. Nine hundred blacks who fled to the camp of Major General Benjamin F. Butler early in the hostilities, hoping for deliverance, were declared "contrabands of war," their status somewhat indefinite. Two slaves who brought intelligence to the Union army in Missouri were returned to their masters, one of them shot and killed as he broke away. More significant, after the northern defeat at Bull Run, Congress passed the Crittenden Resolution to reassure the five loyal slave states— Delaware, Kentucky, Maryland, West Virginia, and Missouri—that their "established institutions" would not be tampered with. As late

---

° It is interesting to note that the Black Muslims today similarly seek "a separate state or territory" for Negroes "either on this continent or elsewhere."

as August 1862 Lincoln, in his oft-quoted letter to Horace Greeley, avowed that "my paramount object in this struggle is to save the Union, and is not either to save or destroy slavery."

The Negro, it became clear, however, was the backbone of southern society, growing its food and cotton, building its military earthworks, driving the horses, and doing the menial tasks without which neither the army nor the system could survive. To promise him liberation and to enroll him in the federal forces was therefore only sensible strategy, which Lincoln yielded to steadily. In April 1862, as noted above, Congress freed the slaves in the District of Columbia, with some compensation to their owners, and two months later in the territories belonging to the United States. In July, prodded by Thaddeus Stevens, the North pledged liberty to "any man or boy of African descent" who rendered service to the Union, such as intelligence, as well as to his mother, wife, and children. Finally, in September 1862, Lincoln issued his monumental Emancipation Proclamation, granting freedom to slaves in the eleven rebel states as of January 1, 1863, when and if occupied by the federal troops. It was a grand event, appeasing the antislave movement and unleashing unbounded hopes in the black community down under. Nonetheless, mindful of the inevitable travail that faced bondsmen shifting from reliance on their masters to reliance on themselves for food, clothing, and shelter, there were some who muted their enthusiasm. "That proclamation," commented Wendell Phillips in summary of this position, "frees the slave but ignores the Negro."

The next decade and a half were spent by men of this persuasion trying to overtake this defect.

II

Leading figure in this losing race, at least until he died in 1868, was the congressman from Lancaster, Pennsylvania, Thaddeus Stevens, referred to by a laudatory biographer as "the most powerful parliamentary leader our system of government has ever evolved." That he failed to unite freedom with a measure of economic security for the Negro attests to the overwhelming difficulties of those who would change matters, since not even President Andrew Johnson possessed so much power as Stevens during those critical years when the issue was being decided. So dominant was his position that he came within a single vote of the two-thirds needed to impeach Johnson and replace him with a Stevens ally, Senator Ben Wade, president pro tem of the Senate.

At first glance no man seemed less fitted to be either politician or crusader than the "old commoner" from Pennsylvania. He possessed all those traits that are not only bound to lose votes but are usually associated with self-centeredness. He was a prodigious gambler, a bachelor who loved and left them without qualm, a nonbeliever in religion. One of the few men with whom he formed durable ties, the Reverend Jonathan Blanchard, wrote him in 1865: "Your lips have been defiled with blasphemy, your hands with gambling, and your body with women. . . . That good you have done the country (and none has done more, if so much) is no offset for vices such as I have named. . . ." Stevens' only permanent attachment with a woman is said to have been with his Negro servant Lydia Hamilton, who was his mistress during the last twenty-five years of his life. Other than that he had few friends, was indifferent to stylish clothes, seldom smiled, and never broke out into laughter.

His appearance, however, was deceptive, for as the *Nation* magazine was constrained to say on his death: "No public man was less of an egotist." He enjoyed immense popularity, holding his audiences with a wit that matched his cynicism, and a bitter tongue that brushed aside sophisticated niceties, plunging to the heart of a problem with "unequalled ardor and enthusiasm." Though handicapped from birth by a club foot, his thin, six-foot frame had the muscular foundation of an athlete; as a young man he was indeed an excellent horseman, swimmer, boatsman. His jaw was tough and determined; his eyes shone from within; and his shaven cheeks, wide brow, thin lips, and strong nose rounded out a face that could be called handsome, but even more, commanding. He was elected and re-elected from his district for various posts with impressive majorities, even when the party on whose ticket he ran did poorly. Somewhere at his core was an admixture of the realist and the true believer—traceable perhaps to his early background.

Born in northeastern Vermont during Washington's first term in office, Stevens was named after the Polish hero who served with the Revolutionary forces, Thaddeus Kosciusko. His father, an impecunious shoemaker, deserted his wife and four sons at an "undetermined date," never to reappear. Bringing up the boys then fell to the lot of the mother, a nurse and a devout Baptist, who evidently acquitted herself well, especially insofar as Thaddeus was concerned. In one of those apocryphalike tales that seem to follow all famous men, it is said of Stevens that at the age of twelve, on a chance trip to Boston, he developed a desire to help the poor whom he saw in their hovels, and a corresponding determination personally to become rich. If this is so, his mother made it possible for him to pursue both ends. She enrolled him in school at Peacham, Vermont, an intensely democratic semifrontier community, and then packed him off to Dartmouth College, from which he graduated in 1814, resolved to practice law. The legal profession carried him both to affluence and a political perch from which to defend the dispossessed.

Having emigrated to the more active bailiwick of Pennsylvania after passing the bar, one of Stevens' early cases involved a murderer whom he defended on the then novel plea of insanity. The case gained him a handsome fee, $1,500, and a reputation, soon to be enhanced by other sensational cases. Within a decade the young lawyer was well ensconced both in his practice and in the iron business, and able to take on occasional litigation on behalf of runaway slaves fleeing from adjoining Maryland, or to purchase, as he once did, a Negro hotel servant for $300 in order to emancipate him. Within two decades Stevens was embarked on a political career, winning a seat in the state legislature on the Anti-Masonic ticket.

It was here that Stevens' voice began to boom in underdog causes. He opposed the Masons because he felt secret societies a threat to democracy. It was not an important chapter in his career but it indicated his bias. Soon he became known as a leading advocate of free public education and in 1835 gained state-wide fame by winning over a hostile House which had intended to repeal a law on the subject. Two years later Stevens again made history of sorts by refusing to sign a new state constitution which limited suffrage to whites only. When he was elected to Congress in 1848, after a gap of a few years in which he concentrated on recouping his monetary fortune, it was as a Whig, aligned with the free soilers who opposed the extension of slavery. He fought the Fugitive Slave Law, denounced the compromise of 1850, damned human bondage as "a curse, a shame and a crime," and evidently took his position seriously, since he quit Congress in 1853 in protest against the moderate position of the Whigs. Returning six years later, having meanwhile helped form the Republican Party in Pennsylvania, Stevens soon became, as James G. Blaine noted, "the natural leader, who assumed his place by common consent." As chairman of the Ways and Means Committee he had broad authority over most bills dealing with the war, including those that allocated funds for it.

The past was a prelude to this one grand "moment"—seven years in which Stevens affected history at a critical juncture. He might have become a Cabinet officer had he been more pliable, but he was no sycophant for Lincoln—on the contrary. He had voted for the man from Illinois at the Republican national convention only as a third choice, and he now committed himself to a strategy very much at variance with that of the President. Where Lincoln would make considerable concessions to the South, including that of retaining the slave system so long as it was not extended, Stevens opposed compromise. If the South secedes, he said, "our next United States will contain no foot of ground on which a slave can tread, no breath of air which a slave can breathe." He was one of a handful who opposed the Crittenden Resolution. Almost from the beginning he favored confiscating all property "used for insurrectionary purposes," and he urged Lincoln to arm the Negroes. Toward the end, while many sought reconciliation, the old commoner—a "sour and angry congressman," one historian calls him—would have desolated the South, arrested its leaders wholesale, taken their lands, and subjected them to exile and capital punishment. Together with a clan of kindred radical Republicans—Senators "Bluff Ben" Wade, Zachariah Chandler, Charles Sumner, among others—Stevens engaged in a game of push and pull with Lincoln, prodding him toward emancipation. On this the President was flexible enough to move forward, once he felt he had mustered a consensus, and the relations between the two men, while cool, never became as embittered as between Stevens and Johnson.

But it was only the first act of the drama, and looking at it from the point of view of abolishing poverty for four million people, the least important act. Off stage loomed an intense internecine conflict within the Republican Party over the rights and prerogatives of the defeated Bourbons, and conversely the rights and prerogatives of the freed slaves. Had Lincoln lived and continued his course he would have been the butt of radical wrath, for his plan of reconciliation virtually excluded the Negro as a factor. In his Proclamation of Amnesty and Reconstruction of December 1863, the President offered all southerners, excluding civilian and military leaders, full pardon and "restoration of all rights of property, except as to slaves." More, they could regain autonomy for their respective states as soon as one-tenth of the voters on the 1860 electorate list (all white, of course) had taken an oath of allegiance and pledged to incorporate an antislave provision in their constitution. Under this plan "phantom" governments were already installed in Virginia and Louisiana when Congress began to balk. To restrain the Administration, Congress passed the Wade-Davis bill requiring the President to appoint provisional governors until the war was over and then to form permanent governments only if a majority of the 1860 voters would swear loyalty, rather than 10 per cent.

With the assassination of Lincoln in April 1865, five days after the surrender of the Confederate army, the new President, Andrew Johnson, continued the restorationist policy. The former tailor from Tennessee, who in 1861 would have executed the secessionist leaders if it had been in his power, had in the meantime changed course. He confided to an interviewer that previously the nation was threatened by an "aristocracy based on $3 billion of property in slaves" in the South. Now it was menaced by an "oligarchy of bonds and national securities" running rampant in the North. To contain the latter he was for re-establishing a stable South as a counterweight, even if that meant restoring the older aristocracy to a measure of authority. Step by step, then, the mutinous southerners were reinvested with property and influence. Though Johnson modified the amnesty provision, limiting its benefits to those with less than $20,000 in property, he left a loophole whereby those with greater affluence could be pardoned by applying to him personally. Some 14,000 southern gentry, including General Robert E. Lee, were thereby restored to their plantations or compensated for them.

By January 1866 white civil administrations were reinstated in all the southern domains but Texas. Many rebel leaders, including six ex-cabinet members of the Confederacy, four generals, and five colonels were elected to the federal legislature, including Alexander H. Stephens of Georgia, former Vice-President of the Confederate States, only recently interred in Fort Warren, accused of treason. The President himself gagged at the prospect of Stephens serving in Congress and urged suffrage rules so as to give the vote to Negroes with $250 in real estate who could read the Constitution. The effect of his over-all policy, however, was to turn the eleven states back to the slaveholders, and leave the Negro naked in his quest for relief. Had his policy been permitted to stand, the South, now entitled to eighty-three members in the House of Representatives, would have been able, with northern allies, to control Congress and the electoral college. "They will at the very first election," charged Stevens, "take possession of the White House and the Halls of Congress," and seek to revive slavery.

The southern Bourbons, had they been more patient, might then and there have rescued from defeat the spoils of victory. But they overplayed their hand. Not content with a disfranchised Negro they sought to shackle him through Black Codes, very much like South African apartheid or Hitler's laws against the Jews. A Negro was required to carry his labor contract on his person or be jailed for "vagrancy." In Mississippi if he was without "visible means of support" he could be imprisoned or sold for a specified period to pay out the fine. In Alabama he could be placed to work under state overseers. In Maryland a freedman convicted of minor crime could be placed in temporary bondage for years. Special laws set wages and hours of work, and imposed prison penalties for those who left the plantation before their employment contract had expired. South Carolina set a fee of $10 to $100 a year for a black man who sought work at anything but agriculture and domestic service, thus propelling the Negro back to his master. Here and there the law provided that blacks could come to town only on sufferance of the employer. A bill in Mississippi, ironically titled an "Act to Confer Civil Rights on Freedmen and for other purposes," forbade intermarriage between whites and Negroes, restricted renting of lands or homes, barred the black from carrying firearms or drinking liquor, and reinstituted all the chattel slavery laws not specifically rescinded. The whip and the pillory came back into general use, terrorist groups such as the Black Cavalry, lineal predecessors of the Ku Klux Klan, were formed by the planters to keep the Negro in his place.

"The rebellion has not ceased," Wendell Phillips exclaimed, "it has only changed its weapons. Once it fought, now it intrigues; once it followed Lee in arms, now it follows President Johnson in guile and chicanery; once its headquarters were in Richmond, now it encamps in the White House."

III

The gulf between the policies of Andrew Johnson and Thaddeus Stevens is clear from the terms used to identify them—"restoration" versus "conquered provinces." Where one would restore the Confederate aristocracy to power, the other would not only destroy it but seize its land so that it would never rise again. Where one would withdraw federal troops, the other would retain them as an occupying force until a new political configuration emerged in the South. And where one would leave the Negro subservient, the other would elevate him to new status, if only to make him a counterweight to the Bourbons. Wittingly or unwittingly the Johnson plan for reconstruction preserved the pattern of poverty in modified form; the Stevens plan, in one of its facets, offered an antipoverty program of wide-ranging impact.

"We have turned, or are about to turn, loose four million slaves," said the old commoner on December 18, 1865, "without a hut to shelter them or a cent in their pockets. The infernal laws of slavery have prevented them from acquiring an education, understanding the common laws of contract, or of managing the ordinary business of life. If we do not furnish them with homesteads, and hedge them around with protective laws; if we leave them to the legislation of their late masters, we had better leave them in bondage."

Speaking to his Lancaster constituency a few months before, Stevens had offered a blueprint for accomplishing multiple objectives. Of the six million whites in the South, he pointed out, only 70,000 families owned as much as 200 acres. Their land added to that owned by the states themselves totaled 394,000,000 acres of the 465,000,000 in the area. By confiscating this property the federal government would leave unhurt more than nine-tenths of the southern whites. On the other hand the seizure would refashion the old Confederacy roof and rafter, breaking the back of its oligarchy, and offering the freedmen a basis for survival. Out of the lands to be expropriated Stevens would give the million black families forty acres each, plus $50 in cash. The rest would be sold to provide pensions for

Union soldiers, to reimburse loyalists for lost property, and mostly—
$3 billion in expected revenue—to pay off the national debt.

This proposal caught the spirit of the black man's aspirations, the
glimmer of hope he had clung to, that freedom meant forty acres and
a mule. The federal armies never appeased his hope nor made any
outright grants of farm land during hostilities, but they occasionally
hinted it was in the offing as they seized abandoned plantations or
state lands under the Confiscation Act of 1862. At Port Royal, South
Carolina, for instance, Negroes employed on abandoned estates were
allowed two acres plus an additional five-sixteenths of an acre for
each of their children on which to grow food. Here and there, such as
on the fifteen-square-mile tract of Jefferson Davis, Negroes were
formed into colonies to work the occupied lands, sometimes with a
Negro regiment to protect them. Near Jackson, Mississippi, in 1863
the Federals took over a large estate, advised the slaves they were
now free, gave them weapons, and left them to divide the land among
themselves, using a plowline to measure. As General Sherman
marched to the sea in January 1865, joined by thousands of refugees
almost as numerous as his own army, he issued a special order setting
aside "the islands from Charleston south, the abandoned ricefields
along the rivers for thirty miles back from the sea, and the country
bordering the St. Johns River, Florida . . . for the settlement of Negroes now made free. . . ." Forty thousand were given temporary
title to forty-acre farms and a pledge that permanent title would soon
be forthcoming from Congress. With tens of thousands of black
troops in the federal forces by now and many forming into Negro militias, it did not seem unreasonable to translate this into license for
securing land. A *Chicago Tribune* correspondent concluded after a
trip to the South in 1865 that "there is among the plantation Negroes
a widely spread idea that land is to be given them by the government,
and this idea is at the bottom of much idleness and discontent."
When General Grant proposed to Johnson in December 1865 that
only white troops be stationed in the South he gave as his reason that
the black soldier was "imbued with the idea that the property of his
late master should by right belong to him, or at least should have no
protection from the colored soldier."

Stevens articulated these Negro dreams—according to some historians because he was a Negrophile, according to others because he
was vengeful, and according to still others to keep the Republican

Party in office. Be that as it may, as a man conversant with the mechanism of power, he believed fervidly that his plan had no chance of success unless the 70,000 "proud, bloated, and defiant rebels" were exiled or rendered powerless.

IV

No sooner had Congress reconvened in December 1865 than Stevens and his radical Republicans sought to undo the President's mischief. The elected Confederate leaders, including Alexander Stephens, were denied their seats. Two months later the old commoner, by resolution, established a fifteen-man joint committee of the House and Senate, with himself as chairman, to oversee reconstruction. The resolution took from the President the right to determine when a secessionist state should be readmitted and conferred it on Congress alone. In short order, usually over presidential vetoes, the jubilant radicals put on the books the Civil Rights Act, assuring legal equality to former slaves, the Freedmen's Bureau Act, continuing this relief organization for another two years, and the Fourteenth Amendment, conferring full citizenship on Negroes and guaranteeing them "due process of law." Discarding Johnson's façade of civilian government, Congress divided the ten states (Tennessee was not included) into five military districts, each ruled by a brigadier general—called "satrap" by southern detractors. Twenty thousand soldiers, reinforced by Negro militias formed from demobilized blacks, occupied the "conquered provinces" much as American troops did in Germany and Japan after World War II, acting as the ultimate legal authority. To punctuate congressional sovereignty, the aggressive Stevens machine imposed a Tenure of Office Act in March 1867 prohibiting the President from removing Cabinet officers without consent of the legislature. In this way it sought to prevent him from replacing the militant Secretary of War, Edwin M. Stanton, who was in charge of reconstruction, with someone less fervent.

What followed was a Roman holiday celebrated in history as an orgy of corruption by "carpetbaggers" (white radicals from the North) and "scalawags" (white radicals from the South), but also by solid progress for the Negro. The Black Codes were rescinded. Six governors and thousands of lesser luminaries were removed from office. Military tribunals replaced civilian courts where necessary to guarantee the Negro's safety. Tens of thousands of white rebels were disfranchised and many abstained from voting so that when registration began in 1867 Negroes on the new voting lists outnumbered whites 700,000 to 650,000. The former slaves did not gain political power anywhere, but from 1868 to 1873 they did hold sizable majorities for periods in the lower houses of three states and from 1869 to 1877 were able to elect fourteen federal congressmen and two senators.

Conventions in the ten states, based on the revised electorate, drew up new constitutions considerably more democratic than those they replaced, including such items as abolition of imprisonment for debt, updated bills of rights, universal public education, and similar reforms. Meanwhile too the Bureau of Freedmen, Refugees, and Abandoned Lands, originally set up by Lincoln to constitute, as Senator Sumner put it, a "bridge from slavery to freedom," was building 40 hospitals, doling out 21,000,000 packets of food (one-fourth to poor whites), establishing 4,329 schools for 247,333 Negro pupils, and arranging for tens of thousands of labor contracts that spelled out employer obligations to black employees not accustomed to wage-labor relationships.

Beyond the trenches of government action, the militant mood was sustained by the Union Leagues and Negro militia, who, if they could, would have edged America toward a "third revolution." The leagues, originating in the North about 1862, transferred their locus to the South with war's end, determined to unite whites and blacks into an anti-Confederate party. They enrolled soldiers, workers of the Freedmen's Bureau, poor whites, and above all, ex-slaves. As James S. Allen has noted in his work on reconstruction they were "in some respects similar to the Jacobin Clubs of the French Revolution. They became units of a well disciplined organization and by 1867 played a decisive role in preparing for the new Constitutional Conventions." There were 800 leagues in Virginia alone, holding meetings in Negro churches and schoolhouses, preaching equality, agitating for confiscation of rebel property and division of land among black folk.

Parallel to the leagues were the Negro militia, formed after 1867 under such picturesque names as the "Whangs" or the "Wide-Awakers." They were usually volunteer groups made up of civilian freedmen around a nucleus of former black soldiers who had served with the federal army. In the tense atmosphere of reconstruction the Afro-Americans had much to defend themselves from: during the 1866 riots in Memphis, Charleston, and New Orleans, for instance, literally hundreds of blacks were shot down by police and white mobs—at New Orleans as they gathered for a Republican convention. Some of the provisional governors gave the militias legal status as well as arms when scheduled elections seemed in jeopardy from Bourbon violence. Fourteen regiments of "nigger K.K.K.'s," as southern newsmen called them, were organized under the aegis of the reconstruction government in South Carolina before the 1870 elections, each with 1,000 men.

V

But despite the Freedmen's Bureau, the militia, the leagues, and a sympathetic Congress, the Negro never received his forty acres and a mule—not even in the area around Charleston where General Sherman had promised this to 40,000 freedmen. Stevens introduced a bill for land confiscation in 1867, based on his proposals of two years before, but even he could muster only negligible support for so drastic a measure. At a time when millions of acres of land were being given away in the West, under the Homestead Act and grants to railroads, Congress refused to vote forty acres to the million black families. To cede virgin land that belonged to no one (except the Indian perhaps) was one thing, but to make grants that involved already established property rights, albeit of yesterday's enemy, was something entirely different. Not even Stevens' fellow radicals were ready to tamper with so hallowed an institution as private property. The only access to land for the ex-slave therefore was through purchase, if he had any money, or through lease from the Freedmen's Bureau. Under the first bill creating the Bureau, the War Department was authorized to lease plots of forty acres or less at a rental of 6 per cent the land's value. Since it had acquired only 800,000 acres of "abandoned lands" it could at best accommodate 20,000 blacks, a piddling number against the million landless families crying for farms.

Too much remained unsettled on the American scene for anything so dramatic as Stevens' confiscation plan to have a chance. In Washington the President was trying to remove Stanton from his post as Secretary of War, an act that brought his quarrel with Congress to a boil and resulted in impeachment proceedings. Down South the Bourbons were challenging reconstruction through a host of terrorist groups such as the Ku Klux Klan, the Knights of the White Camellia, the Constitutional Union Guards, the Pale Faces, who formed an invisible empire to punish impudent carpetbaggers and Negroes. The number of murders they committed ran into the thousands—in 1871, for instance, 300 were killed near New Orleans alone, 163 in one Florida county. The Grant Administration, of course, took countermeasures. It dissolved the Klan in 1869 and the Knights of the White Camellia the following year. It had Enforcement Acts passed in 1870 and 1871, but the number of whites convicted for violence was relatively small and the intimidation continued. From 1870 to 1876 only 1,208 were adjudged guilty—mostly in Mississippi and South Carolina, where the radicals still held sway—while more than twice that many went free.

Up North, too, radical passions were cooling. The rampaging financiers, hailed in history as the Robber Barons, were not particularly interested in the black man's welfare—were in fact a little afraid he might form an alliance with poor-white laborers above the Mason-Dixon line to thwart their ambitions. And these sentiments steadily penetrated Republican ranks. In 1870–71 the radicals registered their last victories, with the Enforcement Acts and the Fifteenth Amendment guaranteeing the right to vote. Simultaneously, however, Congress passed a generous new amnesty reducing the number of ex-rebels barred from office from 150,000 to fewer than 500. When Grant refused to dispatch forces to checkmate the riotous Klan in North Carolina and Klansmen seized by Negro and mountaineer militiamen were freed by the courts, the game was virtually over.

The white supremacists regained in peace what they had lost in war. As Wendell Phillips had foreseen, "land dictates government," and the failure to deprive the Bourbons of their economic base, though they were much chastened and weakened, gave them an opportunity to recoup their losses. In 1869 Tennessee was retaken politically by the dominant whites; by 1876 all but three of the eleven Confederate states were back in business, sovereign and racist.

VI

In August 1865 nine hundred black men meeting near Mobile to discuss their circumstances had concluded by a vote of 700 to 200, in the words of the *Montgomery Advertiser*, "that the freedom which the war had bequeathed to them" was "far from being so flattering as their imagination had painted it." Negroes, "no more than white men, can live without work, or be comfortable without homes." Their northern deliverers, said the black conclave, "had not, as they had expected and been taught to expect, undertaken to provide for their happy existence in their new state of freedom." The only alternative was "to return to the homes which they had abandoned in a moment of excitement, and go to work again under their old masters."

Physical liberation and liberation from poverty, it became apparent in the next quarter of a century, were not the same thing. In point of fact the black man was back in bondage differing only slightly from the past, and in some ways worse. Frederick Douglass could report after a tour of the South in 1888: "The same class that once extorted his [the Negro's] labor under the lash, now extorts his labor by a mean, sneaking, and fraudulent device which is more effective than the lash. That device is the trucking system, a system which never permits him to see or save a dollar of his hard earnings. . . . The highest wages paid him are eight dollars a month, and this he receives only in orders on a store which in many cases is owned by his employer. The scrip has a purchasing power on that one store, and that one store only. A blind man can see that by this arrangement the laborer is bound hand and foot, and he is completely in the power of his employer."

With the aid of the courts and unpunished terror the South was recast in its racist image. Judge J. J. Chrisman, a man of the old school, conceded in 1890 that there had not been a fair vote in Mississippi since 1875: "in plain words, we have been stuffing ballot-boxes, committing perjury and here and there in the State carrying the elections by fraud and violence." Not atypical was the murder of 30 Negroes in the 1878 elections in the state of Louisiana. From 1889 to 1918 some 2,522 Afro-Americans were lynched in southern byways. A new term began to crowd the American lexicon, Jim Crow, its derivation going back to a popular blackface actor in a minstrel show of the 1830's. Negroes were Jim Crowed—segregated—on passenger trains, in waiting rooms, restaurants, hospitals, everywhere. Negro nurses were forbidden to treat white patients, and white nurses black patients. In the well-known Plessy v. Ferguson decision of 1896 the Supreme Court upheld the doctrine of "separate but equal." The states were not required to integrate schools or other facilities so long as facilities were "equal," which in practice almost always meant inferior. In a number of respects, for instance insofar as the prison system was concerned, conditions had grown worse than in the heyday of slavery. Black prisoners, instead of being sent to jail, were leased out to favored politicians, then subleased to farms and factories as unpaid labor. Whipping and other forms of punishment cut the life span of such prisoners so that 32 per cent died annually in Arkansas in 1887, 16 per cent in Mississippi. It was not until 1918 that this convict-lease system was abrogated.

A half century after the Civil War half the Negroes of the nation were still illiterate. Some three-quarters of Negro farmers were sharecroppers or tenants, paying half or more of their crop to a white landlord in return for using his land, mule, and plow. Only the least desirable jobs went to the descendants of slaves, as attested to by the fact that one-third of those employed were domestic servants. "The percentage of skilled Negro craftsmen," write Herbert Hill and Jack Greenberg, "was much smaller than it had been in 1865."

A dark gloom settled over Negro America.

Chapter 11

FARMING THE FARMERS

The year Lincoln promulgated the Emancipation Proclamation, 1862, he also signed the Homestead Act, and agreed to a measure, passed by Congress, to complete the transcontinental railroad. Freedom for the slave, free land, and the wonderful iron horse—so popular with the poor people at the time—these should have formed a triangular partnership against poverty to make the devil quake. Each was the kind of vision a nation is lucky to have once in a generation, let alone three in one year. But three decades later the ex-slave and the western farmer were, each in his own way, mired in the lower depths, and the railroad had graduated to the most hated institution in American history. There was a touch of irony to all this. The Negro remained poor because he could not get "forty acres" of his old master's plantation; the farmer generally remained poor even though he was entitled to 160 acres free under homestead. The railroad promoters were incredibly rich even though theirs was to have been only an auxiliary service.

The Homestead Law, deriving from the Vote Yourself a Farm agitation of George Henry Evans in the 1840's and high on the Republican Party order of priorities, assigned to every citizen who wanted it 160 acres of the public domain, at no cost whatsoever, on the single condition that he live on it for five years. The domain beyond the

Mississippi was so vast it should have assured the nation and its people freedom from want. As Evans and Horace Greeley originally outlined it, land reform would have the double effect of quashing poverty for those who migrated, since they would flourish on their own farms, as well as for the workers who stayed behind, since their bargaining power vis-à-vis their employers would be greatly augmented. Evans, of course, included two provisions in his program that the law omitted, inalienability and limitation of holdings—he would have had it that no land could be attached for mortgage or loan, and that no one could own more than a specified number of acres. Nonetheless the jubilant Republicans who passed the 1862 bill did so convinced that their half loaf would achieve its purpose. Senator Ben Wade—the man who almost became President in 1868—called it "the greatest measure I know of to mold in the right direction the Territories belonging to this nation; to build up a free yeomanry capable of maintaining a republican Government forever."

They might have been justified in this expectation if nothing else had intervened to subvert the law. The trouble was, however, that the Homestead Act was hedged, surrounded, and undermined by other bills and executive decisions that made it impotent, a dessicated reed against a steam roller. A "free yeomanry" did emerge in the sense that millions of additional families gained title to land, but not in the Jeffersonian meaning of a constituency of equals. Until the last few years of the century and the early part of the next, the free yeoman in fact was a pygmy encircled by giants and squeezed mercilessly. There was, first and foremost, the railroad, but there were also the speculator, the mortgage holder, the merchant, the grain-elevator man, the political manipulators who did tricks with money, all conspiring to reduce the farmer to bare subsistence, and on occasion, bankruptcy. During the three decades after the Civil War, the agrarians, as Harold U. Faulkner has recorded, "were in an almost continuous condition of revolt."

As legal documents, the Homestead Act and the bills that supplemented it were among the most generous pieces of legislation on behalf of the common man the American Congress has ever passed. Under the original law, a citizen had only to wait until the government had surveyed the land to stake his claim for a quarter section. If he decided against remaining for five years, he had the right to "commute," purchase the 160 acres outright for $1.25 to $2.50 an acre, and then rent or resell it at will. In the ensuing years Congress sweetened the bill with free-hearted addenda. A timber culture act of 1873 offered an additional 160 acres to anyone who would plant trees on part of his holding. Under a desert land bill of 1877, a settler could acquire 640 acres of dry land at $1.25 each (25 cents down and $1 in three years) if he agreed to irrigate it. Under the timber and stone act the following year, lands valuable for these items, rather than for tillage, could be bought in lots of 160 acres at the appraised value or for $2.50 an acre. In addition, the old pre-emption act of 1841 was still on the books, by which a person could secure 160 acres at $1.25 an acre. A bonanza presumably awaited any hardy soul following Greeley's advice to "go West."

All the other barometers also seemed propitious for rural affluence. On the technological front American inventors designed barbed wire for fencing material, a pivotal development in the prairies, for without it they might still belong to the cowboys and the roaming herds. The windmill partially solved the problem of water. The reaper, the twine binder, the combine, the bundle carrier, the straddle-row cultivator, the seeder, and many other machines made it possible to augment production of grain from 5.6 bushels for every person in the nation in 1860 to 9.2 bushels in 1880. The railroad, simplifying both travel and marketing, increased its trackage from 35,000 miles to 200,000 miles at the turn of the century. The economy, despite the usual interruptions for depressions, was in an unparalleled upswing—population doubled from 1860 to 1890, wealth quadrupled, industrial production was five times as high and deposits in saving banks ten times.

Yet against this background, the western farmer failed to reap his harvest. To begin with, he found himself arrayed against natural adversities more formidable than he had anticipated. If he was an early settler he might be lucky enough to build a log home on a river or creek bottom. More likely, however, he found timber in short supply and had to settle for a sod house half buried in the ground and little more than a dugout. Not only was life rudimentary but it posed constant problems, such as gathering wood for heat (in Kansas many had to substitute sunflower stalks; elsewhere some had to rely on buffalo chips) and finding a supply of water. Fred Albert Shannon, in his *Farmer's Last Frontier*, tells of a Nebraskan who had to dig two miles of wells in the course of thirty years, one of them 280 feet deep. In the northernmost states heavy snowfalls buried homes and barns during the winter for long periods, constituting a serious threat to frontiersmen living in isolated circumstances.

Once a few meager amenities were assured there were other hazards to contend with. There were the blizzards to which many of the immigrants from Europe were not accustomed. The rivers were found to be especially treacherous, often flooding and sometimes wiping out new communities. Warm winds played havoc with wheat and corn at certain stages, and prairie fires sometimes swept everything in their path into oblivion. In addition there were the dust storms which blew for days on end, forcing men and women to wear wet cloths on their faces even inside their homes in order to breathe. There were the buffalo herds stampeding over dry land and, perhaps most frustrating of all, the periodic grasshopper plagues, such as those over the Dakota Territory, Nebraska, Kansas, and parts of Texas in 1874, 1875, and 1876. Carried in by the wind, the grasshoppers were so numerous their weight actually broke the limbs of trees, and they ate everything in sight from onions to wheat, corn, plow handles, and pitchforks. It was said of these pests that "two new grasshoppers arrived to attend each dead one's funeral." Though the pestilences lasted only a few days to two weeks, they so polluted streams and wells that by the time they lifted both men and animals faced dire prospects. The insects were such a menace that Minnesota paid fifty cents a bushel for those caught and burned, Nebraska mobilized all able-bodied men to fight them, and many states plus the federal government raised considerable sums for the relief of farmers caught in their path—an unusual step at the time.

It wasn't only Mother Nature, however, or the bleak circumstances of early home-building that harried the homesteader in the last third of the nineteenth century. The only crop raised in eastern Colorado for many years, it was said not too facetiously, was "bankrupts"; and this was primarily due not to natural mishaps but to the manipulations of railroaders, landboomers, financiers, and a host of others. Placards such as "In God we trusted, in Kansas we busted," and "Going back to the wife's folks," appeared on covered wagons returning eastward in the 1880's and 1890's. This 1889 rhyme of the Farmers Alliance expressed a widespread disenchantment:

> There are ninety and nine who live and die
>   In want, and hunger, and cold.
> That one may live in luxury
>   And be wrapped in silken fold.
> The ninety and nine in hovels bare,
> The one in a palace with riches rare.

What went wrong? According to farm leaders many things, among them:

1. Monopolization of the land, despite homestead, by the railroads and speculators.
2. Overpopulation and overproduction.
3. The extortionate practices of the railroads.
4. The machinations of mortgage holders, grain-elevator men, and merchants.
5. "Expensive" money.

II

It is generally agreed that the settlement of the West was too rapid, too chaotic, too disorderly, too planless. Back in 1827, when the public domain was considerably smaller than it was destined to become with the annexation of Texas, California, and other spoils of the Mexican War, Secretary of the Treasury Richard Rush estimated it would take five hundred years to inhabit it effectively. Settlement was actually accomplished in one-eighth the time in a considerably larger territory. Everyone, it seems, wanted the West occupied quickly. The government for obvious geopolitical reasons preferred to have its open spaces inhabited, and not only was willing to subsidize the railroads to further this goal, but winked an eye at bribery, fraud, and corruption. The railroads wanted to handle the additional passenger and freight traffic, as well as to sell the enormous lands they received as subsidy for laying tracks. The speculators were guided by the usual profit motive. Before the steam roller of these convergent interests the homestead principle was all but pulverized; it was of only marginal significance in frontier history.

The reason was that the best lands and the largest acreage were being siphoned off elsewhere. The popular image of how the West was settled comes from such books as Edna Ferber's *Cimarron*. There is the drama of 20,000 "boomers" in 1889, waiting for the gun to go off to send them on the race for 6,000 homesteads in the Oklahoma District recently purchased from the Indians. And there is the disappointment of some as they discover that the "sooners" had slithered in before them, without waiting for the pistol shot. But the game actually was not played that way—at least not until 1890, when the frontier was considered closed. By and large the millions who took Greeley's advice did not get their land free but bought it from an intermediary as the following figures illustrate. The number of farms in the United States soared from 2,000,000 in 1860 to 4,000,000 in 1880 and 5,750,000 by 1900. Improved acreage doubled, from 400,000,000 to 800,000,000, an increase in farmland three times the size of France. But as of 1890 only 377,000 families had claimed a mere 48,000,000 acres under the Homestead Act, and one-quarter of this had been commuted. It is doubtful if in these twenty-eight years as many as a million people benefited from the law, a meager number considering that the population of the nation had risen by thirty millions in the meantime.

By contrast the railroads and speculators gained title to at least a half billion acres. Some of this vast estate was secured through fraud, of course, but most of it, however ill-advised, was made available to them in perfectly legitimate ways. Under the Morrill Act, for instance, the government assigned 140,000,000 acres to the states as endowments for agricultural colleges. The states in turn could have disposed of them in small tracts, directly to the settler, but it was easier to put them on the market in large parcels, a method clearly favorable to the land jobber. Similarly, the reservation lands seized from the Indians in the various wars against them were usually sold in big blocks—until the Dawes Severalty Act of 1887—instead of to potential settlers. Ingenious men, in addition, could find a host of ways to evade the Homestead Act. One of the law's provisions called for government surveys before the land could be put up for claim. Speculators, moving ahead of the surveyors, simply purchased the best sites under the pre-emption law of 1841, still in existence. Another means, used on a wide scale and winked at by public land officials for "a consideration," was to register titles in the name of dummy entrants. That the public land office was less than exemplary is evidenced by such statements as this one by a federal land commissioner in 1885: "The widespread belief . . . that the land department has been very largely conducted to the advantage of speculation and monopoly, I have found supported by developments in every branch of the service." When Teddy Roosevelt's National Conservation Commission in 1909 reviewed what had happened to the timber and stone law, it found that giant corporations like the Sierra Lumber Company and the Montana Improvement Company had gobbled up for $30,000,000 "timber worth at a very conservative estimate $300,000,000."

The railroads, however, were far and away the greatest beneficiaries of federal and local generosity, for they received their lands free, in addition to what amounted to monopolistic charters, loans, and other emoluments. The carriers were nurtured like delicate orchids—though, it must be admitted, not without popular approval.

From 1850 to 1871 they were plied with gifts of 200,000,000 acres of choice lands, usually alternate sections five to twenty miles on either side of the line. Though the gratuity was pared down to 137,000,000 acres because some of the corporations failed to carry out their share of the bargain, it was still an empire as large as France, five times the size of New York State. The one grant to Northern Pacific alone in 1864 was equal in area to that of the six New England states. According to the governor of Kansas, 80 per cent of the municipal debt in his state in 1888 was committed to spur-railroad construction. Mitchell County offered $180,000 to the Sante Fe to run its line through its territory. Jewel County paid a bounty of $95,000 to the Rock Island. Faulkner estimates that the benefactions "included one-fourth of the states of Minnesota and Washington; one-fifth of Wisconsin, Iowa, Kansas, North Dakota, and Montana; one-seventh of Nebraska, one-eighth of California, and one-ninth of Louisiana."

A considerable part of the public domain, then, was outside the pale of free pre-emption; and when one adds to this the fact that the Homestead Law did not apply to the alternate sections paralleling those given to railroads, which remained government property, the availability of well-situated free land was considerably reduced.

Thus the trend was for migrants to buy their holdings rather than stake a claim. In this, of course, they were encouraged by the carriers, who competed vigorously for the hundreds of thousands of families moving westward. Beguiling advertisements, not unlike those of the newlanders and crimps of colonial days, promised paradise on a gold platter, and offered irresistible services and credit terms. Sante Fe, in offering 2,500,000 acres of Kansas, "proved" with statistics that a man who invested $8,000 in cattle could earn $11,000 profit—more than 133 per cent—each year. Illinois Central boasted that the million acres "of superior farming lands" it was putting up for purchase were situated near "towns, villages, schools and churches," and definitely were "not surpassed by any in the world." The Burlington and Missouri quoted one of its clients to the effect that while he had not "taken much stock in the stories of wonderfully cheap homes in the West" before, he now saw with his own eyes people "living almost in affluence on their prairie farms, who I know left New York State only a few years ago with next to nothing." Settlers concerned about the dry climate in some areas were told fairy tales about rainfall moving westward to make Edens out of deserts. "These vast extents of plowed land," read one advertisement, "not only create a rainfall by their evaporation, but invite rains by their contrasts of temperature." Rhapsodic—but purely fictional— figures were adduced to show that Nebraska, say, was just as wet as Illinois. "Follow prairie dogs and Mormons," read one enthusiastic brochure, "and you will find good land" that would yield 30 bushels of wheat or 70 of corn per acre.

The carriers added kindly deeds to their mellifluous words. Burlington, for instance, furnished round-trip fares at three-fifths the normal rate for would-be land buyers, and a partial rebate if the sale was consummated. Prices varied, but were usually modest, considering the potential. Burlington averaged $5.14 an acre for its Nebraska lands, some of it put on the block for as little as twenty-five cents. Illinois Central's "superior" lands went for $8 to $12. William A. Peffer, a farm leader unsympathetic to the railroads, wrote in 1891 that the average purchase price from the carriers was "about $3 an acre upon the payment of a small portion cash—10 percent or thereabouts." Since the railroads were more interested in settlement than immediate revenue they also proffered alluring credit terms. The man without cash could arrange "long credit" of ten years, paying only 6 per cent interest and none of the principal in the first two years. Or he could have "short credit" for three years at considerably lower cost. With such enticements the trans-Mississippi territories swelled with migrants. The four grain areas—Minnesota, Dakota, Nebraska, and Kansas—inflated from 300,000 to nearly a million by 1870 and two and a half million by 1880.

The expansion began, however, during the war, when demand for farm products was high, currency inflated, and prices soaring. It continued, stimulated by railroad and other propaganda, under less propitious circumstances, while supply was outstripping demand, greenbacks were being called in, and prices were falling. The hopeful came, Allan Nevins tells us, "by thousands in almost penniless estate, with few tools, little household furniture and no conveniences. Many lived for years in dugouts, an excavation perhaps a dozen feet wide in the side of a hill, roofed with lumber and sod, and walled with sod, logs or stone." They cleared the land, planted it, and harvested the crop, working sunup to sundown 365 days a year. But how were they to know about such esoteric phenomena as overproduction—that the more they grew, the more they were depressing prices? "We were told two years ago," cried a Kansas orator around 1890, "to go to work and raise a big crop, that was all we needed. We went to work and plowed and planted; the rains fell, the sun shone, nature smiled, and we raised the big crop that they told us to; and what came of it? Eight cent corn, ten cent oats, two cent beef and no price at all for butter and eggs—that's what came of it. Then the politicians said that we suffered from overproduction."

There were good years and bad years, but Department of Agriculture statistics show that cotton fell relentlessly, from 15.1 cents per pound in 1870–73 to 5.8 in 1894–97. Corn was 75.3 cents in 1869, 54.9 in 1870, and 28.3 in 1889. Oats were 43.3 cents in 1870, 22.9 in 1889; wheat $1.04 in the earlier year and 69.8 cents in the latter one. The farmer's problem, summarized Henry R. Chamberlain, was "to make two spears of grass grow where one grew before. He solved that. Now he is struggling hopelessly with the question how to get as much for two spears of grass as he used to get for one." The plight of the western farmer is conveyed in a single dry statistic: in 1867, a crop of 1.3 billion bushels of cereals (corn, wheat, rye, oats, barley, and buckwheat) was raised on 66 million acres and brought $1.3 billion return; in 1887 the crop was twice as large (2.7 billion bushels), grown on 142 million acres, but it brought in less money—$1.2 billion.

The farmer just was not organized to cope with his problem. A manufacturer could regulate his production, to an extent at least, to conform with the market. Even a laborer could withhold his labor —go on strike—if the price offered for it, the wage, was inadequate. But the individual farmer was caught in a double bind. He had no control over either the size of the crop or the demand for it. Drought or locust plague sometimes reduced the harvest to the vanishing point; increased competition from foreign states during the 1880's plunged the price of corn down from a peak of 63 cents in 1881 to 28 cents in 1890, wheat from $1.19 to 73 cents.

No matter which way the pendulum swung, the American farmer seemed to be at the wrong end. Prices boomed during and immediately after the Civil War, in part because so many tillers were at the front, in part because the government had issued hundreds of millions of unsecured greenbacks, depreciating the value of money; and high prices drew migrants to the West like a magnet. But by 1870 the supply of commodities had overtaken demand, and deflation—due to the redemption of money and bonds in gold, and the circulation of specie—forced the farmer to repay in "hard" money what he had borrowed in "soft" money. Thus while the industrial sector of the nation was enjoying a rampant prosperity from 1870 to 1873, the farmer languished on the sidelines. The enervating depression that followed, however, from 1873 to 1879, caught him square in the midriff. By the time the economy had returned from the doldrums, the overpopulated West faced a new antagonist: greatly expanded competition from Australia, Argentina, Russia, and Canada in the world market. The expected profits from bumper wheat crops in 1882 and 1884 were canceled out by a big drop in exports, causing a corresponding downturn in domestic prices. Finally, after 1887, drought set in in Nebraska, Kansas, and South Dakota. Where rainfall had averaged 21.63 inches in previous years, during the next decade it sometimes fell to as little as two or three inches. According to Hallie Farmer, "settlers who had taken up claims in Cheyenne County, Nebraska, in 1886 harvested no crop until 1893." The state as a whole produced 129,000,000 bushels of corn in 1885 but a mere 13,000,000 in 1894. The increase in prices did not begin to compensate, unfortunately, for the catastrophic fall in supply. "Whereas in 1880," writes Arthur M. Schlesinger, "the value of farms just equaled that of urban real estate, ten years later city real estate had advanced to double the value of farm land. The difference was even greater if other forms of property were included. A contemporary economist estimated that in 1890 the average wealth of rural families did not exceed $3,250 while that of urban families surpassed $9,000."

Surveying the wreckage of early aspirations, Mary Elizabeth Lease, the Populist firebrand from Wichita, Kansas, advised farmers "to raise less corn and more hell."

III

The problem of overpopulation, dire as it was, somehow did not raise agrarian hackles in the same way as the more direct burdens imposed by the railroads and the mortgage holders—perhaps because the latter were so visible. "There are three great crops in Nebraska," a farmer wrote in 1890. "One is a crop of corn, one a crop of freight rates, and one a crop of interest. One is produced by farmers who by sweat and toil farm the land. The other two are produced by men who sit in their offices and behind their bank counters and farm the farmers."

The farmers hailed the railroads originally as friend and ally. Innumerable yeomen invested in railroad stocks, often mortgaging their farms to do so, and local communities offered sizable bounties to have the lines run through their territories. Two hundred and ninety-four towns, cities, and counties in New York State presented the carriers with a total of $30,000,000 to run tracks through their area, cognizant of the fact that access to transportation added value to their property. Similarly, the land grants by the federal government for transcontinental lines were at first considered sound investments, in the best public interest. Laborious and dangerous trips, once taken in covered wagons, would soon be made in the modest luxury of a coach pulled by the "iron horse." The railroads also meant that farmers could send their crops to Chicago or the eastern seaboard with dispatch unknown before. It says something of the early popularity of the railroads that Ignatius Donnelly of Minnesota, a leading figure of the agrarian revolt for decades, felt no pangs of conscience when as a young congressman he took a $10,000 "gift" from the Lake Superior and Mississippi Railroad Company. Encouraging the railroads was a means of settling the state, and on this there was a harmony of interest.

It soon became apparent, however, that the railroad promoters were bribing and manipulating their way to riches on a scale unmatched before, with the cost of their inflated construction charges, bribes to legislators, watered stocks, and fraudulent bankruptcies all passed on to the public—and in particular the farmers—in higher freight rates. Not all of them were as callous as Cornelius Vanderbilt ("What do I care about law? Hain't I got the power?") or Jay Gould ("I can hire one half of the working class to kill the other half"); some, like James J. Hill of the Great Northern, performed valuable services for the farmer, such as promoting foreign markets, teaching modern methods of tillage and road building, providing information on credit. But generally speaking, the robber barons, of whom the rail tycoons were the hard core, were unconscionable in their depredations. Typically, an investigating committee in Wisconsin found that the La Crosse and Milwaukee Railroad had passed around a million dollars in bonds and cash to thirteen senators, thirty assemblymen, the governor ($50,000), and various newsmen to assure a land grant valued at $17,000,000.

The Crédit Mobilier scandal, exposed in 1872, was an extreme example of corruption on the national level, but differed only in details from similar practices on a more modest scale locally. A month and a half after Lincoln signed the Homestead Act, Congress took steps to complete a transcontinental system, entrusting the section from Omaha to California to the specially organized Union Pacific, in which Congressman Oakes Ames of Massachusetts was the key figure. The federal legislature was more than lavish in its endowment. It gave the road 200 feet of right of way for hundreds of miles, the right to use whatever wood, stone, and other materials it found nearby, gifts of alternate sections of land running 20 miles on either side of the tracks, and credits of $16,000 to $48,000 for each mile of track laid. That Congress should be so considerate of a firm that could raise a bare half million dollars on its own is perhaps explained by the fact that Ames spread around $436,000 where it would "do the most good," and promised instant wealth to a host of legislative insiders such as the prominent Senator James G. Blaine and a future President, James A. Garfield. Not content with this beneficence, however, the promoters assigned construction of the line to a company with a fancy French name, Crédit Mobilier, which they controlled. The profit—or loot, whichever you will—from this shady transaction was $44,000,000: it cost $50,000,000 to build the road, but Union Pacific and behind it the federal government and first-mortgage bondholders were charged $94 million. Ames was not wrong when he told envious friends he had hit "a diamond mine."

This was a common practice in the nineteenth-century railroad boom. Central Pacific paid a construction firm dominated by its leading stockholders $120,000,000 to do work that cost $58,000,000. Another means of mulcting the public was to water the stock. Erie Railroad, for instance, boosted its capitalization from $17,000,000 to $78,000,000 with no appreciable assets to show for it. New York Central, it was said, added $50,000 of "absolute water" for every mile of track from New York to Buffalo. In Kansas stock certificates of $300,000,000 were issued for 8,000 miles of rail laid at a cost of $100,000,000. The *Commercial and Financial Chronicle* of May 15, 1869, noted that twenty-eight corporations had increased their capital value in less than two years by 40 per cent.

It was a display of unbridled brigandage that might have been curbed if the promoters had not secured their flanks not only by bribery but by a deep foray into politics. The carriers had their governors in many a state house, both East and West, and senators and congressmen by the bushel at the federal level. Historians are agreed that until the agrarian revolt became strong enough to alter the situation, every western state at one time or another was in the vest pocket of the carriers. Union Pacific and Burlington were joint sovereigns of Nebraska, Santa Fe ran Kansas. At state nominating conventions of both parties, enough hard cash was spread around to guarantee friendly auspices in key places. Passes for free travel were doled out to pliant governors, judges, and legislators with extreme generosity, and newsmen and other influential figures were wooed avidly to guarantee a favorable climate for the rails. "Do they not control the newspapers?" asked the *Progressive Farmer* rhetorically in 1889. "Are not all the politicians their dependents? Has not every Judge in the state a free pass in his pocket? Do they not control all the best legal talent in the State?"

Someone had to pay for the corruption and the excessive profits. The farmer was the obvious choice, since there was little he could do about it. Most of the railroads held monopolies in their territories, and where they did not, they made "pooling" arrangements with competitors to maintain uniform high charges. The farmer therefore was almost totally in their power, subject to high and discriminatory freight rates that kept him shackled to poverty. To ship a bushel of corn to market from Kansas, Nebraska, or Iowa cost the equivalent of another bushel in transport costs, sometimes much more. At a time when corn was 70 cents in the East in 1869, shipping charges from the Mississippi Valley were 52½ cents, leaving the farmer 17½ cents for his product. The *Prairie Farmer* of November 30, 1867, lamented that rates for delivering shelled corn from Iowa to Liverpool were eight or ten times as much as the farmer got for it at his home town elevator. Simultaneously rules were imposed, highly unfavorable to the small farmer. Short hauls were sometimes more expensive than longer ones: wheat, for instance, could be transported from Minneapolis to Chicago for half as much as from Fargo to Duluth, though the distance was twice as far. To prevent the farmer from transferring his produce at a large city to another railroad—at lower cost, perhaps—the carriers insisted that he pay through rates in advance. Even if he had no intention of sending his crop beyond the first big city, he was nonetheless forced to pay for the longer trip. Thus if he wanted to ship wheat from Dakota to Minneapolis he had to pay charges through to Milwaukee, about double the cost, and then try to sell his "transit" right to someone else—usually at a quarter to a half what he paid for it. A rule of the Hill system in the 1880's, emulated by others, provided that grain be gathered in elevators "of at least 30,000 bushels, or cars will not be furnished." Large shippers in league with the carriers received substantial rebates; the small farmer paid the normal price.

At a time when corn brought eighty cents or a dollar a bushel in eastern markets, Iowa farmers were burning it, in lieu of coal, because they were offered only fifteen cents. "How long," cried a Minnesota publication, "even with these cheap and wonderfully productive lands, can . . . any agricultural community pay such enormous tribute to corporate organizations in times like these, without final exhaustion." A letter by a farmer from Muscotah, Kansas, to the *Chicago Tribune* (November 17, 1887) read: "Take whatever course he may, the farmer at the end, toils chiefly for the various organized representatives of capital that crouch and wait and gamble for his surplus earnings. They have only half a crop. The railroad gets half of that for transportation and the crop is sold for half price. . . . Then for lumber, salt, and machinery the farmer pays 25 percent above the cost of production to the manufacturer and 50 percent of the value to the railroad to bring them from the place of production."

IV

Not too far behind the railroads as the object of agrarian wrath were the mortgage holders and merchants. The farmer, beset on many sides, was like the compulsive loser at a roulette table, hoping for one more spin of the wheel to put him back in the game. For this he needed credit—to pay off last year's debts, buy new equipment, or build a barn—and fortunately there were enough loose funds back East to more than fill his needs. Indeed there were agents in each town engaged in a sprightly business, on a commission basis, negotiating loans between the settlers and eastern moneylenders. Massachusetts mortgagors, it is estimated, loaned western tillers $8,000,000 to $12,000,000 annually. New Hampshire, sparsely settled though it was, nonetheless held $25,000,000 in trans-Mississippi land mortgages as of 1899. The amounts from citizens in states like New York, of course, were very much larger. The notes, beautifully embossed in gold and green ink, were meant to reassure the farmer that his credit was good and life was worth another gamble, either in new machinery or additional acreage. In the Dakotas, Kansas, Minnesota, and Nebraska by 1887 there was an average of more than one mortgage per family, and the total indebtedness per capita was three times what it had been seven years earlier. Everyone seemed happy, the farmer because he had money to dam the dikes against adversity, the investor because he was getting 6 to 10 per cent on real estate, and 10 to 18—and more—on chattel mortgages.

The trouble with this system was that rural America in the last third of the nineteenth century was too amenable to cycles of boom and bust. When the farm economy was lively and land values rising, investors were ready with mortgage money. But when the inevitable retrograde set in, the money well dried up and the farmer was left near bankruptcy. The worst of these boom-bust cycles came to a head in the prairie states in 1887, and was indicative of what a farm community had to contend with.

The year began with wild speculation. A farm purchased in Abilene, Kansas, for $6.25 an acre in 1867 was peddled twenty years later for $270 an acre. Land three miles from the center of Kansas City exchanged hands for $5,000 an acre, and seven miles out for $1,500. A Wichita clerk bought a lot for $200 one day and sold it two months later for $2,000. To double what one paid for land in 1881, or even quadruple it, was considered unexceptional. The exhilaration of anticipated profits brought 35,000 people to Wichita from January to May 1887 alone, and resulted in real estate sales of $35,000,000, a pace of business exceeded only in New York City. "Nothing causes the Nebraska farmer more dismay," wrote the editor of the *Nebraska State Journal* with wry humor, "than to return from town after spending a few hours there, and find that his farm has been converted into a thriving city with street cars and electric lights during his absence. But such things will occur now and then and should be regarded with comparative calmness." Within a few weeks the joke had turned sour as it became apparent in the summer of 1887 that the crop that year would be a disaster.

As farmers, with a short crop on hand, found themselves unable to meet their loans, land values dropped as quickly as they had risen, and not a few speculators went under along with their clients. Yeomen sold their cattle for anything they could get, sought chattel mortgages on machinery, horses, or any other property, at interest rates—appropriately increased, since credit was now in short supply —of 20 to 36 per cent. It was not enough, however. In Kansas, the state with the biggest boom and loudest bust, 11,122 foreclosures took place from 1889 to 1893. By 1895 there were fifteen counties where between 76 and 90 per cent of the land had fallen into the hands of loan companies. This was the period when 180,000 inhabitants deserted the state, "going back to the wife's folks," or somewhere else where help was available. Twenty towns were totally depopulated. Though it was not so dismal in other frontier states, the disaster ruined tens of thousands at its epicenter.

A letter to the *Farmers' Alliance* of Lincoln, Nebraska, dated January 10, 1891, tells a not too uncommon story: "The hot winds burned up the entire crop, leaving thousands of families wholly destitute, many of whom might have been able to run through this crisis had it not been for the galling yoke put on them by the money loaners and sharks—not by charging seven percent per annum, which is the lawful rate of interest, or even ten percent, but the unlawful and inhuman country-destroying-rate of three percent a month, some going still farther and charging fifty percent per annum. We are cursed, many of us financially, beyond redemption, not by the hot winds so much as by the swindling games of the bankers and money loaners, who have taken the money and now are after the property, leaving the farmer moneyless and homeless. . . ." Many a moneylender, especially the smaller ones, also went broke but, as this letter indicates, misfortune weighed heaviest on the farmer.

V

The credit system in the southern states operated differently from that in the West but with effects that were, if anything, more enervating. In the shakedown that followed civil war and reconstruction, large holdings were broken up into small units of twenty to fifty acres, some of them purchased by poor whites and ex-slaves, but most of them operated by tenants and sharecroppers. The outright tenant, a minority of this nonowning group, simply paid an annual rent, provided his own tools, seeds, and animals, and kept the crop. The sharecropper, who constituted by far the largest number, leased a "one-horse" or "two-horse" farm (fifteen to forty acres) and received from the landlord the seed, tools, horse or mule to operate it. For this he paid the landlord one half of the cotton or corn he produced; or if he had contributed some of his own animals and tools, one fourth to one third.

It was, of course, a system of marginal farming in which the producer was in constant need of credit to keep alive, but there was no credit accessible from the usual sources. In prewar days the plantation owner borrowed from his cotton factor or the banks. In the West the farmer, poor as he was, could put up his land or machinery for security. But the sharecropper had no property on which to attach a mortgage. Banking in fact became a lost art in the South for a while; as of 1895 there were only 417 national banks in the ten cotton states. More than half the counties in Georgia had none.

Credit was provided, however, in a more primitive form—from the merchant. In return for a lien on the future cotton crop the store owner advanced merchandise to the share tenant until harvesttime, when the crop was brought to the merchant for marketing. No interest was charged but it was generally understood that the tradesman had a two-price system, one for cash and one for credit. Matthew B. Hammond, writing in 1897 after talking with southern store owners, estimated that "prices on a credit schedule are usually from twenty to fifty percent higher than those on a cash schedule. Thus flour selling at $4 per barrel to cash buyers sells for $5 on a credit basis; bacon selling at 10¢ a pound, cash, for 12½¢ 'on time.'" Since the average period of the "loan" was six months, that was in fact 40 to 100 per cent interest per year.

The corollary of this form of credit was a permanent control over the sharecropper's economic life which virtually reduced him to peonage. He had to consult his merchant on what crops he could grow, agree to market them only through the one store owner with whom he did business, and to buy everything he needed from him as well. Since he was never entirely out of debt he lived from year to year under this unfavorable arrangement, seldom seeing any cash, never more than one step from destitution. "Estimates differ," writes John D. Hicks, "but probably from three-fourths to nine-tenths of the farmers of the cotton South were ensnared to a greater or less degree by the crop-lien system."

VI

Just as a rundown body is susceptible to a virus, so the farmer— South and North—in this critical period was susceptible to economic manipulation. Some of it was patent, some subtle. One of the oft-heard complaints in the West was about "grading." Agricultural commodities naturally were of different qualities, or grades. Wheat, for instance, which qualified as "number one hard" had to weigh 58 pounds to a bushel, show good color, be clean, pure, and hard. Since the elevator owners in each town usually had a monopoly on the purchase of grain they could, by grading it lower than it really was, exact an additional profit. Charles A. Pillsbury, of flour fame, frankly conceded that his elevators graded more fairly at the beginning of the purchasing season, when supplies were still small, than at the end when there was plenty of grain available. According to the railway commission of Minnesota in 1890, the farmer was cheated on the average by more than a nickel a bushel through fraudulent grading practices.

A more subtle—and distant—levy on the farmer resulted from the manipulation of the national currency. During hostilities a strapped Unionist regime had withdrawn specie from circulation and issued almost $450,000,000 in greenback dollars which had behind them only the government's promise to pay. The greenbacks naturally declined in value (in terms of gold they were worth 39 cents by the summer of 1864); the prices of food, fuel, rent, and textiles rose correspondingly. The farmer, though he had to pay more for what he bought from the city, felt that it was counterbalanced by the larger sums he received for his crops. Furthermore, inflation helped him pay off mortgage and other debts at extremely favorable terms: a loan of $1,000 when money was "dear" and wheat, say, 50 cents a bushel, cost him 2,000 bushels, whereas when money was "cheap" and wheat went up to a dollar, it cost him 1,000 bushels. Had the government permitted the same amount of greenbacks to circulate after the war—or issued additional ones—the farmer would have been lyrically happy. Instead, Washington withdrew millions of dollars of the unsecured paper money and paid off bondholders in gold. The deflationary policy may have been necessary to protect the dollar but translated into terms that rural America could understand, it meant lower prices for crops and commensurately higher payments—in terms of produce— for debts. What made it all the more galling was the obvious discrimination in favor of bankers who had loaned the government "cheap" money during the war but had been paid in "hard" gold or coin, while the farmer whose debts ran into the postwar period had borrowed "cheap" but had to repay "dear." "The same currency for the bondholder and the ploughholder" was a familiar cry in the hustings for more than a quarter of a century. It culminated in the famous speech by William Jennings Bryan at the Democratic Party convention on July 7, 1896: "You shall not crucify mankind upon a cross of gold."

This chapter in the history of American poverty was unique in that it was a poverty primarily of the native-born (though there were some immigrants from Europe too) and grew side by side with prosperity and technological advance never known before. Like all types of poverty, whatever their cause, it represented the ultimate in hopelessness and degradation. "I take my pen in hand," wrote a Kansas woman, Susan Orcutt, in 1894 to Governor Lorenzo D. Lewelling, "to let you know that we are starving to death. . . . I haven't had nothing to eat today and it is three o'clock!" No more poignant description of the state of affairs then existing can possibly be written.

But the poverty of that period has a greater significance than that of others in one major respect: It was the first one that provoked a sizable and conscious reaction against *laissez faire* itself. It led to a new evaluation of the role of government, opposed to the thesis that that government is best which governs least. It was the first step toward controlled capitalism and the welfare state, for, in the process of organizing themselves, the rural poor of the Populist era laid the cornerstone for the "square deal," "new freedom," "new deal," "new frontier," and "great society" that were to follow.

Chapter 12

HAYSEED SOCIALISM

By an iron law of social dynamics, poverty begets forms of organization fit to its circumstances. The immigrant, for instance, clings to his ethnic societies for succor; the worker, to his unions or labor parties. The farmers, in the three decades following the Civil War, joined forces in a variety of movements, economic and political, which came to a climax with the formation of the People's Party. The Grange, the Greenback Party, the Alliance, the Wheels, the Populists fought feverishly for regulation of the railroads, currency reform, a "sub-treasury plan," and many other planks, with only episodic success. What is significant about their effort, insofar as the war on poverty is concerned, is the part they played in reassessing the role of government. They began a rethinking on the subject that is still going on and still underlies all debate on antipoverty programs.

The conservative view, as expounded most eloquently by Alexander Hamilton, was that government's primary concern should be for the "rich and well-born" who are the backbone of any society. The liberal view, taking its cue from the word liberty, was that government at best was a neutral between contending classes, obligated, insofar as possible, to leave them alone. The agrarian rebels rejected both theses; they disagreed with the first on moral grounds, with the second on strategic.

It was well and good, said the Populist leaders, to speak of *laissez faire*, leave alone, but in point of fact the "corporations and special interests" had grown "rich and powerful" only because of "class legislation and favoritism." That was not what the Constitution meant when it spoke, in its preamble, about promoting "the general welfare." Before anything else, "the first duty of the government is to the weak. Power becomes fiendish if it be not the protector and sure reliance of the friendless. . . ." The federal government has the responsibility, they said, to regulate commerce, issue money, and take other actions in such a way that the "natural rights" of the "many" are protected from the "few." Though it may not sound so today, after a half century in which the legal principle of regulating business has been generally accepted and a third of a century of neo-Keynesian economics, it was a dramatic idea at the time, when robber barons and social Darwinians were reinforcing the conventional wisdom of rugged individualism.

Incensed detractors called it hayseed socialism.

II

The first of the hayseed organizations that swept the prairies went by the unwieldy name of the National Grange of the Patrons of Husbandry. It was founded, said its mentor, Oliver Hudson Kelley, on "the rock of poverty—and there is no harder material."

Kelley, a government clerk assigned to the Commissioner of Agriculture and later to the post office, was asked to make a tour of the South in 1866 to gather "statistical and other information" required by President Johnson. Forty years old, a dignified man of Yankee Boston heritage with high forehead and a massive, near-white beard, Kelley had not distinguished himself in any way up to this point. He had migrated to Iowa, then to Elk River Township, Minnesota, before apprenticing himself to the government; but though he was considered by his associates "an engine with too much steam," he hadn't as yet released the steam for any major social purpose. Now, touring the devastated Confederacy, noting both the antiquated agricultural methods and the melancholy dreariness of farm existence, he wove an idea for an organization that would educate the husbandman in new techniques of farming as well as give him an outlet for social comradery. The following year, with six accomplices, five of them in government service, he founded his Patrons of Husbandry, or as it was popularly called, the Grange. Being a Mason he added a few ritualistic frills, and since he was especially impressed with the dullness of life for the women folk, gave them a prominent role in his order. The offices of Ceres, Pomona, and Flora—roughly equivalent to Faith, Hope, and Charity—were reserved for the fair sex.

In a day when there were no telephones, automobiles, electricity, inside plumbing, or rural mail delivery, and farmers lived in oppressive isolation, the prospectus had considerable appeal. Grange picnics, festivals, songs, lectures, newspapers, and magazines provided social relief and self-education. Aid to rural victims of catastrophe— to farmers in Louisiana and Alabama when the Mississippi flooded in 1874, for instance, or those out West during the grasshopper plague —also added a sense of community. But the Grange needed a touch of evangelism that spoke to farmers' economic interests before it could reach the take-off point. Kelley and his coterie, after reassessing early setbacks, finally supplied it with such slogans as "Down with Monopoly" and "Co-operation." By 1874 there were 20,000 local granges in thirty-two of the thirty-seven states, with one and a half million members, no mean representation considering that there were only three million farms in the nation.

The Grange is best known for the bills it sponsored in many states to domesticate the railroads, commonly called the "Granger laws," the political activity it generated indirectly, and the various cooperative business ventures it founded to undercut middleman profits. The first timid law to regulate rail carriers was passed in 1869, when Illinois farmers' clubs, enraged by the refusal of rail corporations to deliver grain to warehouses of independent elevator companies, pushed through a bill restricting charges to "just, reasonable, and uniform rates." It was followed two years later by laws setting maximum passenger fares and freight levies, which the rail companies, true to laissez-faire maxims, called an abomination of freedom and a violation of the Fourteenth Amendment, since it deprived them of "property" without "due process of law." Their lawyers argued that carriers were private businesses no more subject to regulation than merchants who sold candles and calico. In this initial confrontation the contending sides went beyond legalism and rhetoric. When Illinois railroaders announced they would not respect passenger tariffs set by the legislature, groups of farmers boarded trains, offered the fares, and on being told to get off pulled revolvers and bowie knives on the conductors. But the idea of regulation caught on anyway: Minnesota passed similar bills in 1871; Iowa and Wisconsin in 1874; and the rest of the Mississippi Valley "Granger states" in the ensuing decade.

As expected, the affronted railroads questioned regulation in the courts and the Grange appealed adverse decisions with unabated tenacity. The Illinois Supreme Court ruled regulation unconstitutional in January 1873. Three years later in a landmark decision the United States Supreme Court held in Munn v. Illinois and Peik v. the Chicago and Northwestern Railway Company that "where property has been clothed with a public interest the legislature may fix a limit to that which shall be in law reasonable for its use." The dike had been breached—at least for a decade, until the Court reversed itself.

Grange activity generally attested to that doctrine in physics that all actions cause reactions. Though apolitical presumably, the Grange winked at, even encouraged, efforts by its members to form third-party movements in eleven states, under such sobriquets as "antimonopoly," "reform," and "independent." With the rural tide running in their favor, the Illinois Reformers won office in fifty-three of the sixty-six counties in which they entered candidates, and elected three members to the House of Representatives. Kansas, for a long time the most maverick of states, chose a U.S. senator favorable to the Grange. The *Chicago Tribune*, then a clarion for the poor farmer, editorialized that "if there is any healthier political organization anywhere than that which farmers have originated in the West, we do not know what name it is called by." Under the hailstorm of farmer-power, five Mississippi Valley states enacted further regulatory legislation.

In economic affairs the Grange fostered a wide variety of cooperative ventures to counter merchant monopolies in the small towns and circumvent middleman profits. Illinois granges sold reapers for $175 which private retailers marketed for $275. Small threshers that cost $300 ordinarily were delivered by the Grange for $200; $150 wagons for $90; sewing machines for little more than half price. So extensive were grange cooperative businesses that the *Chicago Tribune* in 1874 carried three columns listing their services—insurance, elevators for grain, gristmills, pork-packing facilities, and many items produced by grange factories. The Iowa grange purchased the Werner harvester patent in 1874 and sold 250 of these machines at half the established price. This grange, at its peak, was operating three plow factories at Des Moines and owned thirty grain elevators. In not a few places the Grange founded cooperatively owned stores to compete with local merchants. When the Montgomery Ward mail-order house—first of its kind—opened in 1872, one of its major purposes was "to meet the wants of the Patrons of Husbandry."

Ebb tide for the Grange began in 1875. Too many hucksters of one kind or another had infiltrated its ranks. "Everybody wanted to join the Grange then," said D. Wyatt Aiken, one of its officials in the South, "lawyers to get clients; doctors to get customers; Shylocks, to get their pound of flesh; and sharpers, to catch their babes in the woods." More important was the collapse of many of the Grange businesses and cooperatives in the wake of the 1873 panic. The success of harvester production in Iowa spurred the Grange to buy up patents to manufacture machinery in seven states, ventures that died a-borning, with much loss of both cash and confidence. Anyway, the Grange nostrums were not sufficiently convincing to the rank-and-file farmer at a time of economic depression. In the distant East 5,000 firms failed, 3,000,000 laborers were without work; in the rural West and South the elevators were full but demand weak. Cotton slumped 20 per cent, wheat fell 15 cents a bushel, flour 50 cents a barrel. Something more meaty than cooperative stores or antirailroad legislation was needed to reverse the tide, and the Grange was not up to this challenge. By 1880 the number of local granges had declined to 4,000.

III

The next phase of the agrarian revolt, overlapping the Grange period somewhat, was an organized campaign for inflation—the Greenback movement. Economists argue that schemes for cheapening money, such as the Greenback scheme, boomerang on the poor since the increase in costs for what they buy cancels out whatever benefit they get from higher prices for their commodities. Be that as it may, however, innumerable farmers believed that putting more money into circulation would redistribute income in their favor, and help them against their creditors. "Inflate the currency," said Solon Chase, chairman of the Greenback-Labor Party in Maine, "and you raise the price of my steers and at the same time pay the public debt."

If the economists are right, there were quite a few important figures fooled by Greenbackism. Included among its adherents in the 1870's were James Buchanan, lawyer and newspaper editor, whom the *Chicago Tribune* called the "political Moses" of the movement. There was General B. F. Butler, who served (though not with great distinction) in the Union army during the Civil War, was elected to Congress five times as a radical Republican, and became governor of Massachusetts in 1882. There was Adlai E. Stevenson, grandfather of the Democratic standard-bearer of 1952 and 1956, who won a seat in Congress on the Greenback platform in 1878 and was Vice President of the United States under Grover Cleveland. There was Peter Cooper, the octogenarian millionaire who endowed Cooper Union in New York as a school for thousands of workers; Ignatius Donnelly, a colorful lawyer from Minnesota and onetime congressman; General James Baird Weaver, an authentic war hero and also a congressman; and many others.

Currency reform initially was a program devised by urban radicals with the broad purpose of undermining capitalism itself. Edward Kellogg, a well-to-do New York dry-goods merchant, published a book in 1849, *Labor and Other Capital*, in which he argued that the roots of economic disaster such as the 1837 panic lay in the rights granted to private bankers to issue money. To assure high interest for the loans they made, these infamous men withheld credit when it suited their purpose, thus choking off expansion, creating unemployment, reducing wages, and promoting general chaos. The fundamental reform needed therefore was to set up a government-run "national safety fund" authorized to print money against real estate security to be offered to borrowers at 1 per cent interest. In this way, said Kellogg, "all agriculturalists, manufacturers, mechanics, planters, in short all who wish to secure a support by honest industry," would be able to lay their hands on all the capital they required, and both they and the nation would prosper.

The dry-goods merchant's plan lay fallow for two decades until the leftist National Labor Union of William H. Sylvis picked it up after the Civil War. Sylvis and his associates, though devout trade unionists, had lost faith in strikes as weapons for social justice because so many had been smashed in the postwar period. They concentrated instead, therefore, on establishing worker-owned cooperative factories, and for a while did fairly well until they ran into the problem of credit. Transferring the banking function to government seemed a way to solve the problem. Under their altered version of the Kellogg plan the private banking system would be abolished, to be replaced by a complex federal operation. Under the new system, any citizen who had the cash would be allowed to buy national bonds at 3 per cent interest and convert them to greenbacks. Anyone who did not have the cash could borrow directly from the government on the usual property security at much lower than the 9 to 12 per cent charged by private sources. An inevitable result of this socialized credit would be the multiplication of producers' cooperatives effectively competing with the private corporate goliaths and in due course embalming the existing capitalist order.

The rural version of Greenbackism did not go quite this far. It also demanded a currency managed by the federal government, but it focused more on manipulating the amount in circulation so as to produce a steady increase in farm prices. During hostilities, almost $450,000,000 in unsecured greenbacks had been printed by the Administration to finance the war effort, and of course had caused predictable inflation. In the aftermath a conflict developed between those who felt the government had no right to issue such money to begin with, and ought to contract the supply until it was fully redeemed, and the farmers—with labor support—who believed quite the reverse, that the regime had not only a right but a duty to keep the cheap money in circulation, and even add to it. When President Grant and Congress paid bondholders in gold rather than the depreciated paper and the Treasury withdrew $77,000,000 in paper from the economic bloodstream, tempers began to boil. Instead of adding to the supply of cheap money, the Administration was contracting it, reducing prices on the one hand and forcing debtors to repay in hard money for the soft money they had borrowed years before. The obvious discrimination in favor of Wall Street banks raised a western cry for "the same currency for the bondholder and the ploughholder," but it was a cry unappeased. The Congress and the Executive were in the hands of the contractionists. They would not restore the paper money taken out of circulation, and during a depression in 1875, when prices were plummeting precipitously downward, they passed the Resumption Act which cut back paper currency to $300,000,000. A compromise a few years later pegged the supply at $347,000,000 but the disquiet was unallayed.

In effect the greenback plank was a reincarnation of all the plans for arbitrating the lender-borrower dispute in favor of the latter, going all the way back to the Land Bank of Deacon Sam Adams in the eighteenth century. It was to be followed by the agitation for monetization of silver and the "subtreasury plan" advocated by the Southern Farmers' Alliance. Basic to all these nostrums was the concept of government as an active force, using whatever devices were at hand, to effect the redistribution of wealth and income in favor of the poor.

The greenback idea as the expression of this philosophy during the 1870's threatened for a while to fashion a third force as a balance of power between a Republican Party that had fallen under the sway of eastern capital and a Democratic Party that was a feeble instrument for social protest. During the 1878 elections the Greenbackers polled a million votes and elected fourteen members to the House of Representatives, including Adlai E. Stevenson. Two years later they mounted their most ambitious campaign for the Presidency, nominating General James B. Weaver of Iowa as the standard-bearer.

Weaver, more than any man of this period, reflects the mood of agrarian dissent from the Grange to the People's Party. Patriarchal in appearance, medium-sized, with white hair and curled mustache, he might have risen much higher in the political firmament if he had not clung so doggedly to panaceas like prohibition and Greenbackism. He had a Lincolnesque frontier background and an aura of incorruptibility. One of thirteen children who had been brought to Iowa by his millwright father in the 1840's, he carried mail for four years, was caught up in the gold fever in 1853 and temporarily shifted locale to California, returned disenchanted to take on a store clerk's job at home, and in 1855 borrowed $100 (at 33 per cent interest) to enter the Cincinnati Law School. Like so many others of his generation who had read *Uncle Tom's Cabin* and the editorials in Greeley's *Tribune*, he became a fervid antislaver, a Republican stalwart who attended the convention that nominated Lincoln, and an immediate volunteer—as private—in the Union army when the President issued the call. Bravery in the battles of Donelson, Shiloh, and Cornith won him steady promotion so that at the end of the war he was brevetted a brigadier general.

A devout Methodist, with a rich voice and an oratorical talent for painting ideas in vivid imagery, Weaver was an impressive personality. "He presents a composite picture," said a contemporary maverick, Mrs. Annie L. Diggs of Kansas, "in which strength and gentleness blend. The cannibalism of politics has snapped and bitten at him in vain. Serene while others are in tumult; clear while others are confused; secure in his orbit while others are erratic; certain while others are in doubt—these characteristics make him a man of value second to none in a great epoch like the present." But they were not enough to endear him, alas, to Republican leaders for whom his extremist views were a patent handicap. He was for regulation of railroads, for money reform, and uncompromising in his views on prohibition, a doctrine that raised hackles in Iowa circles. Had he been more flexible on this score, he might have been nominated for the posts he sought over the years from 1865 to 1875 as lieutenant governor, congressman, and governor, but the Iowa Republicans were in a tailspin away from radicalism. In 1877, finally, Weaver crossed over to the Greenbackers, convinced that the party of Grant and Hayes could no longer serve the farmer and workingman. A pragmatic believer in coalition, he accepted Democratic support and won a seat in Congress, where his reputation for integrity elevated him to presidential timber within the minority movement.

The Greenbackers, meanwhile, through a cacophony of parties and alliances were moving to their banner years, 1878 and 1880. The crusade had begun with the formation of a sterile National Labor Reform Party in 1871–72, under the aegis of radical trade unionists, which for a variety of comic-opera reasons was unable to field a presidential candidate in 1872. The panic of 1873, however, and the Resumption Act of 1875 intensified efforts for the next electoral challenge. Farm parties in Indiana and Illinois, aided by trade unionists such as A. C. Cameron, a former delegate to Karl Marx's First International, launched the Independent Party in March 1875, dedicated to the repeal of the Resumption Act, and ran aged Peter Cooper for President the following year. The millionaire philanthropist polled only 82,000 votes, but by 1878 the Greenback mood had taken wings as a result of the loss of scores of railwaymen's lives in the repression of the coast-to-coast railroad strikes. The Greenback-Labor conference that followed went far beyond the money plank. It called for shorter work days, a public domain policy guaranteeing land only to settlers, discontinuance of contract prison labor, closing the door to Chinese immigration, and government commissions to make statistical reports on labor and business. Cheap money, however, remained the true religion. The Greenbackers polled a million votes for Congress—11 per cent of the national total.

By 1880 the alliance of reformers enlarged itself, this time including Susan B. Anthony, the suffragette leader, as well as the Marxist Socialist Labor Party. It added a new and novel plank to its platform, the graduated income tax—another means of redistributing income in favor of the lower classes—and chose Weaver for its candidate on the first ballot. The General toured the nation from Arkansas to Maine, made 100 speeches, shook 30,000 hands, and spoke to a half million people. But his vigor could not offset the returning sun of prosperity. Crops that year were the best in history, and for a change prices did not slump. Weaver polled only 308,578—3 per cent of the national total; the Greenback movement flew apart as if from a centrifuge, to make way for the next and most dramatic chapter of the agrarian crusade.

IV

The People's Party, like the Alliances, Wheels, and other esoteric mass organizations that preceded it, was an amorphous movement, typically American in its decentralism, but unified in its determination that the government must marshal all its energies to repair the balance between rich and poor. In this it was centralist, even collectivist. America must conclude its courtship with *laissez faire,* and not only regulate but nationalize certain sectors of the economy, including above all, the banking and money function. The Populists were not socialists: their credo was rooted in the American tradition of the Declaration of Independence, which they felt was being subverted by corporate wealth; though they sometimes spoke of revolution, they intended to remove the cancer of monopoly through electoral action and legislation rather than uprising. Otherwise, however, there was a confluence of goals—to abolish poverty—and a considerable similarity in the rhetoric by which they damned the rich.

It is necessary to emphasize this point because there is a tendency in historical folklore to reduce the Populist crusade to the single issue of "free silver," or Bryan's "cross of gold" speech. These barbed words of Mary Elizabeth Lease, whom General Weaver called "our Queen Mary," are more reflective of the Populist mood: "We wiped out slavery," she cried, "and by our tariff laws and national banks began a system of white slavery worse than the first. Wall Street owns the country. It is no longer a government of the people, by the people and for the people, but a government of Wall Street, by Wall Street and for Wall Street. The great common people of this country are slaves, and monopoly is the master. . . . The parties lie to us and political speakers mislead us. . . . We want money, land and transportation. We want the abolition of the National Banks, and we want the power to make loans direct from the government. We want the accursed foreclosure system wiped out. . . . The people are at bay, let the blood-hounds of money who have dogged us thus far beware."

There was a flavor of class conflict to Populist words. "The corporations and special interests of every class created during the past twenty-five years by various species of class legislation and favoritism," said Weaver, "have grown rich and powerful. They are now pleading to be let alone. . . . The world has heard similar lamentations before." But where Marxian socialism attributed monopoly and exploitation to an inherent character of the system, the Populists tended to argue that it was an aberration that could be put straight if the government would mount a massive campaign against the usurpers. "Our system," wrote Henry Demarest Lloyd in his famous *Wealth Against Commonwealth,* "so fair in its theory and so fertile in its happiness and prosperity in its first century, is now, following the fate of systems, becoming artificial, technical, corrupt; and as always happens in human institutions, after noon, power is stealing from the many to the few." And the cure? "Thousands of years' experience has proved that government must begin where it ends—with the people; that the general welfare demands that they who exercise the powers and they upon whom these are exercised must be the same. . . . In nothing has liberty justified itself more thoroughly than in the resolute determination spreading among the American people to add industrial to political independence."

These florid words published at the height of the Populist excitement mark a climax of disenchantment—but with a train gone off track, rather than one on the wrong-sized rail.

The build-up toward the hayseed socialism of the People's Party began with new grass-roots formations similar to the old Grange, called Alliances and Wheels. The first Alliance in 1875 is said to have been born in Lampasas County, Texas, where farmers grouped together to safeguard themselves against horse and cattle thieves. The Alliances actually gained momentum five to ten years later after a series of complex amalgamations, arriving finally at two major centers. The Farmers' and Laborers' Union of America, generally known as the Southern Alliance, was molded by one of those remarkable young men who kept springing up in the countryside in those fateful years, C. W. Macune. Of Scotch-Irish descent, thirty-five, he had given vent to his wanderlust, roaming California, Kansas, and finally Texas, until fate brought him to the Alliance, which he helped revive when it was near collapse.

Up North the guiding spirit of the Alliance movement was Milton George, an Illinois farmer turned newspaper editor. His *Western Rural*, repeatedly castigating the railroads for "literally starving some of our farmers to death," was a rallying point for Alliance-minded yeomen. The two movements might have coalesced when they met in December 1889 but they could not agree on a name, on eliminating the secret rituals of the southern group, and on opening the door to Negroes as demanded by the northerners. Black farmers had to form their own parallel group, the Colored Farmers National Alliance, which at one time claimed—though probably an exaggeration—a million adherents. The two major Alliances had enrolled two million members by 1892 and were publishing more than 800 papers.

The Alliances bore striking resemblance to the Grange, with the one difference that they were more openly political. They avidly recruited women, arranged the usual picnics and social affairs, sent lecturers to the hustings to advise on scientific farming or crop rotation, opened libraries to encourage "a general system of home culture," published innumerable newspapers (150 in Kansas alone), formed cooperatives, engaged in a dozen kinds of collective business enterprises, including grain elevators, insurance companies, and creameries.

But apart from such activities they were forced by circumstance and disposition to accelerate work on the political front. The 1880's were a decade of unprecedented growth for the American economy, outstripping the pace of Europe many times over. Yet both in the cities and villages of the United States the cleavage between the

upper and under classes was widening appreciably. For the disin-
herited the country seemed to be turning itself over, boot and booty,
to the mammoth corporations. The Haymarket riot in Chicago in
1886 was the signal for a campaign of repression and blacklisting of
militant unionists. The same year the Supreme Court nullified the
Peik decision of nine years before, which upheld the right of states to
regulate the railroads. Congress, reacting to rural sentiment, thereupon passed an interstate act, forbidding pools, rebates, and various
forms of discrimination, but it was a toothless law, since the five-man
Interstate Commerce Commission established under its provisions
could neither set rates nor call the carriers to task without taking the
issues to court. Here the circle was completed, for the judiciary, as so
often before, was loathe to interfere with the prerogatives of free
enterprise. The Supreme Court in the Minnesota Rate case, in April
1890, held that only the courts, not the states or Congress, could decide whether a rate was reasonable or not. Angry farmers called it the
"second Dred Scott decision," and the cry for government ownership
of some of the transcontinental lines, in particular Union Pacific,
reached a high pitch.

Of even greater importance to the Alliances was the question of
money reform, now centering on the coinage of silver rather than
printing of greenbacks. Back in 1837 Congress had agreed to mint
silver at the ratio of nearly sixteen to one of gold, 371.25 grains of
pure silver to a dollar as against 23.22 grains of pure gold. In 1873 the
silver dollar was actually worth $1.02 in gold, but with adoption of
the gold standard and limitation of silver coinage in various European nations the amount of silver on the market expanded, with a
consequent drop in price. In 1876 a silver dollar was worth only
ninety cents as compared to gold, seventy-two cents in 1889, and
sixty cents in 1893. The farmer, thinking of salvation in terms of inflation, persistently demanded that the government coin all the silver it
could lay its hands on, thereby depreciating the value of money and
increasing the price of crops.

Other farm demands called for reduction of interest rates, changes
in the patent laws, popular election of senators, federal ownership of
the telegraph, breakup of land monopolies and industrial trusts, abolition of national banks, and similar planks. To win them it was
necessary to challenge the established parties for political office, and
this logic drove the rural heretics to concentrated efforts for local and

federal power. In the South, where for all practical purposes a one-party system prevailed, the Alliance sought to seize the machinery of the Democratic Party. Surprisingly, beginning with "Pitchfork" Ben Tillman's campaign in South Carolina in 1888, the oligarchy was dethroned in one Democratic Party after another. By 1890 Alliancemen were in the saddle at the party's conventions in Florida, Georgia, and the two Carolinas, and had wrested control of five southern legislatures. In addition they had elected three governors, one senator, and forty-four congressmen favorable to the Alliance platform, including a thirty-four-year-old red-headed criminal lawyer from Georgia, Thomas E. Watson, who was to play a major role on behalf of the Negro and Populism for many years. Long after the movement had passed its peak, he was to be its candidate for President.

In the Northwest the rhapsody of politics was played outside the two-party system; Alliance stalwarts put forth tickets under such headings as Independent Party, People's Party, Industrial Party. Since the northern Alliancemen were not as influential as their southern brethren, their record was not so impressive. Even so, the People's Independent Party of Nebraska captured both houses in that state; Minnesota elected a Populist congressman; Kansas and South Dakota chose U.S. senators favorable to the cause. The most noteworthy victory for independent politics above the Mason-Dixon line was in Kansas, where the lower house fell to Populism and no fewer than five congressmen were returned on its ticket.

Hayseed socialism was ripe for national harvest. As with the Republicans a generation and a half before, a new coalition emerged on the shoals of disenchantment, confident it could redirect American destiny. Under the aegis of the Alliances a number of conferences and conventions were called, climaxing in the one at Omaha, meeting—appropriately—on July 4, 1892, to adopt a People's Party platform and choose candidates. The largest contingent of this boisterous assemblage—given to singing at the drop of a note—was from the various Alliances, including the Colored Alliance, but there were also representatives of the Knights of Labor, suffragettes, single taxers, and many others. When Ignatius Donnelly, probably the greatest Populist orator of the period, finished reading the preamble, according to one news story, "instantly there was enacted the mightiest scene ever witnessed by the human race. Fifteen thousand people yelled, shrieked, threw papers, hats, fans, and parasols, gathered up banners, mounted shoulders." The ovation lasted forty minutes.

"We meet," said the preamble, "in the midst of a nation brought to the verge of moral, political and material ruin. Corruption dominates the ballot-box, the legislatures, the Congress, and touches even the ermine of the bench. . . . The newspapers are largely subsidized or muzzled; public opinion silenced; business prostrated; our homes covered with mortgages; labor impoverished; and the land concentrating in the hands of the capitalists. . . . The fruits of the toil of millions are boldly stolen to build up colossal fortunes for a few, unprecedented in the history of mankind; and the possessors of these, in turn, despise the republic and endanger liberty. From the same prolific womb of governmental injustice we breed the two great classes —tramps and millionaires. . . .

"We have witnessed for more than a quarter of a century the struggles of the two great political parties for power and plunder, while grievous wrongs have been inflicted upon the suffering people. We charge that the controlling influences dominating both these parties have permitted the existing dreadful conditions to develop without serious effort to prevent or restrain them. . . ."

At the end there were three general statements of position: first, "that the union of the labor forces of the United States this day consummated shall be permanent and perpetual"; second, that "wealth belongs to him who creates it, and every dollar taken from industry without an equivalent is robbery"; and third, "that the time has come when the railroad corporations will either own the people or the people must own the railroads. . . ."

The platform itself dealt with the three main problems that had brought the Populists together: money, transport, land. The monetary demands called for a national "safe, sound, and flexible" currency, issued by the government directly to the people "without the use of banking corporations," the "free and unlimited coinage of silver and gold at the present legal ratio of sixteen to one," "an increase in the circulating medium" so that there would be not less than $50 per capita, and the "subtreasury" system of loans which had been devised by C. W. Macune of the Southern Alliance.

This latter plank was an interesting scheme—a lineal forebear in some respects to the Agricultural Adjustment Act of 1938. Under it the Administration would circulate its money through subtreasury offices in every county in states that had a half million dollars or more of agricultural produce. A farmer could bring his crop to the elevator or warehouse of these subtreasury offices and receive a loan of up to 80 per cent of the value of his corn, cotton, wheat, etc., at 1 per cent interest. If he wished he might sell his deposit certificate or he might redeem the produce within a year; otherwise it would go under the hammer at a public auction. Macune insisted that this plan was no different from the prevailing system of putting money into circulation, except that instead of bankers depositing bonds with the U.S. Treasury in return for the right to issue paper money (up to 90 per cent of the bonds), agricultural products would be deposited.

The program of the Omaha assemblage also called for the graduated income tax, postal savings banks, government ownership and operation of the railroads, telephones, and telegraph, and the reclamation of land held by railroads and corporations "in excess of their actual needs" as well as holdings "now owned by aliens." The last point may be considered out of character with progressive philosophy, but antiforeignism had deep popular roots not only among conservatives but in many a liberal and radical as well. Other planks included direct election of U.S. senators, a single term for the President, the shorter work week for labor, and termination of subsidies or aid by the government "to any private corporation for any purpose." For good measure, in genuflection to labor union allies, the exultant mavericks denounced Pinkerton labor spies and proclaimed a boycott against Rochester clothing manufacturers who were warring with the Knights of Labor. It was a program catering to virtually every grievance of the under classes, designed to redistribute income, wealth, and power in their favor. Not unexpectedly, as one journalist reported, it was greeted with a "cyclonic ovation." The man selected to present it for the consideration of the American voters—after ruling out Ignatius Donnelly and a few others—was General Weaver of Greenback fame.

Exactly why the populace at large did not react with the same "cyclonic" enthusiasm as the lyrical delegates at Omaha is not clear. It may have been the usual wariness of third parties, or conversely, as the antifusionist wing of the Populists believed, because their leaders were making too many deals to run fusion candidates for Congress with the support of Democrats in some states and Republicans in others. Or it may have been an inability of Weaver to interpret a program so militant. In the opinion of one associate the brevetted General was "no Moses who can frighten Pharaoh into fits or bring convincing plagues upon the monopolistic oppressors of Israel." The Alliance membership alone should have assured two or three million votes, but the actual count was 1,041,028, a disappointing 9 per cent of the total. Nonetheless if the campaign did not tumble the house down it shook the rafters enough to cause the older parties to make obeisances to Populist sentiment. That year, 1892, both the Democrats and Republicans included a silver plank in their platforms.

This, it turned out, was to be the role of the People's Party, a lightning rod to others rather than a magnet drawing state power to itself. Already in the 1892 campaign, the Populists made dozens of deals in this state and that, fusing in one place with Democrats, elsewhere with Republicans of compatible nature. The more militant elements berated such compromises, but the fusionists had a vision that, aligned with the better element in the old parties, they might lead the unwashed to the domicile of power. This notion received some reinforcement in the 1894 congressional elections (a depression year) when Populism polled nearly a million and a half votes, and the silverites, had they wanted to, could have passed a free coinage law in Congress. They shied off only because they knew President Cleveland would veto it.

By 1896 the mood was for one all-or-nothing turn of the card—combine with the Democrats, who were now on the same wave length insofar as silver was concerned, and seize the White House. An unreconstructed minority held out against fusion with the Democrats, but by a vast majority the main body of the People's Party convention accepted a thirty-six-year-old orator from Nebraska, William Jennings Bryan, as a joint candidate. To show their "independence," the delegates refused to nominate the Democratic vice-presidential candidate, casting their lot instead with Tom Watson, the redhead from Georgia.

Populism had now reached its apogee: Bryan failed by 600,000 votes against Republican McKinley. He ran again as a fusion nominee in 1900—with former Greenbacker Adlai E. Stevenson as vice-presidential choice—and gained approximately the same number of tallies. Fusion, said the more fervid Populists, was a suicide impulse. They may have been right, for by 1904 the People's Party had retrogressed to the point where Watson received only 117,183 votes. Populism won 27 seats in Congress in 1896, ten in 1898, and by 1902, none. One by one, the leaders of the movement strayed back into the fold of the old parties—Weaver, for instance, rejoined the Democrats, whom he had abandoned long before the Civil War, and Senator Peffer of Kansas, the Republicans—as farm prosperity cut the ground from agrarian discontent. From 1899 to 1909 agricultural crops increased in value from three billion to five and a half billion dollars, and agricultural property from approximately twenty to forty billion.

The amelioration of rural poverty, forty years after the Homestead Act, cannot be said to have been an act of political design. Certainly it was not the result of Populist victory. But there is no question that the unrelenting crusade in the cotton, grain, and cattle areas of the nation caused sufficient changes to bolster the democratic process, and thereby to offer the farmer a measure of protection he did not enjoy previously.

Surveying the montage in retrospect Mary Lease said in 1914: "I have seen, with gratification, that my work in the good old Populist days was not in vain. . . . Note the list of reforms which we advocated which are coming into reality. Direct election of senators is assured. Public utilities are gradually removed from the hands of the few and placed under the control of the people who use them. Woman suffrage is now almost a national issue. . . . The seed we sowed in Kansas did not fall on barren ground." Mrs. Lease overstated the case, but Populism could boast important victories. Woman suffrage did win, so did the Australian (secret) ballot and direct primaries in many states. Populism's silver plank prodded the powers that be to reform the money system, leading to the Federal Reserve Act. The government did not seize the railroads, but the Interstate Commerce Commission was finally clothed with power to set rates and abolish discriminatory practices, free passes, and other vices of the early era.

The overriding significance of Populism as a cure for poverty, however, was not in what it achieved specifically, but in initiating the national dialogue over government intervention. For the next two-thirds of a century, except for the interregnum of the 1920's and the war periods, this was to be the main item for political discussion. If the cause of poverty is viewed as the absence of power, and the goals of antipoverty as the rectification of powerlessness, the Populist era was the opening curtain in a protracted drama.

Chapter 13

THE FIT AND THE UNFIT

William K. Vanderbilt, the railroad tycoon, once expressed his contempt for what other people thought of his ethics with the pungent phrase, "The public be damned." Many of the buccaneers who made sensational fortunes during the age of industrial expansion believed that wealth was its own justification. It was no one else's business. But in a society where people read newspapers and agitators mounted soapboxes to declaim on behalf of the dispossessed, this callous stance could not be sustained forever.

It was now commonplace to read of financial barons who left their children ten, twenty, fifty million dollars, even some who earned that much in a short span of time. William K. Vanderbilt pocketed a cool fifty million in one frenzied year, manipulating the stocks and bonds of his railroads. Andrew Carnegie, the Scottish immigrant who rose to fabulous heights as a steelmaker, earned twenty-three million dollars in 1900, every penny of it tax free. The rich not only made money but spent it with ostentation and pomp that to many people seemed indecent. Mrs. William K. Vanderbilt lavished a quarter of a million dollars on one ball. A guest at another such affair, even more grandiose, spent $10,000 for a gold costume. Limestone mansions, one more ornate than the other, were built in the best sections of New York. Debutantes and their fathers paid kings' ransoms to capture a duke or a count for a husband. The Vanderbilts gave the Duke of Marlborough two and a half million dollars to refurbish his Blenheim Palace and meet the payroll of hundreds of servants, in return for consummating a loveless marriage with daughter Consuelo.

The cavorting of the *nouveaux riches* and second-generation wealthy might have passed with less censure if it were not for the pervasive poverty in other quarters. Consuelo's family bought her her duke, for example, during the depression period that followed the 1893 panic. In that year, three million laborers were unemployed, and hunger was so rampant one winter that the *New York World* distributed a million loaves of bread to the idle. In Pittsburgh a relief committee raised funds to hire 4,000 men at a dollar a day, and in Denver the jobless were given food and lodging in return for sawing wood. San Francisco engaged its unemployed to sweep and resweep the streets. And though a conference of union delegates, presided over by AFL President Samuel Gompers, pleaded for public works and public relief, not a single state, let alone the federal government, responded. Those who still held jobs were stung with wage cuts of 10, 20, 30 per cent, and the year 1894 saw 690,000 proletarians "hit the bricks" in defensive strikes to recoup their losses, including the most revolutionary strike in American history, the Pullman railroad strike. "General" Jacob S. Coxey was leading his Commonweal of Christ, 20,000 unemployed, to the nation's capital to demand work for the workless.

The conspicuous consumption of the upper classes in the face of such anguish—in this and previous depressions—clearly called for doctrinal rationalization. The public might be damned, but unless appeased it could do unpleasant things with its votes. How could one justify the grandeur of the new mansions amidst the noisome, filthy slums, or the extravaganzas of those who had nothing else to do with their money against the hunger of children? This justification was put forth, with neither defensiveness nor apologia, by an English philosopher, Herbert Spencer, and his American disciples—including Carnegie—in the sophisticated theory of social Darwinism.

The term mistakenly leaves the impression that Spencer plagiarized from Darwin's *Origin of Species;* in fact, social Darwinism antedated the exposition of biological evolution by nine years, and the phrase "survival of the fittest" was first used by Spencer, not Darwin. "Under the natural order of things," he wrote, "society is constantly excreting its unhealthy, imbecile, slow, vacillating, faith-less members" in order to leave room for the competent ones entitled to reward. "The poverty of the incapable, the distresses that come upon the imprudent, the starvation of the idle, and those shoulder-ings aside of the weak by the strong, which leave so many 'in shallows and in miseries' are the decrees of a large, far-seeing benevolence" —the same benevolence that "brings to early graves the children of diseased parents, and singles out the low-spirited, the intemperate, and the debilitated as the victims of an epidemic."

This hard view was arrived at from the assumption that a man's characteristics, both those inherited and those seemingly acquired through experience, are genetic in origin. Nature has decreed that some men are fit for the stormy journey, and by that right should survive, whereas others are unfit and by that misfortune must accept the consequences of poverty. "If to be ignorant," wrote Spencer in his *Social Statics*, "were as safe as to be wise, no one would become wise." He condemned public education as government interference with natural selection, as well as an abrogation of the rights of par-ents to decide which school, if any, their children should attend. For similar reasons it was improper for the government to operate the post office or national mint, for in doing so it interposed itself against the competitive aspirations of its citizens. If Spencer did not de-nounce private charity it was not because he sympathized with help-ing the indigent but because he felt that the wealthy, no matter how ill-advised, ought to be free to give or not to give as they chose. To let the poor flounder or perish by their own inadequacies, while society watched indifferently, was not venal, according to the philosopher of social Darwinism, but simply "the fundamental law of social life."

Spencer, when he came to the United States in 1882, was wined and dined by the wealthy for whom his views were a comforting expiation, and hailed as a prophet. Contempt for the poor was of course nothing new. It had been expressed even by some charity workers and liberals throughout the century, but Spencer gave it a coherent mold. The cudgels for his philosophy were taken up and popularized on this side of the Atlantic by such notable figures as William Graham Sumner of Yale and Josephine Shaw Lowell, a "sci-entific philanthropist." Let nature take its course, they counseled. Meddling by the state in the regulation of industry, imposition of tariffs, subsidies to the poor, even the improvement of sanitation except where a great epidemic impended, was a conspiracy against the natural order, depriving citizens of their inherent right to fulfill themselves.

As Donald Fleming summarizes their views, "nothing must come between a man and his sufferings—neither public assistance from the state nor private charity from individuals." The only "charity" tolerable was that "of helping men to help themselves." Tenderness should be eschewed, the gospel of egalitarianism forcefully repudiated. If people died of hunger or tuberculosis it was no worse than whales eating minnows. Josephine Shaw Lowell, in founding her Charity Organization Society of New York in 1882, argued that relief ought to be limited to those already in an institution—say an almshouse—and made so unattractive that people would want to escape. If it were ever necessary to give temporary aid to the distressed it ought to be in food, not money, and just enough for a single day.

Social Darwinism was an engaging doctrine for the acquisitive classes, for it absolved them of responsibility for the degraded status of the lowly. If they chose they could give funds for philanthropy or charity, but not as an obligation, either moral or legal. Moreover the Spencer-Sumner thesis was a plausible rebuttal to those who charged that unbridled wealth was due to favoritism, bribery, and political manipulation. One could point to the immutable law of the "survival of the fittest" to indicate that the accumulation of wealth was a near-automatic process which the "fit" could hardly avoid. If some people fell by the wayside it was not the fault of the rich but the defect of the "unfit." "The growth of a large business," said John D. Rockefeller, head of the petroleum trust, "is merely the survival of the fittest." Just as "the American Beauty rose can be produced . . . only by sacrificing the early buds which grow around it," so the Standard Oil Company "is not an evil tendency in business [but] merely the working-out of a law of nature and a law of God." For those who had reservations about the ethics of big business, Professor Sumner offered the consoling thought that this universal law "was not made by man," it was part of a changeless order transcending man.

If there were entrepreneurs who echoed such theorems tongue-in-cheek, there were some, like Andrew Carnegie, who elevated it to the high order of gospel—the Gospel of Wealth. Carnegie, a notch above contemporary millionaires in sensitivity to public reaction, published two books and a number of articles expounding a refined version of the social Darwinist credo, which somehow seemed to fit the measure of his own success story. The outstanding philanthropist of his day, the canny steelmaker had been a boy of twelve when he was brought here from Scotland in 1848. Though virtually without education he went to work immediately as a bobbin boy in an Allegheny City, Pennsylvania, cotton factory to help fill the family larder. "Anyone can get along in this Country," he wrote after a few years in his new habitat. "If I don't it will be my own fault." Without knowing it he was already a social Darwinist. At eighteen he moved along to a $35-a-month job as telegraph clerk for the up-and-coming Pennsylvania Railroad in Pittsburgh, where he hitched his chariot to his supervisor, Thomas A. Scott, whose star was also rising. Utilizing connections he had gained on the job, Carnegie became partner to a host of businesses during the Civil War, enough to raise his $2,400 salary to an over-all income of almost $50,000 by 1863. When the war was over, the "Star-Spangled Scotchman" quit the railroad, set up an office in New York for handling rail securities, and in due course transferred to the iron and steel industry where he prospered beyond all expectations. Careful not to fall prey to the bankers, he and his partners financed their own ventures, and built an empire that by 1900 produced three million tons of steel a year, provided $40,000,000 annually in profits, and was valued at nearly a half billion dollars by the Morgan interests which bought it out the following year. In his own shrewd style Carnegie insisted that J. P. Morgan pay him his share, $225,000,000, in gold bonds.

The steelmaker from Dunfermline, Scotland, was not a typical robber baron either in the way he acquired wealth or in the way he disposed of it. Somewhere along the line, perhaps as early as 1868, he concluded that a man's life was divided into two phases, one in which he made his fortune and the other in which he gave it away. He was convinced, as were other social Darwinists, that only the fit could— or should—become rich, but he confided to an English friend, William E. Gladstone, his conviction that no man ought to permit himself to die rich. What he earned should be given away for public benefaction while he was still alive. "The fundamental idea of 'The Gospel of Wealth,'" he wrote in an article with the enigmatic title "The Advantages of Poverty," "is that surplus wealth should be considered as a sacred trust to be administered by those into whose hands it falls during their lives, for the good of others. It predicts that the day is at hand when he who dies possessed of enormous sums, which were his and free to administer during his life, will die disgraced, and holds that the aim of the millionaire should be to die poor. It likewise pleads for modesty of private expenditure." In line with these teachings, Carnegie dispensed ten million dollars to towns and cities for libraries from 1881 to 1900 and another fifty million in the next two decades. His philanthropy included a host of trust funds that donated money for concert halls, parks, museums, swimming pools, scientific research, pensions, scholarships, and educational facilities for children.

If this was a unique twist to social Darwinism—followed only fitfully by others, usually for evasion of steep inheritance taxes—it nevertheless rested firmly on Spencer's and Sumner's foundations. There was no need, argued Carnegie, for social reform—and indeed no benefit from it—since inequality was the law of nature and as durable as the sun. He was disdainful of charity or direct relief, urging that such aid be given "rarely" and never in such amounts as "to do all." Whatever improvements accrued to the less fortunate of society would come from the benevolence of the millionaire class, which must be permitted to accumulate its largesse in untrammeled competition, without government interference. Carnegie ruefully admitted that this was not Christ's way, but he did not believe that Christ's teachings could be implemented under modern circumstances.

The steel magnate, pinched by the assertions of Henry George that the rich were growing richer and the poor poorer, entered into a polemic with the immensely popular single taxer to disprove the claim. George's *Progress and Poverty*, published in 1879, was a runaway best seller which circulated to at least three million readers in the ensuing years and made its author a minor saint among workers of New York who ran him for mayor in 1886. His remedy for poverty, a single tax on land, was based on the same contention as that of Karl Marx, namely that the working classes were being increasingly immiserated. Carnegie vehemently disputed this allegation. "The truth is," he wrote, "that the rich are growing poorer and the poor richer, and that the land is passing from the hands of the few into the hands of the many." Millionaires in fact "can only grow amidst general prosperity. . . . [They] make no money when compelled to pay low wages. Their profits accrue in periods when wages are high, and the higher the wages that have to be paid, the higher the revenues of the employer." To illustrate this inviolate law Carnegie referred to the fact that as of 1880 there were 88,665 paupers in the United States where millionaires abounded, or five per thousand people, whereas in Britain where the industrial gentry were less affluent there were thirty-three paupers per thousand population.

Carnegie was a bit inconsistent when a year after he wrote this article he decreed a 22 per cent wage cut for his employees at Homestead, Pennsylvania, and smashed their strike in one of the bitterest industrial wars of the period. The theory, however, was more durable than the act. Social Darwinism, even in its more moderate form, the Gospel of Wealth, remains a fixture of conservative thinking to this day. There are still millions of people who insist that those who receive government relief are "lazy" and "unwilling to work."

II

Whatever the attractiveness of social Darwinism to those who felt they could "make it" on their own, however, it was counteracted, as the new century dawned, by an increasing recognition that economic life was interdependent. A case could be made that it took a certain talent, ethical or not, for a titan of industry to climb the ladder of wealth. But the argument could not hold for second-generation millionaires whose talent was in being born to the right parents. Reasons —though not overwhelmingly cogent ones—could also be given for rugged individualism as a doctrine for survival on the plains or prairies. But the city was a great web of interrelationship in which no man's fate was entirely in his own hands. Joblessness, industrial accidents, disease, musty housing, low wages, vice, could not be entirely explained in terms of "fitness" or "unfitness."

In the dim horizons, then, a view that was opposite to that of social Darwinism began to assert itself. This metamorphosis in outlook was, of course, evident with the Populists, but it was punctuated with great force by men such as Jacob S. Coxey and his Commonweal of Christ. As the bedraggled band of unemployed, led by Coxey, marched out of Massillon, Ohio, on a chilly Easter Sunday in 1894, it was seeding the ground for welfare state ideas. Flags flying, banners waving, bands playing, this segment of the 20,000 contingent that was converging from all corners of the nation, sang a song to the tune of "Marching through Georgia" that expressed the determination of the jobless that some day, four decades later, would have to be allayed:

Hurrah! hurrah! for the unemployed's appeal!
Hurrah! hurrah! for the marching commonweal!
Drive the lobbies from the senate,
Stop the trust and combine steal,
For we are marching with Coxey.

We are not tramps nor vagabonds that's shirking honest toil,
But miners, clerks, skilled artizans, and tillers of the soil
Now forced to beg our brother worms to give us leave to toil,
While we are marching with Coxey.

Coxey, a dignified man with a wide, thin mouth, large ears, a full head of hair and a prominent nose, had earned a nest egg of $200,000 in sandstone and farming. Like Carnegie he was also a self-made man, though nowhere near as rich, and like Carnegie too he had a bent for pragmatic action. He had also quit school early to go to work in the rolling mills, but he developed along different philosophical lines. At the age of twenty-two he enrolled with the Greenback movement and had moved along with the tide of protest to Populism. Now in the 1890's he conceived of a single idea that he felt would put their principles into effect. Through a friendly spirit in Congress he had introduced a Good Roads Bill in 1892 which would achieve three results: pump a large sum of money into circulation, alleviate rural hunger, and appease labor's demand for an eight-hour day. Under the bill, the Secretary of the Treasury would issue $500 million in currency, hand it over to the Secretary of War, who would then hire any man who presented himself, at $1.50 a day for an eight-hour day, to build roads. Apart from its monetary plank, here was the germ of a plan which four decades later would flower into the New Deal's W.P.A.

The bill, of course, died an unmourned death, but in the meantime it became obvious to Coxey that there was a serious flaw to the measure: it aided the rural populace but did little for city workers. This was especially pertinent in view of the 1893 panic, which tossed men to the industrial scrap heap by the millions. The revised draft that the "General" and his subaltern, Carl Browne, drew up was called the

Non-interest-bearing Bond Bill. If passed it would authorize every state, county, township, territory, and municipality to circulate non-interest-bearing bonds up to half the assessed value of the property in their confines. These bonds would be deposited with the Secretary of Treasury as security for legal tender notes, and the money would then be used to make jobs—paving city streets or country roads, building schools and courthouses. The bonds would be paid off by local taxes spanning twenty-five years.

It was for this federal job-making program that Coxey and Browne organized their army "to send a petition to Washington with boots on." That it had enormous appeal is evidenced by the comment of a journalist that "Coxey compelled all the newspapers of the continent to devote from a column to six columns a day to reporting Coxeyism, that is to say, with echoing the inarticulate clamor for work for the workers." When the army began its march from Massillon, forty-three reporters accompanied it, sixteen sticking it out until the remnants reached the Capitol. Each arrest of a Coxeyite—for breaking into a freight car or similar offense—brought forth glaring headlines. "We are now witnessing a spectacle," said former President Benjamin Harrison, "that our country has never witnessed before." It was not only a new spectacle but a novel idea, presented in human form and blistered feet. Hitherto it was assumed that relief for the jobless ended at the water's edge of private charity or municipal aid. The petitioners with boots on, however, were demanding that work be made for them, and all in like circumstances, by the *federal* government.

That it came to naught—in part because the Pullman strike deprived the Commonweal of easy transport, so that it dribbled down to 1,000 by the time it reached Washington—is really beside the point. For it is doubtless true, as W. T. Stead wrote in *Review of Reviews*, that the Coxeyites though "ridiculed by the classes, have the sympathy of the masses." The idea of federal aid to the unfortunate dug roots slowly, and in time, after bitter experience, edged its way into the mainstream of national consciousness.

It was a rebuttal "with boots on" to social Darwinism, the kind of a rebuttal that would rise to a clamor with the passing decades.

Chapter **14**

THE OTHER HALF

Traditional American history has emphasized what modern sociologists call "upward mobility." Yesterday's indentured servant was tomorrow's independent landowner; yesterday's unskilled worker, tomorrow's skilled artisan or affluent businessman. If he himself did not topple the barriers of poverty, then his son or grandson did. In exceptional cases, as for instance with Andrew Carnegie, determined immigrants might catapult in a single generation from rags to untold riches. Yet with all the upward mobility that made life easier for millions of families, parallel processes usually created ever larger "proletariats"—in the Roman sense of lowest classes. While certain groups were being relieved of poverty, moving upward, others were being frozen into it, and new immigrant stocks were augmenting the impoverished class.

The first seventeen years of the twentieth century, up to World War I, were a remarkable illustration of this general rule. Wealth and poverty pyramided simultaneously, each reaching a new peak. Populist antipathy to monopoly and the Sherman Anti-Trust Act of 1890 notwithstanding, 276 mammoth combines were formed from 1898 to 1903 alone, including the first billion-dollar trust, U.S. Steel. By 1904 James Moody, the financial editor, could write that the economy was dominated by "about 445 active trusts," capitalized at more than $20 billion, or nearly one-seventh the national wealth. Millionaires grew like weeds. There were four thousand such gentry, according to the World Almanac of 1902, and it was estimated that 1 per cent of the people owned 50 per cent of the country's riches. "During the 1840's," Richard Hofstadter tells us, "there were not twenty millionaires in the entire country; by 1910 there were probably more than twenty millionaires sitting in the United States Senate." Not only the super-rich but the middle classes and the two million skilled workers in the American Federation of Labor improved their plight handsomely. There were, to be sure, four short economic dips in the first decade and a half of the century (1903, 1907, 1910, 1914), yet even in the rural West and South the bad years receded to nostalgic memory with the good harvests that followed 1897. From 1900 to 1910 agricultural produce rose in value by almost half and farm property doubled in worth. After three decades of unrest the prairies began to display well-kept buildings, newly painted barns, better roads, more expensive machinery.

But the core of American life was now incontestably the city, and here the cesspool of poverty enlarged alarmingly. The number of cities with 50,000 population increased from sixteen to more than a hundred in the half century ending in 1910. In these drab centers manufacture had taken wing, its product enlarging by more than fifteen times, its wage earners by almost five times. Yet glorious as was this technological saga, its grim side was as appalling, for the city was an aggroupment of colonies—Italian, Irish, Greek, Jewish, Bohemian—famous at home and abroad for deadening privation. Poverty had existed in the urban centers before but never on the scale or with the special nuances that accompanied the explosion of industrialism. "The first city," wrote Josiah Strong in *The Twentieth Century City*, "was built by the first murderer, and crime and vice and wretchedness have festered in it ever since."

Here, to the city, in the early twentieth century flocked the immigrant, a man described by Edwin Markham, with

> The emptiness of ages in his face,
> And on his back the burden of the world.

Thirteen million aliens cramped the steerage of ocean-going vessels from 1900 to 1915, headed for the United States—1,285,000 in 1907 alone. In fifteen years two-thirds as many came as in the previous eight decades. As of 1903, 37 per cent of New York's population was foreign-born, and if those of foreign parentage are included, 80 per cent. The same proportion prevailed in Chicago, and was even higher in Milwaukee. This immigration was the fodder on which poverty fed, and never more so than when it reached its zenith during the "Progressive Era."

The previous generation of immigrants had been natives of England, Scotland, Ireland, Germany, Scandinavia. The new one was predominantly from southern and eastern Europe—masses of Italians, Poles, Russians, east European Jews, Slavs, Czechs—with a cultural background less easily adaptable to the American scene. On arriving at Ellis Island, or similar point of debarkation, they were given brochures by immigrant societies of their own ethnic groups welcoming them to "the best country in the world."

But, true or not for the nation per se, this did not automatically assure personal triumph. To begin with, many immigrants were illiterate in their own tongue—half of those from southern Italy, for instance—and few were literate in English. Under such circumstances they were dependent on ethnic brethren who had come earlier for the thousand and one daily tasks needed for survival. Clustered in steamy slums they relied on immigrant societies and political machines for jobs, social services, apartments, naturalization as citizens. Secondly, they invariably confronted hostility from native workers who considered the "dagos," "mockies," "hunkies" a threat to their own standards.

Strange as it seems for a nation where everyone but the Indian traces his heritage to an immigrant, antiforeignism was a recurring theme in American life, shared not only by rightists but many a liberal and radical as well. Philip S. Foner, in his history of the American labor movement, records the complaint of a native agitator in the 1840's that American workers were unable to compete with aliens because the latter "feed upon the coarsest, cheapest and roughest fare—stalk about in rags and filth—and are neither fit associates for American laborers and mechanics nor reputable members of any society." The American Party, a ritualistic movement of the 1850's, called the Know-Nothing Party because its members always replied "I know nothing" when asked of its activities, campaigned bitterly against Catholic immigrants, especially the Irish and Germans, and was able to win control of the Massachusetts legislature in 1854.

Denis Kearney, who founded the Working Men's Party in California in 1877 "to destroy the great money power of the rich," also called for ridding "the country of cheap Chinese labor as soon as possible . . . because it tends still more to degrade labor and aggrandize capital." Even the radical labor historian John R. Commons had grave misgivings about immigration. In his 1901 report for the Industrial Commission he states agreement with the thesis "that had there been no immigration whatever into this country during the past ninety years, 'the native element would long have filled the place the foreigners have usurped'" and forced wages to a much higher level.

During the Progressive Era—the first decade and a half of the century—this nativist agitation continued, centering as usual on the argument that the alien was eroding American wage standards. The AFL, under Samuel Gompers—himself an alien from England—demanded that the government place greater restrictions on the invasion of laborers from Europe. Proposals that they be given a literacy test, rejected by President Cleveland in 1897, were nonetheless persistently renewed. Both Presidents Taft and Wilson vetoed legislation requiring every new arrival to prove he could read English, yet in 1917 excitement on the subject was so intense Congress overrode Wilson's veto. Simultaneously the labor movement laid down a drumfire against the "yellow peril" so implacable that the Japanese government itself was induced to a "gentlemen's agreement" in 1907 to curb emigration of its nationals.

The immigrant, then, began with many strikes against him in an environment considerably more hostile than he had anticipated. He may have been warmed by the belief that he or his children would in due course melt in the melting pot, but meanwhile he lived in stultifying want.

II

Neither the degree of want nor its significance penetrated public consciousness automatically. For the average American, living outside the enclaves of immigrant poverty, the pleasant image of a nation where the newsboy saves his dimes to become a petroleum magnate, or the grocery clerk marries the boss's daughter, formed a smokescreen around the wretched islands, so that he passed them daily without realizing their debasing and widespread character.

Gradually, however, under prodding by an avalanche of books and articles by sympathetic writers, the smokescreen began to lift. Jacob Riis's *How the Other Half Lives*, published in 1890, was a masterly reportage of the tribulations of slum life drawn from direct observation without interpretive embellishments. Riis's books and articles opened many a complacent eye, and were supplemented by a dozen other authors who published vivid pieces in such magazines as *Scribner's*, *Harper's Weekly*, *The Forum*, *Arena*, and similar liberal journals. Josiah Flynt and Owen Kildare penned sympathetic books on tramps and city bums based on their own experiences; Bessie and Marie Van Vorst lifted the veil on the conditions of factory girls; Charles B. Spahr described *America's Working People* and A. M. Simons opened up *Packingtown*. Simultaneously, groups such as the Charity Organization Society, in collaboration with state and local governments, made surveys of tenement conditions, and the federal government began to publish more detailed statistics on wages and unemployment.

Finally, as a climax to more than a decade of agitation, a young socialist, Robert Hunter, published a book in 1904 under the simple title *Poverty* which, in the words of Robert Bremner, "was the most comprehensive as well as the most controversial treatment of the subject yet attempted in the United States." Its theses were not as universally accepted as those of another young socialist, Michael Harrington, whose *The Other America* caused a similar stir six decades later, but its impact was just as widespread. Hunter, a graduate of Indiana University, had lived among the impoverished for eight and a half years as a social worker. He knew the debilitating effects of their circumstances from firsthand observation and he was able to buttress his theme with a mass of statistics from what are generally known as "reliable sources." Present-day scholars take issue with him on some of his allegations but his poignant picture was a major step in redefining the term "poverty" as "want" or "need" instead of the traditional "pauperism."

A man may be poor, Hunter argued, not only when he has no resources or hopes of accumulating any, i.e., when he is helpless, but even when he has a job and regular income. "Those who are in poverty," he wrote, "may be able to get a bare sustenance, but they are not able to obtain those necessaries which will permit them to maintain a state of physical efficiency." They may receive a paycheck every week in the year, have food on the table, and live in a tenement, yet still be poor. "Only the most miserable of them are starving or dependent on charity," the rest get no help from any source but are nonetheless in want. They have "too little of the common necessities to keep themselves at their best." Jacob Hollander, a professor at Johns Hopkins, later paraphrased the concept in convenient shorthand: the poor were the "inadequately fed, clad, and sheltered"—a shorthand which Franklin Roosevelt borrowed two decades later. The people who lived in this state were not lazy or unfit, yet their development was slowly stunted until it was beyond psychological or physical remedy.

By Hunter's standard there were at least ten million Americans in poverty during prosperous times, perhaps as many as fifteen or twenty million—an eighth to a quarter of the population—and almost all of them foreign-born. There were as many of German stock in New York, he pointed out, as in any German city except Berlin, nearly twice as many Irish as in Dublin, as many Jews as in Warsaw, and more Italians than in Naples or Venice. "No other great nation has a widespread poverty which is foreign to its native people. . . ." Hunter's figures, though much larger, were compatible with an estimate a decade earlier by Professor Richard T. Ely and Charles D. Kellogg, of a New York charity organization, that there were three million *paupers* in the country. Presumably there were three to six times as many "poor" as helplessly indigent. Hunter's computations also seemed to confirm the calculation by Riis that in the eight years before 1890 no less than one-third of the people in America's largest city had been forced to apply for private charity at one time or another.

Dependency, according to the young social worker, was only the terminal stage of poverty. Other symptoms included low wages, child labor, disease, unemployment, inferior housing, industrial accidents, illiteracy. The statistics he adduced for this thesis, culled from a hundred official sources, were an astonishing commentary on a thriving society. The 1900 census recorded that six and a half million Americans, or almost one-fourth of the laboring force, were unemployed at some time during the year, two million of them for as long as four to six months. Of the 606,000 inhabitants of Boston in 1902, 136,000 had to seek charity from "public authorities alone." That same year in Manhattan 60,463 families were evicted from their tenements for nonpayment of rent. So needy was the populace that one out of every ten New Yorkers who died had to be buried in potter's field "at public expense. The United Hebrew Charities reported in 1901 that 75,000 to 100,000 Jews were incapable of providing for their own necessities. According to the Massachusetts Bureau of Statistics a family of five needed $754 a year, and according to the New York Bureau of Labor at least $10 a week to survive, but average wages for the unskilled ranged from $400 to $500, the standard wage being $1.50 a day. Shopgirls earned $5 to $6 a week, and one-third of the southern males over sixteen a similar sum. Good times or not, said the Industrial Commission—a federal agency—wages in 1900 were 10 per cent lower than before the 1893 depression. Years later, economist Paul H. Douglas, in a scholarly tome on the subject, corroborated such allegations by proving that real wages—what they could buy in terms of consumer goods—were no higher in 1914 than they had been in the 1890's. A man could work all year long, in rain or shine, and still not have enough to support his family or maintain himself in "a state of physical efficiency." Not infrequently then, he sent his under-age children into the factories or mines—there were 600,000 so employed in 1900—or had his wife take in homework. In the cluttered apartments of New York City, especially around Mulberry, Mott, Elizabeth, and Chrystie streets, 24,260 homeworkers were licensed in 1903 for underwear, women's clothing, and "the thousand and one other articles" they fabricated on their own premises. Jacob Riis reported in 1900 that he had seen women working all day finishing pants for total earnings of only thirty cents.

Until Hunter and the other researchers of the Progressive Era, the study of poverty had been a superficial one, often centering on effect rather than cause. If studies showed that a large percentage of the poor were alcoholics, drinking was designated as a *cause* of poverty; it did not occur to such charity workers that it might be the other way around, a man drank to forget debased circumstances. The progressive generation put things right side up (or upside down, depending on one's views): there were innumerable factors making for poverty beyond the individual's control. Consider the matter of industrial accidents or factory sanitary conditions. In 1901 some 2,675 railroad workers, or one out of every 399 then employed in this industry, were killed on the job. Among the operating craftsmen the figures were much higher, one of every 137 losing his life and one of every eleven being injured in a single year. The figures for Colorado miners were of similar magnitude. Frederick L. Hoffman, statistician for the Prudential Life Insurance Company, noted there were 30,000 to 35,000 laborers killed while at work during 1908 and two million injured. Occupational diseases, such as silicosis, pulmonary and respiratory ailments, arsenic and lead poisoning, claimed innumerable additional victims. One of the most derogatory industrial words of the period was "sweatshop," signifying a musty, airless, crowded, inflammable, and unsafe factory where workers sweated or froze, and died a premature death. The nation was horrified by the Triangle Shirtwaist Company fire in March 1911, in which 145 employees, mostly young girls, died while trapped in a New York loft that had no outside fire escapes. For each death or long-term injury through accident or disease there was a family left in dire straits, its way of life suddenly and decisively altered through circumstances over which it had little influence.

One of the most stinging descriptions of immigrant workers' conditions was made by a Hungarian churchman, Count Vay de Vaya und Luskod, in 1908 after a visit to McKeesport, Pennsylvania. "Fourteen thousand tall chimneys are silhouetted against the sky along the valley that extends from McKeesport to Pittsburgh," he wrote, "and these fourteen thousand chimneys discharge their burning sparks and smoke incessantly. The realms of Vulcan could not be more somber or filthy than this valley of the Monongahela. . . . Thousands of immigrants wander here from year to year . . . and here they suffer till they are swallowed up in the inferno. Scarce an hour passes without an accident, and no day without a fatal disaster. But what if *one* man is crippled, if *one* life be extinguished among so many! Each place can be filled from *ten* men, all eager for it. Newcomers camp out within sight of the factory gates, while a little farther away others arrive with almost daily regularity—thousands of immigrants to don the fetters of slavery."

Another plague of the immigrant poor, institutionalized into the work system among the Italians particularly, was the mischievous padrone system. Seven thousand agents were said to be operating in Italy alone, luring potential workers to the other side of the Atlantic with all kinds of extravagant promises. Those who took the bait and emigrated found themselves on arrival here under the tender mercies of a padrone, who arranged jobs and secured apartments for them—

—all at a handsome commission. As described by the *Charities Review* the system operated much like a cattle market. A contractor or a railroad company in need of unskilled labor placed an order with a padrone, say for "five hundred dagoes," and the padrone matched his men to the jobs. Untutored and unlettered foreigners who fell under this system often were afraid to reject the job, since they might not be offered work again, and had almost no say about conditions, which sometimes bordered on slave labor. A correspondent for the *Review* described one such group of "isolated camps, cut off from the outside world by mountains" in West Virginia, in which the laborers were surrounded by armed guards for fear they might flee and cost the contractor his $15 investment in them. A man who tried to leave was, in the author's words, "driven back at a run under the muzzle of a rifle, and made to lift alone so heavy a stone that he suffered a severe rupture." Similar conditions were usual for other ethnic groups. "Scarce a Greek comes here, man or boy," wrote Jacob A. Riis, "who is not under contract. A hundred dollars a year is the price, so it is said by those who know, though the padrone's funning has put the legal proof beyond their reach."

The most enervating feature of immigrant life in the slum colonies was the slum itself. A report of the New York Tenement House Committee of 1900 said: "With all the remedial legislation and regulation . . . the present type of tenement house—the six story double-decker—occupying 75 per cent of a twenty-five foot lot, with four families on a floor, gives its occupants less light and less ventilation, less fire protection and less comfortable surroundings than the average tenement of fifty years ago, which was lower in height, occupied less lot space and sheltered fewer people." In 1864, 486,000 persons lived in such hovels; in 1900, 2,372,079 of the three and a half million New Yorkers languished there. In a typical tenement there were fourteen rooms on each floor, but only four received light and air from the street or the back yard. The ten rooms on the side were fed air from a shaft "which is enclosed on all four sides, and is foul and semi-dark." In "summer, the small bedrooms are so hot and stifling that a large part of the tenement-house population sleeps on the roofs, the sidewalks, and the fire-escapes."

A report of the Chicago City Homes Association, written by Robert Hunter on the basis of surveys by himself and other social workers, was more graphic, and if anything more gruesome. Here the tenements were not high, 90 per cent being only one or two stories. But the overcrowding was indescribable, three-quarters of the apartments studied being less than four hundred square feet. The investigators listed case after case of seven or eight people confined to 228 square feet, an area about the size of a modern living room. One day, Hunter records, he visited the home of a man who worked on a street-paving gang and had left early because of heat prostration. In the two-room apartment of a rear tenement (behind another one in the front) lived seven people. "The day was in August, and the sun beat down upon one unintermittently and without mercy. . . . The air was steamy with a half-finished washing, and remnants of the last meal were still upon the table. A crying baby and the sick husband occupied the only bed." As he watched the skillful mother keeping order in her household, writes Hunter, he "understood a little of what it meant to live in such contracted quarters. To cook and wash for seven, to nurse a crying baby broken out with heat, and to care for a delirious husband, to arrange a possible sleeping-place for seven, to do all these things in two rooms which open upon an alley, tremulous with heated odors and swarming with flies from the garbage and manure boxes, was something to tax the patience and strength of a Titan."

In the three districts researched, "darkness, lack of air, uncleanliness, and poisonous gases" were universal complaints. One out of every twelve families lived in a dank, airless basement. The plumbing was abominable; in the rear 769 apartments, 667 had no sinks. Despite laws to the contrary, hundreds of privies amounted to nothing more than holes in the ground without sewer connections, each serving eight or nine people. Many of the water closets were either in halls, basements, or under the sidewalks, releasing insufferable stenches that eternally pervaded the apartments. In two Italian and Jewish neighborhoods, only 3 per cent of the homes had bathtubs. The streets, alleys, and sidewalks were in such broken state that 1,554 court cases were pending for personal injuries sustained on defective sidewalks alone. Worst of all, there was "a surprising number of stables in the three districts." District one had had only one hundred more rear houses than stables—537 stables with 1,443 horses.

Here are some typical entries in the social workers' log books describing specific buildings on certain streets:

Polk Street—Cellar and first floor used for stables.

Twelfth Street—Stable complained of as the worst in America. Three cows kept in dilapidated house. Three cows and four horses kept in stable; shocking condition.

Taylor Street—Manure pile has been in yard over a year. Bitter complaints.

Liberty Street—Manure seven feet high in yard.

Blue Island Avenue—Manure-box bottom is broken out and manure falls to yard ten feet below. Yard wet and dirty.

Throop Street—Keep poultry in cellar, great odor.

"If I should be asked," said Dr. S. A. Knopf before the New York Tenement House investigation of 1900, "what conditions are most conducive to the propagation of tuberculosis and especially pulmonary consumption, I would have to reply, the conditions that prevail in the old-fashioned tenement-houses as they still exist by the thousands in this and other large cities." During the previous four years, he noted, there were as many as twenty consumptive cases reported in a single building, and many more unreported.

What this state of affairs did to the human soul is not reducible to arithmetical statistics, but a New York agency reported the following corollary effects: "Keeping children up and out of doors until midnight in warm weather, because rooms are almost unendurable; making cleanliness of house and street difficult; filling the air with unwholesome emanations and foul odors of every kind; producing a state of nervous tension; interfering with the separateness of home life; leading to a promiscuous mixing of all ages and sexes in a single room, thus breaking down the barriers of modesty and conducing to the corruption of the young, and occasionally to revolting crimes."

It was no wonder then that "prostitution has spread greatly among the tenement houses." Daughters of "honest and reputable parents," said the New York Tenement House Committee, often envied the ladies of joy who plied their trade in the same buildings, living high off the hog while they themselves came home tired after a ten- or twelve-hour day in the sweatshop. "The fall of many girls . . . has, undoubtedly, been due to this contamination." The slum took vengeance on its people in a dozen different ways. It enticed disenchanted youth into a life of crime. It drove some insane: half the inmates of New York State's insane asylums were foreign-born slum dwellers. It drove others to the poorhouses, the last staging ground of poverty. Two-thirds of those in city poorhouses were aliens.

Statistics on economic growth or national income clearly did not tell the whole story. "To many thoughtful men" of the period, Harold U. Faulkner notes, "it seemed that America in making her fortune was in peril of losing her soul."

Chapter 15

HALFWAY HOUSE

Though there was an interlude in the 1920's when, according to some people, America went "back to normalcy," the period from the 1890's to World War II is known as the Age of Reform. It was an age when the mood of America made a 180-degree turn from the conservatism of the previous three decades to a new form of liberalism. The public became aware of the miseries of the poor as never before and an increasing number demanded that something be done about it.

The Age of Reform, like ancient Gaul, may be subdivided further into three parts: the Populist period, the Progressive Era, and the New Deal, each with its own distinct characteristics. In the Populist decade (the 1890's) the surge of reform came from rural America but was turned back at the water's edge without significant victories. In the Progressive Era (1901–1914), against the background of the urban and immigrant poverty described in the last chapter, the reform movement became national in scope, under the aegis of middle-class youth, and penetrated the highest places of government. That its achievements were indecisive is attested to by the fact that the New Deal (1933–1939) was necessary twenty years later. The New Deal in turn evolved in the midst of the worst spasm of poverty in American history, engulfing not only workers and farmers but the middle class as well, and resulting in the most deliberately conceived antipoverty program up to that time. The three periods form a continuum in which the United States, sputtering like a tin lizzie, made the transition from *laissez faire* to controlled capitalism, from rugged individualism to a measure of collectivism and welfarism.

The middle period, the Progressive Era, is noteworthy for its inchoate, confused, and disorganized character—like an army in the field caught by a surprise attack, not entirely sure where to make its stand. The two Presidents whose names are associated with progressivism, Theodore Roosevelt and Woodrow Wilson, began life as conservatives and were driven to the reformist stance by the winds around them. The President who served in between, and fell to ignominious defeat in 1912, William Howard Taft, was never able to adjust to the crescendo of reform. Progressivism, clearly, was a pragmatic response by writers, social workers, thinkers, and some political leaders to what Walter Weyl called the "disequilibrium between social surplus and social misery." In a milieu where wealth and monopoly were pyramiding sensationally, poverty stood out all the more glaringly. As a matter of conscience, then, many intellectuals raised their voice in protest, at first issue by issue, until the movement found philosophical direction from the pens of brilliant young men like Weyl, Herbert Croly, and Walter Lippmann, as well as a few older ones like Louis D. Brandeis. A new generation of middle-class youth, as Charles Forcey writes, "turned away from the dream of automatic progress by the free-wheeling exercise of individual rights to a conviction that only the conscious, cooperative use of governmental power can bring reform." But they implemented this conviction in a variety of different ways on a number of different fronts. Theirs was a cacophony of songs played by a dozen pianists— muckrakers who exposed the brigandage of the trusts and the exploitation of the common man in vivid journalism; zealous social workers who ministered directly to the poor in new settlement houses; theoreticians who painted the bright tomorrow; city and state reformers who fought corruption; the two Presidents who carried the mood into the halls of federal power.

The awakening of conscience, however, was also a response to the ground swell of agitation outside the ranks of progressivism. It was stirred and goaded on by the efforts of the dispossessed themselves, in tens of thousands of strikes for union recognition, and by the emergence of a new left more determined than ever to lay low the specter of capitalism. Whereas the average number of walkouts in the mid-1890's was 1,300 per year, the figure rose to 4,000 by 1903. Some of them were incredibly bitter, especially those of the Western Federation of Miners and the Industrial Workers of the World (IWW) led by radical socialists and syndicalists. In the fifteen-month strike by miners in Cripple Creek, Colorado, in 1903 and 1904, for example, 42 were killed, 112 wounded, 1,345 held in bullpens for many months —denied the right of habeas corpus—and 773 forcibly deported. "To hell with the Constitution!" cried General Sherman Bell whose troops were being paid by the employers to subdue the strikers. "We're not following the Constitution." Fourteen hundred soldiers policed Lawrence, Massachusetts, during the walkout of immigrant textile workers in 1912, and 876 employees, mostly foreign-born, were arrested during the first month of the Chicago clothing strike in 1915. The skilled and semiskilled flocked to the AFL, which quintupled its ranks from 1898 to 1904, from 278,000 to 1,676,000. The unskilled and foreign-born could be found with the socialist-controlled garment unions or the IWW. At the meetings of the Lawrence unionists in 1912 one could hear a multiplicity of foreign tongues—Italian, Russian, Portuguese, Syrian, Lithuanian, German, Armenian. The plaint of the proletarian on the picket line was captured in this chorus of Ralph Chaplin's "Solidarity Forever":

It is we who plowed the prairies, built the cities where they trade;
Dug the mines and built the workshops; endless miles of railroad
    laid;
Now we stand outcast and starving, 'mid the wonders we have made;
    But the union makes us strong.

Also speaking for the poor in a way that excited many beyond its ranks was a growing socialist movement. The Socialist Party, born through a number of fusions in 1900–1, began with 4,536 members and kept doubling and redoubling in size every couple of years. By 1912 it boasted 117,984 members (the largest Marxist party in American history), plus many times that number of non-dues-paying sympathizers. It published thirteen daily newspapers, eight of them in foreign languages, forty-two weeklies (one, *Appeal to Reason*, with a circulation of a half million), and was able to elect 1,039 party members to public office, including 56 mayors, 1 congressman, and 300 local aldermen. Eugene V. Debs, the Socialist standard-bearer, in 1912 polled 6 per cent of the votes, 900,000, as against 6,250,000 for President-elect Wilson. The intellectuals who were either members of the Socialist Party or stood between it and progressivism included such luminaries as John Dewey, Stuart Chase, Paul Douglas, Roger Baldwin, Jack London, Floyd Dell, Max Eastman, Harry Overstreet, Alexander Meiklejohn, and Jacob Potofsky. Many a convert from socialism became a publicist for progressivism, for instance Walter Lippmann, and many a disillusioned progressive sought shelter under the umbrella of socialism.

It is against this panorama of class conflicts between workers and employers, and the revolutionary preachings of socialists and Wobblies (as IWW members were called), that the palliatives of the Progressive Era were applied. That socialism loomed weightily in the thinking of the reformers is indicated by the frequency with which they referred to it. Even Roosevelt, in his youth a social Darwinist, was constrained to note in 1907: "There are plenty of people who call themselves socialists, many of whose tenets are not only worthy of respect but represent real advance."

II

The middle-class dissent that accompanied this rise of radicalism was a discordant drama played out simultaneously on five stages. It was a mood as much as a movement, generating itself like a self-winding watch. The first symptoms of this mood manifested itself in cities and states where mavericks sought to dislodge the corporate giants and predatory machines from political power. Hazen S. Pingree, an affluent shoe manufacturer, threw the rascals out in Detroit as early as 1889, and was elected three times thereafter. His avowed purpose was to take business out of politics, in particular the utilities and street railways. Pingree's reign was distinguished by the open help he gave streetcar workers while on strike, and by his much-heralded "potato-patch plan," which assigned vacant lots to 1,000 impoverished families on which to grow vegetables. Samuel M.

(Golden Rule) Jones, reform mayor of Toledo, also a wealthy man, argued for government ownership of the utilities as the first step toward a national cooperative commonwealth. Though he had never read Marx he came to the conclusion on his own that "private ownership is a high crime against democracy." Other reformers who seized local bastions included Tom L. Johnson in Cleveland; Seth Low, president of Columbia University in New York; Brand Whitlock, who succeeded Jones in Toledo; Newton Baker, who succeeded Johnson; Ben Lindsey of Denver; Mark Fagan of Jersey City; Joseph Folk of St. Louis; Hovey Clarke of Minneapolis; and two Socialists in Milwaukee, Emil Seidel and Dan Hoan. In Galveston, Texas, after the flood that devastated one-third of the city in 1900, a commission plan of government was introduced, and copied by 200 cities within the next decade. A widespread belief existed, especially in the Midwest, that if citizens could regain control over their cities and towns democracy could be made to work on behalf of the underprivileged.

The mounting tide billowed into state government. Robert M. La Follette, the most consistent progressive of the first quarter of the century, was elected governor of Wisconsin in 1900 against a machine that had been entrenched for twenty-five years, and promptly set about to introduce direct primaries and impose higher taxes on the railroads. "A small, wiry man," Russell B. Nye describes La Follette, "with a shock of black (later iron-gray) hair and a tendency towards swift and sharp gesture, [he] was honest, serious, almost inhumanly intense and thoroughly uncompromising." La Follette's contemporary reform governors included Joseph W. Folk of Missouri, Albert B. Cummins of Iowa, Hiram Johnson of California, Charles Evans Hughes of New York. Many of the innovations they introduced in the political schema seem minor or irrelevant in retrospect, but they were burning issues at the time. To take party nominations out of the hands of the bosses they passed legislation for "direct nomination" by the people through primaries; Wisconsin enacted such a law in 1903, seven other states in 1907. To checkmate legislative power, Oregon introduced the referendum and initiative in 1902, modeled after the system in Switzerland. The referendum permits voters to pass on measures introduced by the legislature; initiative is a mechanism by which the populace itself can propose bills either for vote of the people or for the law-enacting bodies. Within a decade fifteen states followed Oregon's example on "direct legislation." Other efforts to democratize the creaking political process included recall of officials who had become persona non grata with the public, limits on election expenditures, direct election of senators, and women's suffrage. It is often forgotten that as late as 1914 only eleven states granted the ballot to the distaff side, all in the progressive West, beyond the Mississippi.

More symbolic of the progressive mood than the local reformers, and indicative of its national scope, was the bank of journalists and writers whom Theodore Roosevelt disparagingly called muckrakers. The name derives from the "man with the muckrake" in *Pilgrim's Progress*, who only looked downward to the filth on the floor. Presumably—or at least so TR thought—the fraternity of literary figures who exposed corruption with incandescent brilliance could only look downward to the seamy side of things. But it was a side that the public wanted to explore, for their articles and books were immensely popular. Their hammerlike effect, says Arthur M. Schlesinger, resulted in state passage of "more social legislation in the first fifteen years of the century than in all previous American history." Lincoln Steffens, first of the muckrakers, wrote in *McClure's* on corruption in St. Louis; Ida Tarbell on the peculations of the Standard Oil Company; Ray Stannard Baker on the greed of the railroads; Charles E. Russell on the beef trust; Samuel Hopkins Adams on patent medicines; David Graham Phillips on "the treason of the Senate." An avalanche of muckraking novels, the best-known being Upton Sinclair's *Jungle* (1906) which led to passage of the Meat Inspection Act, and of historical iconoclasm such as Gustavus Myers' *History of the Great American Fortunes* and Charles Beard's *Economic Interpretation of the Constitution*, added mightily to the literature of exposure. "Muckraking, indeed," claims John Chamberlain, "provided the basis for the entire movement towards Social Democracy that came to its head in the first Wilson administration."

A third force in the middle-class awakening of conscience, but more integrally related to the poor, was the social worker. Unlike the charity dispensers of the early nineteenth century, social workers like Jane Addams, Robert Hunter, Julia Lathrop, Stanton Coit, and Edward T. Devine conceived of charity only as a down payment toward social justice. Playgrounds, nurseries, financial relief, education for the immigrants were offered because government was not yet ready to provide such facilities or was doing so inadequately. "We have a day nursery at Hull House," explained Jane Addams, the most prominent of social workers. "We would a great deal rather have someone else establish the nursery, and use our money for something else; but we have it because there are not enough nurseries in that part of the city. We have a free kindergarten, because we cannot get enough of them in the public schools of our ward. We have a coffeehouse, from which we sell cheap foods in winter at cost, not because that sort of thing is what the settlement started out to do, but because we feel the pressure for it. One of the residents goes every day to court, and has the children handed over to her probational care when they are first arrested—not because we want to do that, but because we have no children's court and no probation officer."

Exactly how much the social workers contributed to the amelioration of poverty is a subject of controversy. The socialist novelist Jack London said that "they do everything for the poor except get off their backs." But the career of Jane Addams, though admittedly atypical, attests to the fact that like the muckrakers they instilled a measure of humanity into a society whose veins had hardened with self-interest.

The founder of Chicago's famed Hull House was born in Stephenson County, Illinois, where her father was the leading local figure—banker, miller, state senator seven times. Though frail in health and advised by her doctors, after an operation, that she could never bear children, Jane Addams had no worries for the future insofar as money was concerned. But like many another young person of similar circumstances she was troubled, after the usual college schooling and two trips to Europe with her friend Ellen Starr, by a sense of emptiness, purposelessness. She recalled how as a child of seven she had visited the slums of Freeport near her home town and promised herself "that when I grew up I should, of course, have a large house, but it would not be built around the other large houses, but right in the midst of horrid little houses like these." On one of her pilgrimages abroad, while sitting in a cathedral at Ulm, Germany, the idea came to her that she too should build a cathedral, not for religious purposes, "but a cathedral of humanity, a place where beauty, in its broadest sense, could be brought into the lives of the poor and lowly."

Miss Addams did not have to *build* her cathedral in a slum. On Halsted Street in Chicago was a big house that a real estate dealer,

Charles Hull, had deeded to his secretary, Helen Culver. Miss Culver, in turn, passed it on to Jane Addams in 1889 for use as a settlement house. It was not the first one; Jacob Riis had founded Neighborhood House in New York the year before. Other pioneers included Lillian D. Wald and her Henry Street Settlement, Stanton Coit and his Neighborhood Guild, Robert A. Woods and his South End Settlement in Boston. Within fifteen years there were a hundred such houses, but none so successful as Hull House. In the first year alone 50,000 impoverished Chicagoans, mostly immigrants and immigrant sons, entered its portals to use its facilities.

Like the other settlements, Hull House sponsored classes in English, formed clubs for the youth, trained people in technical crafts, held discussions on literary subjects, initiated singing, gym and other societies, provided a library, and gave shelter to working girls who needed it. Most important, it became an institution prodding the authorities for reforms.

On noting the unsanitary conditions in which milk was being dispensed from cans, for instance, the Hull House social workers enlisted the aid of a University of Illinois agriculture specialist to help Miss Addams write a circular on the "Milk Supply of Chicago." It led to other studies and eventual improvement in the production and handling of milk. The Hull House founder prevailed on the powers to establish the first juvenile court; here young delinquents were dealt with not as hardened criminals but with the leniency due first offenders. When the settlement learned that children in its area were paid four cents an hour for sewing garments, it lobbied for an anti-sweatshop bill and succeeded in getting it passed—though the Supreme Court of Illinois ruled one of its provisions, the eight-hour day, unconstitutional.

Almost any human problem, large or small, attracted Jane Addams' attention. Once she petitioned the city to do something about the stink of uncollected garbage and the malfunctioning of sewers on the West Side. Hardened politicians turned a deaf ear to this demand until the newspapers took up the cry, whereupon the mayor appointed Miss Addams herself as garbage inspector at $1,000 a year. "She arose at 6 A.M.," writes William Leonard in a *Chicago Tribune* eulogy on the occasion of her centennial, "to see that the collectors got to work on time, followed the wagons on their rounds and to the dump, made the contractor increase the number of wagons

from nine to seventeen, made landlords provide garbage recep-
tacles."

From boys' clubs and girls' boarding facilities, Jane Addams'
movement reached far afield into the arenas of politics and social
reform. The West Side was then a hellhole of vice and corruption,
containing 255 saloons and ruled by Alderman Johnny Powers. Miss
Addams mobilized her followers three times for election campaigns
to unseat her nemesis, though in vain. She agitated for prison reform;
she joined with the National Child Labor Committee to win a shorter
work day and a minimum wage for children; she crusaded for the
first social insurance the country has ever enacted, workmen's compensation for employees injured in work-related accidents; and she
served four years on the Chicago School Board. Because of her
humanitarian efforts she was often called on to act as an arbitrator in
labor disputes—for example, in the Pullman strike of 1894, the team-
sters' walkout of 1905, the garment union strike of 1910, and ten or
twelve others. As a feminist she worked arduously for women's
suffrage, and as a pacifist she became president of the Women's International League for Peace and Freedom, formed in 1915 to fight
war. In 1931 she was awarded a Nobel peace prize for her efforts.

Taking each act or campaign on its own, Miss Addams' life seems
remarkably uncentered, a helter-skelter of motion without plan. But
the social worker whom she typified lived by the hope that if he
could implant the seed of human concern in one small place it would
spread roots everywhere. Let the nation pass a reform bill on child
labor, for instance, and the drum beat would roll on until all other
needed reforms were passed and America became a povertyless
Shangri-la. The social workers were in the van, seeking to ameliorate
degrading conditions while leading the campaign for government
action on minimum wages, safety standards of work, better housing,
unemployment compensation, social insurance, and the various
other planks that would eventually translate into the welfare state.

III

Moving from the fringes, where the middle-class zealots, the muckrakers, political reformers, and social workers were occupied, to the
core of power, where Presidents and Congress functioned, the senti-

ment for reform was much diluted. By a process of osmosis the humanistic *élan* inevitably infiltrated the White House, but the idea of federal action against poverty was still novel. It had taken a few decades for Americans to become accustomed to tepid regulation of the monopolies, and even that was still vigorously contested. To pass welfare laws that *gave* something to those in want, especially if they were not paupers on the verge of starvation, seemed to many an invasion of property rights in violation of every sacred constitutional guarantee. If the spirit of Populism then kept marching on, like John Brown's body, in the Midwest and the hinterlands generally, it was conspicuously absent from Washington the day Theodore Roosevelt took the oath of office following the assassination of William McKinley.

Roosevelt was a worthy graduate of the social Darwinist school, as ill disposed to reform as his predecessor. Of upper-class parentage, educated at Harvard, he was "liberal" only in the sense that he muddied his fingers in politics, an arena eschewed by contemporary young people of his class. For the rest he voted and spoke as expected of aristocrats. His record in the New York legislature, as police commissioner of New York City, Assistant Secretary of the Navy, and governor of New York State, was flamboyantly illiberal. When the New York legislature voted on granting the twelve-hour day to streetcar men, Roosevelt denounced the heretical bill as "socialistic and un-American." His answer to the problem of radicalism was to urge "taking ten or a dozen of their leaders out, standing . . . them against a wall and shooting them dead." He had hailed President Cleveland's suppression of the Pullman strike, advocated an obnoxious prison labor contract plan, fought pensions for teachers, and damned Bryan and the Populists as a "semisocialistic agrarian movement." On taking the helm he retained the McKinley cabinet intact, a cabinet generally conceded to be an appendage to Mark Hanna and Wall Street.

But the nation was pirouetting to the left, and the hero of San Juan Hill was sufficiently malleable to dance a few steps in the same direction. In his first message to Congress, December 1901, interwoven between statements damning murderous anarchists, suggestions for educational and monetary barriers against immigration, and a strong defense of corporate bigness, Roosevelt conceded that the old laws for controlling wealth were "no longer sufficient," and proposed legis-

lation to protect women and children in industries directly or indirectly dependent on the federal government. Touring the Midwest
and New England in mid-1902 he called for a "square deal" for
everyone—labor, business, and the public—a gentle theme that has
been repeated more or less by every President since then. In practice,
the square deal meant government regulation to trim the edges of excess, whether by management or labor organizations. Typically,
after nearly 150,000 anthracite miners under John Mitchell had been
on strike for five months in 1902 and the nation faced a coal famine,
Roosevelt tried to mediate the dispute with the railroad barons who
owned three-quarters of the mines. When they balked at submitting
the issues to arbitration, he threatened to send in 10,000 federal
troops to dispossess the mine owners and see that coal was produced.
There were no constitutional provisions specifically authorizing
such action but the President was clearly irked by the "arrogant stu-
pidity" of the corporations and such irrelevant statements as those of
George Baer of the Reading Railroad that "anthracite mining is business and not a religious, sentimental or academic proposition." It was
a unique action in that for the first time a Chief Executive was calling on the military forces not to smash a union—as Cleveland had
done during the Pullman strike—but to "protect the public interest."
The operators yielded to the threat and though the miners were not
jubilant with the award—it gave them the shorter hours and a 10 per
cent wage increase, but no union recognition, their central demand
—Roosevelt had established an image of resisting big business.

The image was further enhanced in 1903–4, when the Roosevelt
Administration prosecuted Northern Securities, a holding company
for three giant railroads, the Northern Pacific, Great Northern, and
the Chicago, Burlington and Quincy, on the grounds that 30 per cent
of its capitalization was "pure water"—stocks that had no assets behind them. The merger of the Morgan and Hill interests was ordered
dissolved, and when the order was sustained by the Supreme Court,
Roosevelt's reputation as a trust buster soared toward the zenith.
Concomitantly Congress, at Roosevelt's urging, passed the Elkins
Act, which declared illegal secret rebates by railroad companies to
their large customers. Under this law the old Rough Rider prosecuted Standard Oil and secured a $29,000,000 fine against it. All told,
in seven and a half years in office, Teddy Roosevelt entered twenty-
five indictments against the monopolies, including the sugar and

beef trusts. It was not a large number considering the pace at which combinations were forming, but it was so novel to see a President act against big business that Roosevelt won hearty plaudits from the public. He hastened to explain that he was not against wealth and combination as such, but simply against "misconduct" and against the "unscrupulous man, whether employer or employee" who challenged public interest. Neither then nor to his dying day, ironically, did Roosevelt ever argue that trust busting was an answer to poverty or society's ills generally, but his formula for the regulatory state was a stern departure from the approach of state and federal officials of the past, who resisted regulation as a matter of principle.

Roosevelt's second term in office is distinguished by the enactment of other regulatory measures and a few pieces of social legislation. The Hepburn Act granted more power to the Interstate Commerce Commission. The Pure Food and Drug Act provided for federal inspection of meat plants and barred the use of "deleterious" drugs and chemicals in food, liquor, and medicines. Two other bills limited hours of labor for trainmen and placed liability for work-related accidents in the transport industry on management. Until then the railroad worker had to prove that the carrier was negligent to receive compensation; now he was entitled to it automatically, no matter who was to blame. Another Roosevelt innovation was the 1907 statute that banned political contributions by corporations. The willingness to use state power against entrenched wealth, even though sporadic and in fact exceptional, lent an aura of progressivism to Roosevelt's Administration. It was buttressed by his strong stand on conserving timber lands, the program for irrigation in sixteen semi-arid states, and by the President's own vigor, charisma, and canny knack for public relations. By way of extenuation for not having done more, Roosevelt once wrote that "the men who wish to work for decent politics must work practically"—a thesis similar to the present liberal argument that "politics is the art of the possible."

When he turned over the scepter to his friend and Secretary of War, William Howard Taft, Roosevelt had hopes that the regulatory state would pass a national workmen's compensation law, grant further rights to the I.C.C. for checkmating the railroads, and place controls over the sale of stocks. But Taft lacked either flair or flexibility. He did, it is true, institute twice as many antitrust prosecutions as his predecessor, including indictments against Standard Oil of

New Jersey and American Tobacco. Under his tutelage Congress also passed laws for postal savings banks and parcel post service, and rushed through the Sixteenth Amendment to the Constitution which made it legal to impose an income tax. A number of minor social bills scurried through Congress, laws for safety standards for mines and railroads, an eight-hour day for government workers, abolition of phosphorous matches. But by this time progressivism had taken bolder theoretical form and the various states had passed hundreds of pieces of social and welfare legislation. By contrast with the prevailing climate, Taft's record seemed sterile and timid, so much so he was repudiated at the polls with only eight electoral votes—the worst defeat ever administered an incumbent President.

The mood of the country was overwhelmingly reformist by 1912, the two progressive factions—Wilson, the Democrat, and Roosevelt, the nominee of the Bull Moose third ticket—receiving three votes to every one for Taft. Sentiment against the financial titans was so great the Democratic convention had passed a resolution by four to one proclaiming its determination not to choose "any candidate for President who is the representative of or under obligation to J. Pierpont Morgan, Thomas F. Ryan, August Belmont, or any other member of the privilege-hunting and favor-seeking class." Through eight months of hectic hearings that year, the Pujo Committee of Congress focused attention on the "vast and growing concentration of control of money and credit in the hands of a comparatively few men." The "money trust," it said, dominated the American economy, with five banks alone, through interlocking directorates, ruling 112 corporations with a capitalization of twenty-two billions. Both Roosevelt's New Nationalism and Wilson's New Freedom, though differing on methods, agreed that the monster must somehow be controlled.

A second strain in the progressive sentiment reaching its apogee that year was that of social justice. The cry was strongest at the state level where legislation on behalf of the weak gained momentum. As of 1912 there were bills on the books of thirty-eight states setting minimum age restrictions on the employment of minors—usually fourteen to sixteen years. The laws also prohibited their employment in dangerous trades or on night shifts, limited hours of labor, and made detailed provision for schooling. Twenty-eight states had established maximum hours of work for females, and dozens were now enacting workmen's compensation bills whereby an injured laborer was entitled to compensation without having to prove he was blameless. These grass roots laws were, as usual, under attack in the courts as invasions of "property rights," but they accurately reflected the public cry for state protection for the powerless.

The 1912 campaign, then, was essentially a debate on how, not whether, to put the concepts of regulation and social justice into practice. The differences between Roosevelt and Wilson were sufficiently subtle for Wilson to have once commented: "When I sit down and compare my views with those of a Progressive Republican I can't see what the difference is, except that he has a sort of pious feeling about the doctrine of protection, which I have never felt." Roosevelt would not checkmate bigness per se, but restrict its effects when it became harmful to the public interest. "We are for the liberty of the individual," he wrote in 1910, "up to, and not beyond, the point where it becomes inconsistent with the welfare of the community." The corporations could be made responsible, he held, through revising the Sherman Act so that a "national industrial commission," similar to the Interstate Commerce Commission, monitored the honesty and conduct of the trusts to check overcapitalization and other vices. Wilson, guided in his thinking by an old friend of La Follette's, Louis Brandeis, proposed to "return in some degree at any rate, to the practices of genuine competition." Monopolies would be broken up by federal action so that the smaller entrepreneurs might flourish with less handicap.

On the question of social justice and reform the Bull Moose program was the more specific. It included direct primaries for the choice of presidential candidates, direct election of senators instead of by state legislatures as still prevailed in some states, women's suffrage, initiative, referendum and recall, and a host of welfare measures—national workmen's compensation, child labor bills, minimum wages and an eight-hour day for women, safety and health standards "for the various occupations," and a pledge of sickness, unemployment, and old age social insurance. In capsule form this was a lineal cousin to the future New Deal. Wilson's program was less detailed and laid its major emphasis on winning freedom for the people against "the curse of bigness," but it too promised to use government power to "exalt the lowly and give heart to the humble and downtrodden."

The transformation of Wilson, like Teddy Roosevelt, from conservatism to progressivism is an interesting affirmation of the adage that the times make the man. Wilson, a college professor and university president, son of a Presbyterian minister, was also conservatively oriented at the time he assumed his first post in 1910 as governor of New Jersey. During the 1907 panic, he denounced the levying of fines against malevolent corporations on the grounds that it put money "into the public treasury where there is generally a surplus and where it is likely to lie idle." Like Roosevelt he had been zealous in condemning socialism and showed little love for labor unions that espoused the closed shop. Newly elected as president of Princeton, Wilson publicly sided with capital during the 1902 anthracite strike, charging the union with a shady ambition "to win more power." Walter H. Page was not wrong when he described Wilson as "a right-minded man of a safe and conservative political faith. He would not have the government own the railroads; he would not stir up dis-content . . . he would not speak the language either of Utopia or riot."

Wilson, however, bowed to prevailing sentiments. "We have been proud of our industrial achievements," he said in his first inaugural address, "but we have not hitherto stopped thoughtfully enough to count the human cost, the cost of lives snuffed out, of energies over-taxed and broken, the fearful physical and spiritual cost to the men and women and children upon whom the dead weight and burden of it all has fallen pitilessly the years through." This was a paraphrase of the familiar progressive credo that society has as much obligation to conserve its "human resources" as its material resources. During his first couple of years in office Wilson tried to accomplish this objective in the roundabout way of filling the leaks in the regulatory dam. But in due course he shifted emphasis to legislation that more directly affected human welfare. By the time the United States entered World War I the scope of government intervention had been expanded in both respects. The Federal Reserve Act of 1913 established a "bank of banks," divided into twelve districts, and designed both to make the supply of money more elastic and to ensure cooperation during panics. The Clayton Anti-Trust Act authorized more vigorous action against trusts and exempted unions from prosecution under its terms, a harassing technique often used under the old Sherman Act. The Federal Trade Commission Act set up a government institution to root out "unfair methods of competition." It is true, as critics charged, that Wilson appointed to the Federal Reserve Board and the Federal Trade Commission men of conservative bent, and that the number of antitrust prosecutions in eight years of Wilson's stewardship was only about the same number as during the four years of Taft's. All of which punctuates the point that frequently in American history the composition of enforcement committees has cut the ground from under progressive legislation. But if regulation was the answer to whatever it was that ailed America, Wilson filled out its structure appreciably.

On the social front Wilson signed into law the income tax bill introduced by a young Congressman from Tennessee, Cordell Hull, which imposed graduated rates ranging from 1 per cent (on incomes above $3,000 for single people and $4,000 for married ones) up to a maximum of 6 per cent on earnings of a half million or more. On the welfare side too, Wilson approved the Seamen's Act of 1915, introduced by La Follette, which improved conditions for merchant sailors. The Adamson Act set a limit of eight hours a day for railroad employees. The Keating-Owen Act—later declared unconstitutional—took a roundabout way of prohibiting the employment of youngsters under fourteen. Workmen's compensation received abbreviated attention from Wilson's Congress in August 1916, when it passed such a law for those employed by the federal government. The Federal Farm Loan Act of 1916 gave rural Americans something they had agitated for for decades, easier credit. It provided for the establishment of twelve federal land banks empowered to sell bonds to the public and loan the monies raised to farmers—through cooperative associations—at rates of 5 to 6 per cent interest.

The middle-class reformers, after a decade and a half, could point to a considerable enrichment of American life. The slums continued, it is true, but a network of parks, schools, playgrounds, roads, sewerage systems surrounded them to make urban living more tolerable. There were three and a half million automobiles on the highways by 1916, and gas light was rapidly giving way to electricity. Real wages were only slightly higher than in 1913—1 per cent—but at least they were not plunging in the other direction, and soon, spurred by war, they would go up some more, and almost half the workers would be working a forty-eight hour week.

Yet the mechanism for keeping balance between rich and poor was already in disarray—and in half a generation would be a shambles.

Statistics for 1917 showed that only one and a half million families (out of twenty-one million) earned enough money to pay any kind of income tax, while the number of millionaires had risen from 7,509 in 1914 to 19,103 and would soon rise still more. The prosperity on the farm, two decades old, was about to be washed overboard by another cycle of overproduction, and the regulatory dams—I.C.C., F.C.C., and Federal Reserve—would prove much too sievelike to check the greatest onrush of poverty in American history.

Taken together the package of regulatory and welfare measures neither checked the advance of unbridled wealth nor gave the poor an adequate cushion against economic insecurity.

IV

On balance, the most noteworthy contribution of the Progressive Era toward an antipoverty crusade was in the intellectual probings by some of the keenest minds of the century—Herbert Croly, Walter Weyl, Walter Lippmann, Louis D. Brandeis, Charles McCarthy, among others. Of these, Croly—"the greatest publicist of his generation," according to Waldo Frank—was the most prominent. A slight, medium-sized man, unusually shy, far from good-looking, and "morbidly sensitive," he wielded vast influence with Teddy Roosevelt before and during the 1912 Bull Moose campaign, and on all liberals when he, Weyl, and Lippmann began publishing the *New Republic*. The core of his philosophy, set down in *The Promise of American Life*, published in 1909, was a theory of a "new nationalism." Reduced to essentials, it was a formula for class reconciliation as against the socialist doctrine of class struggle, a formula that all other progressives and liberals have accepted as axiomatic ever since.

Invidious poverty amid enormous and, to some extent, unearned riches, said Croly, must "breed class envy on the one side and class contempt on the other," dividing the community "irremediably." Some means must be found through the good offices of government to bridge this chasm. The muckrakers, he argued, contributed little to this process, for their exposures of corruption implied that society's sickness was due to personal wickedness. Croly, by contrast, like the Marxian socialists whom he disparaged, ascribed the current difficulties not to men, per se, but to "the system." Americans were trying to squeeze a square political peg, built for an agrarian culture and unrestrained individualism, into the round hole of an integrated industrial economy. If it were up to him, said Croly, he would remodel the Constitution, for its decentralized division of powers among federal, state, and local governments was generations out of date. He restrained himself from proposing so drastic a step only because the document was considered too holy to tamper with. Other means, therefore, would have to be devised to get around the barrier.

Croly wasted no words of sympathy on the small entrepreneur, hero of American tradition. If "the small competitor of the large corporation is unable to keep his head above water, he should be allowed to drown." Bigness and inequality, he said, were here to stay and it was time Americans divested themselves of the foolish Jeffersonian notion of "equal rights for all and special privileges for none." That you could not have "liberty" and "equality" both was evidenced by the pragmatic circumstance that the corporate wizards had used the liberty of *laissez faire* to become untrammeled goliaths. He did not deny that the monopolies had strewn their mischief throughout the economy, but he claimed that there could be "fruitful" bigness and "fruitful" inequality providing that government intervened to "maintain a proper balance" between capital and labor. Croly's "national reconstructive policy" to accomplish this balance called for a strong centralized government in the tradition of Alexander Hamilton, promotion of labor unions, regulation of big business. This was the path, said the author of the New Nationalism, to conserve and protect the nation's human resources.

From this philosophical perch the mentor of progressivism came down to specifics. The Sherman Anti-Trust Act should be repealed outright since the trusts, properly regulated, were a boon to the nation rather than a liability. There was an apparent similarity between this estimate and that of J. P. Morgan, but where the financiers would leave corporate wealth unmolested, Croly would place it under "official supervision" through such devices as federal incorporation. Those that were "natural" monopolies, such as the railroads, would be nationalized by the government, not as a step toward socialism, but as a means of appropriating "the fruits of . . . monopoly for public purposes." Since power and wealth were two sides of the same coin, Croly proposed a number of measures of "constructive discrimination" against wealth in order to curb its power.

One would be an inheritance tax of 20 per cent as a means of redistributing the national riches.

Insofar as the unions were concerned constructive discrimination would work the other way around, as "substantial discrimination in their favor." Here the purpose was to increase the power of unions since they were "the most effective machinery which has as yet been forged for the economic and social amelioration of the laboring class." What he proposed was something akin to the future Wagner Act, recognizing and protecting the rights of unions to organize and bargain, and guaranteeing them a union shop requiring all employees to become members. Just as with the small businessman, Croly had little patience for workers who did not want to belong to the labor movement. The unions were entitled to full strength in dealing with management, and the union shop was one means of assuring it. On the other hand Croly went even further than the present Taft-Hartley Act in placing shackles on unions that operated against the public interest. Those would be stripped of their prerogatives, and the government might even establish dual organizations to function against them—"counter-unions."

The redistribution of power was the vehicle for redistributing income and wealth, and in the end both labor and "responsible" capital would be better off. Clearly there were resemblances here both to socialism and the fascist corporate state, especially since Croly stressed the need for strong leadership such as was offered by Teddy Roosevelt. To the pundit of progressivism, however, this was not socialism but a nationalist means of avoiding it, and though it was collectivist in spirit it catered to "constructive individualism."

Walter Weyl, author of *The New Democracy* (1912), and another titan of progressive theory, stoutly reinforced many of Croly's themes, but laid more stress on humanitarian reforms. A handsome man, militantly independent, outgoing, a wizard with statistics, a linguist and widely traveled, Weyl was more at home with laborers and socialists than Croly. As a drifter of twenty-nine, he offered his services to John Mitchell of the United Mine Workers during the bitter 1902 strike (other volunteers included Louis D. Brandeis, Clarence Darrow, John R. Commons, and Henry Demarest Lloyd) and prepared the stark statistics of mine-worker exploitation for President Roosevelt's Board of Arbitration. Though his resistance to socialist blandishments was lifelong, he was a sympathetic critic, and his writings are larded with references to Engels, Edouard Bernstein, John Spargo, and other Marxist thinkers.

But Weyl also believed in the reconciliation of classes and "fruitful" inequality. Want could be eradicated even while the gap between rich and poor remained substantial, he said, so long as society stimulated consumption. "Where wealth is growing at a rapid rate," he wrote, "the multitude may be fed without breaking into the rich man's granary." There was no need to take away the rich man's fortune so long as the national pie grew larger each year and was judiciously allocated. Weyl, like Croly, would socialize monopolies at a certain point and replace *laissez faire* with stern regulation.

The wizard of statistics, however, was more specific—and more passionate—about the social reforms needed for the "conservation of human resources." "Sooner or later," he said, "we must insure our population against sickness, accident, and invalidity, and must devote enormous sums to the prevention of these calamities." Universal state insurance "compels society to recognize that it itself is the loser from each preventable sickness." In the same vein he advocated abolition of the sweatshops, regulation of factory conditions, free education from kindergarten to university, and steps to limit consumption of tobacco, alcohol, opium, cocaine. The humanist strain is evident in a passage by Weyl on the social cost of sweatshops: "From the point of view of society this cheapness is dearness and sheer wastefulness. It would be wiser to pay a few cents a gross more for our artificial flowers. It would be cheaper to pay our bounty in dollars than in the life and health of the workers." Where Croly placed his stress on "constructive discrimination" in favor of the unions, Weyl laid the outline for a welfare state, socialized medical insurance, laws against woman and child labor, maximum hours, minimum wages, free education, abolition of night work, full Negro suffrage. The impetus for this reformist crusade, he felt, would come not from either the rich or the poor—who together constituted but twenty million of the ninety million American population—but from the seventy million in the middle who would be mobilized for the New Democracy.

Walter Lippmann, youngest of this triumvirate of progressive theoreticians, was, like Weyl, of German-Jewish background, but more of an active figure than his contemporaries. Leader of the Harvard Socialist Club, a fervid member of the Socialist Party, secretary to a Socialist mayor for four months, he quit the Socialist movement in 1912 because it was not radical enough. But the next year he published *A Preface to Politics,* which sought a moderate substitute for socialism. His main contribution was to wed the progressive *élan* with Freudian psychology, arguing that political leaders could sublimate the dark, malevolent forces within them to create the good society. It was, he said, a fiction that the misery of the poor was due to "a deliberate and fiendish plot" initiated through "the will, the intelligence and the singleness of purpose in the ruling class." The new businessman could be molded, with judicious government prodding, toward greater social responsibility. "That subtle fact—the change of business motives, the demonstration that business can be conducted as medicine is—may civilize the whole class conflict."

Other progressive philosophers sought to civilize the class conflict by returning as much as possible to the principles of free competition. Boston attorney Louis D. Brandeis sponsored and adhered to this theory to the end of his days, leaving a deep imprint not only on the Wilson but the Franklin Roosevelt administration. Also of German-Jewish parentage, a tall, thin man with narrow face, dark eyes, and vigorous gestures, Brandeis was a successful lawyer in his mid-forties when the Progressive Era began. Though his clients included many businessmen he was a liberal of the old style, dedicated to individual freedom and respect for privacy as guaranteed in the Constitution. His general sympathy for labor was tempered by a legalistic accent on freedom: he defended the rights of unions to organize but only in open shops where individual workers could join or not join as they pleased. He spoke often of social justice, espoused child labor and other reform legislation, favored municipal ownership of street railways, but the central focus of his social philosophy was the curbing of monopoly. It was not only "bigness" that appalled him but the diluted initiative and inefficiency of large institutions. He caused a furor testifying before the Interstate Commerce Commission when he charged that railroads could save a million dollars daily through more efficient management. The money trust he said was responsible for the execrable conditions of workers in the mills of the United States Steel Corporation who labored long hours seven days a week. For a whole decade he fought successfully against a J. P. Morgan—inspired merger of the New York, New Haven and Hartford Railroad with the Boston and Maine. It was the "curse of bigness" Brandeis believed that inhibited national development and

caused social misery. Against the bigness of business he would coun-
terpose the power of the state through antitrust prosecution and, if
necessary, price-fixing and fair trade laws.

A cousin to the Brandeis philosophy was the New Individualism
espoused by the sharp-tongued senator from Wisconsin, Robert M.
La Follette, and his associate, Charles McCarthy. The old frontier
individualism, they said, could no longer serve as the basis for
democracy in a highly integrated industrial society. If democracy
was to survive, rampant individualism had to be checked. Some of
the methods adopted might resemble socialism in that they restricted
laissez faire, but McCarthy and La Follette insisted that the New
Individualism could be achieved within the context of private
ownership of property. McCarthy and La Follette would save capitalism from its own vices by setting up a countervailing force—the
people. The cure for the sickness of democracy was greater participation by the people. "Get and keep a dozen or more of the leading
men of a community interested and well-informed upon any public
question," said La Follette, "and you have laid firmly the foundations of democratic government." As McCarthy spelled it out, there
were two prongs to the new individualist attack: one negative, one
positive. With the people controlling the mechanism of political decision through direct primaries, women's suffrage, initiative, referendum, recall, and popular election of U.S. senators, they would
effectively regulate capital and big business. This could be accomplished through antitrust laws, higher corporate taxes, banking and
insurance acts, corrupt practices bills, programs to conserve natural
resources. On the positive side, the legislatures would enact the welfare bills that would place a cushion under poverty—workmen's
compensation, old age pensions, woman and child labor laws, medical care insurance, and similar measures. Roosevelt undoubtedly had
La Follette in mind when he declaimed against "rural toryism." But
in a different form the arguments between the "new nationalist" liberalism and the "new individualist" brand were to continue into the
New Deal and beyond.

In the theoretical speculations of Croly, Weyl, Lippmann, Brandeis, La Follette, and McCarthy were the hilly outlines of America's
twentieth-century answer to poverty. Essentially what they were
calling for was a new capitalism, spurning the class struggle in favor

of class partnership. This was at one and the same time the response
to the challenges of both socialism and rugged individualism.

It is the prescription that, except in the 1920's, has been followed
for better or worse ever since.

Chapter **16**

PERCOLATION AND PANIC

For the better part of two decades a lively consensus seemed to be forming in America which stressed the need for a strong President, control over business, and welfare reforms. Without these essentials, said the oracles of the New Nationalism and the New Freedom, the specter of poverty would haunt the nation into eternity. But with America's entry into World War I and the "golden twenties" that followed, a new mood settled over the land, one of self-glorification, "Americanism," and conservatism. Why this was so is not entirely clear, but historians have noted that except for the period after the Spanish-American War every war that the United States has been engaged in has been followed by a relapse to conservative government. Arthur Schlesinger, Sr., has also pointed out that from 1765 to 1947 liberal and conservative times have followed each other, the former lasting an average of 16.2 years, the latter 14.8 years.

At any rate the idea of "reform" in the 1920's was not social insurance but the Volstead Act, which prohibited the sale of liquor. Big business, instead of being whipped into line, was running the government as flagrantly as it did during the Mark Hanna–McKinley days. And the two Presidents who occupied the White House for most of the time were, by comparison with Teddy Roosevelt and the erudite Wilson, Jukeses trying to solve Einstein's equations.

230

Warren G. Harding, an amiable journalist from Marion, Ohio, was a man of limited education and even more limited vision, who had been catapulted to the Senate and then the Presidency by old guard bosses who, like himself, reflected the narrow materialism of the times. His speeches reminded H. L. Mencken "of a string of wet sponges." The nation was returning, he said at his inauguration, to "normalcy"—or as his speechwriter had written it, to "normality"— by which he meant the rule of business and the trusts.

Calvin Coolidge, Harding's running mate, and successor on his death two years later, was, in the words of Samuel Morison, "a mean, thin-lipped little man, a respectable mediocrity, [who] lived parsimoniously but admired men of wealth, and his political principles were those current in 1901." Born in Vermont, a graduate of Amherst, a lawyer who ascended in slow stages from low office to the governorship of Massachusetts, his most noteworthy achievement before attaining the vice-presidency was breaking the Boston police strike of September 1919. His total philosophy was summed up in the single aphorism he tossed out to newspaper editors in 1925: "The business of America is business."

Yet the 1920's over which these two Presidents reigned was a remarkably prosperous period, and even more remarkably—to the bedevilment of progressive theorists—witnessed a sizable reduction in human want. Rexford G. Tugwell, a key figure of the early New Deal and certainly unsympathetic to Harding-Coolidge policies, conceded in a book co-authored with Howard C. Hill, that while ten million families were still in poverty as of 1929, four million had climbed out of the rut "from poverty to comfort." Further, if poverty was defined as an annual income below $2,000 per family, the lot of the ten million too had improved, since eight million had moved from "the minimum subsistence level" to the "upper ranges" of want.

Tugwell, of course, cited such statistics not as commendation but as an indictment. That ten million families, "over one-third of the total population," should still live below the level of decency in such a rich country during such an affluent period was adduced as impeachment of the "new era." But the facts were indisputable, and many a pundit was drawing the conclusion that at last, under the benevolence of "rugged individualism," America was headed for the want-less society. Coolidge was expressing what hundreds of leading economists and theoreticians believed when he said three months before he left office that "the country is in the midst of an era of prosperity more extensive and of peace more permanent than it has ever before experienced." A half year later Herbert Hoover, the "great engineer" and humanitarian who followed Silent Cal, exuberantly noted that "we in America today are nearer to the final triumph over poverty than ever before in our land. The poorhouse is vanishing from among us." The respectable and widely acclaimed economist Irving Fisher boasted that America was at "a permanently high plateau" of prosperity. And *True Story* magazine buoyantly plunked down the money for a *New York Times* advertisement on May 7, 1929, which read: "You business executives sitting at your desks, you have been making a fairy tale come true. Within ten years you have done more towards the sum total of human happiness than has ever been done before in all the centuries of historical time."

If history, Rip Van Winkle style, could have dozed off, after this ebullient outburst, for the next decade, the 1920's might have offered the final and convincing confirmation of social Darwinism. For in the 1920's the edifice of the progressive era was either undone or subverted, yet the nation had the boomtime look of an oil gusher. The gross national product, that ultimate materialist measurement of greatness, rose from $70 billion in the depression year 1921 when almost five million were unemployed, to $103 billion in 1929, and prices remained fairly stable. Even if comparison is made with the predepression year 1920, the real advance in GNP was still on the order of 45 per cent. Government data on per capita earnings showed that it had risen almost a fifth; others placed it at a third. And the 2,046 largest manufacturing firms showed a whopping profit of more than 11 per cent annually from 1922 to 1929. As a song of the day put it, "Happy Days Are Here Again."

Anyone could see it for himself just by looking around at the automobiles on the streets and the radios in the homes. As of 1920 only seven million horseless carriages rolled along American roads; nine years later there were twenty-four million. In 1921 citizens purchased ten million dollars' worth of a newfangled instrument, the radio, and in 1929 forty times that much. There were other wonders to behold and savor: the silent movies and the talking pictures; the electrical appliances; the spread of electricity and the telephone; the development of air flight. Almost anything could now be bought on the installment plan, and workers were joyously assuming debts, confident the bubble would never burst. The numbers of insurance policies and savings accounts burgeoned. So many people had surplus funds to invest on a sure-fire roulette wheel called the stock market that the number of brokers accommodating the demand rose from 30,000 to 71,000 in a single decade. The standard statistics of common stocks, set at 100 for the year 1926, skyrocketed to 148 by June 1928 and 216 by September 1929. Toward the end of the decade John D. Rockefeller, Jr., was paying an income *tax* of $6,278,000 on an income that must have been astronomical, and Henry Ford and his son Edsel, $5,100,000. If the wide-eyed masses could not yet afford to rent the apartments on Park Avenue, with gold-plated bathtubs, advertised for $45,000, their daughters could splurge on lipsticks at $2.50 a tube, and their sons on a package of three razor blades for a half dollar.

II

The "new era," as they called it after 1923, seemed to many the product of its own genius. Success was its own justification. But in calm retrospect it was obviously rooted in the special circumstances of World War I. The United States, having hung back from the fray for the first two and a half critical years, turned Europe's misfortune into its own grand opportunity. The minor depression of 1914 blended for the next five years into an incredible expansion, as Uncle Sam supplied a mountain of raw materials and finished goods to the embattled Europeans. Iron ore production rose from forty-one million long tons to seventy-five million; copper, oil, zinc, everything soared accordingly. Export of steel quadrupled; that of wheat tripled; and explosives rose by 125 times. The farmer could hardly satisfy demand, and was constantly seeking to put new acreage into production. Cotton, deep in slump in 1915 when it was selling for 8½ cents a pound, shot up to a record 36 cents by 1920; wheat zoomed from 97 cents a bushel to $2.73. So great was the demand for American goods that exports in 1917 exceeded imports by three and a half billion dollars—eight times the favorable balance in 1914.

The boom continued even when the United States joined hostilities, despite the fact that military expenditures cost about twenty-five billion and loans to the Allies another ten billion. Unlike

Europe, where both victor and vanquished were prostrate, the colossus of the West suffered negligible hardship, at least insofar as material things were concerned. Not a single inch of U.S. territory was devastated. Normal life was interrupted almost imperceptibly by rationing, government wage controls, pressure to buy liberty bonds, and federal operation of the railroads. Everyone who wanted work could get it, and real wages, though they failed to keep up with prices for a number of years, made a major breakthrough eventually so that by 1920 they were 12 per cent higher than prewar. The number of people earning $50,000 a year or more rose from 7,500 in 1914 to 25,000 in 1918.

When the war ended, the United States was ready for a second round of expansion. New York now had replaced London as the banking center of the world. The United States was no longer a debtor but a creditor nation, increasing its foreign investments by leaps and bounds. With Europe clamoring for goods and loans to recover from the maelstrom, and Americans ready to buy the wonderful gadgets for which the nation became famous, economic progress was sensational. In a sense no one was to "blame" for the boom, it sprouted from the tragic tree of war.

Despite the historical background, however, the Republican administrations of the 1920's attributed prosperity to the inherent strength of a capitalism freed from government restraint. "The driving force of American progress," said Coolidge, "has been her industries. They have created the wealth that has wrought our national development." From this it followed that what was good for business was good for the nation, and that the salvation of the poor lay not in such flimsy measures as doles or guaranteed minimum wages, which only stunted ambition and efficiency, but in helping industry. As the rich became richer, wealth would inevitably percolate down to the poor. On the other hand, to lay heavy taxes on business or reduce its profits would only hold back the economy and make the poor poorer. Cynics called this percolation or "trickle-down" philosophy a "theory of feeding the sparrows by feeding the horse."

In the smugness of prosperity there was a change in the configuration of power, and this change reflected itself in the conventional wisdoms. The same war that unleashed the new affluence also unleashed reaction—as it was to do after World War II and Korea. Under Woodrow Wilson, apostle of the New Freedom, thousands of antiwar socialists and Wobblies had been incarcerated during hostilities, and afterward—still under Wilson—thousands of additional leftists were put behind bars or deported to Europe under the 1920 Palmer raids. The postwar strike wave, reaching its climax in the strike—and rout—of 365,000 steelworkers in 1919, started the labor movement on a decade of decline. From five million members it shrank to three and a half million, the first time unions failed to grow in a period of prosperity. Flexing the big business muscle, Judge Elbert H. Gary told his U.S. Steel stockholders in 1921 that while unions "may have been justified in the long past . . . there is, at present, in the opinion of the large majority of both employers and employees, no necessity for labor unions." Not even Andrew Carnegie had said it so crassly. Soon five hundred employer organizations were embarked on an open shop campaign to prevent unionization of their industries, and to blacklist thousands of militants who tried it.

The defensive liberals tried to put up a barrier against conservative advance. A progressive bloc formed in Congress around Senators La Follette and Norris (both nominally Republicans) and outside the august halls, around a potpourri of groups such as the Conference for Progressive Political Action and the Nonpartisan League, which coalesced into the Progressive Party of 1924 and ran La Follette for President. But the aging Senator, who was to die the following year, polled only five million votes, one-sixth the total, and with his defeat the floodwaters of conservatism poured through unchecked. Coolidge presented the alternatives of progressivism and his own position in these terms: "whether America will allow itself to be degraded into a Communistic and Socialistic state, or whether it will remain American."

Wallowing in prosperity, with liberalism and radicalism routed, Americans talked not of reform but of "Americanism." Never before was this word bandied about so often, or the term "un-American" used so venomously against ideas and men—"labor agitators," for instance—the respectable class did not like. Given the conservative mood, the Ku Klux Klan came back into fashion, winning the governorships of Oklahoma and Oregon, and virtually seizing the state of Indiana. Anti-Semitism took wings, especially after Henry Ford published the faked "Protocols of the Elders of Zion" which "proved" that the Jews were in a conspiracy to take over the world. And even an anti-Catholic sentiment took hold, particularly in the South. Prosperity or no, an ugly chauvinism stalked the land. Antiforeignism, its obverse side, expressed itself in laws of 1921 and 1924 that limited immigration drastically. The number of aliens admitted to the promised land fell from 800,000 in 1921 to 150,000 annually by the end of the decade; from 1927 to 1935, in fact, more Europeans left the country than entered it.

In this setting citizens became complacent about trusts and big business. "As the years have gone by," wrote the well-known social writer Arthur Train, "and the millionaire era has become the billionaire era, the virus of acquisition has built up its own anti-toxin." Some dissent, it is true, was heard when the railroads were turned back in 1920—under very generous terms—to private ownership. Labor wanted the industry nationalized, as in most European countries, and William G. McAdoo, Wilson's Treasury Secretary who had run the roads, suggested they remain under federal suzerainty for another five years. But there was nothing like the agitation against the carriers that had prevailed a generation back. Merchant ships, acquired by the Shipping Board in wartime, were sold to the corporations under Harding for $30 a ton—one-eighth their original cost—with only muted opposition. Income taxes were lowered in such a way that those earning less than $5,000 found their levy cut by 1 per cent, whereas those in the million-dollar bracket reaped a bonanza of 31 per cent.

The consolidation of corporate wealth was actively encouraged by the government with little public outcry. One method, the brainchild of Secretary of Commerce Herbert Hoover, was to prod the firms into 2,000 new associations which, as Eric F. Goldman points out, "virtually ignored the antitrust laws." Another was to wink an eye at the mushrooming holding companies. The sixteen largest utility groups, according to the Federal Trade Commission report to the Seventieth Congress, controlled 53 per cent of the industry in 1924–25, as against 22.8 per cent a decade earlier. Thirty-seven hundred firms had disappeared into the void under the flood of mergers. Consolidations in auto, steel, movie, and retail businesses reached such proportions that by 1930 two hundred firms, controlled by 2,000 individuals, held in their hands almost half the nonbanking resources of the nation. Aided by the courts, which interpreted the antitrust laws liberally enough for almost any holding company to squeeze through, and by the benevolence of the Attorney General, the concentration of capital reached astronomic heights, all the laws against trusts notwithstanding.

For a brief historical moment the concept that what's good for business is good for America captivated the nation. Despite warnings by economists like Stuart Chase the belief spread that economic growth was irreversible, and that the riches would percolate down from the affluent to the lowly indefinitely.

III

Anyone who looked behind the façade of stock market speculation and flapper girls, of short skirts and long profits, however, could detect soft spots forming into festering sores. Textiles, certain branches of iron and steel, shipbuilding, bituminous mining, and above all agriculture were in a depressed state long before the climax of Black Thursday. At the boom's zenith, according to the Brookings Institution, 19 per cent of the country's productive capacity was idle and two million workers unemployed, many castoffs of technological advance. The maldistribution of income, again according to Brookings, was worse than even Tugwell had stated it. Allowing for $2,000 a year per family as the minimum "to supply only basic necessities," three-fifths of the nation was at the poverty level: two-thirds of this number at the "deprivation" level, while one-third—six million families—were living on less than half the minimum, $1,000. Thirty-six thousand families at the top of the ladder received as much income in 1929 as eleven million at the bottom.

Most dire was the plight of the farmer, who had never seen a glimmer of the golden twenties—for him they were an undiluted catastrophe from the outset. "Everyone seems to be prosperous and making money," said Senator George W. Norris of Nebraska, "except the farmer." With the end of the war, demand had slackened and from 1919 to 1921 prices had fallen by almost half. Two and a half dollar wheat in 1917, dollar wheat two years later, pigs at fifteen cents a pound down to seven cents, horses that brought $200 each "could hardly be disposed of in 1922 at fifty dollars." In a trip around the country R. L. Holman noted in 1921 that "one can see field after field growing up in rag weeds, indigo weeds, or other weeds peculiar to the locality." That old devil overproduction had again caught up the yeoman in a viselike grip, and neither he nor the price level ever recovered until the special ministrations of the New Deal. Land values fell from $79 billion in 1920 to $58 billion in 1927, and somewhere between a million and two million farm families deserted their holdings. "The farmer is on the way to peasantry," cried William E. Dodd in 1928.

In the paraphrase of Bruce Bliven of the *New Republic*, this was the agricultural consensus: "During the war the government told us to increase our acreage, to feed the soldiers overseas. When we protested that we could not finance such an effort, Washington told us: 'Never mind, the money will be provided.' . . . Then what happened? After the war, Washington suddenly ordered all loans called in. We were in no position to pay, and they went ahead anyhow. . . . The Federal Reserve Board put the screws on the banks, compelling them in turn to put the screws on the farmers. As a result, the latter lost their newly acquired land, and were very lucky if they didn't lose everything else they possessed in the world, in the bargain."

After the war the Senate Committee on Agriculture introduced a bill to set up the government as a huge middleman to stabilize prices. It was defeated, according to Senator George W. Norris, by "very powerful political influences." Subsequently the McNary-Haugen bill, modeled on a plan by the president of the Moline Plow Company, ran into the devastating opposition of Coolidge, Hoover, and the billionaire Secretary of the Treasury, Andrew Mellon; it failed of passage even though it had the backing of the Secretary of Agriculture. Under this plan the government would establish a federal farm board, with a $400,000,000 revolving fund, to buy surplus commodities and withhold them from the market until prices improved. The excess produce would be dumped abroad at whatever it would bring, the difference to be absorbed by a tax—"equalization fee"—on the farmers themselves. The bill was introduced again in 1926, once more failing of passage, and in 1927, though it carried both Houses, was vetoed by Coolidge. The President in turning down this legislation lectured the yeomen on the values of being thrifty: "The ultimate result to be desired," he said, "is not the making of money, but the making of people. Industry, thrift and self-control are not sought because they create wealth, but because they create character. These are the product of the farm. We who have seen it, and lived it, know."

If the condition of the husbandman was not enough to dispel the great illusion of endless prosperity, the stock market crash of October 1929 was more definitive.

IV

Herbert Clark Hoover had been President for less than eight months when the stock market crash opened the curtain on a long decade of depression. "The most disastrous decline in the biggest and broadest stock market of history rocked the financial district," was the way *The New York Times* described the sudden downward plunge of stocks on "Black Thursday," October 24, 1929. It was only the opening salvo. Five days later, after a group of bankers, meeting at the offices of J. P. Morgan & Co., had assured the nation that the economy was "sound," the stock market plunged deeper into the morass. "Stock prices virtually collapsed," reported the *Times*, and again repeated that it was "the most disastrous trading day in the stock market's history." Soon all kinds of unpleasant records were being broken. While bankers and political officials kept reassuring the public, business firms went bankrupt, banks closed their doors, unemployment reached new peaks, and many a family faced literal, not figurative, starvation.

It was Hoover's unhappy destiny to reap this whirlwind. As the months slipped by and the depression deepened, he would become the most unpopular President of this century. Shanty colonies put up by the unemployed on the outskirts of town would be called "Hoovervilles," the old newspapers used to cover the indigent as they slept "Hoover blankets," and rabbits "Hoover hogs." Hoover, however, unlike Harding or Coolidge, was not only a man of great stature but until the panic of 1929–33 cut the ground from under him, one of the most highly respected and popular figures in the nation. Both intellectually and administratively he was the equal of any modern Chief Executive. He was not, as commonly believed, an extreme reactionary; he was considered, in fact, the most "liberal" member of the Harding-Coolidge cabinets. Mary Elizabeth Lease, the Populist agitator of the 1890's, called him "one sent by God." He had flirted with the Bull Moose in 1912. Later he had tried to buy into the *New Republic* magazine, the voice of liberalism. In his own view he was the "true liberal," a label he proudly wore not as a gimmick for votes

—he never ran for public office until 1928—but as a sincere expression of what he believed was progressive politics. If the image he projected in the 1930's was of a dour, unconcerned, heartless representative of Wall Street, no one can disparage his work as a humanitarian during and after World War I. He may be criticized for seeking to use food as a political weapon—particularly against the Bolsheviks—but his relief work throughout Europe was highly impressive. John Maynard Keynes, to whose economic views Hoover was titanically opposed, said of Hoover's activities with the American Relief Administration that "never was a nobler work of disinterested goodwill carried through with more tenacity and sincerity and skill, and with less thanks either asked or given." Had he been President in 1865 or 1895 he would have served with honor, but in 1929 he was living proof of the obsolescence of nineteenth-century liberalism applied to twentieth-century conditions.

Herbert Hoover was the self-made man personified, and this undoubtedly contributed to his exaggerated faith in individualism. His father, a devout Quaker and village blacksmith in West Branch, Iowa, where Herbert was born, died when he was six; his mother, a gifted woman, also a Quaker and well known as a preacher, died three years later. The three orphaned children were divided up among relatives, Herbert, the middle one, winding up with an uncle on his mother's side, a doctor and land speculator who was moderately well-to-do. Working for his uncle as an office boy, Herbert was able to acquire an education at a small Quaker academy, then at the newly opened Stanford University in California, where again he worked part time and summers to pay his own way.

At college he associated with and helped organize the poorer students and, in the only other job besides President to which he was ever elected, was chosen treasurer of the school body in 1893. He graduated with an engineering diploma two years later in the midst of another terrible depression, so that instead of working at his profession, he was forced to take on a common laborer's job in a Nevada mine, shoveling ore at $2.50 a day. It was not long, however, before he had become assistant to a prominent San Francisco engineer and from there moved along to his first foreign assignment as an engineer for British gold mines in Australia. At the age of twenty-four he was earning $7,500 a year. By forty, after marriage and a host of jobs in China, Italy, Central America, Russia, Burma, and elsewhere, he was linked with a couple of dozen mining companies and was already a millionaire.

Perhaps it was Hoover's Quaker background or his knack for administration, but when he found himself stranded in Europe at the outbreak of World War I, he organized a private relief agency for tens of thousands of fellow Americans who were also unable to get home. Before he had completed this task he was called on to perform similar duties for ten million starving Belgians and Frenchmen. With the approval of the American ambassador to London, Walter Hines Page, Hoover formed the Commission for Relief in Belgium and distributed to the needy five million tons of food and clothing valued at a billion dollars—no mean task considering the blockade that hampered shipments. When the United States entered the fray, President Wilson called on Hoover to act as food administrator back home, and again he acquitted himself nobly. After the war, duty called him once more to Europe, this time to provide food for relief in twenty-three countries.

Hoover was no innocent dispensing food for its own sake; it was for him part of a program—parallel to that of President Wilson's—for rebuilding the old continent as a liberal capitalist haven, secure from the virus of Bolshevism. "My job," he later asserted, "was to nurture the frail plants of democracy in Europe against . . . anarchy or Communism. And Communism was the pit into which all governments were in danger of falling when frantic peoples were driven by the Horsemen of Famine and Pestilence." The same motivation undoubtedly caused him to assume another relief project in the fall of 1921, when he was Secretary of Commerce, to feed ten million Russians in the Volga Valley.

These and other relief activities built Hoover's image as a great humanitarian. Like General Eisenhower three decades later, he seemed to be a man above politics, with no known affiliations. He had been an advocate of Wilson's Fourteen Points and, with reservations, of the League of Nations; when asked in March 1920 for his political philosophy he described himself as "an independent progressive" equally hostile to "the reactionary group" in the Republican Party and to the "radical group" among the Democrats. When he announced his availability for the Republican presidential nomination shortly thereafter, it was as "a forward-looking liberal," a designation that no doubt contributed to the fact that the old guard passed him over, despite his immense national following, for the non-descript Harding.

Nor was this image tarnished during Hoover's tenure as Secretary of Commerce. He took what was a relatively insignificant assignment and built it to equal stature with that of the Secretary of the Treasury, the key job in Coolidge's Administration. He introduced, for instance, an Office of Simplified Practice to help standardize packaging and products, issued reports on business trends as never before, prodded corporations to form voluntary associations for their industries, did yeoman's work to find markets for American business. Though the winds of the Teapot Dome scandal swirled around him, Hoover himself emerged as a man of integrity, dedicated to business efficiency. He was the Republican Party's natural and overwhelming choice when the party factotums met in Kansas City in 1928, and he ran off with the election with 444 electoral votes against 87 for the colorful Alfred E. Smith of New York.

The man at the tiller, then, as the Great Depression approached, was neither incompetent nor base. He was a poor orator and something less than dynamic in his public stance, but he was not mediocre and though he believed in individualism, it was with certain qualifications. Unrestrained individualism, Hoover agreed, led to social injustice, but in the American system it was moderated by "equality of opportunity." In his credo the "strong" must not be permitted to overwhelm the "weak," but every man must be given a fair chance at the start of life's race to "take that position in the community to which his intelligence, character, ability, and ambition entitle him. . . ." This was, Hoover argued, "no system of *laissez faire*," but an underpinning for "economic justice as well as political and social justice."

It was from this philosophical perch that most of Hoover's practical reactions followed. He opposed socialism because it did not work, as proved, he said, by the experience of Russia. And he opposed state ownership, as he declared when he vetoed Senator Norris' plan for a government power plant at Muscle Shoals, because it put government into business to compete with private citizens. Oddly enough Hoover's Administration intervened in the economy more than any President's before him, though it was done grudgingly, late, and primarily on behalf of big business because of his twin fixations on "voluntarism" and the percolation theory.

The depression simply overwhelmed Hoover and fixed him into a kind of immobility; it was as if an irresistible reality were clashing with an immovable philosophy. Within a few weeks after Black Thursday thirty billion dollars of paper value had "vanished into thin air," a sum larger than the national debt at the time. As the banks began calling in their loans to stock speculators, tens of thousands were wiped out, hundreds committed suicide. Gruesome jokes were told of free revolvers being given out with every share of newly purchased stock, and of the hotel clerk who asked registrants whether they wanted rooms "for sleeping or jumping." Dixon Wecter tells the apocryphal story of a ruined shopkeeper who scribbled on his door "opened by mistake."

The statistics of economic decline that followed the crash can only be described as macabre. From October 1, 1929, to August 31, 1932, according to Frank A. Vanderlip, former president of the National City Bank of New York, 4,835 banks failed, costing depositors more than three and a quarter billion dollars. Not uncommon was the plight of a Mrs. Cearman, a Midwesterner, who "beat with her fists upon the closed plate-glass doors and screamed and sobbed without restraint. She had in a savings account the $2,000 from her husband's insurance and $963 she had saved over a period of twenty-five years from making rag rugs." She ended up in an insane asylum a few days later. The value of all stocks listed on the New York exchange fell from ninety to sixteen billions. A share of General Motors fell from a high of 91¾ to a low of 7⅞; Radio Corporation of America from a peak of 114¾ to as little as 2½; United States Steel, 261¾ at its highest in 1929, 21¼ at its nadir in 1932. The consequence, of course, was a great merry-go-round, loans called in where stocks had been put up as security, curtailment of spending, reduction in manufacture, layoffs of workers, further cuts in spending, further loans called in. The full effects were not felt immediately, but by late 1932 industrial production had fallen by one-half, construction by six-sevenths. Farm prices, already depressed, fell another three-fifths by March 1933, and a million more families abandoned their homesteads.

Wherever one turned was a wasteland of shattered lives. By March 1930 there were four million out of work, a year later eight million, and when Franklin Roosevelt took office in March 1933, at least thirteen million. Some estimates were as high as sixteen or seventeen million, with a similar number working only short hours. As of 1934—a year after the New Deal applied its magic potions—there were two and a half million proletarians who had not been employed for two years or more, and six million who had been out of work for at least a year. Those still lucky enough to hold jobs had their pay cut by 20, 30, or more per cent, a fact reflected in a 60 per cent drop in payrolls in just four years. The number of city dwellers who were dispossessed from their apartments ran into many hundreds of thousands. "This depression," commented Colonel Leonard Ayres in *The Economics of Recovery*, "has been far more severe than any of the twenty depressions that we have experienced in this country since 1790."

V

The statistics of the Great Depression, grim though they may seem, were merely pale reflections of human misery. "My four motherless children and I, the father," wrote a citizen to Governor Pinchot of Pennsylvania, "are on the verge of freezing and starving. Being several months out of work, I have no money to buy coal, food or winter clothes for my school children. . . . The landlord attempts to evict me from his premises. Two of my children are ill. So please, Mr. Governor, be kind and render your assistance . . . please assist us from cold and hunger, Mr. Gov. Pinchot."

Another read: "There are nine of us in the family. My father is out of work for a couple of months and we haven't got a thing [to] eat in the house. Mother is getting $12 a month of the county. If mother don't get any more help we will have to starve to death. I am a little girl 10 years old."

According to the Department of Labor, at least 200,000 waifs were wandering the land without means of support, and Hoover himself admitted there were "at least 10,000,000 deficient children in this country." One local hospital reported: "This week we have had four children admitted with the diagnosis of starvation. One who was found eating out of a garbage can, has died since admission." In a single day in April 1932, Boston police picked up thirteen unidentified bodies, men who had died of hunger or committed suicide. At the city dump on 32nd Street and Cicero Avenue in Chicago large lines formed every day waiting to sift through the refuse as garbage trucks unloaded their waste. At the other end of the country, according to a letter quoted by G. Hutchins in her *Women Who Work:* "An expectant mother lives in Hoovertown [a shantytown of unemployed named in honor of Hoover], on the edge of the industrial section of Los Angeles, with no shelter except a piece of canvas stretched over the bed. She and her husband have been out of work for months. For food, they eat the decaying vegetables given away by the wholesale markets as unfit for sale." An item in the Troy, New York, *Record* told an extreme but not uncommon tale: "The body of a man found Wednesday morning huddled beneath a pile of straw in the barn at The Knolls was identified yesterday as that of Ignatz Wlosinski. . . . An autopsy revealed that the man had died of starvation and exposure. . . . Authorities believe Wlosinski had been on the road and had crawled into a pile of straw at the barn in an attempt to escape from Tuesday night's bitter cold. When found he was about four feet beneath the surface of the straw."

At noon on February 14, 1933, a fifty-one-year-old man in overalls entered a bank at Garden City, Kansas, drew a revolver and told the assistant cashier: "I've got to have some money. . . . I'm sorry but I'm desperate. I'll pay this back when times get good." Scooping up $1,838 the farmer, a man named Ross Mundell whose farm was being foreclosed, repaired to the home of a friend and asked him to hide the money for the use of his children. "I'm going down the road now and kill myself."

In a small book called *The Great Depression*, David A. Shannon has compiled a sample of newspaper clippings, mostly from *The New York Times*, telling the story in its most graphic terms. "Fifty-four men were arrested yesterday morning," read a dispatch of October 7, 1932, "for sleeping or idling in the arcade connecting with the subway . . . but most of them considered their unexpected meeting with a raiding party of ten policemen as a stroke of luck because it brought them free meals yesterday and shelter last night. . . ." An announcement by the Soviet trading firm Amtorg that it had six thousand skilled jobs available in Russia brought "100,000 applications." According to Mrs. Elizabeth A. Conkey, Commissioner of Public Welfare, "several hundred homeless unemployed women sleep nightly in Chicago's parks." Oscar Ameringer, a Socialist publicist, told a congressional committee in February 1932: "While Oregon sheep raisers fed mutton to the buzzards, I saw men picking for meat scraps in the garbage cans in the cities of New York and

Chicago. I talked to one man in a restaurant in Chicago. . . . He said that he had killed 3,000 sheep this fall and thrown them down the canyon, because it cost $1.10 to ship a sheep, and then he would get less than a dollar for it. He said he could not afford to feed the sheep, and he would not let them starve, so he just cut their throats and threw them down the canyon."

While farmers were destroying cattle and crops that were unmarketable, police in dozens of towns reported items such as these: "Attracted by smoke from the chimney of a supposedly empty summer cottage near Anwana Lake in Sullivan County, Constable Simon Glaser found a young couple starving. Three days without food, the wife, who is 23 years old, was hardly able to walk." Or, "Found starving under a rude canvas shelter in a patch of woods on Flatboard Ridge, where they had lived for five days on wild berries and apples, a woman and her 16-year-old daughter were fed and clothed today by police and placed in the city almshouse. . . . They were huddled beneath a strip of canvas stretched from a boulder to the ground. Rain was dripping from the improvised shelter, which had no sides." A check on Chicago schools in June 1931 revealed that "11,000 hungry children were being fed by teachers." The superintendent of schools sent an urgent plea to the governor of Illinois: "For God's sake, help us feed these children during the summer."

If there was one feature that lent a distinction of sorts to the Great Depression, albeit a negative one, it was its universality. As Helen M. and Robert Lynd expressed it in their classic *Middletown*, "The great knife of the depression . . . cut down impartially through the entire population cleaving open lives and hopes of rich as well as poor." It was no longer the urban immigrants who held the citadel of poverty almost as a monopoly, or the working class and farmers. Caught in the web was a majority of every class, including professionals, academics, and businessmen. The man selling apples on the street corner was as likely to be a former certified public accountant as a drill press operator. This was, future sociologists would say, a "majority" poverty. Thus Langlan Heinz, forty-four years old, told a Brooklyn court trying him for vagrancy in May 1932, he was a graduate of the University of Colorado and had held responsible jobs in China, Panama, Venezuela, as a civil engineer. But his resources were now depleted and for the previous forty-six days he had been sleeping on a cot in a vacant lot near Flatbush Avenue. "Firemen at a firehouse near by gave him occasional shower baths, he said, and housewives and school children in the neighborhood gave him food." Of the 455 qualified chemists registered for employment at a New York relief agency, 109 were "said to be destitute, 130 others are in need and 158 have funds for a short time." At least 10,000 college alumni were unemployed in New York alone, according to a *New York Times* estimate of July 27, 1932. The story of the Donner family, released by a study group in Dubuque, Iowa, years later points up the problems of small businessmen. In 1918, after a career in insurance, Donner (first name not given) took over a printing firm in Chicago, whence he had moved as a youngster. The firm, employing twelve to thirty people, prospered and gave the Donners a fair income of $300 a month. In 1929, however, the bank that held his funds went under. To keep afloat he begged and borrowed from friends, and held on through 1930 and 1931. Finally the family of four had to sell its business and return to Dubuque to live with Mrs. Donner's parents. For five months the husband was unemployed, until finally he secured a job as common laborer on the Dubuque lock and dam project. In this and other jobs his income fell from $300 a month to $90. Franklin Roosevelt was to point out in 1938 that big businessmen had grown bigger during the depression, as bankrupt small firms were swallowed like minnows by larger ones, but the petit bourgeois and their technicians had cascaded to penury as never before.

The glow of the 1920's faded; the tune of the day was "Brother, Can You Spare a Dime?" In his 1930 play, *The Green Pastures*, Marc Connelly summarized it pithily: "Everything nailed down is comin' loose."

VI

Herbert Hoover would not admit that his vaunted free enterprise system was "comin' loose." It was simply "readjusting"; prosperity was "just around the corner." To question "the basic strength of business," he said in November 1929, "is foolish." In a speech to Congress on December 3, 1929, he explained the sudden downturn in these words: "The long upward trend of fundamental progress . . . gave rise to over-optimism as to profits, which translated itself into a wave of uncontrolled speculation in securities, resulting in the diversion of

capital from business to the stock market and the inevitable crash."
All that was needed was to restore "confidence" and the wheels
would soon be moving again. Some months later Secretary of the
Treasury Mellon airily observed that he saw nothing "in the present
situation that is either menacing or warrants pessimism." The
Hoover clan forged its own credibility gap long before the term
gained currency. "Business and industry have turned the corner,"
said the President on January 21, 1930, and a few months later reas-
sured everyone that "we have now passed the worst." The Assistant
Secretary of Commerce cheerily informed a radio audience that the
stock crash was only of minimal importance since it affected a mere 4
per cent of the population. The song was replayed like a broken
record throughout the next three years, joined by a chorus of financiers and businessmen who sang it with equal lustiness. "Business is
Good, Keep it Good, Nothing can stop US," read a billboard plastered across the nation by the National Association of Manufacturers.

Meanwhile the Great Depression was gaining momentum, and
everyone was crying for jobs and relief. The Communists, reduced to
a sect of 7,545 members during the twenties, called a national demonstration March 6, 1930, around the slogans "Don't Starve—Fight"
and "Work or Wages!" According to the *Daily Worker* account, almost a million proletarians and ex-proletarians responded, in more
than a dozen cities, a hundred thousand each in New York and Detroit. Two months later another national protest brought out only
about a third as many people, but it led to the formation of a Communist-controlled National Unemployed Council. Parallel to it, the Socialists established their Workers Alliance, and an unaffiliated radical, A. J. Muste, the National Unemployed League. Before long the
three groups, as well as many local ones, were conducting a guerrilla
war against the depression, involving literally millions of people in
small acts of resistance, such as sitting in a relief station to assure aid
for an unemployed family, demonstrating in front of city halls, occasionally raiding a food warehouse, and in thousands of instances preventing marshals from evicting tenants. Typically, as reported by an
Associated Press dispatch of January 20, 1931, from Oklahoma City:
"A crowd of men and women, shouting that they were hungry and
jobless, raided a grocery store near the City Hall today. Twenty-six of
the men were arrested."

The Unemployed Council of New York boasted that in a four-year period they moved 77,000 evicted families back to their apartments. Twice the Communists led small unemployed detachments to Washington, reminiscent of Coxey's Army forty years before. In 1932 a detachment of 20,000 World War veterans, also Communist-led, bivouacked in Washington demanding early payment of a bonus promised them for 1945. Their placards dramatized the gulf between official thinking and popular misery: "Heroes in 1917—Bums in 1932," "We Fought for Democracy—What Did We Get?" Hoover could think of no better answer to this plaint than ordering the men and their families home, and when many had left, sending in General Douglas MacArthur, with tanks and cavalry, to burn their camp down. Fifty-five people were injured.

Lest anyone conclude that all such agitation was the work of outside subversive plotters, Mauritz A. Hallgren reported in *The Nation* that "genuine rebellion is smoldering here [Detroit]. Wherever one goes through the working class districts one hears positive, angry expressions of dissent, unafraid expressions of sympathy for the radicals." The question, Can capitalism survive? was on so many tongues, a leading newspaper syndicate wrote a series of articles on the subject based on interviews with financiers and business officials. Everyone answered in the affirmative but the question itself indicated that there was a little doubt in many places. The Communists simply articulated a widespread malaise. Sherwood Anderson, the noted author, stated it best in a letter to President Hoover on August 11, 1932: "What I am trying to say to you is that men like me do not want to be radicals. I am, myself, a story-teller. I would like to give all my time and thought and energy to story-telling. I can't."

The agitation on the farm was equally disconcerting for the White House; not even the Populist 1890's approached it in intensity, and certainly not in violence. At its extreme the protest took two forms, "strikes" to withhold produce from the market and forceful resistance to foreclosure sales. A Farmers' Holiday Association in Iowa laid siege to Sioux City, Council Bluffs, and other cities in 1932. With guns, clubs, and fists the farmers declared themselves "on strike" to prevent milk and produce from reaching market. The effort was not successful, but it led to a nationwide movement engaging in similar actions throughout the farm states. More effective was the campaign against foreclosures. Sometimes repossession sales were stopped entirely. When New York Life Insurance tried to foreclose a fa.m in Cedar Rapids with a $30,000 mortgage on it, the farmers seized its attorney and prevented the sheriff from "doing his duty." An appeal by the Circuit Court judge "to let the law take its course . . . was applauded by a hail of stones and clods." More often, however, the technique was to turn the forced sale to the farmer's advantage. Characteristically, the farm of Charles Grady of Champaign County, Illinois, with a $2,750 mortgage on it, was put on the block and "sold" for $4.75—no one dared bid any higher. An indebtedness of $1,200 on another farm was retired for $16.46, tractors falling under the hammer for twenty-five cents, horses for a dime, wagons for fifteen cents. After the "sale" the property was leased free to its former owner for ninety-nine years. Forced sales were carried out against one-tenth of the farms in the country, according to Ernest A. Dewey in *Commonweal* magazine, but there were many occasions when the courts, banks, and insurance companies declared "a virtual moratorium on farm mortgage foreclosures" for fear of mob action.

No President could have disregarded the social tempests of the 1930's, but Hoover's method of dealing with them was along the philosophical lines of Grover Cleveland. The nineteenth-century President, in vetoing a $10,000 drought relief bill in 1887, expressed the conviction that while "the people support the Government, the Government should not support the people." Hoover's principles lay in the same direction, and while he introduced a variety of relief measures—more than any presidential predecessor—they pivoted, as already noted, around the twin themes of voluntary action and "percolation," helping the rich so that they might make jobs for the poor. "A voluntary deed by a man impressed with the sense of responsibility and brotherhood of man," said the Chief Executive, "is infinitely more precious to our National ideals and National spirit than a thousandfold poured from the Treasury of the Government under the compulsion of law." Hoover had used government funds a decade before for direct relief in Europe, but for his own country he considered "works of charity" the proper—and "loftiest"—solution. Ironically, during a drought in Arkansas in December 1930, he urged Congress to allocate $45,000,000 to save the animals, but was patently displeased when the Senate added $20,000,000 to feed human beings. He applauded when the Red Cross refused a $25,000,000 grant from Congress to aid drought victims.

The first patient to be tended, even before the stock market crash, was the depressed agricultural industry, whose mortgaged indebtedness had doubled within a decade. Responding to the agitation of western progressives, Hoover called a special session of Congress but warned in advance that government subsidies, "price fixing, or any other such nonsense" was out of the question. Instead he sponsored an Agricultural Marketing Act to encourage *voluntary* formation of marketing cooperatives. In addition to other functions, the co-ops would seek to create price stability by purchasing commodities when prices were low and holding them until the market improved. A half billion dollars of government money was made available for loans to fulfill this task. Additionally, "stabilization corporations" were authorized to do pretty much the same thing but under direction of a federal board. Neither plan worked. In the gloom-ridden Hoover years there just was not enough money in the cities, no matter how hungry were its people, to buy up rural surpluses. The co-ops found themselves with glutted elevators and warehouses, unable to sell their produce or repay their loans. And the three stabilization corporations, after purchasing mountains of cotton, grain, and wool in 1930–31 had to stop buying. Hoover refused to walk the last mile toward "government compulsion" to check overproduction, and with that lapse agriculture slipped further into the quicksand.

The "great engineer" was not callous. He more than doubled, for instance, expenditures on public works such as the Boulder Dam, and thereby created 600,000 additional jobs. With his engineer's slide rule, he sought to stimulate and co-ordinate private giving for charity, but no more. In October 1930 Hoover appointed a President's Committee for Unemployment Relief, to raise funds and formulate plans for local communities. Ten months later, under the directorship of Walter S. Gifford of American Telephone and Telegraph and a blue ribbon group of financiers and businessmen, the committee set about to raise $175,000,000 through theater and sports benefits, as well as advertising campaigns. The drive unfortunately coincided with a 10 per cent wage cut by Ford, U.S. Steel, General Motors, and others who were represented on the committee, but Gifford moved ahead undaunted. "Between October 19th and November 25th," read one copywriter's masterpiece, "America will feel the thrill of a great spiritual experience." The spiritual experience, however, netted less than a hundred million dollars nationwide, or $3 for each of the thirty million estimated then to be in need.

The fervor for self-help and charity was so pervasive in the upper echelons of society that when Senator La Follette in 1931 proposed a measure for direct federal relief, Senator Gore of Oklahoma denounced it, amid applause, as "the beginning of the dole. . . . Of all the diseases known to pathology, the passion for a pension such as this is the most debilitating." Senator Goff of West Virginia warned about impinging on state sovereignty. Even the president of the American Federation of Labor, William Green, went on record against such nostrums as unemployment insurance on the grounds that it was "a hindrance to progress," a "dole" which affronted "the dignity of the workingman" and would only "subsidize idleness."

Private initiative, taking its cue from the President, performed with characteristic American ingenuity. The most poignant symbol of the day, apart from the breadlines, for instance, was the man on the street corner selling nice shiny apples for a nickel apiece. Some promoter at the International Apple Shippers' Association had thought up the idea of supplying the indigent with apples on credit, to be hawked from boxes on the sidewalk—no overhead involved. Within a nonce there were 6,000 apple entrepreneurs in New York alone, eking out a few dollars daily, until a year later when Manhattan began to curb the practice because of the havoc and sanitation problems it created. During 1931 someone thought up the "Give-a-Job" campaign, urging neighbors, still working, to employ those jobless for whitewashing a cellar or cleaning a yard. Another fashion in relief was called "Block Aid"—dwellers in the same block made weekly collections for their less fortunate friends. A million or more people seceded from the economy to form 154 barter associations in twenty-nine states, exchanging products directly or with special scrip, without the use of legal tender. One such group in California numbered 200,000. All such schemes, however, including those of the President's committee, were like garden hoses against a forest fire. Cynics had adequate proof that the brotherhood of man was chimerical without a federal warrant or an unemployed demonstration, or both, behind it.

By 1931–32 the ship of voluntarism was listing heavily. The local relief system, which began with the dead weight of Elizabethan principles three centuries before, was now financially and morally on the shoals. There were 3,072 counties in the country, each with dozens of city and township relief boards, conflicting in their rules and benefits. Ohio with eighty-eight counties showed 1,535 agencies, each one trying to collect its own funds and, if possible, pass the burden elsewhere. In a detailed analysis for *Survey* magazine, Thomas E. Murphy, secretary of the Public Welfare Commission of Rhode Island, showed how much of the Elizabethan hangover still existed. The laws on public relief in many states still used the word "pauper" under titles such as "The support of paupers and the keeping out and discipline of paupers." Even the settlement provisions of colonial days remained on the books. A man seeking relief had to prove "settlement" of ten years in Rhode Island, five in Maine and New Hampshire, a year in New York, Iowa, Michigan, Minnesota. The Alabama law set restraints on paupers "strolling from one district to another."

Disarmed by such atavistic machinery and unaided by the federal government, local relief all but collapsed by 1932. H. L. Lurie, director of Jewish Social Research in New York, told Congress: "Relief has been continuously and gradually reduced so that whole families are getting an average of $2.39 a week relief in New York City, with $3 and $4 and at the most $5 a week . . . in other cities." The agencies, he said, were unable to pay for rent, gas or electricity. On the average, they gave succor only to 32 per cent of "the totally jobless." How the rest lived was anyone's guess, though an educated estimate by two university professors, Henry Bamford Parkes and Vincent P. Carosso, put the figure of those living in Hoovervilles at one million and the number who had returned to relatives on the farm at a half million. There were in addition, say the two historians, two million "homeless migrants," including 200,000 children.

There were 700,000 jobless in Chicago, 40 per cent of the labor force, 130,000 families. But the city did not have the money to pay its teachers, let alone its paupers. New York, Detroit, Boston, Philadelphia were similarly at the brink of bankruptcy, all trying to borrow money from the corporations to help the jobless. Detroit automakers made one such loan to the city on condition it dole out no more than seven and a half cents a day for food for each individual. Niles, Ohio, reported it was supplying victuals to one-fourth its population, 4,377 people, at 1½ cents a meal; and Tulsa, Oklahoma, announced, "A charity ration costing six cents per day per person is feeding ten thousand unemployed and their families 'and giving them all essential food values.'" To prove how meagerly a person could live the mayor of Syracuse put himself on a nine-cent-a-day diet—for one week.

It was an intolerable situation but Hoover rebuffed all efforts by

Senator La Follette, Congressman Fiorello La Guardia, and others to introduce national relief. The way to help the poor was not through a temporary and degrading expedient such as government handouts, but by getting the wheels of industry to roll again. "The sole function of government," said Hoover, "is to bring about a condition of affairs favorable to the beneficial development of private enterprise." Private enterprise had, of course, shown itself singularly unable, even with a friendly regime in Washington, to ward off the depression. But Hoover, after first conceding that the causes of the cataclysm "lie to some extent within our own borders," blamed it all on the world depression, which caused foreign nations to dump their goods and securities in the United States and undercut the American economy.

Hoover's counteroffensive against misery and unemployment was therefore an oblique one. He called together the titans of industry in November 1929, and subsequently, to urge them to "maintain social order and industrial peace" by holding the line on production and retaining present wage levels "temporarily." When, after two years, these appeals to voluntarism failed to produce improvement, the great engineer finally agreed to government intervention. To stimulate overseas purchase of American goods, he declared a moratorium on foreign war debts and reparations. Internally an avalanche of credit was thrown into the economy to buttress its tottering ramparts. A half billion dollars of loan capital was subscribed by the big bankers for the National Credit Corporation, which in turn loaned it to small banks near collapse. One hundred and twenty-five millions were made available for loans to farmers through federal land banks, to help them ward off mortgage foreclosures, and a similar fund was established to save institutions that loaned money to home owners.

The primary instrument for counterattack was the Reconstruction Finance Corporation. Passed in January 1932, the R.F.C. bill provided three and a half billion dollars for loans to banks, insurance companies, and similar institutions to help them ward off disaster. Cynics called it a "breadline for big business." One of those who received a handsome handout on this "breadline"—$90,000,000——was the large Chicago bank that had been headed by former Vice President Charles G. Dawes, who by strange happenstance had moved from that post to the presidency of the R.F.C. Dawes had written to Hoover the year before commending him for his courage in vetoing the bonus bill for veterans, but he did not consider that inconsistent with the "millionaires' dole"—as Congressman La Guardia put it—for his own bank and similar financial titans.

Finally, as a rider to the R.F.C. bill, $300,000,000 was made available to the states after July 1932 to finance relief of the poor. By the time Hoover left office in March 1933, the R.F.C. had lent $201,000,000 of this money, and another $224,000,000 for local public works, as against a billion and three-quarters to 7,500 banks, railroads, and other businesses. There was a fleeting moment in late summer of 1932 when this panacea seemed to be working, as the economy took a brief turn for the better. But optimism vanished into the void as the wheel turned again in the opposite direction.

The month Franklin D. Roosevelt replaced Hoover, after applying a humiliating defeat to the incumbent President of 472 electoral votes to 59, there were more people unemployed and more banks going under than at any time in American history.

Chapter 17

NEW WINE—OLD BOTTLES

The antipoverty programs prior to the New Deal ordinarily were subpoints under broader programs, leaving the mistaken impression that nothing had been done about poverty until recent times. The sale of Tory land during the Revolution, for instance, was a means of punishing the enemy as part of the struggle for independence. That it ameliorated the condition of tenants or landless farmers was coincidental. The Northwest Ordinance and the public-domain policy after the Revolution also helped many needy people but they too had wider geopolitical and security aims. The emancipation of the slaves was a byproduct of an internecine war to save the Union. The Homestead Act was more directly linked to the whittling of want but it was buried within a complex of other issues—secession, slavery, industrial expansion.

In that sense the New Deal was unusual, for in 1932–33 poverty was *the* issue, the only issue. The nation was in no danger of territorial atomization by forces either within or without. All it had to contend with—no small challenge, to be sure—was its own stalled motor, incapable of lifting its people above the shoals of insecurity.

The New Deal therefore takes on a magical luster in the folklore of America, for it was a sensational step against the dispiriting blight of the Hoover years. It invoked the psychological vision that someone

256

upstairs really cared. It shredded bugaboos about the limitation of government prerogative, and set such cushions under insecurity as unemployment compensation and old age pensions. It raised hopes and mended hopelessness. The area it covered in renewing optimism can be gauged from the alphabet soup of agencies it ladled up to deal with the crisis: A.A.A., N.R.A., F.E.R.A., C.W.A., N.Y.A., T.V.A., C.C.C., P.W.A., W.P.A., F.H.A., U.S.H.A., N.L.R.B., F.C.A., H.O.L.C., S.E.C., R.E.A., and a host of others. Most important, it turned America from *laissez faire* to controlled capitalism, a legacy that has proved to be irreversible.

The New Deal Administration did all this with deliberate determination, more so than any administration before or after. Its results, however, call to mind the man with a size ten foot who invariably wore size eight shoes. When asked why, he replied: "Because it's so good to take them off at night." The New Deal was a wonderful relief from the torment of uncertainty that preceded it, like taking off tight shoes. But among the things it did not accomplish or approach was the abolition of poverty. The government's own figures showed that there were six times as many unemployed in early 1939, when the experiment ended, as in 1929, and almost two and a half times as many as in the first full depression year, 1930. With all the fanfare and alphabetical agencies, joblessness had only been whittled from a high of thirteen million to ten million. Industrial production, the gross national product, farm income, and workers' wages were not yet in sight of the peaks in the golden twenties by quite a distance. The British economist John Maynard Keynes had told Roosevelt early in his ordeal that he had the singular opportunity of applying "the technique [of large government spending] which has hitherto only been allowed to serve the purposes of war and destruction" in the "interests of peace and prosperity." It was "war and destruction," nonetheless, that finally absorbed the jobless and brought the nation a thirty-year spiral of prosperity which still bathes the New Deal in retrospective glow. "The New Deal," writes William E. Leuchtenberg, "left many problems unsolved and even created some perplexing new ones. It never demonstrated that it could achieve prosperity in peacetime." Without World War II and the postwar military expenditures of almost a trillion dollars, the Roosevelt bundle of panaceas would today appear much less glossy.

II

"I pledge you, I pledge myself," Franklin Delano Roosevelt told the Democratic Party convention which had just nominated him, "to a new deal for the American people." The catchy phrase, soon on everyone's lips, came from a remark by Mark Twain's Connecticut Yankee that when six men out of a thousand can crack the whip over 994 others, it is time for the "dupes" to seek a "new deal." The tall, handsome, boyishly exuberant nominee with an exciting inflection in his voice, plucked such phrases from the air with the instinct of an evangelist, "but what they mean (if anything)," said Elmer Davis, a future New Deal official, "is known only to Franklin D. Roosevelt and his God."

Politicians, of course, prefer to leave as much to ambiguity as expediency permits, but in this instance the candidate himself had no clear perception of the road ahead. Working on his behalf was a crew of professors, whom *New York Times* writer James M. Kieran had dubbed the "brains trust"—later modified to "brain trust." At its center was Raymond Moley of Columbia University, assisted by Rexford G. Tugwell and Adolph A. Berle, who in the nomenclature of the past were New Nationalists. But Roosevelt's intellectual accomplices also included a New Freedom wing, led by the aged Supreme Court Justice Louis Brandeis, the Harvard law professor Felix Frankfurter, and a veritable legion of protégés. Within this charmed circle there were as many nuances of liberalism as there were liberals.

The kernel of genius that animated Roosevelt was not his own mastery of complex economic and social problems, but his knack of choosing the politically feasible solutions. In the summer of 1932 he was not yet called on to choose, for he was running against the most unpopular President of the century. It was enough to inspire public imagination with pleasant generalities and catch phrases such as New Deal or concern for the "forgotten man at the bottom of the economic ladder." Conspicuously absent, not yet formulated in fact, were references to the national recovery program, deficit financing, the curtailment of farm production, T.V.A., social security, federal housing, or the other epoch-making specifics that would soon grind out headlines in the nation's press. The New Deal was still a drawing board without a blueprint.

The political ambiguity raised goose pimples of suspicion in sophisticated progressive ranks. As Walter Lippmann saw him, "Franklin Roosevelt is no crusader. He is no tribune of the people. He is no enemy of entrenched privilege. He is a pleasant man who, without any important qualifications for the office, would very much like to be President." The liberal *Nation* editorialized: "One thing stands out clear and unchallengeable. That is the unashamed renunciation by Franklin D. Roosevelt of his last pretension to progressivism. He has joined the old guard of political sharpers." One of the reasons for this outburst, though not the exclusive one, was the proclamation by Roosevelt's running mate, John N. Garner, that "the constantly increasing tendency towards socialism and communism is the gravest possible menace. The government should use every means within its power to prevent their further spread." This sounded more like a replay of the Coolidge-Hoover discs than a call to a new deal. The *New Republic*'s estimate of the campaign was that it was "an obscene spectacle" all around.

The suspicion was compounded by Roosevelt's patrician background. Unlike Hoover, the self-made man, Roosevelt was born with a gold spoon that never tarnished. His family tree on the paternal side was American back to the 1640's, when Claes Martenszen Van Rosenvelt came to Nieuw Amsterdam from Holland, and on his mother's side to 1621, when the French-Dutch Delano family (originally De La Noye) set foot on Plymouth Rock. Genealogists claim he was distantly related to eleven American Presidents, including Teddy Roosevelt, his fifth cousin.

The only son of a second marriage by James Roosevelt, fifty-two at the time, and Sara Delano, a twenty-six-year-old former debutante, Franklin lived in a milieu that if not flamboyantly rich was considerably better than comfortable. As befits the offspring of the country squire of Hyde Park along the Hudson, he was educated by governesses and tutors, had his own pony and sailboat, and had been taken on pilgrimages to Europe eight times before he had learned how to shave properly. School meant Groton, the elite haven run by the Reverend Endicott Peabody; Harvard, the mecca of so many upper-class youngsters; and a stint at Columbia Law School. Though he failed to finish his law studies—because of poor grades—he passed a subsequent bar examination and went on to a desultory career with a New York law firm, meanwhile dabbling in sundry public and charitable activities which gave the Roosevelts a reputation for *noblesse oblige.* The salaries he earned, in this and other jobs, were frosting to a cake that was already sufficiently sweet. While in Washington, as Assistant Secretary of the Navy under Wilson, ten servants manned the household. When he died he left a fortune of two million dollars, plus a half million in insurance, twice as much as the legacies left by Coolidge, Wilson, and Taft combined.

Franklin Roosevelt's liberalism, then, was a branch grafted to a root of conservative background. It was enriched by his marriage to Eleanor Roosevelt, niece of Teddy and also a remote cousin, who was more advanced in this respect than he. As a New York State senator from his home district around Hyde Park, he made a good but not remarkable record as a progressive—he favored social legislation, women's suffrage, direct election of senators, party primaries. After a visit to Woodrow Wilson in 1911 he campaigned hard for the New Freedom candidate (against his fifth cousin, Teddy), and as a sign of his predilections was rewarded not with a post to challenge his social sense but with the one in the Navy. In 1920 he was chosen as vice-presidential candidate on the Democratic slate, then lapsed into obscurity after August 1921, when he was caught in a siege of infantile paralysis. Friendly biographers insist that the experience of living in a wheel chair and wearing braces (for the rest of his life) mellowed him. Nonetheless when he returned to politics, under the encouragement of his wife and his close associate, Louis Howe, to win the state governorship in 1928, he still lacked that incredible zeal for innovation that was to characterize his first five and a half years at the White House. He was a likable man, warm, with a dazzling smile and a distinctively long cigarette holder that he held at a jaunty angle, an excellent mixer, charmingly impulsive, yet as Lippmann had observed neither a tribune nor a crusader.

What distinguished Roosevelt was his "temperament," and this indeed was the hallmark of the New Deal just as "mood" had been the essence of the progressive period. Where Hoover clung tenaciously to preconceived doctrine, FDR began with a predisposition for flexibility. "The country needs and, unless I mistake its temper, the country demands bold, persistent experimentation," he said at Oglethorpe

University. "It is common sense to take a method and try it. If it fails, admit it frankly and try another. But above all, try something." He bent with the winds to an extent that few anticipated. In an interview with the publisher of the *New York Graphic*, Roosevelt recited a conversation with "an old friend who runs a great western railroad. 'Fred,' I asked him, 'what are the people talking about out here?' I can hear him answer even now. 'Frank,' he replied, 'I'm sorry to say that men out here are talking revolution.'" Revolution, it turned out, was not on the agenda, but the New Deal took form from such talk, whittling it from radical to reformist dimension. The unemployed demonstrations, the farmers' strikes, the sitdown strikes, the union organizing campaigns, the panacea movements of Huey Long, Francis Townsend, Father Coughlin, the agitation of progressives like Senator Hugo Black for a thirty-hour week, all this continued throughout his first five or six years in office and affected him mightily. When a traditional economist urged him to let nature take its course in resuscitating the economy, his horrified response was, "People aren't cattle, you know!" He was no enemy of the capitalist system—on the contrary—but he could not understand the myopic fixation on "sacred, inviolable, unchangable" economic laws. While Republicans "prate of economic laws," he argued, "men and women are starving." Roosevelt was, as Richard Hofstadter claims, both a "patrician" and an "opportunist," yet his temperament precluded letting men hunger without doing something more dramatic than waiting.

If Roosevelt started, then, with a tenuous philosophy, his bent for action and his bias against shibboleths made it possible to fill the empty phrase "New Deal" with enough content to rescue many millions from disaster. His very inconsistency was what gave his experiment such vitality.

It raised the hackles of right-wing critics such as John T. Flynn, and not entirely without justification. Roosevelt, for instance, had campaigned on the pledge of a balanced budget, then outspent his predecessor so handsomely he doubled the national debt from $19 to $38 billion within four years. He had criticized the last-ditch plea by Hoover's Farm Board for "farmers to allow twenty percent of their wheat lands to lie idle, to plow up every third row of cotton and shoot every tenth dairy cow" as a "cruel joke"; then went ahead to do the same thing in A.A.A.—but on an even larger scale. He spoke of states' rights and opposed further centralization of government, then centralized the federal regime as never before.

For Roosevelt, however, the idea was to get results. Being inconsistent was less of a sin than being ineffective. Out of pragmatic concern he reversed course many times, especially as pressures built up. Roosevelt was a catalyst for change, not an initiator on his own. He picked between the plans devised by other men, often with little knowledge of the subject himself. "I don't find," wrote Raymond Moley, "that he has read much about economic subjects. The frightening aspect of his methods is FDR's great receptivity." This "great receptivity" was both his weak and strong point, weak because it frequently punctuated inconsistency, and strong because it gave him the flexibility for options he might not have taken otherwise. If there was any principle that became fixed, again in reversal of previous pronouncements, it was the definition of the function of government given by Lincoln seven decades before: "To do for the community of people whatever they need to have done, but cannot do at all, or cannot do so well, for themselves."

III

Not surprisingly, then, the Roosevelt era is divided into two halves, the New Deal period of grandiose change from 1933 to the first days of 1939, and a period of social quiescence thereafter, unrelated to the original New Deal *élan*. In turn the New Deal itself is dramatically subdivided into a first and second New Deal, each taking a different path toward combating poverty.

The first New Deal began with FDR's inaugural exhortation—"the only thing we have to fear is fear itself"—and one hundred days of the most frenzied legislative and executive activity in American history. There was no way to go that Saturday as the new President took his oath of office but up. Earlier in the day Governor Lehman of New York had put an executive padlock on the state's banks to prevent further runs on their resources. The nation's depositors, duly alarmed by the failure of more than a quarter of its savings institutions, had been withdrawing dollars from their accounts in ever-increasing amounts—$1.2 billion in the final two weeks of Hoover's

Administration alone. It was better to put money under the mattress or bury it in a garden strongbox than leave it with the banks. Thus one bank after another ran short of cash and closed its doors, and one state after another—nine before New York, including Michigan and California—was forced to declare a bank holiday. That fateful morning the New York Stock Exchange shut down, as did the Chicago Board of Trade and a half-dozen commodity markets. Here and there, as millions found themselves penniless, their monies inaccessible, local communities made plans for issuing their own paper. A hotel in Pasadena loaned scrip to guests without funds. Almost anything seemed to serve as a medium of exchange: stamps, Canadian dollars, Mexican pesos, IOU's. The Princeton University paper issued twenty-five-cent scrip for students and Dow Chemical minted coins for its workers out of a magnesium alloy. The economic machine of free capitalism was grinding to a shattering halt, its brakes shrieking.

At this nadir, Roosevelt could have cloaked himself with the powers of an economic czar, and ruled by decree for an extended period. Indicative of the willingness of Congress to defer to him was the fact that the emergency bill he proposed on March 9 passed the House unanimously after a mere thirty-eight minutes of discussion, though no copies of it were available, except the single draft in the Speaker's hands. Conditions were so dire, the public so anxious for "action," that any proposal made by the new President would have skidded through. With his wry humor, Will Rogers commented that the whole country was with FDR even if he did wrong, so long as he did something: "If he burned down the Capitol, we would cheer and say, 'Well, we at least got a fire started anyhow.'"

In light of this universal mandate, FDR's response to the bank crisis was surprisingly moderate, so moderate that it had the hearty endorsement of Herbert Hoover's fiscal advisers. The day after inauguration, Sunday, Roosevelt invoked an old Trading with the Enemy Act to forbid trade in foreign exchange or export of gold, and declared a four-day national bank holiday during which no currency or gold could be paid to depositors. Many had expected that the President would nationalize the credit institutions, but the banking bill, hastily passed at the special session, used more traditional nostrums: it authorized the printing of more currency so that solvent banks could ward off a "run," imposed penalties on hoarding, and set plans for reopening those banks deemed liquid and reorganizing those in difficulties. To reassure bankers and budget balancers, the President followed this with an economy measure one day later that cut $400,000,000 out of payments to veterans and slashed federal salaries another $100,000,000. It was only three months later that a striking new concept was added to the banking system, and then over the original opposition of Franklin Roosevelt, though his name is linked with it in history. Under the initiative of Republican Senator Arthur Vandenberg of Michigan and southern Democrat Henry Steagall, a Federal Deposit Insurance Corporation was formed to guarantee individual bank deposits up to $5,000.

This first foray against the depression was noteworthy in illustrating FDR's methodology: to act quickly, but to conserve as much of a national consensus as possible. Where the pressures for radical steps, such as nationalization, were meager he preferred the fundamentalist solution. The next patient to be ministered to, the sickest of all by far, was the man without work. Here fundamentalism had already been tried by Hoover, and found wanting. Roosevelt's formula, therefore, as expressed by the man to whom he delegated most of the job, Harry L. Hopkins, was simplicity itself: "Feed the hungry, and Goddamn fast."

Hopkins was that brash, exuberant type who gave the New Deal so much of its color. Tall, thin, with sallow complexion, always showing signs of the sickness that followed him from youth, a chain smoker, outspoken, often brusque, he was almost unknown when he took his job at the head of the Federal Emergency Relief Administration (F.E.R.A.). But within four years he would become the most powerful figure within the Roosevelt entourage, virtually an assistant President. A nonbeliever who had been divorced and psychoanalyzed, Hopkins embodied the New Deal mood—to get things done without moralistic preaching or sentimentality. Brought up in Sioux City and Grinnell, Iowa, "Skinny" or "Hi" Hopkins never stopped boasting of his impecunious origins. Dad Hopkins, a convivial harness maker, storekeeper, and traveling salesman, who loved to bowl and tell salty stories, was beloved by the Grinnell College students, but he was no great shakes at making a fortune. The mother, a pious Methodist who packed her five children off to church every Sunday, sometimes terrified the elder Hopkins lest she siphon off some of his bowling winnings for the weekly collection. Harry inherited his penchant for social work from his mother and his prankishness from his father. A fair student in economics and sociology, a good basketball player until laid low by a bad siege of typhoid, he was most of all a born organizer. When his hero, Woodrow Wilson, president of Princeton, passed through Grinnell, "Skinny" arranged for a band to greet the future President at a cost of $1.50. On graduating from college he was about to embark on a journalism career when a professor steered him to a counseling job in New Jersey. From there he went on to a host of jobs in the social welfare industry until fate brought him to the attention of Governor Roosevelt of New York, who needed a man to administer the state relief program. Hopkins was no doctrinaire party follower; in 1917 he was so outraged at the major parties in New York City he lent his support to the mayoralty candidacy of Socialist Morris Hillquit. But Hopkins was FDR's kind of maverick, buoyant and earthy, and his immediate choice as head of the Federal Emergency Relief Administration when Congress allocated $500,000,000 for relief in May 1933. Hopkins didn't disappoint his mentor. Within two hours, while workmen were remodeling an office and his desk was still in the hallway, he spent $5,000,000. Within a day he had made grants to seven states, prompting the *Washington Post* to predict that the half billion would be gone within a month.

Before F.E.R.A. passed on to the alphabetical Valhalla two and a half years later, it had allocated some three billion dollars for direct relief. Where Hoover had tarried and finally made $300,000,000 available in loans, Hopkins siphoned ten times that much money to the states, and through them to local governments, as nonrepayable grants. At its peak in February 1934 the F.E.R.A. program was paying 70 per cent of national relief costs and providing succor for eight million homes—twenty-eight million people. To cut red tape and bring aid to about one-fifth the American people in so short a time was in sharp contrast to the usual sluggish government performance. Moreover in the wink of an eye Hopkins established new principles of public welfare which would make old-time charity workers blink with dismay. Federal relief, he announced, was not an act of charity but a direct obligation of the government; the citizen was entitled to it as a matter of right, not a gift. Secondly, he arranged for cash payments rather than grocery chits, with the recipient himself making the decision on how to spend the money. Finally, he insisted that relief must include funds not only for food, but for rent, clothing, and medical care. Leftists criticized the program as inadequate; rightists sneered at it as a dole that would dry up human initiative. But it was a mammoth undertaking that plowed new ground.

As an offshoot of F.E.R.A., Hopkins and his assistants designed a national plan of "made work." The Civil Works Administration initiated 180,000 projects within four months, repairing schools, cleaning playgrounds, improving roads, beautifying parks, operating a pest- and erosion-control program. The criterion for each one was not how useful it was to the public in the long run, but how quickly it could provide temporary jobs in the winter of 1933–34, a circumstance that brought forth the charge of "boondoggling." Made work, however, was popular not only with the public at large but above all with the four million hired. "The joy of men having even this brief opportunity to earn a decent living," said a C.W.A. administrator in Michigan, "knew no bounds." It lent a certain dignity to the recipient which direct relief, with its demeaning "means" test, obliterated. Half of those employed, in fact, were either unwilling to accept the "dole" or ineligible for it, and the pay was based on the prevailing wage in the area, with a minimum of thirty cents an hour. Many a local politician charged that offering the unemployed the same rates of pay as already existed for the employed threatened area pay structures; and General Hugh Johnson of N.R.A. made the same point relative to wage scales in his codes for industry, but Hopkins stood his ground. He had been told by FDR to disregard the plaints of politicians and he proceeded along his merry way to spend $933,000,000 in one short winter. Presidential emissary Frank Walker, returning from a trip around the country to evaluate the program, reported that it had done more to improve morale than any other New Deal activity. An old friend he had met digging ditches on a C.W.A. project told him: "I hate to think what would have happened if this work hadn't come along. I'd sold or hocked everything I could. And my kids were hungry. I stood in front of the window of the bakeshop down the street and I wondered just how long it would be before I got desperate enough to pick up a rock and heave it through the window and grab some bread to take home."

A second prong in the New Deal assault on poverty was an allocation of $3.3 billion for the Public Works Administration (P.W.A.), designed to revive the construction industry. Harold L. Ickes, a self-styled "curmudgeon" who had been Bull Moose chairman in Illinois and later a La Follette Progressive Party supporter in 1924, was placed in charge of the program. It was for him the culmination of a reformist dream: "By God," he exclaimed in an uninhibited moment, "I never thought I'd live to see this. Why, this is a second honeymoon." Unlike F.E.R.A. and C.W.A., P.W.A.'s purpose was not to provide jobs directly but to get the heavy industry wheels turning again. In carrying out this function Ickes was often so cautious he caused consternation with the Hopkins firebrands. Nonetheless P.W.A. primed the industrial pump and created jobs for a half million workers. When it was dismantled during World War II it had spent four billions on 34,000 projects, among them the Tennessee Valley Authority irrigation and reclamation scheme, completion of the Hoover Dam and the New York Triborough Bridge, innumerable sewage systems, city auditoriums, schools. In its first six years its monies built more than two-thirds of the nation's new schools, hospital facilities with 121,760 beds, the Lincoln Tunnel in New York, the port of Brownsville, Texas, and a variety of military projects including fifty military airports, tens of thousands of miles of strategic highways, the aircraft carriers *Yorktown* and *Enterprise*, and a host of submarines, destroyers, airplanes, light cruisers. One of P.W.A.'s innovations was slum clearance and public housing for the lower classes—though Ickes himself conceded that his Housing Division had "very much disappointed him." It had constructed only 25,000 units in four and a half years, primarily because the courts made it difficult to seize land under the right of eminent domain.

A third, though lesser, measure for ameliorating want was the Civilian Conservation Corps, hatched by Secretary of Labor Frances Perkins and Senator Robert F. Wagner as a means of warding off juvenile delinquency. Radicals denounced this plan as a militarist plot, since it was put under the aegis of the War Department. Young men who applied—it was not compulsory—were brought together in camps to do various jobs and were given some military drilling and training concurrently. They were paid $30 a month plus food, lodging, and uniforms on condition they turn most of that money over to their families back home. From 1933 to 1941 more than two and a half million young people, mostly in their teens, had been through the C.C.C. mill for periods varying from six months to two years. For those opposed to C.C.C. "militarism" or physically unfit for it, the National Youth Administration, established in 1935, paid small monthly stipends for young people desirous of continuing their studies and offered forty-four hours of work a month to others at $15 pay. The millions of N.Y.A. beneficiaries were also given access to vocational guidance classes to prepare them for industrial jobs and to community centers to keep them off the streets in underprivileged areas.

Taken together, all the measures for relief and jobs were a startling breakthrough in the walls of tradition, even against the principles of Teddy Roosevelt and Wilson. Two ancient pillars were devastated as if by a blockbuster—the fixation on local and private responsibility for hunger, and the hoarier one of a balanced budget. Every year from 1920 through 1930 the federal account had shown a pleasant surplus; every year under Roosevelt it showed a healthy deficit (in 1943 after "Dr. New Deal" had been replaced by "Dr. Win-the-War," of $57 billion). Yet the nation did not, as some had said it would, come apart at the seams.

During the 1930's, a new term, compensatory spending, was entering the lexicon of all Western countries with prodigious force. Put forth by British economist John Maynard Keynes, the theory of compensatory spending called for government pump priming to stimulate demand—and thereby production—even if it resulted in large budgetary deficits. Keynes brushed aside the senescent thesis that economic health was measured in balanced budgets and deficits were visitations of the devil; the worst thing in the world, he said, was not to have a deficit but to have a sick economy. In bad times, therefore, the government was duty bound to compensate for the decrease in buying by its own increased spending, though it meant borrowing against the future—"deficit financing." The money, to be sure, could not be tossed around helter-skelter for it might end up in a static bank account that did no one else any good; it had to be carefully injected so that it turned into venture capital, such as P.W.A., or individual spending, such as relief. If it did, prosperity was inevitable and the government, when times improved, could impose higher taxes, both to pay off part of its indebtedness and to prevent the economy from overheating. The British theorist pointed out to Roosevelt's Secretary of Labor, Frances Perkins, that—in her paraphrase—"a dollar spent on relief by the government was a dollar given to the grocer, by the grocer to the wholesaler, and by the wholesaler to the farmer, in payment of supplies. With one dollar paid out for relief or public works or anything else, you have created four dollars' worth of national income."

Very few New Dealers had read Keynes. Roosevelt himself knew almost nothing about his theories when Frances Perkins arranged for a meeting between the two men, and was somewhat disparaging of the economist. "I saw your friend Keynes," he told her. "He left a whole rigmarole of figures. He must be a mathematician rather than a political economist." Keynes was equally unimpressed with FDR; he had "supposed," he said, that "the President was more literate, economically speaking." But Keynesianism, which has as many varieties and offshoots as Freudianism, became the guideline for the American economic order during the New Deal. In 1937, when Roosevelt curtailed spending and sharply reduced work relief projects to lay low fears of inflation, the economy took a tailspin—as Keynes had predicted—and the cuts were quickly restored. Marriner Eccles, a Utah banker who was appointed governor of the Federal Reserve Board in November 1934, expressed the leitmotiv of both liberal and conservative administrations ever since: "The Government must be the compensatory agent in this economy; it must unbalance its budget during deflation and create surplus in periods of great business activity." This second feature, planned surpluses, has been brought about only six times in the last thirty-five years, thrice each under Harry Truman and Dwight D. Eisenhower, but the spending and deficit parts have become permanent embellishments of the capitalist society. Interestingly enough, Eccles had never heard of Keynes before promulgating his views, and subsequently read him only in pithy extracts. Compensatory spending evidently suggested itself as a solution even to many who hadn't read Keynes.

IV

Along with putting money in the hands of the jobless, the New Deal was confronted with the more fundamental problem of how to crank up production. Such measures as aid to the unemployed, the emergency bank bill, the Emergency Farm Mortgage Act, the Truth-in-Securities Act, the Home Owner's Loan Act, useful as they were, could only be stopgaps until industry and agriculture recovered their momentum. They were repairs on a roof while the foundations of the building were tottering.

Periodically President Roosevelt went on the radio in his famous fireside chats to buoy confidence, but there were many people in the 1930's who had serious doubts that production would ever return to previous levels. Senator Hugo L. Black, for instance, had thrown a thirty-hour bill into the legislative hopper because he was convinced that full employment would never come back and that the only remedy was to share the work. (Roosevelt, incidentally, was horrified at this piece of reform, on the theory it was unconstitutional, and even more that it could not be applied to many industries such as dairying because it interfered with the "rhythm of the cow.") Senator James F. Byrnes urged that "we accept the inevitable, that we are now in a new normal," with millions doomed to joblessness to the end of their days. Raymond Moley thought the nation would be paying relief to millions "permanently." As late as 1937 Hopkins was arguing that it was "reasonable to expect a probably minimum of 4,000,000 to 5,000,000 unemployed in future 'prosperity' periods."

The New Dealers approached the problem of recovery therefore with the realization that drastic steps had to be taken far beyond the bounds of tradition. At the one end were those who urged vigorous trust busting and reform; at the other a group that felt the nation must move toward coherent economic planning—a division in other words, though more sanguine, along the lines of the New Freedom and the New Nationalism of progressive days. The New Freedom contingent was mentored by Supreme Court Justice Brandeis and Harvard law professor Felix Frankfurter, both friends of the President who manned his ramparts with seventy-five to a hundred protégés. According to their diagnosis, recovery was stalled because of the corporate monopolies who mercilessly squeezed the small entrepreneurs. There was nothing wrong with the American economy that a little free competition and decentralization wouldn't cure. If the government would curb monopoly through antitrust action and discriminatory taxes against the big corporations, the wheels of industry would soon be turning again in normal cadence. "We must come back to the little unit," said Brandeis, and as a corollary to whittling the power of the titans the government should strengthen that of the less privileged through various reforms and welfare measures.

On the collectivist side the key figure behind the scenes, though joined by many others, was the former Columbia professor Rexford G. Tugwell, who served in these early days as Assistant Secretary of Agriculture but whose influence was far broader than this post implied. A tall, strikingly handsome man, Tugwell's origins were in upstate New York where his father operated a prosperous fruit farm. After high school Tugwell enrolled in the Wharton School of Finance and Commerce, taught at a number of colleges before coming to Columbia University in 1920. Then, after a dozen years in the classroom, he moved along with Raymond Moley into the Roosevelt brain trust. Rabid conservatives like Mark Sullivan considered him a near-Bolshevik. John T. Flynn, while conceding that Tugwell "had a first-rate mind and wrote well," quoted a poem he had written in college, "The Dreamer," to indicate that he was cold-hearted, contemptuous, and possessed of a trace of megalomania. The last line read: "I shall roll up my sleeves—make America over." But in fact Tugwell, like Roosevelt, believed he was saving the capitalist system by imposing discipline and coordination on it, rather than weakening it. In a 1934 book on *The New Dealers*, by an anonymous "unofficial observer," he is described as "a collectivist in the sense that Mr. J. P. Morgan is a collectivist, in that he realizes that technological advance tends toward larger and more elaborately interrelated business units. . . . The only question is whether the profits of collectivism shall flow into the pockets of speculators, bankers and idle rich who live on inherited wealth, or whether they shall be widely enough distributed to enable the private ownership of property and the individualistic basis of capitalism to survive at all."

Tugwell was not the only one talking about "planning"; it was a concept in fact with widespread currency. As espoused by communists and left-wing socialists it was linked with revolution and the nationalization of industry. The more moderate right-wing socialists would nationalize only the heavier industries and do their planning in a mixed economy which permitted private profit in large areas of the economy. Beyond them, in the center, was a considerable number of liberals—historian Charles A. Beard, George Soule, Senator Robert M. La Follette, Jr., to name three—who propounded planning schemes within the context of private capitalism. Even big business had its share of planning advocates, notably Gerard Swope, president of General Electric, who urged formation of national trade associations to be supervised by the Federal Trade Commission. Swope's blueprint, incidentally, included mandatory requirements on each firm to provide unemployment compensation for employees. Tugwell's nostrum, then, was not so unique as it might seem; it differed from Swope's in only two major aspects. Tugwell, in addition to joining businessmen into industrial associations, would create a Central Industrial Integration Board to coordinate such economic activity as the allocation of capital, production, prices, wages, social conditions, the distribution of markets; and, secondly, this board would include government members who would have the final say in reconciling individual industry proposals into a nationwide coherent plan. Such a program would not destroy capitalism, it would simply discipline it.

Confronted with the deep divisions among his advisers, Roosevelt, in his first New Deal, sided with the planners against the trust busters. When the National Industrial Recovery Act was passed on June 16, 1933, he called it "the most important and far-reaching legislation ever enacted by the American Congress." He also gave fervid support to the Agricultural Adjustment Act, in which Tugwell also had a hand, which sought through planning to raise prices and income on the farm. Thus, for the next two years, until the courts ruled both measures unconstitutional and FDR's own ardor for collaboration with big business cooled perceptibly, the United States trod a collectivist path never before envisaged.

The heart of the program finally accepted—a cross between Tugwell's panacea and Swope's—lay in Title I of the Recovery Act. Under the aegis of a National Recovery Administration (N.R.A.) businessmen in each industry were to establish associations and draw up codes of fair practices, dealing with prices, wages, hours, exchange of information, selling methods, etc., subject to presidential approval. N.R.A. would not enforce any national plan but confine itself to helping each segment of the economy recover separately. In essence, what it amounted to was a pledge by government that if industry raised wages and reduced hours, thereby increasing the demand for goods, it would be allowed to set prices for its products without antitrust prosecution. There was a little in it for everyone, except of course the consumer, and he presumably would benefit from higher earnings on his job. In the backdoor maneuvering that preceded enactment of the bill, William Green of the American Federation of Labor exacted a last-minute concession—Section 7A—which recognized labor's right to collective bargaining. Thus Herbert Croly's 1909 dream of a "constructive" partnership between business, labor, and government seemed, after a quarter of a century, gloriously close to fruition.

The man chosen to head N.R.A. and supervise its code writing was General Hugh Johnson, who had labored with Tugwell in drafting the bill. The General was a gruff, blustering warrior, not without charm, whose record at West Point had been punctuated by "chronic insubordination" and in his early Army days by periodic bar room battles, in one of which he broke the jaw of an inebriated private. Nonetheless he had served with Pershing in the expedition to northern Mexico, had been involved in writing and applying the wartime Draft Act, and was a close associate of Bernard Baruch. After the war he had joined the Moline Plow Company with another future New Dealer, George N. Peek, had continued to help Baruch in sundry projects, and at the 1932 Democratic convention surfaced, together with the elder statesman, in a "Stop Roosevelt" drive. The same year he distributed to friends in Wall Street a prospectus for an economic dictatorship that would rule without Congress, and to which he gave the esoteric name "Muscle-Inny." When Baruch made peace with FDR, Johnson was requisitioned for the election campaign and subsequently brought into the brain trust by its chief, Raymond Moley.

Johnson threw himself vigorously into the task of integrating and codifying the practices of hundreds of American industries, but first results were not encouraging. Of the ten major industries only one responded quickly. The men who drafted the cotton textile code drew applause, to be sure, when they agreed to eliminate child labor in the mills, raise wages, cut hours, and bargain collectively, in return for joint action to restrict production. But other industries dragged their feet; instead they increased output furiously as a hedge against the day when they would be shackled by higher labor costs—so much so in fact that an artificial boom developed. Industrial production languishing at the index figure 56 in March jumped to 101 by July, with corporate issues on the stock market rising accordingly. Taken aback by a boomlet that presaged another inevitable bust when the supply of goods outstripped demand, Johnson and his general counsel, Donald Richberg, decided to put pressure on the industrialists through a "blanket agreement," setting forth a thirty-five-hour week for blue collar and forty-hour week for white collar workers, with 40 cents an hour minimum wages for the former and $12 to $15 a week for the latter. This blanket code was to serve until specific ones could be devised for each industry. But since it was not enforceable by law it could be enforced only by public opinion. In the ensuing months Johnson organized a hoop-la campaign of parades, speeches, chats by the President over the radio, and mass media publicity, that made the Gifford campaign for charity under Hoover a pale effort by comparison. Every company with two or more employees who signed up was given a placard with the Blue Eagle symbol, carrying the slogan "We Do Our Part," and consumers were urged to buy only those goods that displayed this memento of cooperation. Not everyone jumped to the lash—the most important holdout was Henry Ford—but within a short time two and a quarter million companies employing sixteen million workers (later twenty-two million) joined the crusade. Caught in the revivalist surge, various states passed "Little N.R.A." bills with the same objectives for firms not deemed in interstate commerce.

Under this pressure the major job of codifying industrial practices accelerated in tempo. All told, under Johnson and Richberg, who succeeded him in September 1934, 576 basic and 189 supplementary codes were drawn and approved as the nation found new economic shelter under a Blue Eagle umbrella. A hasty review of its effects one year after it went into operation showed on the plus side that hourly wages in manufacturing had risen by 31 per cent, weekly earnings— held back by reduced hours—by 14 per cent. This represented a true increase in living standards since the cost of living went up only half as much, by 7 per cent.

On the minus side, however, there was an explosion of complaints about price fixing and an irrepressible squeeze on the small companies. A National Recovery Review Board selected by Roosevelt in March 1934 to sift these charges concluded that in "virtually all the codes we have examined one condition has been persistent . . . the code has offered an opportunity for the more powerful and more profitable interests to seize control of an industry or to augment and extend a control already obtained." Theoretically the codes were to be written with the participation of the whole business community, labor, the consumer, and the government. But in actuality, according to the board—headed by famous civil liberties lawyer Clarence

Darrow—the legal eagles for big business had done most of the drafting, and had written into the documents trade practices, limitations of production, price levels, and other features that drove the small and marginal entrepreneurs to the wall. "It may safely be said," wrote Darrow, "that not in many years have monopolistic tendencies in industry been so forwarded and strengthened." As an example he pointed to the motion picture business, where the chain movie houses had written the code disfranchising the 13,571 theaters out of 18,321 run by independents. In cotton, woolens, carpets, sugar, the codes were copies "down to the last comma, of the trade-association agreements written during the Administration of Herbert Hoover." In lumber the small company was all but ruined by the code. Moreover, by opting for maximum profits instead of maximum employment, the moguls retarded rather than helped the process of recovery. Darrow was so incensed he personally called on the President to socialize industry and have done with it.

From all corners the crescendo of criticism mounted against N.R.A. Thousands of letters to the editor pinpointed flagrant instances of chiseling, of undercutting wages or price agreements. A favorite ruse for evading the hours provisions was to have workers punch their time cards after eight hours and return to their labors for another two or three hours without record—or pay. Machinery for enforcement was so meager that evasion, it was said, was as widespread as that of bootleggers under Prohibition. Yet, indicative of Johnson's bias on this score was the fact that the first culprit chosen for prosecution was a minor restaurant owner in Gary, Indiana.

The labor movement, lyrical at first that at long last collective bargaining was being enshrined as national policy, soon gave way to a mood of despair as it became obvious that for the most part Section 7A was a paper concession and laborers' cries for union recognition went unheeded. The unions, expecting that the wage and hour sections of the codes would be written in a collective bargain between themselves and the industrial associations, found to their dismay that they were bypassed by government-appointed Labor Advisory Councils which did the job for them. Management simply refused to recognize the unions. Moreover Johnson's idea of collective bargaining encompassed as bargaining partners not only legitimate unions but company unions and even individuals. Taking advantage of this tailor-made loophole, the solons of industry sponsored, for purposes of bargaining, four hundred "labor" organizations that they themselves controlled.

As bitterness mounted, Roosevelt, always the consummate politician receptive to pressure, designated first a National Labor Board, then a National Labor Relations Board, to hold secret elections for determining bargaining agents. But though the boards were headed by good men, friendly to the workingmen's cause, they had no power of enforcement. A truculent management, especially in the mass production industries, refused to heed board decisions. When desperate workers "hit the bricks," Johnson often told them they were striking against the government and ordered them back. Given this runaround, hundreds of weak labor organizations disbanded or were driven out of existence. The climax came in July 1934 when a half million textile employees in twenty states called a national walkout for recognition and a thirty-hour week but were commanded back by the President himself, in one of the worst defeats for labor of the times, with no gains. What was originally hailed as "labor's Magna Carta" was sneered at as the National Run-Around, and the Blue Eagle was impiously renamed Blue Buzzard.

N.R.A. was battered by taunts from left, right, and center. Hoover majestically called it "fascism, pure fascism," a sentiment echoed by the Communists when they published a pamphlet on the "fascist Blue Eagle." The New Deal, wrote Communist Party leader Earl Browder, "is a policy of brutal oppression at home and imperialism abroad . . . carrying out more thoroughly than Hoover, the capitalist attack against the living standards of the masses." Newspapers berated N.R.A. incessantly, and even Harry Hopkins, in a typical colloquialism, told Johnson: "Hugh, your codes stink." Tugwell, of course, was distraught. For him the Recovery Act was only a "beginning" toward consistent planning. It lacked the stiff penalties needed to make it work and in practice granted business rather than government the decisive voice to coordinate the economy. Even Roosevelt conceded to Frances Perkins that "the whole thing has been a mess . . . an awful headache."

The undoing of the Blue Eagle turned out to be a chicken. In February 1935 Roosevelt pleaded with Congress for a two-year extension of the Recovery Act on the grounds that it was the major factor in putting four million people to work. Under it, he said, "the age-long curse of child labor has been lifted, the sweatshop outlawed, and millions of wage earners released from starvation wages and excessive hours of labor." This too-glowing assessment, however, was irrelevant, for while Congress was deliberating, the Supreme Court in May handed down its decision in the Schechter appeal. The Schechter brothers were poultry jobbers in Brooklyn who had been hailed before the bar for selling diseased chickens and paying chicken killers subpar wages under the Live Poultry Code. The Court ruled that N.R.A.'s powers to regulate industry, apart from the fact that the Schechters were in intrastate not interstate commerce, were unconstitutional. "America stunned," read a headline in the *London Daily Express*, "Roosevelt's two years' work killed in twenty minutes." An angry and disconsolate President could have recast the legislation, as he did with the A.A.A., to make it legally acceptable. But by this time he had wearied of big business machinations against him. He had tried, he felt, to forge a broad coalition for planning economic recovery, with business in the key role, and he sometimes irritated his liberal friends in order to win good marks with the men of industry. In one brief period, for instance, he took the side of management in a number of important labor disputes, he removed militant reformers from the Agricultural Adjustment Administration, and came out against adding a "prevailing wage" section to the work relief law. Yet the United States Chamber of Commerce attacked him strenuously and some of the most important corporate chiefs, spurred by the Du Pont family and General Motors, had formed the American Liberty League in August 1934 for the specific purpose of fighting the New Deal. Smitten by these reactions, Roosevelt lost faith in his coalition and, despite Tugwell's exhortation that what was needed was more and better planning, not less, the President let the experiment sink quietly into oblivion.

V

Coincident with the N.R.A. and its codes, the New Deal had a special plan for agriculture. The plan was, if viewed in a vacuum, an absolutely weird concept for "recovery," since the New Dealers did not propose to increase production, as with industry, but to reduce it significantly. For the millions on relief or C.W.A. it was an upside-down world to wake up one day and find that Secretary of Agriculture Henry A. Wallace had ordered the slaughter of six million little pigs and 200,000 sows to remove them from the market. Why kill pigs when people were hungry? Or to learn that during the first year of agricultural planning, while the needy in the cities were without clothes, the government had paid $100,000,000 to cotton farmers to trample and plow under ten million acres of their crop. Forever after, this image of killing pigs and plowing under cotton and grain was fixed as the image of the New Deal in many American minds, even though almost all of the destruction occurred in the first year.

Yet there were millions of people starving on fertile farms not because they could not produce enough hogs or grain or cotton, but because they had produced too much. During the 1920's the progressives believed they could solve this dilemma by dumping farm surpluses on foreign markets. But the depression was now world-wide and there was as little chance of selling food abroad as at home. Theoretically, of course, the government could itself buy what the farmer produced and simply give it away, like Santa Claus or Robin Hood, to the needy. That, however, is not the way a market economy works; not even the New Deal extremists advocated planning of this type. Hoover, in his last months, had called on the yeomen voluntarily to let millions of acres lie fallow. The New Deal accepted this kernel of a program, but surrounded it with carrot-and-stick compulsion.

Around the time of the 1932 nominating convention, when the brain trusters were probing for ideas, Tugwell became enamored of a scheme, worked up by Professor Milburn L. Wilson of Montana State College, called the "Domestic Allotment Plan." In essence it proposed to pay farmers "attractive rentals" for acres taken out of production. By estimating what the nation was likely to consume, the government could reduce agricultural acreage enough to keep supply and demand in harmony and thereby increase prices to yield a proper income for the farmer. The money paid to the farmers would come from the coffers of millers, canners, and other processors of agricultural commodities, against whom government would levy the necessary taxes.

The Tugwell-Wilson position was only one of many considered by New Deal thinkers. Everyone was agreed that prices for farm commodities had to be raised, but different factions within the Department of Agriculture disputed the best way to do it. One, led by

George N. Peek, Hugh Johnson's associate at Moline Plow and soon to be chosen the first administrator of the Agricultural Adjustment Administration (A.A.A. or Triple-A), would stabilize the situation by making marketing agreements for higher prices, and dumping surpluses abroad—the old McNary-Haugen plan. Another faction would set prices by legislation or executive decree. Roosevelt, in his usual conciliatory style, plugged for a bill encompassing all options but permitting the farmers themselves to make the final decision. The first Agricultural Adjustment Act passed in May gave the President these flexible prerogatives.

What the farmer himself wanted was made fairly clear from what he was doing in the hustings. On April 27 five hundred men of the Farmers' Holiday Association sitting in the courtroom of Judge Charles C. Bradley of Le Mars, Iowa, raucously demanded that he suspend foreclosure sales. When the Judge rebuked the men for wearing their hats, they dragged him from the court, put a rope around his neck, and threatened to lynch him unless he relented. The lynching did not come off but the association scheduled a national farmers strike for May 13 and continued to agitate for compulsory control of production and fixing of prices. When they seemed to be making no progress, they engaged in such niceties as pouring kerosene in cream, setting dynamite in dairies, and splashing on the highways the milk of those who refused to cut back production. The violence on the farms exacerbated the bitter internecine fight within the Department of Agriculture between the Tugwell allotment group (including such lawyers as Jerome Frank, Adlai Stevenson, Thurman Arnold, Abe Fortas, Alger Hiss) and George Peek's clan, with Roosevelt throwing his weight to the Tugwell forces. Peek, the administrator of Triple-A, was quietly eased out of office and the emphasis from then on was on the Tugwell-Wilson approach.

It was already too late in the summer of 1933 to head off planting, and cotton in particular seemed to be headed toward a bumper, sixteen-million-bale surplus. Twenty-two thousand government agents, most of them volunteers, descended on the cotton area, therefore, to sell farmers on the idea of accepting $6 to $20 an acre in cash for plowing up ten million of the forty million acres under seed. With the hog market also in despair payments were made to compensate for the slaughter of six million little pigs. Wallace conceded it was "a shocking commentary on our civilization" to kill animals and plow under farm produce, but it was no worse, he said, than plowing workers out of the factories. At least, in the former case, some of the "surplus" food, cattle, and cotton was rescued and doled out among the poor—about $300,000,000 worth from 1933 through 1935.

The planned scarcity in the farm sections proceeded in a more orderly fashion after 1933, with the main emphasis placed on taking acreage out of cultivation—the domestic allotment plan. Triple-A decided in Washington how many acres of each commodity should be withdrawn, and committees selected by the farmers in every county then made the allotments based on how many acres had been planted by the individual husbandman in previous years. The system was meant to produce a fair price that "would give agricultural commodities a purchasing power" equivalent to what was enjoyed in the base period August 1909 to July 1914. This was called "parity."

Triple-A was buttressed in its scheme by another alphabetical proliferation, a subsidiary of the Reconstruction Finance Corporation called the Commodity Credit Corporation. As told by Bascom N. Timmins, biographer of chairman Jesse Jones, the idea came to fruition when a large Mississippi planter complained to the President that with cotton at nine cents he was close to ruin. Informed of this problem, Jones, a Texas banker, replied: "All right, we'll make it worth ten cents. . . . We will offer to lend ten cents a pound anywhere in the cotton-growing areas." Thus was born the C.C.C., which in the course of the next six years loaned more money to farmers on this price-support basis than R.F.C. doled out to any other group with the exception of bankers. The plight of the yeoman was alleviated further through a host of other mechanisms which offered him billions in loans to refinance debts and redeem property about to be foreclosed. But the focal point of farm planning remained in Triple-A and its program of government-induced scarcity.

Statistically the operation went moderately well, by contrast with the questionable results of N.R.A. Though the gains reflected other factors as well as Triple-A, Administration figures showed that the purchasing power of agricultural commodities in 1934 was one-third higher than at its nadir in March 1933. To be sure, there was a certain amount of chiseling as well as a legal way around the allotments through more intensive planting, but over-all the farmer was now able to buy 73 per cent of what he had before World War I, as against 55 per cent at the low point of farm fortunes in March 1933.

It was not, however, an undiluted success, even by the New Deal's own standards, for it had a painful backlash on tenants and share-croppers, the lowliest creatures on the rural totem pole. If land had to be removed from harvest, the easiest way for landlords to do it was to take it out of the acreage reserved for tenants and croppers. One landlord in Oklahoma boasted, typically, that "in '34 I had I reckon four renters and I didn't make anything. I bought tractors on the money the government give me and got shet o' my renters." The tenants formed radical organizations such as the Socialist-controlled Southern Tenant Farmers' Union to defend themselves, and the land-lords responded with violence reminiscent of that used by the Klan sixty years before. But the New Deal was too preoccupied elsewhere to concentrate effectively on this problem and there was soon an army of "Arkies" who had been "tractored off the land" to join the "Okies" who had been blown off by dust and drought. As Norman Thomas observed: "It remained for us to invent 'bread lines knee-deep in wheat.' " Within a few years there were a million migrant farm people sputtering along America's byways in the hideous cir-cumstances described in John Steinbeck's *Grapes of Wrath.*

The extreme faction in the Department of Agriculture tried to stay this disaster by imposing rules whereby landlords would have to re-tain not only the same number of tenants but the same individuals; Roosevelt and Wallace, however, overruled them. Instead, a Reset-tlement Administration (R.A.), another alphabetical wonder, was hastily put together in April 1935 under the tutelage of Tugwell to provide new and better farms for the impoverished. It was a valiant idea, yet without practical effect, for though Tugwell hoped to re-settle a half million families, lack of funds kept the number down to a meager 4,441. Some years later, under the Farm Security Administra-tion, better results were achieved, yet they met nothing like the need. The effect of Triple-A, despite its accomplishments, was to plow under the weakest rural elements, just as N.R.A. erased many a small entrepreneur from the business community.

Nonetheless, simply from the academic point of planning, A.A.A. enjoyed a better fate than its associate on the drawing boards. Like N.R.A., it too was declared illegal in 1935, but makeshift legislation permitted the government to make payments based on "conserva-tion" and prevention of "soil erosion" rather than crop curtailment. In 1938, with a more beneficent Supreme Court on the bench, a second Agricultural Adjustment Act was passed along the original principles but with some modification. Instead of curtailing the acreage it curtailed the crop. Quotas for production and "parity prices" were set, and if the market price was lower than parity the government made up the difference. To assure observance of the quotas, farmers who sold beyond them were penalized with additional taxes.

Even John T. Flynn, the right-wing critic of the New Deal, admitted in 1940 that "very obviously the farmer's condition is improved." Income was higher, though still far from previous peaks, and the number of farms electrified under New Deal rural electrification rose from 13 per cent to 33 per cent of the total. But the number of farms and farmers began a steady decline, and the number of farmers in penury remained—and remains—a blight amid national prosperity. Norman Thomas' "bread lines knee-deep in wheat" were still disturbingly conspicuous.

VI

The New Deal, like every antipoverty program before or after, was sensitive to divergent pressures and therefore discordant in its results. Since the pressures were pluralistic the programs that evolved were eclectic. Roosevelt, Rex Tugwell tells us, "was first of all a practicing politician," and as such a weather vane for the storms around him. He began his first New Deal with the apocalyptic hope of forging a harmonious and enduring partnership between business, labor, farmers, government—the penultimate of class collaboration. He threw sops around like a lion tamer to four pet lions, seeking to keep a proper and viable balance between them. He placated—or tried to placate—business with Hugh Johnson and George Peek, the AFL with Section 7A, the jobless with Harry Hopkins. And like a good Leninist he operated on the thesis of "two steps forward, one step backward."

His relief program, for instance, took two great leaps beyond the ancient Elizabethan straitjacket, but just when it appeared that a new federally centralized structure would sweep aside the chaotic local systems, he pulled back to let the old one stand. "Has not the time come," asked social worker Edith Abbott in a *Nation* article of

January 9, 1935, "when the Federal Relief Administrator can announce a plan or policy that will assure the setting up of a permanent Federal Welfare Department with continued federal aid not only for old-age pensions, unemployment compensation, and mothers' pensions but also for general home relief?" Her title "Don't Do It, Mr. Hopkins!" implored the F.E.R.A. chief and his boss Roosevelt not to go back to the past—but they did. FDR was willing to listen to Miss Abbott but he also had a cocked ear for the local politicians back in Cedar Rapids or Gary who had other ideas.

Such a tuning board had to be retuned to the sounds around it. After a year of the first New Deal, the sounds were distinctly different from the ones heard on March 4, 1933, when everyone was applauding. Within a year the configuration of pressures shifted quite a few notches to the left, a surprising development considering all the relief measures. But as historian William E. Leuchtenberg has observed: "The revolutionary spirit burgeons not when conditions are at their worst, but when they begin to improve." The agitation of the organizations of unemployed, guided by Communists, Socialists, and Musteites, did not abate in 1934–35 but accelerated. Hardly a relief station or a city hall was immune from picket lines and sit-ins as the jobless demanded more relief or protested a bureaucratic decision. Antieviction fights such as this one reported in the Muste paper of May 1, 1934, multiplied by the tens of thousands:

> "This constable is for sale. How much is the bid? Sold for 8 cents." The Pennsylvania Unemployed League in Pittsburgh sold the constable at a mass eviction fight. The eviction was stopped by a mass demonstration. When leaving the house, "an accident" occurred to the constable and landlord. They went to the hospital. "Who threw the bricks?" Shrugged shoulders was the reply. No more evictions for six months.

When the three unemployed groups, the National Unemployed Council, the National Unemployed League, and the Workers Alliance, merged in 1936 they claimed a combined membership of 800,000.

More important, the employed workers, previously quiescent, suddenly erupted in pent-up fury. As a tidal wave of mass-production workers formed a few thousand new unions, inside and outside the AFL, strikers on picket lines in 1934 were five times as numerous as two years before. Four violent strikes rent the quiet of class peace and acted as prelude for the bitter sit-downs two years later. The national walkout of 475,000 textile operatives called forth an outpouring of 11,000 national guardsmen and resulted in the wounding of many hundreds, and the killing of ten proletarians. Flying squads roamed the streets of Minneapolis like revolutionary militia as Trotskyists led two militant trucker strikes. On the West Coast, longshoremen and maritime workers under the leadership of a colorful Australian, Harry Bridges, tied up the ports for months. In Toledo the unemployed defied a court order in order to help Auto-Lite workers win a bloody victory, lending considerable stimulus to the nascent automobile union. Fear of sudden radical domination of the labor movement prompted a group of moderates around John L. Lewis and one-third of the AFL convention in 1934 to demand the chartering of industrial unions and a drive in the mass-production industries. The following year the pressure for such unionization resulted in a labor split and the formation of the rival Congress of Industrial Organizations. Not since 1919 had there been such ferment in the ranks of labor, and within a year or two even the furious tempest of 1919 would be exceeded. The radical left, in particular the Communists, were still a meager guard of a few tens of thousands, but their number was doubling and redoubling, and they had access to many millions of working-class stalwarts ready to listen to the message of revolution.

Franklin Roosevelt remained immensely popular, but there was a left flank forming to which he could not be oblivious. Indicative of the way typical progressives were responding to events was the statement by Minnesota Governor Floyd Olson that unless capitalism could find a cure for depression "I hope the present system of government goes right down to hell." Olson clamored for seizure of the "key industries" by the government and a Cooperative Commonwealth, planks that put him in the radical rather than liberal camp. In California, where even the weirdest ideas were commonplace, the old muckraker Upton Sinclair scared the pants off Roosevelt and the conservatives when he organized EPIC (End Poverty in California). EPIC proposed the launching of rural communes on leased or purchased land, and a system of "production-for-use" in leased factories. This plan for giving the unemployed jobs instead of relief was so popular Sinclair beat New Dealer George Creel in the

1934 Democratic primary for governor by a margin of 436,000 to 288,000. Forced to make a choice between a conservative Republican and the novelist of *Jungle* fame, the New Dealers cemented an alliance with the former to bring Sinclair down to defeat in the November elections.

Almost any panacea, demagogic or sincere, could find a quick audience of millions of people. A sixty-seven-year-old doctor, Francis Townsend, formed the Old Age Revolving Pensions, Limited, in January 1934, calling for a government pension of $200 a month for everyone over sixty who agreed to spend the money within a month. The organization boasted 1,200 clubs before the end of the year and solicited, by its own estimates, twenty-five million signatures for the pension plan—even its detractors admitted at least ten million had signed. The silver-tongued priest Father Charles Coughlin, whose radio addresses drew audiences of thirty to forty million each week, conceived a National Union for Social Justice which pronounced capitalism dead, declaimed against the conspiracy of bankers, and urged something akin to the corporate state. Millions flocked to this banner too, even though Coughlin, who had begun as a fervid Roosevelt supporter in 1933—"Roosevelt or ruin, Roosevelt or Morgan"— began releasing a stream of anti-New Deal vitriol. Many a union leader—Homer Martin, president of the auto union, for instance— and many an old progressive made common cause with the priest from Royal Oak, Michigan.

The most serious concern to the Roosevelt entourage, because it was so politically minded, was the 27,000 Share Our Wealth clubs inspired by Senator Huey ("Kingfish") Long of Louisiana and claiming seven and a half million sympathizers. A demagogue, considered a semifascist by critics—witness his choice as organizer of Gerald L. K. Smith—old Huey was a rabble rouser of worrisome dimensions. With mussed-up red hair and an angelic round face, he could bring any crowd to its feet with his cry for confiscating all individual wealth above a certain amount and dividing it among the poor. As governor of the state he had effected quite a few reforms, though in unorthodox and dictatorial style. His slogans—"Share Our Wealth," "Every Man a King"—therefore had a certain credibility, and his rubelike pose enormous appeal, especially to farmers. Huey promised that in "my first days in the White House" he would appoint John D. Rockefeller, Jr., and Andrew Mellon to officiate at the disbursal of their own and other fortunes, so that every "deserving family" would have enough for a car, a home, a radio, and a steady livelihood. If it was weak economics, it was strong propaganda, enough to give New Dealers the jitters. A quiet poll taken by the Democratic National Committee indicated that the Kingfish would get three to four million votes as a third-ticket presidential candidate in 1936, enough perhaps to swing the election to the Republicans.

The 1934 elections assuaged New Deal fears—the Democrats carried the House of Representatives, in a surprising upsurge, by 322 to 103 for the Republicans and 10 Progressives. But with the N.R.A. faltering, businessmen—especially through the newly formed rightist Liberty League—rising to the attack, and criticism mounting from all quarters, Roosevelt decided in 1935 to shift gears. The first New Deal gave way to the second New Deal, the Tugwell planners to the Brandeis-Frankfurter reformers.

VII

When the National Industrial Recovery Act was passed, a jubilant Raymond Moley pointed out to Roosevelt that he was breaking decisively with Wilsonian New Freedom and the Brandeis philosophy of "atomizing" big business. The President replied that he understood this very well and was pleased with the direction his Administration was taking. He congratulated Congress, it will be recalled, for having passed the most important legislation in American history. The road to recovery, it seemed, was to be through restructuring economic institutions to make them compatible with some kind of national planning. What was being rejected was the Brandeis philosophy, as Moley put it, "that America . . . could once more become a nation of small proprietors, of corner grocers and smithies under spreading chestnut trees."

Two years later, however, Brandeis, Frankfurter, and their protégés from Harvard were high in the saddle, drafting New Freedom bills with the same boisterous intensity that characterized the "first hundred days." Frankfurter now was a frequent visitor, often spending the night at the White House after long private discussions with FDR. His protégés, Thomas (Tommy the Cork) Corcoran, an outgoing, witty Irishman, and Benjamin Cohen, a retiring Jew from

Muncie, Indiana, were preparing legislation for a "second hundred days" with blistering haste. Though most Americans were so enamored of Roosevelt as the friend of the "common man" they did not realize a transition was taking place, the nation in fact was branching off in another direction.

Common to both New Deals was the acceptance of John Maynard Keynes's gospel of deficit spending, but where the first one sought to save capitalism through class partnership and rudimentary planning, the second one tried to narrow the power gap between classes through reform and "regulated competition." Stealing the thunder of the left and Huey Long, Roosevelt now disparaged "our resplendent economic autocracy," the men of "entrenched greed" who plotted "the restoration of their selfish power." Against Huey's "Share Our Wealth," New Dealers thundered, "Soak the rich," which was not exactly the same thing but at least was of the same political lineage. The Kingfish himself intoned an "amen" over the Roosevelt tax package.

At the heart of the second New Deal, most of it originating in 1935, were five measures: the Wagner labor bill, a public-utility holding company act, the "soak-the-rich" tax measures, a banking law, and the social security law. The Wagner Act, assented to by Roosevelt at the last moment with misgivings, was designed to give labor an orderly weapon to cope with management. It recognized the right of unions to organize and bargain collectively, legalized union and closed shops, prohibited company unions, and provided machinery—the National Labor Relations Board—to enforce these strictures. It differed sternly from the labor policy under the N.R.A. codes in that it added the element of government compulsion, and called for a single bargaining agent in each unit, thus eliminating internecine competition. It eventually became a highly useful mechanism for orderly labor relations, obviating strikes to win bargaining rights, but it had little effect on the war on poverty during the 1930's since it did not receive Court approval (by five to four) until April 1937, after millions had already joined labor's expanding ranks and the country was consumed by sit-down strikes.

The Public Utilities Holding Act, passed in August 1935, was tailored to eliminate pyramiding holding companies which endlessly widened monopoly domination. A single holding company, controlling a group of operating firms, would itself be controlled by a super-holding company, and it in turn by a super-super-holding company many steps removed from the original producer. It was an excellent device for centralization of corporate power and mulcting the public through unconscionable rates. Under the bill these octopi were to be cut down to size, at the second level, and after three years were to be limited to single integrated systems. The Federal Power Commission was also authorized to oversee rates and business practices. Although widely hailed as a precursor for general trust busting and regulation, the act did little to redistribute income and wealth: in 1937 the utilities enjoyed their best year. The banking act, a complex piece of legislation which jogged through the same month, reorganized the Federal Reserve Board and gave it wider authority over credit and currency, but if it had any impact on reducing poverty it was indirect and long-term.

More directly on target was a bill purporting to redistribute income. A new tax law was under study before the "second hundred days" but it was given the green light only after the decision in the Schechter case. "I want to save our system, the capitalistic system," Roosevelt said, and for this "it may be necessary to throw to the wolves the forty-six men who are reported to have incomes in excess of one million dollars a year." To flatten the peaks of wealth the New Deal suggested inheritance levies on individuals who received them (rather than on the estates), a graduated tax on corporations, imposts on undivided corporate profits, an intercorporate dividend tax, and steeper income taxes in the higher brackets. Considering that the tax structure was filled with loopholes, such as depletion allowances, and was generally regressive in nature, weighted against lower-class consumers instead of those able to pay, this was an indicated channel for reform. It brought forth, however, paeans of criticism about "Raw Deal" and "Soak-the-Successful" legislation, and by the time it had been whittled down in congressional compromise it had become meaningless except as a precedent for the future. The inheritance tax was rejected in favor of an estate tax; most of the other features were feeble and symbolic. It raised only $250,000,000 in revenue, and any redistribution of income it effected was not visible in the next few years—the share of the highest 1 per cent of the population even rose slightly.

The most significant long-term achievement of the second hundred days was a many-faceted social security bill which put a cushion under poverty more extensive than ever known before, and is still relatively unmodified. The bill actually was placed in the hopper months before and had been under study even longer. The reform mood in the White House, however, and nagging concern lest the leftists, on the one hand, and Coughlinites, Townsendites, and Long followers on the other, steal a quick march, gave it added impetus. Moreover this was a reform to which Roosevelt was personally committed. In conversation with Frances Perkins the President talked convincingly of "cradle to the grave" insurance covering not merely industrial workers but everyone, including "the farmer and his wife and his family." When Harry Hopkins argued that work relief was preferable to unemployment insurance it was FDR who insisted that both curatives be used: "Let a man have something definite by law for some weeks and then arrange it so he can have work relief afterward." Yet the bill, as it emerged from the gauntlet of congressional debate and Roosevelt's fears as to constitutionality, was decidedly inferior to plans long in operation in Europe.

The law provided four types of aid, two through insurance and two from the government till. Except for domestics, public servants, farm laborers, and a few others, employees henceforth were to contribute 1 per cent of their pay into a compulsory, federally administered pension fund. The employer would match this amount and out of the monies accumulated those who retired at age sixty-five or beyond would be paid an annuity of $10 to $85 a month, depending on previous earnings. For those at retirement age who were outside the bounds of this system and indigent, the federal government and states were to team up with matching funds to offer relief of $30 (later $40) a month maximum. Because of the parsimonious nature of state contributions the two million elderly receiving this pauper's pittance at the end of the decade averaged only $20 monthly—$240 a year.

A third feature of the bill called for aid to the blind and crippled, dependent mothers and dependent or neglected children, in similar amounts and with similar matching features. Finally, there was unemployment insurance based on a peculiar federal-state partnership. A 3 per cent tax on the employer's payroll was levied by the national government, but 90 per cent of this might be deducted against contributions exacted by an approved state plan. The effect, of course, was that all the states soon had their own unemployment compensation schemes, each one with its own maximum benefits and rules.

The federal government paid administrative costs and set certain minimum standards.

The defects of the social security system were obvious to any social worker. The Communist *Daily Worker* called it "one of the biggest frauds ever perpetrated on the people of this country," and many liberals undoubtedly concurred with this estimate. "In short," wrote the *New Republic*, "the law is almost a model of what legislation ought not to be." For one thing it persevered in catering to states' rights even though it created gross inequities as a result. A blind man in one state might receive $10 a month, $30 a month in another just across the river. An unemployed man in one state might be paid benefits for fifteen weeks, in another twenty. Roosevelt talked forcefully at other moments about "horse and buggy" notions inherited from a long-since-past agricultural era, but he kept compromising—either because of exigency or proclivity—with the same horse-and-buggy drivers. Another defect of the social security bill was its entire lack of benefits in case of sickness or for family allowances, not to mention general medical care. Still another was the number of people excluded from coverage, not merely farmers and those self-employed, but wage earners as well. Finally there was the fact that the old age pensions were not federal gratuities but compulsory insurance over which the recipients enjoyed no control, except the dubious one of voting for good candidates at the polls. By comparison with European standards the bill was generations behind, and still is today after many amendments. Nonetheless, by comparison with barren pre-New Deal days when only one state, Wisconsin, paid unemployment compensation and less than three-fifths of the states boasted any kind of old-age assistance, it was a major leap in public welfare.

So too with the lesser reforms that followed the five major ones of the second hundred days. What Teddy Roosevelt and Wilson celebrated primarily in rhetoric, Franklin Roosevelt breathed into life. He did it under pressure, and he diluted their utility, but as he had promised in 1932, he was going to "do something." The Walsh-Healey Public Contracts Act prohibited child labor and established a forty-hour week and minimum wages in those industries doing business with the government. The Fair Labor Standards Act, which took three years to push through the sclerotic veins of Congress, set maximum hours of work for industry generally of forty-four hours a week, tapering down to forty within two years, and minimum wages of twenty-five cents an hour, rising to forty cents after seven years. It also finally abolished child labor. The Rural Electrication Administration, based on a 1935 law, offered farm communities low-cost loans to string electric power beyond the city "white way" to the villages, and modified rural life in a way that would have made the nineteenth-century Grangers jump with joy. The Wagner-Steagall housing act, while it resulted in only small doses of slum clearance and public housing in its initial years, opened a new dimension in welfare programs.

These and other reforms, whatever their weaknesses in the eyes of social workers and political philosophers, lent a humanistic aura to the New Deal that no administration in this century has been able to match.

In addition to the reforms, the government continued, even widened, its policy of work relief; had it not done so, indeed, its formula for reform would have appeared hollow, for there were still ten to eleven million out of work at the end of 1938. The Work Relief Act of April 1935 substituted a giant program of "made work" for direct relief, on more favorable terms to the jobless. Under the Works Progress Administration (W.P.A.), again entrusted to Harry Hopkins, the federal government in the next seven years spent $10.5 billion in creating jobs, augmented by $2.7 billion contributed by local and other governmental agencies. At its peak it gave succor to 3,800,000 jobless, including writers, artists, and musicians, as well as workers and farmers—all told, to 8,500,000 workers. The recipients of "work relief" were paid prevailing wages for the hours worked and earned $50 to $60 a month, more than double what direct relief recipients were then receiving (about $25 monthly, and in Arkansas and Mississippi only $3 to $5). Hopkins chose only those projects in which labor costs were the major component, so that $86 out of every $100 spent went for wages. Among its physical achievements W.P.A. could point to 600 airports, 100,000 bridges and viaducts, the building and repair of 110,000 schools, libraries, playgrounds, hospitals, and other structures, innumerable sewerage systems, a half-million miles of roads and streets. On the social side were 150 volumes produced by writers in a series on Life in America, hundreds of millions of lunches for school children, a harvest of vocational classes, free musicals and plays, free medical examinations.

The press berated the "boondogglers" and published pictures of men leaning on shovels or huddled around fires, but it is no exaggeration to say that without this infusion of money and jobs, the nation would have faced catastrophe. Nonetheless, the second New Deal, like the first, did not abolish poverty, or come close. In addition to the ten or eleven million unemployed as of the end of 1938, and despite W.P.A. and "compensatory spending," the economy had not yet returned to the levels of the golden twenties. In 1939–40, when the states were again providing three-fifths of the funds for direct relief, the two million "on the dole" were receiving less than in 1933–34 under F.E.R.A., and unemployment benefits in 1940 averaged a mere $10.56 a week.

On January 4, 1939, the New Deal was gently and officially laid to rest with Roosevelt's message to Congress: "We have now passed the period of internal conflict in the launching of our program of social reform." The task now, he said, was "to invigorate the processes of recovery in order to preserve our reforms." From here on in, the social improvements wrought by the "second hundred days" were to be "preserved," not expanded. The agitation in the streets had already spent itself; the Townsend, Long, and Coughlin movements were dimming memories, the farm strikes and eviction struggles now only episodic flareups. The Communists, far and away the largest force on the left, were safely on FDR's bandwagon, having made a great transmigration in 1935 toward a "new line" of critical support. A revived labor movement, sparked by the CIO sit-down strikes of 1937, was three times as large as in 1933 and even more important, strongly ensconced in the mass production industries. The search for industrial justice became more orderly and less militant. Roosevelt could back away from his mighty experiment with little fear for his political future.

The summary of New Deal achievements made in mid-1936 by the *New Republic*'s editors applied with equal force in early 1939: "If one compares it with the measures necessary for a thorough renovation of our society, for creating an economy of abundance, it is sadly deficient, and even, in some respects, reactionary. If one compares it with its own promises and pretensions, and with what it might have done, given the popular support it aroused at the beginning, it is less blameworthy, but still a chapter of lost opportunities." Disregarding John T. Flynn's shrill invective from the right, he was nonetheless accurate when he later wrote of Roosevelt that "the war rescued him." The war orders beginning to arrive from Europe and America's own rearmament gave the economy a nourishment that would soon exceed anything done for it in the 1930's.

For those inclined to probe the causes of the "chapter of lost opportunities," a statement by George Peek stands as a fitting epitaph: "The truth is that no democratic government can be very different from the country it governs. If some groups are dominant in the country, they will be dominant in any plan the government undertakes."

The war put America back to work, where C.W.A., N.R.A., P.W.A., W.P.A. had failed. The Cold War kept it at the workbench thereafter.

Chapter 18

YE HAVE ALWAYS?

For a quarter of a century after the second New Deal passed into limbo the problem of poverty remained comfortably outside the national consciousness. Yesterday's jobless found work as Dr. Win-the-War took over from Dr. New Deal and a cold war followed a hot one. In their modest but improving comfort Americans forgot the nightmare of the Great Depression, almost as if it had never happened.

Contrary to the fears of Harry Hopkins, Raymond Moley, Senators Byrnes and Black that there would always be a large residue of unemployed even in good times, the war and cold war gobbled up all or almost all workers not captured by the military draft. The number without work declined during hostilities to eight million in 1940, then five and a half million, two and a half million, one million, and finally to 670,000 in 1944. On the farm too the warm winds of prosperity wafted over the land as income doubled and the number of farms continued to decline. Over all, the state of economic health in 1945 showed an impressive increase to almost twice the prewar gross national product, in just about the same time it had taken the country to fall apart from November 1929 to March 1933.

This miracle, elusive in the 1930's despite planning and reform, was the result of enormous injections of government funds into the economy. Almost two hundred billions went for munitions, another fifty billion for Lend-Lease to foreign allies (most of it to Britain), and more than twenty billion for new factories built by the government but operated by private industry. By January 1945 Roosevelt could report, in a message to Congress, that nearly half the output of goods and services fabricated by the nation was being bought by the federal government. The purchase of 300,000 planes, 65,000 marine vessels, 17,000,000 rifles, 90,000 tanks, stoked the fires of industry as no similar effort had ever done before. The expenditure on munitions in a single year, $64 billion in 1944, was considerably more than all the monies appropriated for New Deal programs from 1933 through 1938. Inevitably then the economy boomed and corporate profits, less than 1 per cent of net worth in 1934 and only 6 per cent in 1940, pyramided to 16 per cent in 1944. Gone was the reverence for balanced budgets. Where a three- or four-billion-dollar deficit had been considered shocking by conservatives during the New Deal, fifty billions in red ink during 1944 and 1945 were accepted as a matter of course; and if there was any outcry over the sixfold rise in the public debt—from 40 to 250 billions—it was so muted no one paid attention to it.

The aim of wartime spending, of course, was not to shrivel poverty but to defeat Hitler, yet if this was not "compensatory spending" and "deficit financing" as preached in orthodox Keynesianism it had the same effect. A government that spent eighty to eighty-five billions a year, no matter what the purpose, was priming a big pump, and its kindly liquids were bound to overflow to those in need. Europe's "compensatory spending" was counteracted by vast destruction and virtual economic collapse; at the end of hostilities former bank officials in Germany were picking up cigarette butts in the streets of Berlin and many a declassed bourgeois lady could be bought for a Hershey bar. The situation in "victorious" England and France was only slightly better. But America, for the second time, was blessed by the gods. Not a single one of its buildings had been blown up, its economy was rich and firm beyond comprehension, and if there were any hardships during hostilities—beyond the terrible ones of death and injury for more than a million soldiers—they were limited to buying cigarettes and meat on the black market during price controls, or putting up with the restrictive decisions of the War Labor Board on wages.

When the titanic conflict was crowned with victory there were some, notably the Communists but quite a few liberals as well, who believed another depression was the order of the day—if not on the 1929 scale, then that of 1921. Eugene Dennis, head of the Communist Party, talked of "the next cyclical economic crisis" as if it were predestined and warned that it would "enormously accentuate the dangers of fascism in the United States." But these were monumental miscalculations that overlooked three significant circumstances: first, that the government was going to continue massive outlays for armaments many times higher than prewar; second, that bank vaults and tin boxes were bulging with forty-five billions in war bonds and a hundred billion more in savings, ready to be converted into washing machines and automobiles; and finally, that organized labor instead of being battered into quiescence as in 1919 would exact four rounds of sizable wage increases. With money pouring from three directions into the economy's trough, demand for goods remained high even in reconversion, and prosperity reigned triumphant.

The cold war that followed the hot one, after an uneasy year or two, continued the magic formula of pumping military—and related—dollars into the economy. From 1946 through 1967, according to Senate Foreign Relations Committee Chairman William Fulbright, "we have spent over $1,578 billion through our regular national budget. Of this amount over $904 billion, or 57.29 per cent of the total, has gone for military power. By contrast, less than $96 billion, or 6.08 per cent, was spent on 'social functions' including education, health, labor and welfare programs, housing and community development. The Administration's budget for fiscal year 1968 calls for almost $76 billion to be spent on the military and only $15 billion for 'social functions.'" Economic and military aid to foreign allies, which related to American global objectives, accounted for a hundred billion more of government spending.

No one, of course, planned the Cold War as an antipoverty program. Nonetheless it has been one, despite the fact that the most ardent cold warriors in Congress have consistently opposed welfare measures. Richard P. Oliver of the Bureau of Labor Statistics estimated in September 1967 that employment generated by military spending, including military personnel, factory workers directly engaged in war production, and Department of Defense civilian employees, came to about 10 per cent of the labor force, or seven and a half million people. The total amount of employment created by pumping these sums into the economy, however, is much greater since, as the economists put it, a dollar spent by the government has a "multiplier" effect. That means it changes hands two or three times more as it is spent and respent by the grocers, butchers, and landlords who receive it, thus producing large numbers of additional jobs. It is conceivable therefore that had defense spending remained at the picayune billion-dollar-a-year level of prewar, unemployment might have been almost as ominous a specter as in the gloomy 1930's. Supported however by a trillion dollars of postwar military expenditures, the economy faltered only four times in the quarter of a century after the war and unemployment never reached more than a 7 per cent figure. In fact the word "depression" all but passed out of the language and economic downturns were referred to by the milder term "recession."

A generation of postwar Americans began to regard the military-induced prosperity as the norm of economic behavior, while the commonplace depressions that once wracked the nation every decade, sometimes oftener, were considered "abnormal," as if they were accidental aberrations. Typical of the self-satisfaction was the handsome glorification of the "American system" by the editors of *Fortune* in a volume called *U.S.A. The Permanent Revolution.* The U.S., it said, had its faults but it modified itself constantly and peacefully like a computer that not only works better than the human brain but corrects its own errors. The average American, looking no deeper into the mystery of prosperity than his own improved circumstances, conceived of this system as inherently superior not only vis-à-vis the Communist one but that of other capitalist nations as well. If this was not the best of all possible worlds, it was close enough to merit the highest accolade.

In this atmosphere of smug contentment the nation lost sight of its poor, as if they had vanished with the winds. At best they were a subliminal footnote. The New Deal reforms were not undone, for the most part; in fact, they were amended to conform with current conditions. Minimum wages under the Fair Labor Standards Act were raised under President Truman from forty cents to seventy-five cents an hour. Old-age and survivor's benefits were increased an average of 77½ per cent in 1950 to match the rise in living costs since the social security law was enacted in 1935, and an additional seven million farm workers, domestic employees, and self-employed were brought under its coverage. A National Housing Act of 1949 allocated funds for slum clearance and low-cost housing. A GI Bill of Rights, more generous than the post-World War I bonus, allowed discharged servicemen a year of unemployment compensation plus tuition and subsistence allowances if they chose to go to college or trade school, as twelve million did. But Harry Truman's Fair Deal was abortive in plowing new fields and often ineffective against the dilution of old reforms. A proposal for national health insurance and sick benefits for all citizens, for instance, received a congressional cold shoulder. Unemployment insurance was tightened by the Eighty-first Congress to make it more difficult for applicants, and the Taft-Hartley Law, passed in 1947, significantly weakened the old Wagner Act by banning the closed shop, allowing employers to sue unions, imposing an eighty-day cooling off period on strikes where national interest was involved, and requiring union leaders to sign non-Communist affidavits. Efforts to continue Roosevelt's Fair Employment Practices Commission to protect Negroes against job discrimination were talked to death in Senate filibusters.

While a pained Western Europe moved markedly to the left, designating Socialist or Socialist-Communist-Catholic coalition governments to rule it, the pendulum in America swung just as markedly to the right. Old New Dealers like Wallace, Ickes, Morgenthau, Hopkins, Sherwood, Welles disappeared from the scene; liberal groups found themselves beleaguered, berated, and sometimes besmirched as "Communists" by the House Committee on Un-American Activities (HUAC) and eventually by Senator Joseph McCarthy. The mood of militancy that had sustained the New Deal had long since spent itself—it would take half a generation to revive. Typically, the labor movement, its roster now fifteen million and its coffers filling quickly, was well on the way to domestication, and with the expulsion of Communist-controlled unions from the CIO in 1949–50, reached a long-term plateau of moderation. True, there was an outburst of strikes in 1946 when four and a half million workers paced the picket lines—a half million more than in 1919. But this time employers seldom tried to smash the unions, run in "scabs," or draw up blacklists. The temper of the times was accommodation, not class struggle, and the strikes by and large were settled with hefty wage boosts—accompanied by government sanction for even heftier price increases. "The strikes and strike threats of

1945–6," observed *Fortune*, "generated violent emotions, but it was an impressive fact that for the first time a great wave of strikes stirred up almost no physical violence. The strikers of 1945–6 were not desperate men. On the public platform their leaders sounded off with booming phrases directed at the enemy Capital; but privately they, like the strikers, were calm, cool, even friendly warriors."

The proletarians who had shaken the rafters from the Civil War on were relatively appeased. The farmer was doing moderately well, his Populism and milk strikes a dim memory as he crossed over to the conservative side of the political spectrum. The immigrant was a minuscule factor in national affairs, his sons and daughters having long since disappeared into the melting pot. The city workers, as already noted, were winning major victories through their new unions and, in the mass production industries, moving steadily to middle-class standards and middle-class biases, just like the "aristocrats of labor"—the craft unionists—of another day.

The Socialists for all practical purposes ceased to function as a viable force. The Communists plummeted from a peak of about 100,000 to 40,000 in 1950–51 and fewer than 10,000 eventually, with a concomitant decline in sympathizers (whom the rightists called fellow travelers) of even greater proportions. The third-party campaign of former Vice President Henry Wallace in 1948 was a still-born venture, with Wallace polling 1,158,000 votes for President, slightly fewer than the States Rights' candidate, J. Strom Thurmond, whose efforts were confined to the South. It was a shattering setback in the wake of which the largest liberal contingent disappeared, and a resurgent right, more aggressive than that of the 1920's, seized the initiative. Investigations of "Communists" by HUAC, the loyalty-oath campaigns, the shrill ramblings of Senator McCarthy, the restrictive legislation by Senator Pat McCarran which required Communist, "Communist-front," and "Communist-infiltrated" organizations to turn over their membership lists to the government, all combined to cast a pall on dissent and reformism.

The poor, then, both visible and invisible, had few allies and little refuge from which to seek succor. Their numbers were not negligible: as late as 1953 a quarter of all the families or "spending units" in the country survived on less than $2,000 a year. A study by the Federal Reserve Board the following year revealed that more than fourteen million families—26 per cent of the total—owned no liquid assets of any kind to fall back on for a rainy day. "Majority" poverty, as John Kenneth Galbraith would soon note, had been trimmed to "minority" poverty and was therefore less visible than in the 1930's. But it was by no means a minor problem, especially among such minorities as the Negroes, whose average income was approximately half that of their white counterparts. Robert Lampman, perhaps the leading researcher on the subject, estimated that low-income people in the United States might "reasonably range" between 16 and 36 per cent. As of 1958 a fifth of the families in the nation averaged less than $1,500 a year and two-fifths, less than $3,500.

Yet America forged for itself the self-indulgent thesis that it had done just about all that could be done to banish poverty. Twenty years after the war, during the 1964 presidential elections, Barry Goldwater, the Republican standard-bearer, was telling his followers that "it is like greyhounds chasing a mechanical hare. You can never catch up. There will always be a lowest one-third or one-fifth." If there were poor people around, it could not be charged to their lack of education or other factors but to "low intelligence or low ambitions." If the vote for him was any barometer, tens of millions of people—27,174,898—agreed.

II

A new proletariat surfaced in the mid-1950's and with it began another chapter in the war on poverty.

On December 1, 1955, a Negro seamstress, Mrs. Rosa Parks, took a seat on the Cleveland Avenue bus in Montgomery, Alabama, and refused to give it up to a white man when ordered to do so by the bus driver. Mrs. Parks, long active in the National Association for the Advancement of Colored People (NAACP), was arrested, initiating a chain of events as consequential as William Lloyd Garrison's decision to publish the *Liberator* in 1831. Within twenty-four hours the Negro leaders of the city had gathered and proclaimed a boycott of the city buses. Seventeen thousand blacks organized car pools or walked back and forth to work, rain or shine, for 381 days, rather than accept humiliating second-class status any longer.

Among the men who launched the Montgomery Improvement Association, which directed the effort, was the short, stocky, twenty-six-year-old minister of the Dexter Avenue Baptist Church, Martin Luther King, Jr., whose life had been undistinguished until this moment. Studious, well-read, a devotee of nonviolence, which deepened as he came into contact with Bayard Rustin and Glenn Smiley of the pacifist Fellowship of Reconciliation, King was the personification of the "new Negro" rising everywhere on the American scene. Of ministereal lineage—his father and maternal grandfather were also ministers, as was his brother—he had attended the small, integrated Crozer Theological Seminary of Chester, Pennsylvania, had taken his doctorate at Boston University, and returned to his birthplace, Atlanta, where from 1947 to 1954 he served in his father's church until assigned to the one in Montgomery. As part of the younger generation of blacks, conditioned in war and, more and more, college educated, King thought of religion as something more than an exercise in theological rhetoric. Before long he had formed a social and political action committee to register Negroes for voting and to help in whatever way possible the labors of the NAACP.

An oratorical spellbinder, with florid use of language, a resonant voice, and a flare for the pungent phrase, King was able to galvanize the Montgomery boycotters to a sense of quiet determination not seen for a long time. Moreover, the nonviolent character of the protest dramatized to all the nation—and the world—the heavy burdens of the American Negro. When King's home was bombed on January 30, 1956, he pleaded with his followers not to reciprocate: "Don't go get your weapons. He who lives by the sword will perish by the sword." Shortly thereafter twenty-four ministers, including King, were arrested and convicted of sponsoring the boycott. The young Baptist was sentenced to 140 days in jail and fined $500, but the boycott continued during the appeal, and in December 1956 the Supreme Court upheld a decision of the lower federal courts that declared the Alabama law on bus segregation illegal. After more than a year the 17,000 Negroes had won their fight and in the process launched a new black movement, led for the first time by Negroes themselves. (Even the NAACP had been formed at the turn of the century by white socialists and liberals.)

Inspired by King and Montgomery, three militant civil rights forces were soon organizing marches and demonstrations all over the South—King's own Southern Christian Leadership Conference (SCLC), founded in Atlanta by a hundred clergymen; the Congress of Racial Equality (CORE), headed by James Farmer, a long-time pacifist who had formed it originally when he was race relations secretary of the Fellowship of Reconciliation in 1942, and who now revived it; and the Student Nonviolent Coordinating Committee (SNCC), established with King's aid in 1960 and guided by such young men as Robert Parris Moses, John Lewis, and James Foreman. These Negro zealots, risking their lives frequently and going to jail even more frequently (King himself was arrested thirty times), led hundreds of demonstrations, marches, bus rides, sit-ins in the next seven years to enforce equality of treatment and the Supreme Court decision on school desegregation. Thousands of them fell to policemen's clubs or were arrested—300 in Selma, Alabama, from September 15 to October 2, 1963, for instance. Negro and white sympathizers were murdered. Churches were bombed. Police dogs were called out against demonstrators in Birmingham. Innumerable economic reprisals were visited upon blacks by white citizens councils. But the agitation continued, climaxing in the 1963 "March on Washington for Freedom and Jobs," which drew 200,000 Negroes and white sympathizers, and in the walk from Selma to Montgomery two years later. "In the sixties," writes Benjamin Quarles, "the Negro question assumed a new urgency . . . brought about in large measure by Negroes themselves." Reaction against American racism around the world was so intense Secretary of State Dean Rusk commented that the United States was conducting its foreign affairs "with one of our legs in a cast."

In its first phase the black revolt centered on the South and primarily around the issue of social and political equality—equal treatment on buses, in restaurants and hotels, desegregation of schools, the right to vote. But the focus shifted, as many of these prerogatives were partially won, to economic equality, in jobs and in income. As King put it, it didn't do the Negro much good to have the right to sit at a lunch counter if he didn't have the price of a hamburger in his pocket. The horizons of the movement also broadened to include the North and urban America generally, where the new proletariat lived in segregated ghettos and worked at menial tasks, excluded from skilled and semiskilled jobs open to white neighbors.

The proletariat of pre-World War I was somehow linked to immigration of foreigners—the white indentures, the captured black slaves, the foreign-born white workers. The latest proletariat was a product of *inner* migration. In 1910, when the total Negro population was fewer than ten million, all but 800,000 lived in the South, three-quarters of them on farms. The industrial surge that followed World War I and the depression drew more than a million northward out of the Old Confederacy, so that by 1940 there were four million above the Mason-Dixon line. With the enormous need for man power during World War II, the figures rose precipitously as Negroes moved to assembly lines in Detroit, shipyards in Camden, steel mills in Gary; and it continued after the war as mechanization drove hundreds of thousands of sharecroppers and tenants off the land. From 541,000 sharecroppers in 1940, black and white, the number declined to 112,000 in 1959. Almost three million Negroes left the South in this period, most of them clustering in crowded ghettos such as Chicago's South Side or New York's Harlem. By 1968, 69 per cent of the 21,500,000 blacks in America were residents of metropolitan areas and the migration north and west had resulted in so great a population transfer that almost half lived outside the South. In many American cities, especially as the white middle class began its own trek to the suburbs, the Negro population was more than half the total—in Newark and Washington, D.C., for instance. Parallel to the black migration was also an influx of the Spanish-speaking; in New York the Puerto Rican complex of 100,000 in 1940 rose to 700,000 at census time in 1960.

Confined to abysmal slums as bad in many respects as those of the late nineteenth century, the new proletariat showed all the characteristics of older ones. Its members were the first fired from jobs, the last to be hired. Their rate of unemployment was double that of the white working class, their income half as high. As of 1966 one-third of all Negro families earned less than $3,000 a year as against only 13 per cent of whites in similar low estate. Moreover, as the National Advisory Commission on Civil Disorders, headed by Governor Otto Kerner of Illinois, reported in 1968, by and large the incomes of these slum dwellers failed to rise despite inflation and general prosperity. The Department of Labor survey of low-income areas in nine large cities showed Negroes with a 9.3 per cent rate of unemployment, in contrast to 3.3 per cent for whites, and if the "underemployed"—those working part-time, for instance—are included, one of every three Negroes belonged to this category. Of the thirty million people designated poor by the Social Security Administration in 1966 (those with incomes under $3,335 per family) the chance of a white man's being on the list was one in eight, that of a black man two in five. In twelve of the fourteen largest cities in the United States the number of Negro and Spanish-speaking people living in dilapidated housing units ranged from a quarter to half the total. Three decades after the first national housing act the slums of the inner city showed remarkable resistance to extermination; they still boasted more inhabitants, according to Charles L. Farris, president of the National Association of Housing Officials, than the total population on the farms.

What the Kerner Commission wrote of the new proletariat in 1968 was simply a rephrasing of what had been written about other proletariats in bygone days: "The culture of poverty that results from unemployment and family disorganization generates a system of ruthless exploitative relationships within the ghetto. Prostitution, dope addiction, casual sexual affairs, and crime create an environmental jungle characterized by personal insecurity and tension."

All of this had been known, of course, to social workers and liberal writers on the subject for some time. Robert Lampman had done an incisive study for Congress in 1959; the National Urban League made a "Survey of Unemployment in Selected Urban League Cities" two years later that came to many of the same conclusions. But the notion that economic deprivation was at the root of the civil rights explosion penetrated the stream of American consciousness with lugubrious hesitancy. Everyone was aware that the Negro was ostracized socially, that he was brutalized by police, deprived of voting rights in the South, segregated in the school systems despite a Supreme Court decision a decade back. But the conventional wisdom held that this was a "southern" problem and that it related primarily to noneconomic matters, such as the indignity of discrimination.

The accelerated pace of racial riots in the North, however, coming each hot summer, finally focused attention on the black man's *poverty*. Minor incidents of real or alleged policy brutality in 1964 spurred spontaneous and violent outbreaks in New York, Rochester, Brooklyn, Philadelphia, Jersey City, Elizabeth, Paterson. The following year shock waves ran through a complacent nation when disorders broke out in a section of Los Angeles known as Watts, during which 4,000 persons were arrested, 34 killed, hundreds injured, and

$35,000,000 in property destroyed. In 1966 the locus of "black rebellion" shifted to America's second city, Chicago, where a tiny event, refusal by police to permit Negro youths to turn on a fire hydrant on a hot July day, led to an insurgency that necessitated the calling out of 4,200 national guardsmen, and to the Hough area of Cleveland, where chaos ruled for four long nights a week later. It reached a momentary climax the next summer in Newark, Detroit, and almost 150 other cities in which tens of millions of dollars' worth of property was burned down and thousands of blacks arrested. A survey of seventy-five of these disturbances showed 83 killed and 1,897 injured.

It reached another climax less than a year later, in April 1968, following the assassination of Martin Luther King, Jr., in Memphis, where he was planning a demonstration on behalf of predominantly Negro garbagemen striking for union recognition and higher wages. Black outrage flared in Washington, where fires broke out in sight of the White House; in Chicago, which had been immune to the 1967 riots; and in many other cities. Though the toll in dead was less than in the summer of 1967 the government was forced to call out more than 26,500 army troops and 47,000 national guardsmen. "Not since the Civil War," commented *The New York Times*, "has this country experienced an epidemic of domestic violence as widespread as it was this weekend."

The killing, looting, vandalism, and arson, especially in 1967 and 1968, disturbed and alienated many Americans. A few attributed the events to a conspiracy by followers of Stokely Carmichael of SNCC, whose "black power" slogan rang through the ghettos like a clarion. Yet in the sober aftermath, it was obvious that the so-called black rebellion had been spontaneous, leaderless. That so many people in so many places should have risen in anger punctuated the point that discrimination was not merely a racial problem, nor confined to the South, but essentially a poverty problem and nationwide in scope. The fact that many of the participants were among the better educated and better paid does not alter this conclusion; it simply emphasizes that the Negro poor, like the white poor at the turn of the century, were gaining leadership from elements higher up in the economic scale. It was a traumatic thought, three decades after the New Deal and against the background of depressionless affluence, that such a situation should exist.

III

In the rhythm of antipoverty protest, dissent in the streets interacts with the cries of lone reformers until finally it reaches the citadels of power to be translated into action.

In 1958 an economics professor, John Kenneth Galbraith, published a gently written book with the deceptive title *The Affluent Society*. Privation, he wrote, has been ended "as a general affliction" by "increased output which, however imperfectly it may have been distributed, nevertheless accrued in substantial amount to those who worked for a living. The result was to reduce poverty from the problem of a majority to that of a minority. It ceased to be a general case and became a special case." But poverty, though it has no "firm definition," still survives either as "case poverty" or "insular poverty." The former is the result of "some quality peculiar to the individual or family involved—mental deficiency, bad health, inability to adapt to the discipline of modern economic life, excessive procreation, alcohol, insufficient education, or perhaps a combination of several of these handicaps." Insular poverty shows itself as an "island" of privation amidst general affluence, such as in the worked-out mining areas of West Virginia, or the ghettos.

Galbraith's book, in witty, nonacademic language, opened the door a large crack. The idea began to percolate that there *could* be poverty amid affluence, and years later a spate of books appeared with precisely such titles—*Poverty Amid Affluence, Poverty in the Affluent Society*, etc. But Galbraith's book brought few crying towels from the cedar chest and evoked no new crusades.

Ensconced in the White House in 1958 was the pleasant, round-faced hero of World War II, General Dwight D. (Ike) Eisenhower. The President, whose political allegiance to the Republicans had been made known only on the eve of his first campaign in 1952, had a penchant for golf and Western stories, but a lackadaisical attitude toward change or Franklin Roosevelt's type of experimentation. He could not, had he wanted to—and it is doubtful that he did—have torn down the welfarist façade established by the New Deal. It was now part of the "American Way." But he had no intention of carrying it much further either. His Agricultural Act of 1956 gave some succor to farmers, whose price levels had fallen after the Korean War, by paying them bounties for taking unproductive lands out of cultivation. Another amendment to the Fair Labor Standards Act, made necessary by inflation, raised the minimum wage scale in covered industries to one dollar an hour. Public housing bills were passed in 1957, 1958, and 1959 with approximately three billions from the federal exchequer to implement them, and a road-building law was enacted in April 1958 to fight the recession then gnawing at the economy. The National Defense Education Act, spurred in part by realization that the United States might be behind the Soviet Union in the field of science after Sputnik had been sent into the skies, authorized loans and graduate fellowships for students. Old age and retirement benefits were again increased, with slightly higher levies on employers and employees. And under two civil rights acts, in 1957 and 1960, a commission was established to give modest protection to Negroes in the South who were denied the privilege of a ballot. Except for the last two measures, however, all of this was an updating of the New Deal rather than a grandiose assault on poverty.

The accession of John F. Kennedy to the Presidency in 1961 coincided with the student surge that crystallized into freedom rides, demonstrations against HUAC, the birth of SNCC, the reformation of an old socialist group into the radical Students for a Democratic Society, and outspoken sympathy for Castro's revolution within youthful legions—a mood and a movement that C. Wright Mills in a 1960 article designated the "New Left." Kennedy's style—buoyant, vigorous, poetical in its prose—catered to the disaffection of this new generation without embracing its radical implications. His inaugural address rang with such idealistic sentences as: "If a free society cannot help the many who are poor, it cannot save the few who are rich," and urged Americans to "ask not what your country can do for you: Ask what you can do for your country." In one of his first messages to Congress he painted a dolorous picture of cities "engulfed in squalor"—the deficiency in classrooms and education; the lack of sufficient medical care, hospital beds, nursing homes, doctors, dentists; the pollution of water; the "substandard homes" of twenty-five million Americans; the need for medical care for the aged. He seemed to be underscoring a crescendo of concern voiced by Robert Lampman in his quiet studies, and the barrage of pamphlets by the Conference on Economic Progress, in which Leon Keyserling, chairman of Truman's Council of Economic Advisers, was the key figure. A December 1959 brochure by the Conference advocated a $23.5 billion increase in the national budget during the ensuing two years for education, health, relief, and other welfarist steps in order to whittle down the number of people—seventy-seven million—living either in "poverty" or "deprivation."

The catalyst, however, for the latest war on poverty was a little book, actually a large brochure, published by Michael Harrington in 1962, *The Other America*. Like Robert Hunter, whose 1904 opus caused a similar stir, Harrington was a youngish socialist whose sympathies for the dispossessed were based not only on contact but on ideology. Born in St. Louis in 1928, he had studied at Holy Cross, Yale, and the University of Chicago. Two years later he was working with a legendary Catholic pacifist, Dorothy Day, helping to edit her radical publication, the *Catholic Worker*. Here he met not only anarchists, Gandhians, and socialists—one of whom recruited him to a small leftist group—but the hundreds of down-and-out proletarians who sought shelter in Miss Day's New York quarters on Chrystie Street. As he later put it, it was on Chrystie Street that "I first came into contact with the terrible reality of involuntary poverty and the magnificent ideal of voluntary poverty." Moving on to other fields, Harrington's work took him to the Workers Defense League, the Fund for the Republic, where he served with project teams looking into trade union developments and blacklisting in the entertainment industries. He wrote articles for *Commonweal* and *Commentary*, edited two socialist papers, and in between traipsed across the country compiling data on poverty. Published in a small edition, *The Other America* drew little acclaim until a year later when Dwight Macdonald digested its theme for the pages of *The New Yorker* and sent it flying onto the best-seller lists. Among those who were influenced by this "brilliant and indignant book," as Arthur Schlesinger, Jr., called it, was President Kennedy.

The Other America quoted its share of statistics, but Harrington's graphic exposition and lively style had a way of making the poor seem real. While writing the book, Harrington relates, he was arrested during a civil rights demonstration: "A brief experience of a night in a cell made an abstraction personal and immediate: the city jail is one of the basic institutions of the other America. Almost everyone whom I encountered in the 'tank' was poor: skid-row whites, Negroes, Puerto Ricans. Their poverty was an incitement to arrest in the first place. . . . They did not have money for bail or for lawyers. And perhaps, most important, they waited their arraignment with stolidity, in a mood of passive acceptance. They expected the worst, and they probably got it." Anyone who has ever lived in the "culture of poverty" could recognize this "stolid" acceptance of an inhospitable fate.

Similarly the rest of the poverty cast comes out in majestic tragedy through *The Other America*'s descriptive prose: the "rejects" who lose their jobs through automation or plant shutdowns, the rural poor, the blacks—"If You're Black, Stay Back"—the aged, the sick, the welfare recipients, the alcoholics. The poor, says Harrington, "tend to become increasingly invisible. Here is a great mass of people, yet it takes an effort of the intellect and will even to see them." They are invisible because for the most part they live "off the beaten track," out of range of the turnpike tourist or the visitor from suburbia. "To be impoverished is to be an internal alien, to grow up in a culture that is radically different from the one that dominates society." Where opportunity beckons other children who can prepare themselves for an increasingly complex industrial system through adequate education, the youngsters of the other America are frozen to their status, generation after generation, because they cannot acquire the required schooling or preschooling. Today's poor, Harrington concludes, "are the strangest poor in the history of mankind. They exist within the most powerful and rich society the world has ever known. Their misery has continued while the majority of the nation talked of itself as being 'affluent' and worried about neuroses in the suburbs. They dropped out of sight and out of mind; they were without their own political voice."

What *The Other America* drove home to men of conscience was not merely that poverty existed parallel to affluence, but that nothing society was presently doing percolated down to those in need. Neither business prosperity, "compensatory spending," nor welfare elevated the impoverished beyond subsistence. Kennedy's New Frontier team was struck by the point, as Schlesinger records, that "by reasonable definitions—an annual income of $3,000 for a family or $1,500 for an individual—one-fifth of the nation lived in an underworld of poverty beyond the reach of most government programs, whether housing, farm price supports, social security or tax reduction." With the President's blessings, then, Walter Heller, chairman of the Council of Economic Advisers, was assigned to devise a program that would reach that "underworld." It was to be, he was told, the central plank of Kennedy's 1964 message to Congress. Before it could be presented, however, the President was assassinated in Dallas and responsibility for the "unconditional war" on want passed to Lyndon B. Johnson.

IV

The tall Texan, first southern President in a century, had shown little affinity for the downtrodden in the two previous decades, resembling in this respect Teddy Roosevelt, Wilson, and to a lesser extent Franklin Roosevelt. His political career in fact reflected the chameleon more than the crusader. He had come to Washington originally, in 1931 at the age of twenty-three, as secretary to a rich Texas congressman whose social views were as backward as those of an Indian maharajah. After four years he passed over to the New Deal legions, serving as state director of the National Youth Administration under the left-of-center Aubrey Williams. Then, hitching his star to Congressman Sam Rayburn, at that time considered a liberal, Johnson ran in Texas' Tenth Congressional District as a New Dealer against six opponents who considered Franklin Roosevelt anathema, and beat them all. In Washington he drew the attention of the political potentates, including Roosevelt himself, for his firm support of reform. Treated like an adopted son by the President, Lyndon sometimes kicked the traces even of his sponsor, Rayburn, as for instance when he voted against a measure that would raise the price of Texas' petroleum or when Rayburn in 1940 tried to initiate a "stop-Roosevelt" drive.

Following Roosevelt's death, however, Johnson shifted severely rightward. He cozied to the oil and construction interests of his home state, especially Brown & Root Inc., and was rewarded by generous donations to his campaign chests. Business interests that shunned him previously were attracted to him after he voted for the Taft-Hartley Act and gave similar assurances of fidelity. Though he seldom moved completely into the ranks of reaction, lest he sever links with the national party, Johnson displayed an aptitude for caution, compromise, and conservatism consonant with postwar America. In August 1948 he won a primary fight for the Senate by a shaky eighty-seven votes, after the mysterious appearance of 202 additional ballots from a remote precinct. Two years later, mainly through the efforts of Senator Robert Kerr, an oilman from Oklahoma, Johnson was installed as whip for his party, and after another two years, when the Democratic floor leader, Senator Ernest McFarland, was defeated by Barry Goldwater in Arizona, LBJ rose to the coveted top post at the youngish age of forty-four.

Johnson's record, though not of the extreme right, was not meant to endear him to liberals. During the Korean War he was critical of Truman's "makeshift mobilization," questioning whether the nation could have both guns *and* butter if it was to provide the matériel for its armies. He based this view on the belief that "we may well be at war for ten or twenty years more." He voted consistently against civil rights legislation until 1957, and in favor of the restrictive immigration act introduced by two Congressional tories, McCarran and Walter. He gained some liberal support from associate senators by working for those moderate measures that caused little furor back in Texas: higher minimum wages, housing, and social security. But when it came to questions of oil, or gas, his leanings were in the other direction. His image became that of a wheeler-dealer who worked closely with Republican President Eisenhower as well as the southern powerhouse, Richard Russell, and was forever patching up compromises. He seemed to many people to be a man with no commitment except to personal career. When Kennedy chose him as running mate in 1960, organized labor, and in particular Walter Reuther, were so horrified they considered bolting the Democratic ticket. He was definitely not a liberal favorite when fate propelled him into the White House.

Yet Johnson had been in office only five days when he urged "a civil rights law so that we can move forward to eliminate from this nation every trace of discrimination and oppression that is based upon race or color." Forty-two days later, in a forty-minute State of the Union message that had taken six weeks and twenty-four writers to draft, he made the most ringing appeal on poverty in a quarter of a century: "Unfortunately, many Americans live on the outskirts of hope, some because of their poverty and some because of their color, and all too many because of both. Our task is to help replace their despair with opportunity. And this Administration today, here and now, declares unconditional war on poverty in America. . . . It will not be a short or easy struggle, no single weapon or strategy will suffice, but we shall not rest until that war is won." Within a few months he was talking of the Great Society—a term coined by speechwriter Richard Goodwin—which would bring "an end to poverty and racial injustice, to which we are totally committed in our time." It was inspiring talk, all the more so because it was assumed that his legislative wizardry would be able to guide new bills through Congress more easily than Kennedy might have.

Johnson did not disappoint the liberals. His program coupled a promise of an $11 billion tax cut with the Great Society—medical care for the aged, help to the distressed Appalachia area, area redevelopment, youth employment, higher unemployment compensation and minimum wages, special school aid, more libraries and nursing homes, housing, a mass transit bill, and civil rights measures. "These programs," he observed, "are obviously not for the poor or the underprivileged alone." They were, however, a single package, each item related to the other as the New Deal planks had been, zeroing in on poverty from a half-dozen angles. Congress did not respond to the package in the same way as in the "hundred days" of the New Deal, but an antipoverty bill was passed in August and after the 1964 elections a sense of urgency overtook the legislature so that a comparable "hundred days" under Johnson was written into legislative history. Johnson boasted on April 8, 1965, that it was "a record of major accomplishments without equal or close parallel in the present era," and certainly insofar as the postwar period was concerned he was correct.

Foremost on the Great Society escutcheon were medical care for the aged, a new type of education bill, a voting rights law, and the omnibus antipoverty program put under the direction of Kennedy's brother-in-law, Sargent Shriver. These were innovations that had not been tried either in the New Deal or successive administrations. The medicare-social security bill of 1965 provided ninety days of hospitalization, and an additional one hundred days of nursing home care, both to be financed out of social security, plus a voluntary system whereby for $3 a month the senior citizen was additionally covered for doctor's care, X-rays, and similar costs. It was a complex patchwork requiring varying contributions from the aged patient—for instance, the first $40 of hospitalization costs, plus $10 a day after the sixtieth day—but after a quarter of a century of sterility in the domain of reform it seemed to head the nation on a new course.

The aid to education law was also a breakthrough in that it allocated about a billion dollars to those elementary and high school districts where a large number of the children were from poor families. The Higher Education Act consigned a couple of billion dollars for loans to college students as well as grants to libraries, adult education programs, and the like, the aim being, of course, to prepare low-income and middle-income youngsters for better-paying careers.

Neither medicare nor the education laws were directly linked with agitation in the streets, but there was no question that the Voting Rights Bill of 1965 was umbilically related to the uproar in Selma, Alabama, where Johnson was forced to dispatch 1,862 national guardsmen. "This was not Johnson's idea of the Great Society," Rowland Evans and Robert Novak observe in their book on LBJ. "Lyndon Johnson, even more than John F. Kennedy had been, was out of sympathy with the politics of demonstration." The furor, however, had to be appeased, particularly after the killing of Unitarian minister James Reeb. Under the new law, passed despite a filibuster by southern Senators, poll taxes and literacy tests were abolished as preconditions for the ballot—common devices for disfranchising Negroes—and federal examiners were authorized to register prospective black voters in states or counties where they were obviously being discriminated against. Another bill on civil rights gained congressional approval a few days after the assassination of Martin Luther King, Jr., in 1968, this one outlawing discrimination in the sale or rental of all but single-family homes by January 1, 1970.

The center of the Great Society stage, however, was held by the Economic Opportunity Act passed in August 1964, usually referred to as the antipoverty law. It was expected to be, in the words later used by Vice President Hubert Humphrey, the "quiet revolution," and many people actually believed that in a limited number of years it would banish impoverishment forever. Resuscitated liberals, fed a meager fare for two decades, began to recall LBJ's early New Dealism, and not even the Vietnam war—at first—could hold back the flood of accolades. The richest country in the world was finally mounting "the only war worth fighting."

The law itself, however, was not as lavish as its image. Shriver, a pleasant man with a real estate background in Chicago, never tired of telling audiences that it was "not a hand-out program—or an individual case-work program." The eight million helpless poor—those on general assistance, the blind, the dependent children and their families, the aged not insured under social security—won no additional benefits from the antipoverty program. It was geared instead for those who were employable but for some reason or other lacked the skill or desire to integrate themselves into the economy. Title I established a job corps, much like the New Deal C.C.C., authorized to enroll 100,000 young people aged sixteen to twenty-one to do conservation work while improving their basic education. Another 200,000 youth were to be given "work-training" of various types, 90 per cent of the costs to be borne by the federal government; and a "work-study" program, reminiscent of the N.Y.A. of the 1930's, offered fifteen hours of work a week for 140,000 college students from low-income families. In a complex and ever more automated economy where the educational requirement for jobs was rising rapidly, the purpose of Title I was to rescue the school dropout from his fate and make it possible for those lacking the wherewithal to continue their studies in college. In justifying the program Senator Hubert H. Humphrey, soon to become Vice President, pointed out that "thirty percent of all children who enter high school . . . have turned their backs on one of the greatest advantages the United States offers its citizens—twelve years of free schooling. . . . The facts show that education holds the key to escape from the mire of poverty."

The second major feature of the bill—"the heart of the War on Poverty"—was the community action programs, which can be described only as nationalized social work of the same kind Jane Addams was conducting at Hull House seven decades before. In its second report to Congress the Office of Economic Opportunity listed more than 6,000 grants for such diverse projects as "Upward Bound," an "educational program to motivate non-college bound high school students," health centers, "Operation Head Start" to give preschool training to three-quarters of a million disadvantaged children, legal services to the poor, 500 multipurpose neighborhood centers, help for the forgotten Indians and migrants. In addition there was the "Volunteers in Service to America" (VISTA), which provided youthful volunteers for work in the poor areas among migrants, Indians, and the underprivileged generally; a program to make loans available to farmers, cooperatives, and small businessmen (about $50,000,000) and adult education.

In absolute terms, the training and action programs were breathtaking in the magnitude of areas covered and the several million people who gained some benefits from them. But relatively, in comparison to the need, the programs were modest to a fault. All told, only $800,000,000 was appropriated in the first year and about twice that much in each of the next two. Even if one includes the seven billion dollar authorization for public housing over a four-year period, the public works programs for the depressed eleven-state Appalachia area, and the "model cities" projects passed in ensuing years for redeveloping the inner cities, the "war" was, as Martin Luther King pointed out, more nearly a "skirmish."

V

"The present poverty program," wrote Christopher Jencks in the *New Republic*, "is mainly an extension and amplification of policies established under previous Administrations. The chief novelties are in the name and in the administrative form." Its most "conspicuous fact," he continued, was "the elimination not of poverty but of ignorance, incompetence and so forth. The problem may have been redefined, but the solutions have not." Three years after the "war" had started *Business Week* described how the "New Poor" were swelling the ranks: "Both the number of people on welfare and the cost of supporting them are rising, despite prosperity, a Great Society, and a war on poverty. In 1956, about 5.8 million Americans lived on 'the welfare' at a cost of $3 billion to federal, state, and local governments. In 1966, there were eight million on the rolls and the bill was $6.5 billion." For every person on public welfare, it was estimated by economists, there was another one eligible for it who either did not apply or was excluded for some reason. By January 1968, 8,600,000 needy Americans were on relief—one of every twenty-three citizens—a 50 per cent rise since 1957.

"This means," said Mary E. Switzer of the Department of Health, Education and Welfare, "we have an extremely ominous situation. We have a rift between the haves and have-nots in this country that I have not seen in all my lifetime." In affluent Cook County—mostly Chicago—6 per cent of the population existed on welfare, 82 per cent of them Negroes. The average grant per person in Illinois was $41.85 a month for food, rent, clothing and all other expenses except medical aid. By the federal government's own measurement of poverty this was only a third of what a single person needed as a minimum and two-thirds what a family of four required. In Mississippi the average monthly dole was $9.35, in Alabama the munificent sum of $12.75.

Senator Joseph S. Clark of Pennsylvania, who toured impoverished homes in Washington, D.C., and the Mississippi Delta in 1967, recorded for the *Progressive* magazine stark instances of "starvation in the affluent society." Five blocks from the Capitol on Defrees Street he talked with a seven-year-old boy who had soup for breakfast and soup for lunch, nothing more. A community-action worker who guided Clark and Senator Robert Kennedy around the area commented: "There are hundreds of others in this neighborhood who get up in the morning hungry and who go to bed at night hungry. It's been that way ever since I've been here, years and years." South, in Belzoni, heart of the Delta, "we found a mother of fifteen children," Clark records, "nursing a three-day-old child which she had delivered herself. There was no food in the house, she said, and no money. She didn't know what she would do." Near Greenville, Mississippi, he came across a "tumbledown collection of shacks ironically called Freedom City, housing the families of displaced plantation workers. Surviving, somehow, in this appalling squalor were forty-eight children who subsisted entirely on grits, rice, soybeans, and 'whatever is donated,' plus the customary one can of meat per month. Eggs, milk, and fruit juice, the mothers told me, were unknown."

A group of distinguished doctors who made a similar trek to the Delta told a Senate subcommittee they "saw children whose nutritional and medical condition we can only describe as shocking. . . . In child after child we saw evidence of vitamin and mineral deficiencies; serious untreated skin infections and ulcerations; eye and ear diseases; the prevalence of bacterial and parasitic diseases," etc. etc. "We saw homes with children who are lucky to eat one meal a day—and that one inadequate so far as vitamins, minerals, or proteins are concerned."

Dr. Donald E. Gatch told an antipoverty hearing in November

1967 that underfed Negro youngsters in South Carolina were dying of hookworms, roundworms, and other parasitic diseases. A study of 212 persons in Beaufort County revealed that two-thirds were suffering from parasites, including 90 per cent of the children under five. "There's just no damn sense in this country to have a bunch of hungry people. But the hunger and parasite problem isn't on anybody's priority lists."

The *Chicago Sun-Times* dispatched a young reporter, Morton Kondracke, in May 1967 to detail what had happened to the riot-torn cities of the previous two years. In Los Angeles and San Francisco he found "there is debate whether conditions . . . are any better at all. In Cleveland, there is virtual unanimity that conditions are disastrously worse."

Summarizing it all in a letter of February 6, 1968, Michael Harrington wrote: "In January 1964 Lyndon Johnson declared an 'unconditional war' on poverty. In 1967 the Department of Labor's Manpower Report stated that the life in the slums had become worse in the intervening three years. . . . It is scarcely an impressive record. Yet even the already derisory appropriations for the fight against poverty—never as much as a half-percent of our national income and indeed only a tiny fraction of the annual *increase* in that income—are now to be slashed drastically. Head Start, the Job Corps, Medicaid—all are to be cut back even from their present inadequate levels. Public housing remains far below the level proposed by Robert Taft twenty years ago, while the decay of our cities accelerates." He might have added that Taft's proposal for health insurance for *everyone* had been trimmed by the Great Society to health insurance for about one-tenth the population, and that thirty years after the New Deal, according to the Kerner Commission, "only about 800,000 [subsidized federal housing] units have been constructed, with recent production averaging about 50,000 units a year." By contrast government insurance guarantees had "made possible the construction of over ten million middle- and upper-income units."

A still more damning indictment was made by a committee of twenty-five prominent people appointed by Walter Reuther's Citizens Crusade Against Poverty to study hunger. In a book-length summary issued in April 1968 the Citizens Board of Inquiry into Hunger and Malnutrition in the United States showed, on the basis of extensive research, that there were some ten million hungry people in the country and that "the situation" far from being ameliorated "is worsening." The hunger was centered in 256 counties throughout the country, most of it in the South but not a single state being immune. "If you will look," said the board, "you find America is a shocking place. No other western country permits such a large proportion of its people to endure the lives we press on our poor. To make four-fifths of a nation more affluent than any people in history, we have degraded one-fifth mercilessly."

Reciting one instance after another of babies and youngsters ten and twenty pounds underweight because of hunger, or of 470,000 Mississippians living wholly on federal food stamps, eating two meals a day and often nothing at the end of the month, the study group made a number of worrisome over-all observations:

1. That malnutrition has been increasing sharply in the past decade, but government programs for those in need have dropped 1.4 million people from their rolls.

2. That hunger was so widespread in the 256 counties named that nothing but a presidential declaration of emergency could cope with the problem.

3. That less than a fifth of the twenty-nine million poor people (by its estimate) receive food stamps, surplus commodities, or similar aid.

4. That between ten to fourteen and a half million people suffer premature death, infant death, anemia, and many other afflictions because of malnutrition.

The response of the hungry man to all the welfare and antipoverty measures, the Board concluded, would be: "Your programs don't work! The food is not enough to nourish me. The food stamps cost more than I can pay. The school lunch programs are for children of suburban schools. The welfare check is too small for survival. I am still hungry."

A nation whose gross national product was fast approaching the trillion dollar mark annually, and which was spending $30 billion a year on a war in Vietnam and almost three times that much on its military plant generally, did not find the $11 to $25 billion needed to bring the impoverished one-fifth of the nation to a $3,000 a year level per family. Robert Theobold and other economists had been agitating for a decade that the nation forget about trying to save the poor through finding jobs for them and simply assure everyone a minimum guaranteed annual income. An ad hoc committee formed by the Fund for the Republic, making note of the cybernation, weaponry, and human rights revolutions—the "Triple Revolution"—warned "that the traditional link between jobs and income is being broken," and urged that the United States "undertake an unqualified commitment to provide every individual and every family with an adequate income as a matter of right." As a dilution of this proposal some economists, including traditional conservatives such as Milton Friedman of the University of Chicago, an adviser to Barry Goldwater in 1964, suggested a "negative income tax" whereby those with earnings less than the poverty level would receive a reverse payment *from* the government.

There were ideas aplenty for solutions but no national will to implement them. In the interim the Vietnam war had heated up and expenditures on it had risen by geometric progression. Johnson and Shriver had to fight just to save the antipoverty program already on the legislative books; expansion was out of the question. One of the most attractive features of the original bill, that poor people themselves would participate in decision-making at local levels, had to be scrapped under conservative pressures in favor of full authority for the political machines. During the 1968 primary campaign for the Democratic nomination for the Presidency, Senator Eugene McCarthy noted that, while the Kerner Commission established by the President to study the 1967 riots had "recommended the creation of more than 500,000 jobs in 1969, 300,000 of them to be financed by private industry and 250,000 by the public sector," the Administration "proposed only 100,000 jobs in 1969, all to be financed by private business," even though there were 700,000 "non-whites" alone unemployed. More than half the $2.7 billion authorization for aid to elementary and secondary schools remained unspent in the wave of economy enforced by the Vietnam war. Before long the President talked of "austerity," tax boosts, restraint in wage demands, and Congress demanded and was assured of cutbacks in spending, most of which were to be deleted from social programs. Sargent Shriver moved on to greener pastures as Ambassador to France. The antipoverty program, like the tens of thousands who died 10,000 miles from home, was a casualty of war. The 10 percent surtax passed in 1968 went to finance military hostilities, not to mitigate poverty.

As Bill D. Moyers, former press secretary to President Johnson, observed, one of the costs of the Vietnam war has been "the hastening of the end of that broad consensus which in 1964–5 promised for the first time to provide resources equal to the afflictions of poverty, prejudice and the decay of American life. The hope that emerged in those years has become a casualty of the debate over Vietnam, and men upon whom it depended for leadership are too querulously divided by the issues of war to sustain unity of purpose at home." He warned that "three wars this century have been followed by periods of reaction to social reform and resistance to meeting public needs," implying that the same thing may be happening again.

It was an ominous sign that the poor people's march organized by Ralph Abernathy, Martin Luther King's successor as leader of the Southern Christian Leadership Conference, led to no new social legislation. The thousands of marchers, encamped in "Resurrection City," the improvised town they set up within sight of the White House, went home in the summer of 1968 grim and empty-handed. And in the election campaign that followed some weeks later the poverty issue was eclipsed by the shrill cry of all three Presidential candidates—Richard Nixon, Hubert Humphrey, and George Wallace—for "law and order." Humphrey, it is true, continued to speak of the need for antipoverty action but both the public and the political aspirants placed higher emphasis on public order and containing "rowdyism" in the streets than on the problem of human want.

The Great Society, in retrospect, lapsed into a coma two years after its birth and died a year later. It will probably be reincarnated by a new President under a new name in the not too distant future, but its failure puts to rout the thesis that men are poor because society cannot *afford* to raise them out of their poverty, because there is a paucity of economic riches. They are made poor or kept poor either by the indifference or the deliberate intent of other people.

They are poor because they are powerless, or powerless because they are poor, because there still remains within the social psyche an implacable resistance to brotherhood. It is easier to forget the poor than to remember them, easier to hide behind arguments of social Darwinism that they are "unfit" than to take the positive measures needed to alleviate educational, medical, economic, and political inequality.

SELECTED BIBLIOGRAPHY

Except for a few magazine or privately published articles that may be of special interest to the reader, this bibliography is limited to books. No attempt has been made to list the numerous newspaper clippings and magazine articles that were consulted, though many were very useful. A number of general works in history, economics, philanthropy, and other fields are set down under the heading "General" because they were reference sources for a variety of subjects and for different periods of time.

General

BEARD, CHARLES A. and MARY B. *The Rise of American Civilization.* Macmillan. 1927.

———. *A Basic History of the United States.* New Home Library. 1944.

BINING, ARTHUR CECIL. *The Rise of American Economic Life.* Scribner's. 1943.

BREMNER, ROBERT H. *From the Depths.* New York University. 1956.

———. *American Philanthropy.* University of Chicago. 1960.

COMMONS, JOHN R., et al. *History of Labour in the United States.* 4 vols. Macmillan. 1918–40.

FAULKNER, HAROLD UNDERWOOD. *Economic History of the United States.* Macmillan. 1928.

FONER, PHILIP S. *History of the Labor Movement in the United States.* Vols. 1, 2, 3, 4. International Publishers. 1947, 1955, 1964, 1965.

LENS, SIDNEY. *Radicalism in America*. Thomas Y. Crowell. 1966.

McMASTER, J. B. *History of the People of the United States*. 8 vols. Appleton-Century. 1914–34.

MORISON, SAMUEL ELIOT. *The Oxford History of the American People*. Oxford. 1965.

NEVINS, ALLAN, and COMMAGER, HENRY STEELE. *America, the Story of a Free People*. Little, Brown. 1943.

Chapter 1. Cat with Nine Lives

DANIELS, ROGER. "Some Historical Aspects of Poverty in America." (Mimeographed. Institute for Research on Poverty. Madison, Wisconsin.) 1965.

JACOBS, PAUL. "America's Schizophrenic View of the Poor." *Nation*. Sept. 20, 1965.

LAMPMAN, ROBERT J. "Ends and Means in the War of Poverty." (Mimeographed. Institute for Research on Poverty. Madison, Wisconsin.) 1965.

SHRIVER, SARGENT. "Poverty." (Brochure.) Reprinted from the *Encyclopedia Americana*.

Chapter 2. Roots and Resemblances

DORFMAN, JOSEPH. *The Economic Mind in American Civilization*. Vol. 1. Viking. 1946.

HALE, WILLIAM HARLAN. *The March of Freedom*. Harper. 1947.

JERNAGAN, MARCUS W. *Laboring and Dependent Classes in Colonial America*. University of Chicago. 1931.

MARX, KARL. *Capital*. Vol. 1. Charles H. Kerr. 1906.

NETTELS, CURTIS P. *The Roots of American Civilization*. Crofts. 1938.

ONEAL, JAMES. *The Workers in American History*. Rand Book Store. 1921.

PARRINGTON, VERNON LOUIS. *Main Currents in American Thought*. Harcourt, Brace. 1930.

SIMONS, A. M. *Social Forces in American History*. Macmillan. 1913.

WRIGHT, LOUIS B. *The Cultural Life of the American Colonies 1607–1763*. Harper. 1957.

Chapter 3. Antipoverty—Old Style

ABBOTT, EDITH. *Public Assistance*. Vols. 1–5. Russell & Russell. 1966.

ADAMS, JAMES TRUSLOW. *The Epic of America*. Little, Brown. 1931.

———. *Provincial Society*. Macmillan. 1927.

ANDREWS, CHARLES M. *The Fathers of New England*. Yale. 1919.

———. *The Colonial Period of American History*. Yale. 1934.

APTHEKER, HERBERT. *The Colonial Era*. International Publishers. 1959.

BRIDENBAUGH, CARL. *Cities in the Wilderness*. Ronald Press. 1938.

"British Convicts Shipped to the American Colonies." *American Historical Review*. October 1896.

CALVERTON, V. F. *The Awakening of America*. John Day. 1939.

CHITWOOD, OLIVER PERRY. *A History of Colonial America*. Harper. 1961.

CREECH, MARGARET. *Three Centuries of Poor Law Administration: A Study of Legislation in Rhode Island*. University of Chicago. 1936.

CUMMINGS, JOHN. *Poor Laws of Massachusetts and New York*. Macmillan. 1895.

DEUTSCH, ALBERT. "The Sick Poor in Colonial Times." *American Historical Review*. Vol. 39.

HACKER, LOUIS M. *The Triumph of American Capitalism*. Simon and Schuster. 1940.

JOHNSON, E. A. J. *American Economic Thought in the Seventeenth Century*. P. S. King & Son. 1932.

JOHNSTON, MARY. *Pioneers of the Old South*. Yale. 1918.

MORRIS, RICHARD B. *Government and Labor in Early America*. Columbia University. 1946.

ROCHESTER, ANNA. *American Capitalism, 1607–1800*. International Publishers. 1949.

WASHBURN, WILCOMB E. *The Governor and the Rebel: A History of Bacon's Rebellion in Virginia*. University of North Carolina. 1958.

WERTENBAKER, THOMAS S. *The First Americans: 1607–1690*. Macmillan. 1927.

Chapter 4. The Holy Experiment

BRONNER, EDWIN B. *William Penn*. Columbia University. 1962.

CHURCH, LESLIE F. *Oglethorpe: A Study in Philanthropy in England and America*. Epworth Press. 1932.

ETTINGER, AMOS A. *James Edward Oglethorpe, Imperial Idealist*. Clarendon Press. 1936.

FISHER, SYDNEY G. *William Penn*. Lippincott. 1932.

———. *Quaker Colonies*. Yale. 1919.

FISKE, JOHN. *The Dutch and Quaker Colonies in America*. Houghton Mifflin. 1899.

JORNS, AUGUSTE. *The Quakers as Pioneers in Social Work*. Macmillan. 1931.

MYERS, ALBERT COOK. *Narratives of Early Pennsylvania, West New Jersey, and Delaware, 1630–1707*. Scribner's. 1912.

PENN, WILLIAM. *No Cross, No Crown*. A. Sowle (London). 1682.

SHEPHERD, WILLIAM ROBERT. *History of Proprietary Government in Pennsylvania*. Columbia University. 1896.

Chapter 5.   Free but Not Equal

ALDEN, JOHN RICHARDSON. *The American Revolution: 1775–1783*. Harper. 1954.

APTHEKER, HERBERT. *The American Revolution*. International Publishers. 1960.

BURNETT, EDMUND CODY. *The Continental Congress*. Macmillan. 1941.

COLEMAN, MCALISTER. *Pioneers of Freedom*. Vanguard. 1929.

DOS PASSOS, JOHN. *The Men Who Made the Nation*. Doubleday. 1957.

FISKE, JOHN. *The Critical Period of American History*. Houghton Mifflin. 1916.

GREENE, EVARTS BOUTELL. *The Revolutionary Generation: 1763–1790*. Macmillan. 1943.

HACKER, LOUIS M. *Alexander Hamilton in the American Tradition*. McGraw-Hill. 1957.

HARDY, JACK. *The First American Revolution*. International Publishers. 1937.

HIBBARD, BENJAMIN HORACE. *History of Public Land Policies*. University of Wisconsin. 1965.

JAMESON, J. FRANKLIN. *The American Revolution Considered as a Social Event*. Princeton University. 1926.

MILLER, JOHN C. *Triumph of Freedom, 1775–1783*. Little, Brown. 1948.

PAXSON, FREDERIC LOGAN. *History of the American Frontier*. Houghton Mifflin. 1924.

SCHACHNER, NATHAN. *Thomas Jefferson*. Appleton-Century-Crofts. 1951.

WILTSE, CHARLES MAURICE. *The Jeffersonian Tradition in American Democracy*. University of North Carolina. 1935.

Chapter 6.   Bitter Fruit

ABBOTT, EDITH. *Historical Aspects of the Immigration Problem*. University of Chicago. 1926.

CAREY, M. *The Crisis.* H. C. Carey & I. Lea. 1823.

———. *Essays on the Public Charities of Philadelphia.* S. Clarke. 1829.

ERNST, ROBERT. *Immigrant Life, New York City, 1825–63.* King's Crown Press. 1949.

HANDLIN, OSCAR, and FLUG, MARY. *Commonwealth: A Study of the Role of Government, Massachusetts, 1774–1861.* New York University. 1947.

HUBERMAN, LEO. *We, the People.* Harper. 1932.

JONES, MALDWYN ALLEN. *American Immigration.* University of Chicago. 1960.

REZNECK, SAMUEL. "The Depression of 1819–22, a Social History." *American Historical Review.* Vol. 35.

SCHLESINGER, ARTHUR M., JR. *The Age of Jackson.* Little, Brown. 1945.

WARE, NORMAN. *The Industrial Worker, 1840–1860.* Peter Smith. 1959.

Chapter 7. Of Time and Patience

BEECHER, LYMAN. *Autobiography.* Harper. 1864.

BOUCICAULT, DION. *The Poor of New York.* Samuel French. 1857.

FAULKNER, HAROLD UNDERWOOD. *American Political and Social History.* Crofts. 1939.

KNAPP, SAMUEL L. *Life of Thomas Eddy.* Conner & Cooke. 1834.

KROUT, JOHN ALLEN. *The Origins of Prohibition.* Knopf. 1925.

MARTINEAU, HARRIET. *Society in America.* Saunders and Otley (London). 1837.

SCHNEIDER, DAVID M. *History of Public Welfare in New York State.* Vol. 1. University of Chicago. 1938.

TYLER, ALICE FELT. *Freedom's Ferment.* University of Minnesota. 1944.

Chapter 8. Vote Yourself a Farm

COMMONS, JOHN R. *A Documentary History of American Industrial Society.* Vol. 7. A. H. Clark Co. 1910–11.

———. "Horace Greeley and the Working Class Origins of the Republican Party." *Political Science Quarterly.* Vol. 24.

———. "Labor Organization and Labor Politics." *Quarterly Journal of Economics.* Vol. 21.

GOODRICH, CARTER, and DAVISON, SOL. "The Wage Earner in the Westward Movement." *Political Science Quarterly.* June 1935.

GREELEY, HORACE. *Recollections of a Busy Life.* J. B. Ford. 1868.

SHANNON, F. A. *The Farmer's Last Frontier*. Farrar & Rinehart. 1945.
——. "The Homestead Act and the Labor Surplus." *American Historical Review*. Vol. 41.
SOTHERAN, CHARLES. *Horace Greeley and Other Pioneers of American Socialism*. Mitchell Kennerley. 1915.
ZAHLER, HELENE SARA. *Eastern Workingmen and National Land Policy*. Columbia University. 1941.

Chapter 9. "No More Dat!"

BARTLETT, IRVING H. *Wendell Phillips, Brahmin Radical*. Beacon. 1961.
FLEMING, WALTER L. *Documentary History of Reconstruction*. Arthur H. Clark. 1906.
HAMMOND, M. B. "The Southern Farmer and the Cotton Question." *Political Science Quarterly*. Vol. 12.
HART, ALBERT BUSHNELL, editor. *American History as Told by Contemporaries*. Vol. 14. Macmillan. 1901.
HILL, HERBERT, and GREENBERG, JACK. *Citizen's Guide to Desegregation*. Beacon. 1955.
HYMAN, HAROLD, editor. *The Radical Republicans and Reconstruction*. Bobbs-Merrill. 1967.
JOHNS HOPKINS UNIVERSITY STUDIES, Series 37, No. 3. *American Colonization Society*. 1919.
MACPHERSON, JAMES M. *The Negro's Civil War*. Pantheon. 1965.
PHILLIPS, ULRICH B. "The Economic Cost of Slaveholding." *Political Science Quarterly*. Vol. 20.
——. *Life and Labor in the Old South*. Little, Brown. 1929.
STAMPP, KENNETH M. *The Peculiar Institution*. Knopf. 1956.
WESTON, GEORGE M. *The Poor Whites of the South*. (Pamphlet undated.)

Chapter 10. Forty Acres and a Mule

ALLEN, JAMES S. *Reconstruction: The Battle for Democracy (1865–1876)*. International Publishers. 1937.
APTHEKER, HERBERT. *The Negro in the Civil War*. International Publishers. 1938.
——. *A Documentary History of Negro People in the United States*. Citadel. 1951.
CHADWICK, FRENCH ENSOR. *Causes of the Civil War*. Harper. 1906.

DOUGLASS, FREDERICK. *Life and Times of Frederick Douglass.* Pathway Press. 1941.

DU BOIS, W. E. B. *Black Reconstruction.* Harcourt, Brace. 1935.

HESSELTINE, WILLIAM B. *Lincoln's Plan of Reconstruction.* Quadrangle. 1967.

KORNGOLD, RALPH. *Thaddeus Stevens.* Harcourt, Brace. 1955.

LESTER, J. C., and WILSON, D. L. *Ku Klux Klan, Its Origin, Growth and Disbandment.* Neale. 1905.

MILLER, ALPHONSE B. *Thaddeus Stevens.* Harper. 1939.

MILTON, G. F. *The Age of Hate: Andrew Johnson and the Radicals.* Coward-McCann. 1930.

PHILLIPS, ULRICH B. *American Negro Slavery.* Appleton. 1918.

SCHLUETER, HERMANN. *Lincoln, Labor, and Slavery.* Socialist Literature Co. 1913.

WASHINGTON, BOOKER T. "The Negro's Life in Slavery." *Outlook.* Vol. 93.

Chapter 11. Farming the Farmers

BUCK, SOLON J. *The Agrarian Crusade.* Yale. 1920.

FARMER, HALLIE. "Frontier Populism." *Mississippi Valley Historical Review.* Vol. 10.

HICKS, JOHN D. *The Populist Revolt.* University of Nebraska. 1931.

———. "The Political Career of Ignatius Donnelly." *Mississippi Valley Historical Review.* Vol. 8.

HOLBROOK, STEWART H. *The Age of the Moguls.* Doubleday. 1954.

McVEY, F. L. *The Populist Movement.* S. Sonneschein & Co. (London). 1896.

MYERS, GUSTAVUS. *History of the Great American Fortunes.* Modern Library. 1937.

NEVINS, ALLAN. *Emergence of Modern America, 1865–78.* Macmillan. 1954.

ROCHESTER, ANNA. *The Populist Movement in the United States.* International Publishers. 1943.

SCHLESINGER, ARTHUR. *Political and Social Growth of the American People, 1865–1940.* Macmillan. 1941.

TARBELL, IDA M. *The Nationalizing of Business, 1878–98.* Macmillan. 1936.

WOODBURN, JAMES ALBERT. "Western Radicalism in American Politics." *Mississippi Valley Historical Review.* Vol. 13.

WOODWARD, COMER VANN. *Tom Watson, Agrarian Rebel.* Macmillan. 1938.

Chapter 12. Hayseed Socialism

BRUCE, ARNOLD R. *American Parties and Politics*. Holt. 1927.

BUCK, SOLON J. *The Granger Movement*. Harvard University. 1913.

COMMONS, JOHN R. *Documentary History of American Industry*. Vol. 9. A. H. Clark Co. 1910–11.

DESTLER, CHESTER M. *American Radicalism, 1865–1901*. Connecticut College. 1946.

HAYNES, FRED EMORY. *James B. Weaver*. State Historical Society of Iowa. 1919.

NASH, HOWARD P., JR. *Third Parties in American Politics*. Public Affairs Press. 1959.

POLLACK, NORMAN, editor. *The Populist Mind*. Bobbs-Merrill. 1967.

Chapter 13. The Fit and the Unfit

CARNEGIE, ANDREW. *Autobiography of Andrew Carnegie*. Houghton Mifflin. 1920.

———. "The Advantages of Poverty." *19th Century*. Vol. 29.

GEORGE, HENRY. *Progress and Poverty*. W. M. Hinton. 1879.

GOODALE, FRANCES ABIGAIL, editor. *The Literature of Philanthropy*. Harper. 1893.

LOWELL, JOSEPHINE SHAW. *The True Aim of Charity Organization Societies*. Forum Publishing Co. 1895.

MADISON, CHARLES A. *Critics & Crusaders*. Holt. 1947.

McCLOSKEY, ROBERT GREEN. *American Conservatism in the Age of Enterprise; A Study of William Graham Sumner, Stephen J. Field, and Andrew Carnegie*. Harvard. 1951.

McMURRY, DONALD L. *Coxey's Army*. Little, Brown. 1929.

SCHLESINGER, ARTHUR M., JR., and WHITE, MORTON, editors. *Paths of American Thought*. Houghton Mifflin. 1963.

SPENCER, HERBERT. *First Principles*. D. Appleton. 1888.

———. *Social Statics*. D. Appleton. 1865.

VEBLEN, THORSTEIN. *The Theory of the Leisure Class*. Macmillan. 1899.

Chapter 14. The Other Half

ALLEN, FREDERICK LEWIS. *The Big Change*. Harper. 1952.

BUEL, J. W. *Metropolitan Life Unveiled*. Historical Publishing Co. 1882.

DAUGHERTY, CARROLL R. *Labor Problems in American Industry.* Houghton Mifflin. 1933.

FAULKNER, HAROLD U. *The Quest for Social Justice, 1898–1914.* Macmillan. 1931.

HOFSTADTER, RICHARD. *The Age of Reform, from Bryan to FDR.* Knopf. 1955.

HOLLANDER, JACOB H. *Abolition of Poverty.* Houghton Mifflin. 1914.

HUNTER, ROBERT. *Poverty.* Macmillan. 1907.

―――― (text). *Tenement Conditions in Chicago.* Report of the City Homes Association. 1901.

MUMFORD, LEWIS. *The Culture of Cities.* Harcourt, Brace. 1948.

PENMAN, JOHN SIMPSON. *Poverty, the Challenge to the Church.* Pilgrim Press. 1915.

RIIS, JACOB. *How the Other Half Lives.* Scribner's. 1890.

――――. *The Battle with the Slums.* Macmillan. 1902.

STRONG, JOSIAH. *The Twentieth Century City.* Baker and Taylor Co. 1898.

Chapter 15. Halfway House

CHALMERS, DAVID MARK. *The Social and Political Ideas of the Muckrakers.* Citadel. 1964.

CROLY, HERBERT. *The Promise of American Life.* Macmillan. 1909.

DOUGLAS, PAUL H. *Real Wages in the United States.* Houghton Mifflin. 1930.

DULLES, FOSTER RHEA. *Labor in America.* Thomas Y. Crowell. 1949.

DUNCAN-CLARK, S. J. *The Progressive Movement.* Small, Maynard. 1913.

FORCEY, CHARLES. *The Crossroads of Liberalism.* Oxford University. 1961.

JOSEPHSON, MATTHEW. *The President Makers.* Harcourt, Brace. 1940.

――――. *The Robber Barons.* Harcourt, Brace. 1934.

KOLKO, GABRIEL. *Triumph of Conservatism.* Free Press of Glencoe. 1963.

LA FOLLETTE, ROBERT M. *La Follette's Autobiography.* The Robert M. La Follette Co. 1913.

LIPPMANN, WALTER. *A Preface to Politics.* Mitchell Kennerley. 1913.

MOWRY, GEORGE E. *The Era of Theodore Roosevelt and the Birth of Modern America, 1900–1912.* Harper. 1958.

NYE, RUSSELL B. *Midwest Progressive Politics.* Michigan State University. 1959.

PARKES, HENRY BAMFORD, and CAROSSO, VINCENT P. *Recent America: A History.* Thomas Y. Crowell. 1963.

PERLMAN, SELIG, and TAFT, PHILIP. *History of Labor in the United States, 1896–1932.* Macmillan. 1935.

RESEK, CARL, editor. *The Progressives*. Bobbs-Merrill. 1967.

SHANNON, DAVID A. *The Socialist Party of America*. Macmillan. 1955.

TODD, A. L. *Justice on Trial*. McGraw-Hill. 1964.

WALLING, WILLIAM ENGLISH: *Progressivism—and After*. Macmillan. 1914.

WEINBERG, ARTHUR MYRON, editor. *The Muckrakers*. Simon and Schuster. 1961.

WEYL, WALTER. *The New Democracy*. Macmillan. 1912.

Chapter 16. Percolation and Panic

ABBOTT, EDITH. "Don't Do It, Mr. Hopkins!" *The Nation*. Vol. 140.

ADAMS, GRACE. *Workers on Relief*. Yale. 1939.

ALLEN, FREDERICK LEWIS. *Since Yesterday*. Harper. 1939.

BOYER, RICHARD O., and MORAIS, HERBERT M. *Labor's Untold Story*. Cameron Associates. 1955.

GOLDMAN, ERIC F. *Rendezvous with Destiny*. Knopf. 1952.

HALLGREN, MAURITZ A. *Seeds of Revolt*. Knopf. 1933.

HILL, HOWARD C., and TUGWELL, REXFORD G. *Our Economic Society and Its Problems*. Harcourt, Brace. 1935.

HOFSTADTER, RICHARD. *The American Political Tradition*. Fletcher & Son. 1967.

LYND, ROBERT S. and HELEN M. *Middletown, A Study in Contemporary American Culture*. Harcourt, Brace. 1929.

MITCHELL, BROADUS. *Depression Decade*. Rinehart. 1947.

RUBINOW, I. M. *The Quest for Security*. Holt. 1934.

SELDES, GILBERT V. *The Years of the Locust: America, 1929–1932*. Little, Brown. 1933.

SHANNON, DAVID A. *The Great Depression*. Prentice-Hall. 1960.

SOULE, GEORGE. *Prosperity Decade*. Rinehart. 1947.

WECTER, DIXON. *The Age of the Great Depression*. Macmillan. 1941.

Chapter 17. New Wine—Old Bottles

DAVIS, FORREST. *Huey Long: A Candid Biography*. Dodge Publishing Co. 1935.

DORFMAN, JOSEPH. *The Economic Mind in American Civilization*. Vol. 5. Viking. 1959.

FLYNN, JOHN T. *The Roosevelt Myth*. Devin-Adair. 1948.

GUNTHER, JOHN. *Roosevelt in Retrospect.* Harper. 1950.

HACKER, LOUIS M. *A Short History of the New Deal.* Crofts. 1934.

HOPKINS, HARRY L. *Spending to Save: The Complete Story of Relief.* Norton. 1936.

ICKES, HAROLD L. *The Autobiography of a Curmudgeon.* Reynal & Hitchcock. 1943.

JOHNSON, HUGH SAMUEL. *The Blue Eagle from Egg to Earth.* Doubleday. 1935.

LENS, SIDNEY. *Left, Right and Center.* Regnery. 1949.

LEUCHTENBERG, WILLIAM E. *Franklin D. Roosevelt and the New Deal.* Harper & Row. 1963.

LINDLEY, ERNEST K. *The Roosevelt Revolution, First Phase.* Viking. 1933.

PERKINS, FRANCES. *The Roosevelt I Knew.* Viking. 1946.

RAYBACK, JOSEPH G. *A History of American Labor.* Macmillan. 1959.

SCHLESINGER, ARTHUR M., JR. *The Politics of Upheaval.* Houghton Mifflin. 1960.

SHERWOOD, ROBERT E. *Roosevelt and Hopkins.* Vol. 1. Harper. 1948.

STERNSHER, BERNARD. *Rexford Tugwell and the New Deal.* Rutgers University. 1964.

TUGWELL, REXFORD G. *The Democratic Roosevelt.* Doubleday. 1957.

———. *FDR: Architect of an Era.* Macmillan. 1967.

UNOFFICIAL OBSERVER. *The New Dealers.* Simon and Schuster. 1934.

WALLACE, HENRY. *New Frontiers.* Reynal & Hitchcock. 1934.

ZINN, HOWARD, editor. *New Deal Thought.* Bobbs-Merrill. 1966.

Chapter 18. Ye Have Always?

BAGDIKIAN, BEN H. *In the Midst of Plenty: A New Report on the Poor in America.* Beacon. 1964.

BENNETT, LERONE, JR. *What Manner of Man, A Memorial Biography of Martin Luther King, Jr.* Johnson Publishing Co. 1968.

BRODERICK, FRANCIS L., and MEIER, AUGUST, editors. *Negro Protest Thought in the Twentieth Century.* Bobbs-Merrill. 1965.

EVANS, ROWLAND, and NOVAK, ROBERT. *Lyndon B. Johnson: The Exercise of Power.* New American Library. 1966.

Fortune, Editors of. *U.S.A. The Permanent Revolution.* Prentice-Hall. 1951.

GALBRAITH, JOHN KENNETH. *The Affluent Society.* Houghton Mifflin. 1958.

GOLDMAN, ERIC F. *The Crucial Decade—and After: America 1945–1960.* Vintage. 1960.

HARRINGTON, MICHAEL. *The Other America*. Macmillan. 1962.

HENTOFF, NAT. *The New Equality*. Viking. 1964.

HUMPHREY, HUBERT H. *War on Poverty*. McGraw-Hill. 1964.

JACOBS, PAUL, and LANDAU, SAUL. *The New Radicals*. Random House. 1966.

KING, MARTIN LUTHER, JR. *Stride Toward Freedom*. Harper. 1958.

OSTRANDER, GILMAN M. *A Profile History of the United States*. McGraw-Hill. 1964.

QUARLES, BENJAMIN. *The Negro in the Making of America*. Macmillan. 1964.

Report of the National Advisory Commission on Civil Disorders. Bantam. 1968.

ROBERTS, CHARLES. *L.B.J.'s Inner Circle*. Delacorte. 1965.

SCHLESINGER, ARTHUR M., JR. *A Thousand Days: John F. Kennedy in the White House*. Houghton Mifflin. 1965.

SHERRILL, ROBERT. *The Accidental President*. Grossman. 1967.

SILBERMAN, CHARLES E. *Crisis in Black and White*. Random House. 1964.

SORENSEN, THEODORE C. *Kennedy*. Harper. 1965.

WEISBROD, BURTON. *The Economics of Poverty: An American Paradox*. Prentice-Hall. 1965.

ZINN, HOWARD. *SNCC*. Beacon. 1964.

INDEX